MAYER CENTER SYMPOSIUM XVIII | READINGS IN LATIN AMERICAN STUDIES

Materiality
Making Spanish America

EDITED BY JORGE F. RIVAS PÉREZ

DENVER ART MUSEUM

This volume is published in memory of Charles G. Patterson III (1944–2020),
who joined the Denver Art Museum as its first conservator in 1991 and
served as the museum's first director of conservation until his retirement in
2010. Carl was a longtime supporter of the Mayer Center
for Ancient and Latin American Art and a dear friend.

✤ ✤ ✤

CONTENTS

Foreword

The Denver Art Museum's Latin American art collection is one of the best in the world and the most comprehensive of its kind in the United States. It began with Anne Evans's gift of *santos* from southern Colorado and northern New Mexico in 1936, and has grown rapidly over the intervening years thanks to generous donors including the Frank Barrows Freyer Collection, Robert C. Appleman, the Stapleton Foundation of Latin American Colonial Art (made possible by the Renchard Family), the Frederick and Jan Mayer Collection, and the Colección Patricia Phelps de Cisnersos. The collection now encompasses work created from the 1500s to the present.

Since 1968 the department has expanded thanks to the support and enthusiasm of longtime museum trustee Frederick Mayer and his wife, Jan. The growth of the Latin American art collection and programming received a major boost with an endowment from Frederick and Jan in 2001. This gift made it possible to establish the first curatorial position exclusively dedicated to Spanish colonial Latin American art in the United States.

The Mayers also founded the Frederick and Jan Mayer Center for Ancient and Latin American Art at the Denver Art Museum, dedicated to increasing awareness and promoting scholarship in these fields by sponsoring academic activities including annual symposia, fellowships, study trips, research projects, conservation, and publications. Since 2001, the Mayer Center has held a symposium nearly every year. My gratitude goes to Jorge Rivas Pérez, Frederick and Jan Mayer Curator of Latin American Art, for his dedication in organizing the 2018 Mayer Center Symposium. The topic, *Materiality: Making Spanish America*, brought together scholars from Europe, Latin America, and the United States in Denver on November 1 and 2, 2018. Those papers are presented in this volume.

The Mayers have generously supported the museum's larger mission for the past fifty years. Though Frederick left us far too soon in 2007, Jan has continued this spirit of generosity and enthusiasm for the museum. We offer our thanks to her for her ongoing dedication to the museum as a whole and to the study of ancient and Latin American art in particular.

Christoph Heinrich
Frederick and Jan Mayer Director
Denver Art Museum

✦ ✦ ✦

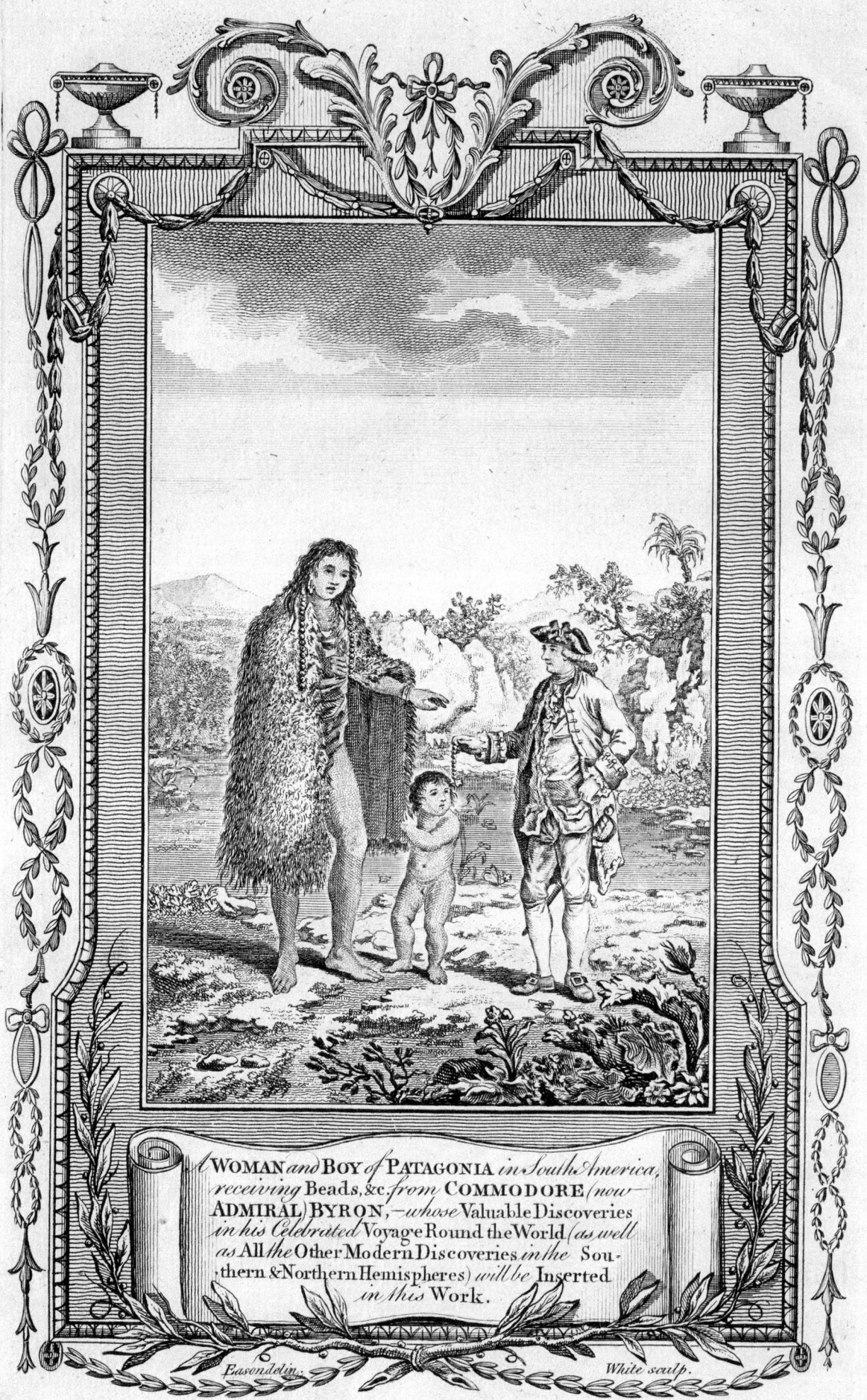

London Published by Alexr. Hogg at the Kings Arms No. 16 Paternoster Row.

A WOMAN and BOY of PATAGONIA in South America, receiving Beads, &c. from COMMODORE (now ADMIRAL) BYRON, — whose Valuable Discoveries in his Celebrated Voyage Round the World (as well as All the Other Modern Discoveries in the Southern & Northern Hemispheres) will be Inserted in this Work.

Eason delin.

White sculp.

Spanish America
A Material Perspective

In the early sixteenth century, encounters between Europeans colonizers and the Indigenous peoples of the Americas initiated a chain of important transformations in their respective material worlds. Although in recent years our understanding of those material encounters has advanced, in particular through studies on subjects such as hybridity and acculturation, the material culture of Latin America from the fourteenth to the early nineteenth centuries is still understudied. We know very little about how Indigenous people employed and adapted—or resisted—European goods, materials, technologies, and visual repertoires, and how these choices transformed their material world and shaped their cultures, economies, and societies. Thanks to archaeological research and documentary sources, we know that the appropriation of foreign materials such as glass beads (fig. 1), glazed pottery, and iron tools—often obtained through gift exchange or colonial trade practices (fig. 2)—led to the transformation of the Indigenous material world with profound implications for the societies of Latin America.

Indigenous artisans shaped the colonial material world through their significant and diverse contributions, and they responded to the unique dynamics and conditions of each region of Spanish America. Rather than acting merely as passive spectators or full participants in European production structures, Indigenous artisans played a role in the definition and negotiation of new colonial industries. The introduction of new types of goods, technologies,

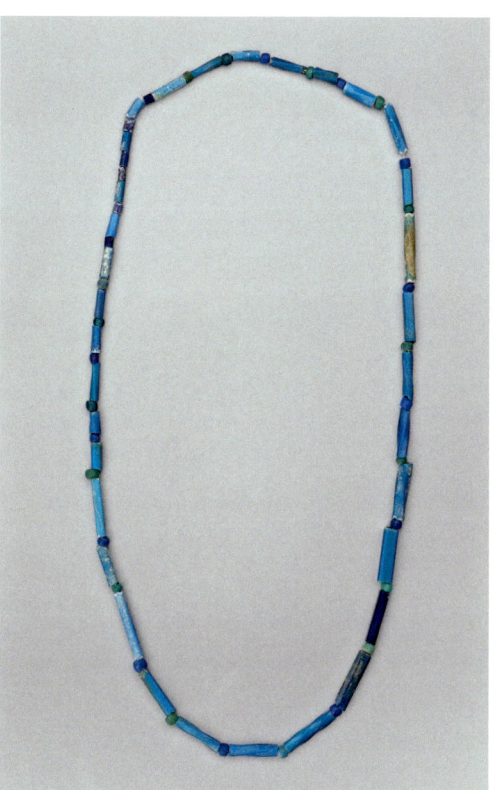

Opposite: Fig. 2. Unknown artist, *Woman and Boy of Patagonia in South America receiving beads from Admiral Byron.* England, 1750–1799. Engraving on paper, 11½ × 7 in. Denver Art Museum: Gift of the Collection of Frederick and Jan Mayer, 2013.382

Fig. 1. Unknown artist, *Necklace of Nueva Cádiz beads.* Spain, 1500–1550. Glass and seeds, 34 in. Denver Art Museum: Gift of the Collection of Frederick and Jan Mayer, 2013.329

Fig. 3. Unknown artist, *St. Anthony*. Mexico, 1600s. Feathers glued on paper, mounted on copper, 17 × 13½ in. Denver Art Museum: Gift of the Collection of Frederick and Jan Mayer, 2011.424

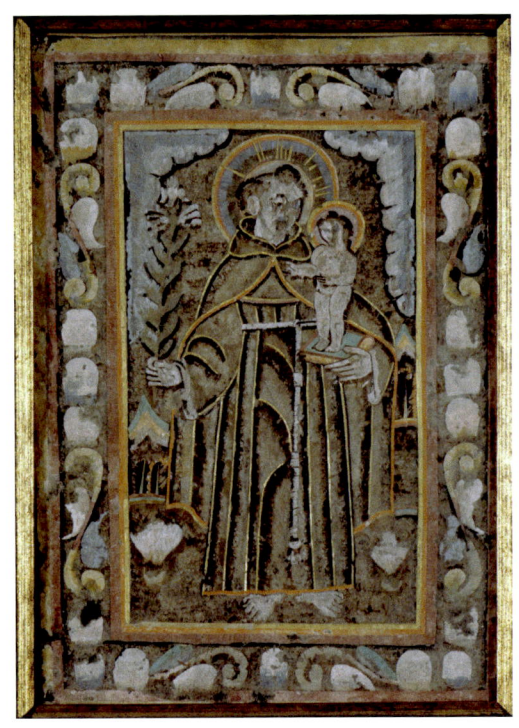

Fig. 4. Unknown artist, *Tonalá vase.* Jalisco, Mexico, 1650–1750. Earthenware, 4⅛ × 2⅞ in. Denver Art Museum: Funds from Carl Patterson in honor of Jorge Rivas, 2018.304

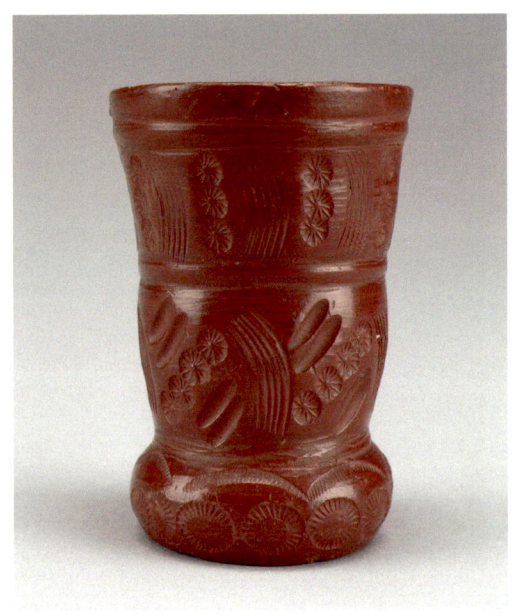

Opposite: Fig. 5. Nicholas Guzman, *Saints Cripsin and Crispinian with Christ.* Puebla, Mexico, 1704. Oil paint on canvas, 66½ × 44½ in. Denver Art Museum: Gift of the Collection of Frederick and Jan Mayer, 2015.541

and production processes, as well as production organizations—namely guilds and different types of workshops—had a profound impact on the preexisting productive world. From the beginning, the agency of Indigenous artisans resulted in hybrid goods that departed from material traditions. These new hybrid creations, such as feather work paintings (fig. 3) and Tonalá pottery (fig. 4), became important industries that supplied luxury goods for colonial elites and the export market. It is difficult to find an upper-class Spanish inventory from the sixteenth to eighteenth centuries that does not list any luxury good from the Americas. This is a clear demonstration of the impact of manufactured goods from the Americas in the global context of the Spanish Empire.

The guild structure played a notable role in the making of the material world in Spanish America. The European guild model evolved over time, and Indigenous peoples (and later, free individuals of African descent and mixed race) became important players not only in

the productive tissue of their communities, but also in the complex structure of brotherhoods and other associations that linked the Catholic church to artisans (fig. 5). Despite racial prejudice and legal barriers, by the end of the Spanish age, mixed-race individuals of Indigenous or African descent largely dominated the production of consumer goods. Often thanks to intermarriage and family alliances, certain trades became the exclusive domains of specific social groups. For example, by the late eighteenth century in Caracas, the silversmith trade was largely in the hands of a tight-knit community of mixed-race families of African descent (fig. 6).

Men and women from different colonial strata surrounded themselves with a world of objects, some of which had practical use, such as clothing, furniture, and tools; others were treasured solely for their aesthetic or symbolic value. Domestic spaces became remarkable repositories of objects, both those produced locally and coming from around the globe. The trading routes established between the Philippines and China with Spanish

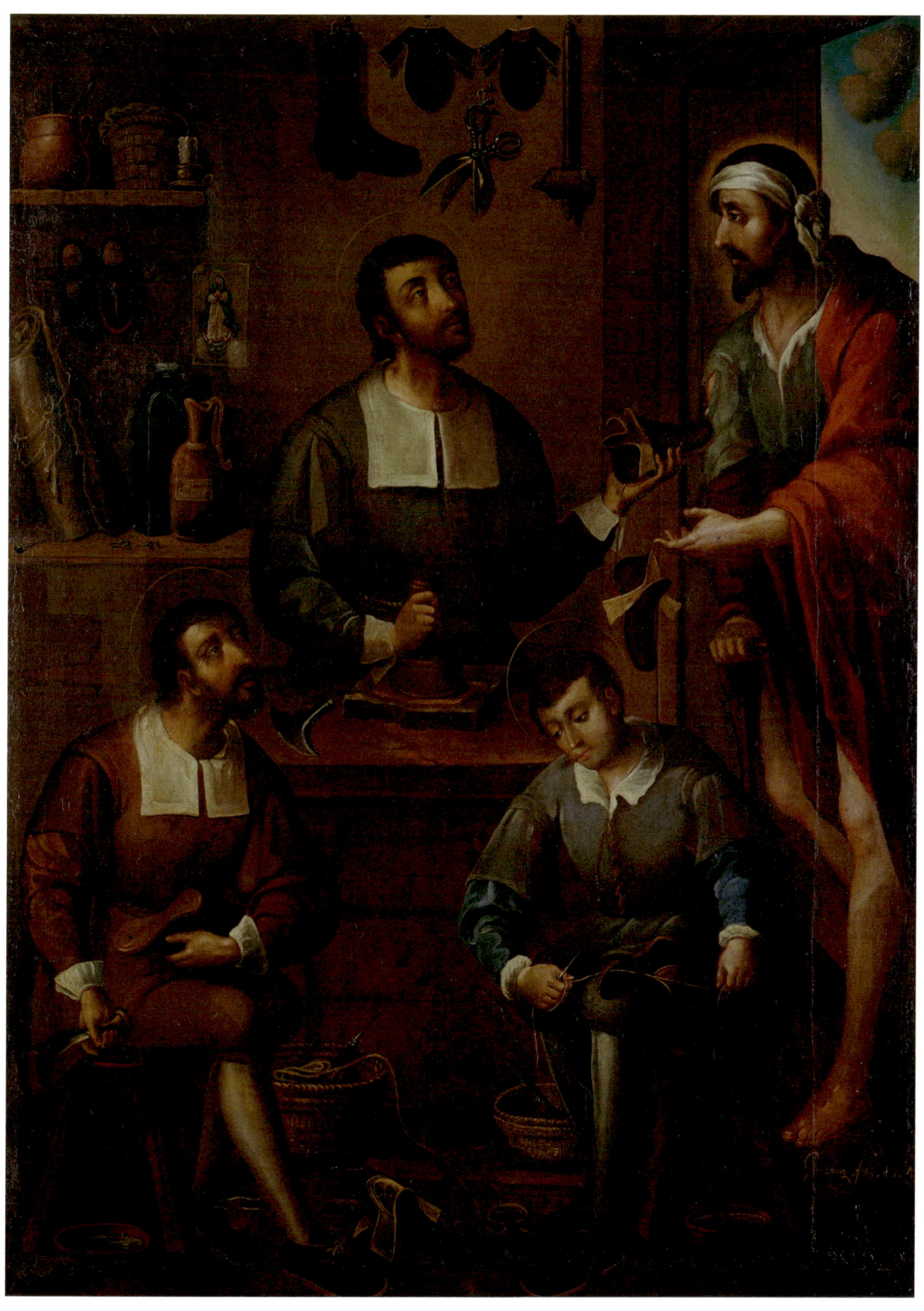

America, further connecting with Europe, set a model for global transoceanic trade, which influenced the material world of the Americas (fig. 7). Although documents show the consumption of imported goods permeated across social classes, unfortunately, very few artifacts from the lower strata of society survive today.

The secluded world of religious communities in convents and monasteries, some of them cloistered—thus detached from mundane affairs—was not very different from the rest of the society. Although we know less about the materiality of religious communities, their interconnections with the external world and with other religious establishments facilitated the flow and production of objects. There is plenty of material evidence and documentation to help us understand the objects produced in the workshops of convents, monasteries, and missions, both for internal consumption and for supplying the outside world (figs. 8 and 9).

The winds of "Enlightenment" that changed European thinking also reached Spanish America. Home to ethnically diverse populations, the great viceregal capitals of Mexico City and Lima became important cultural hubs beginning in the seventeenth century. In this context, the local intelligentsia, including scholars such as Carlos de Sigüenza y Góngora (1645–1700), among others, began to envision a new societal model beyond the terms of the authoritarian Spanish colonial structure. Under that new vision, the material culture and history of the prehispanic past had a preeminent place when ideas of freedom and independence began to incubate among the *criollo* elite. Those ideas, fostered in part by the study of the Indigenous material world, later crystalized during the wars for independence and the creation of free nations in the 1820s. These new nations adopted Indigenous and hybrid elements as they constructed national identities.

It is important to outline the reach of this volume in the context of recent scholarship on colonial Spanish American art and material culture. For most of the last quarter century, the "fine arts"—chiefly painting, and to a much lesser degree sculpture—have been the subject of most studies in the field. Other topics such as material culture and the decorative arts have generated less scholarly attention. The limitations on reach and scope for studying production from the

Fig. 6. Domingo Tomás Núñez, Venezuelan, active 1735–1801, *Sacrarium.* Venezuela, about 1790. Silver, 6⁷⁄₁₆ × 5⁷⁄₈ in. Denver Art Museum: Gift of Patricia Phelps de Cisneros in honor of Gisela and Carlos Padula, 2019.73

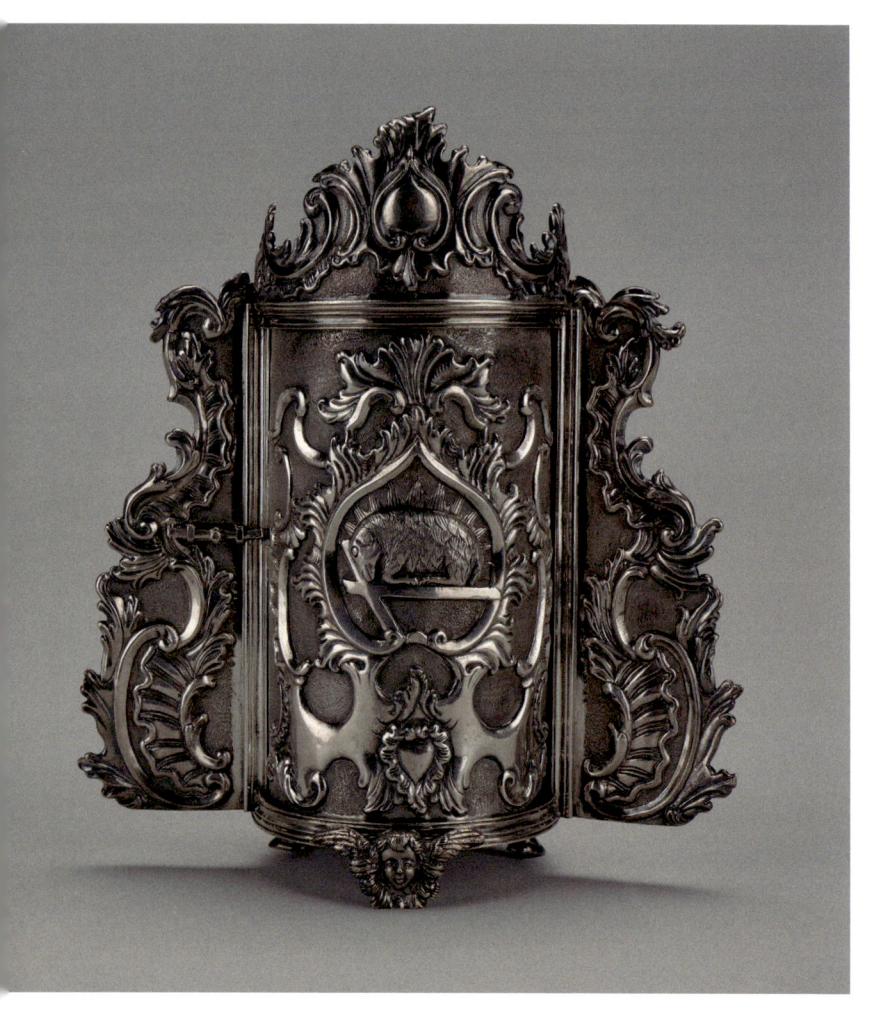

Opposite: Fig. 7. Diego de Reinoso, *Double-sided carving of Saint Michael and the Virgin and Child with Saints Dominic and John the Baptist.* Mexico, about 1696. Alabaster, 7 × 3⅜ × 3⅜ in. Denver Art Museum: Gift of Robert J. Stroessner, 1991.1150

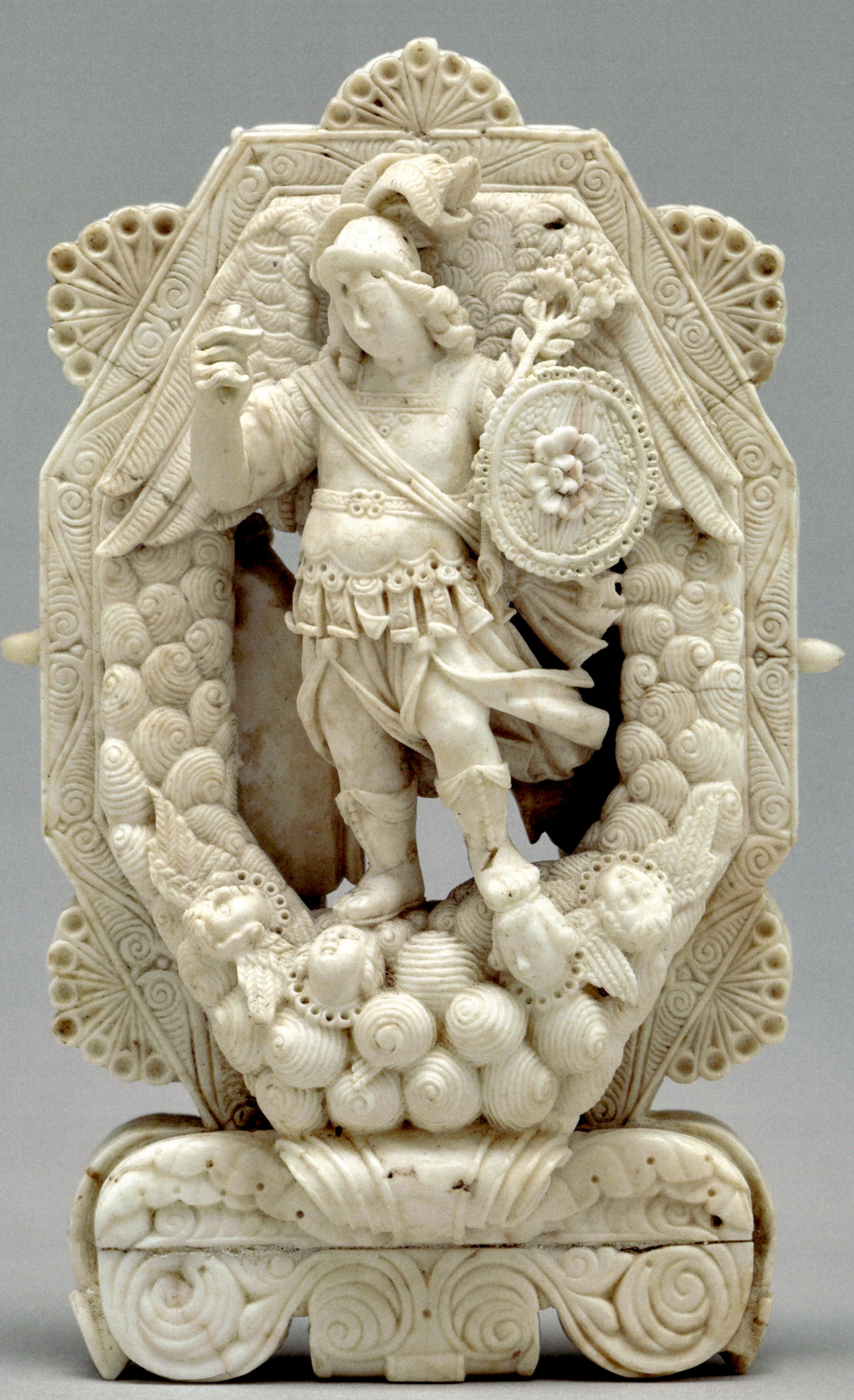

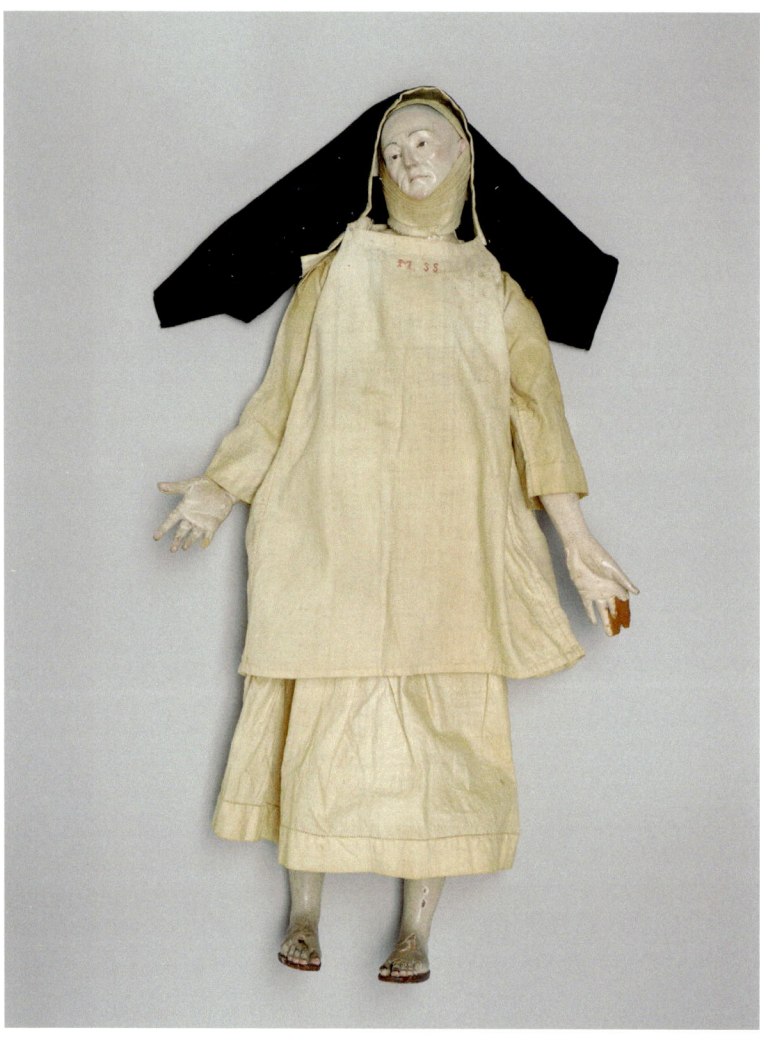

period have affected how the Spanish age has been reconstructed and presented. Thanks to new interdisciplinary and theoretical approaches, and more focused studies, some of the old (and often merely descriptive) narratives of the material world have been revised and amended. However, and most importantly, as new research areas are gaining traction and generating interest among scholars, studies with a more sensitive approach are reshaping the field with a broader and more encompassing perspective. I am confident that the topic of the eighteenth Frederick and Jan Mayer Center for Ancient and Latin American Art Symposium at the Denver Art Museum, held in November 2018, and of this resulting volume, will enrich this new vision on the history of the materiality of Spanish America.

Above: Fig. 8. Unknown artist, *Nun Doll.* Ecuador, 19th century. Fabric, porcelain, wire, cork, and twine, 19½ × 8 × 3½ in. Denver Art Museum: Gift of the Stapleton Foundation of Latin American Colonial Art, made possible by the Renchard family, 1990.593

Right: Fig. 9. Unknown artist, *Coca Box (Coquera).* San Javier de Chiquitos Mission, Bolivia, 18th century. Cedar, 11 × 7⁴⁄₅ in. Denver Art Museum: Funds from Carl Patterson in honor of Richard A. Haynes, 2017.417A-B

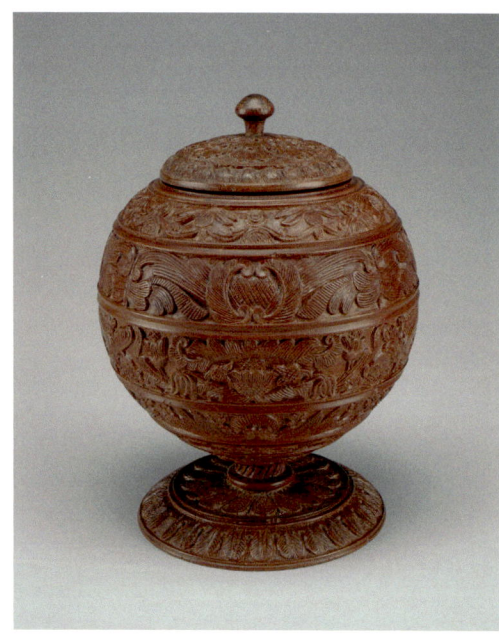

Thomas B. F. Cummins opens the volume exploring how *tocapus* were altered to coincide and intersect with European forms and objects in complex and divergent ways after the Spanish invasion of Peru in *The Tocapu: Guaman Poma Meets Alberti,* or, *"The more that one tries . . . to interpret . . . the more confused one becomes . . . there is no hope." The Meaning of Objects from the Indies in Early Sixteenth-Century Castilian Households* addresses the reception and dissemination of goods from the Americas in early sixteenth-century Spain. In this chapter, Antonio Urquízar-Herrera considers the role that artifacts collected and sent to Spain by early explorers and settlers played in building the image of the Americas. Urquízar-Herrera also argues that later changing perceptions of their cultural value led to their dispersal from Spanish collections. In *Sculpture at Home in Baroque Lima,* also focused in the domestic environment, Rafael Ramos Sosa delves into the role of sculpture in daily life in viceregal Lima, a field still understudied.

In *Material Matters: Global Trade at the Edge of the Spanish Colonial Empire,* Donna Pierce focuses on the commercial exchange of Asian luxury goods, chiefly porcelain and fine textiles, at the northern border of the Spanish Empire. She further discusses how local artists appropriated and transformed Asian visual repertoires in the colonial arts of New Mexico. The material culture of arms and armor in the early colonial Americas, a topic that has received scarce scholarly attention, is the subject of Jonathan Tavares's essay *Adapting European Arms to the Americas: the Material Culture of Conflict in Colonial New Spain, 1500–1800.* Through the examination of rare surviving objects and written historical accounts, Tavares presents an overview of the consumption, adaptation, and production of arms and armor in Spanish America.

Based on material evidence, in *Materiality between Mind and Hands: Some Approaches to Native Creativity in Colonial South America,* Gabriela Siracusano explores the aesthetic parameters and material traditions that guided Indigenous artists of colonial South America in the production of religious art. By studying the artifacts represented in hagiographic images—the instruments of conquest and native weapons—Emmanuel Ortega presents insights into the material world of Franciscan hagiographic martyr portraiture—a paint genre that gained traction among religious orders in New Spain. In *Consuming the Host: The Materiality of Franciscan Anxiety in Eighteenth-Century New Spain,* Ortega seeks to explain how Franciscans sought to represent

for posterity their efforts in Christianizing the native populations of the Americas.

By using as a case study Bishop Baltasar Jaime Martínez Compañón's index, in *Cognitive Ecologies and Cabinetization: The Bishop of Trujillo's Eighteenth-Century Index,* Olaya Sanfuentes presents the complex story behind Martínez Compañón's investigation into Peruvian natural and cultural history as a model of material culture research during the Age of Enlightenment in Spain. Also dealing with collections, in *Ammonites, Gourds, Watercolors, and Lithograph Prints: Scientific Objects and Images for a Cultural History,* María Paola Rodríguez Prada brings closure to the volume by commenting on the circumstances that surrounded the founding of the National Museum of Colombia in the 1820s, shortly after independence from Spain.

―――――――――

I am grateful to these scholars for their participation in the symposium and for their contributions to this volume. With fresh views of local stories and rigorous scholarship, this book highlights the importance of studying these issues in the wider context of the materiality of the Americas. Considered together, these individual studies offer new perspectives on the material culture of the Spanish era and, I hope, will open new paths for further research.

Jorge F. Rivas Pérez
Frederick and Jan Mayer Curator
of Latin American Art
Denver Art Museum

✛ ✛ ✛

THOMAS B. F. CUMMINS

The Tocapu: Guaman Poma Meets Alberti

"The more that one tries . . . to interpret, . . . the more confused one becomes. . . . There is no hope."

Tocapu is a Quechua word (the language of the Inka) that is used to indicate a specific kind of design that appears on a great variety of Inka and colonial media. The tocapu consists of various distinctive and extremely beautiful geometric abstract forms that are almost always arranged within a grid pattern layout as can be seen in an exquisite Inka *uncu* (tunic) in the collection of Dumbarton Oaks (figs. 1a–c).[1] Apart from this general characterization, however, what the tocapu means or signifies is not so easy to define. Nonetheless, many scholars have claimed over the past sixty years in various arguments or assertions that the tocapu represents some form or system of Inka writing.[2] There is, in fact, no Rosetta stone for interpreting, or even fully understanding, what the tocapu is, nor the system through which it may signify.[3] The tocapu certainly did convey information/ ideas of a kind, and tocapus are ubiquitous in the Inka and viceregal period, painted or woven on a variety of objects. However, unlike in Mexico where Aztec, Mixtec, and Maya systems of pictographs and glyphs are clearly glossed for a European to understand,[4] there are no colonial Andean manuscripts that try to explain tocapus. In fact, there are very few manuscripts in the

sixteenth and early seventeenth centuries that even illustrate the tocapu and how it appeared in Inka culture.

There are, to be sure, many more objects on which tocapus appear, but almost all illustrations for which there is a specific context occur in two manuscripts by Martín de Murúa and one by Felipe Guaman Poma de Ayala.[5] These three manuscripts are intimately related, and they are the most important corpus of tocapu designs in colonial manuscripts.[6] Most important, the tocapus in these three manuscripts appear mostly

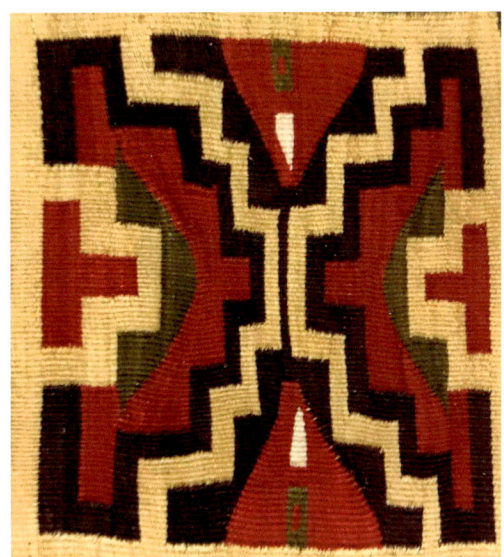

Fig. 1a. Unknown artist, *Tocapu,* detail of Inka royal *uncu* (tunic). Peru, about 1530. Camelid wool weft, warp cotton, tapestry weave. Dumbarton Oaks Research Library and Collections, Washington, DC (P.C. B.518).

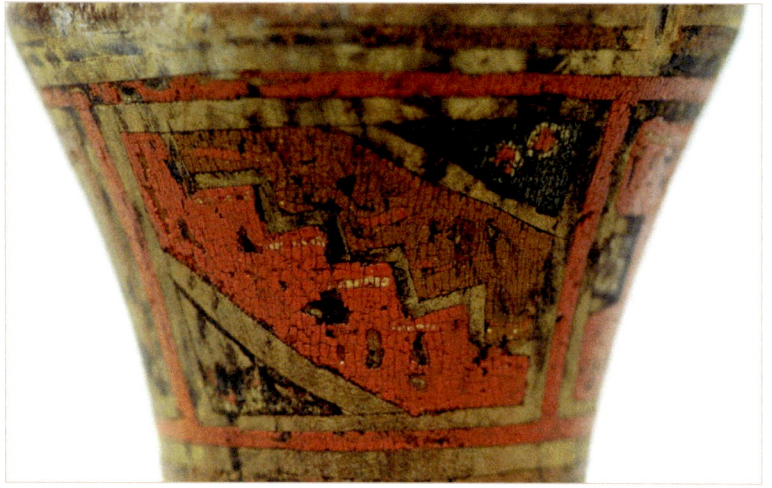

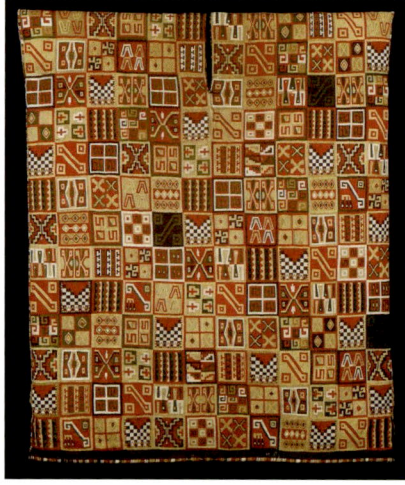

in the royal uncus of the Sapa Inka (literally "unique Inka," designating the Inka ruler). Unfortunately, as will be argued, one set of tocapus in particular, those drawn by Guaman Poma de Ayala for his own manuscript, have been employed as a major source for several different modes of interpretation, depending on what scholars believe that they see.[7] This chapter is not intent on trying to interpret the tocapus in these manuscripts in terms of some "secret Inka form of writing"; rather, it will focus on the problem of using Guaman Poma de Ayala's images as some sort of interpretive key and to indicate a specific source that was surely the inspiration for how Guaman Poma de Ayala depicted many of the tocapus in his portraits of the Inka kings in *El primer nueva coronica y buen gobierno* (hereafter, *Nueva coronica*). This source is a sixteenth-century published history of the conquest of Peru, and it does present a graphic system that was secret and used for encoding and transferring sensitive information, but in a context and method radically different than what any Inka used. We must therefore look at the tocapus drawn by Guaman Poma de Ayala through this lens and with a different and unexpected perspective, one developed by Leon Battista Alberti.

The Tocapu

What is the tocapu, and is it the same thing before and after the Spanish invasion? I will not answer this question with any definitive answer as I have discussed the issue previously, except to say that the tocapu underwent similar transformations as did the *khipu* in the viceregal period.[8] That is, there is no universal code that allows us to interpret the tocapu just as there is none for the khipu. For example, Gary Urton has worked extremely hard for the past thirty years trying to break the "khipu code." However, it now also seems clear that there is in fact no Rosetta stone for the khipu just as there is none for the tocapu, nor can any one khipu be deciphered independent of corroborating texts. And this independent decoding of khipus has not occurred, partially because it is presumed that there is a single abstract operating system or code separate from mnemonics. Of course, binaries and a decimal system are operative presumably for accounting purposes, but there are non-systematic (non-decimal) khipus, and there were khipus that did not record statistical information for the Inka or colonial Andeans. The tocapu, like the khipu, cannot be interpreted as a source for information that is otherwise unknown. Neither Inka system reveals its contents. We only can recognize their expressive possibilities. Moreover, we have brief descriptive historical accounts for each system that reveal very little for how either system functioned. And for khipus, there is one statistically possible association of a set of specific written accounts and a set of particular khipus; however, their linked association is based on a number of assumptions and not on any direct historical evidence or even precise dating.[9] One cannot not extrapolate from this coincidence a systematic means to extract information from other contemporary khipus.

It is important, however, to acknowledge that the khipu underwent an historical and possibly morphological and epistemological change after the Spanish invasion, as Sabine Hyland, Gene A. Ware, and Madison Clark have convincingly suggested.[10] In fact, there were immediate ontological changes to both the tocapu and the khipu. For example, in one of the *Cartas Annuas* of 1602, it is told of how a blind man confessed in Cuzco using a khipu of six varas of spun cord into which he placed signs made of stone, bones, and feathers through which he recounted his sins over four days.[11] By the eighteenth century if not earlier, the khipu was aligned with alphabetic text, and if the khipu that Raimondo di Sangro, Prince of Sansevero, depicts in his book has an origin in colonial Peru, then tocapus, khipus, and alphabetic text are interrelated (fig. 2).[12] This early eighteenth-century print of a supposed logosyllabic khipu has tocapu-like designs woven into it in addition to having embedded objects such as tiny pan flutes and silver stars. This new form, or imagined form, of the Inka khipu by di Sangro is not too dissimilar to the description of the blind man's confessional khipu with embedded objects in the Jesuit letter of 1602. Nor is it too dissimilar to the 1783 Collata khipus described as incorporating phonetic signs,[13] or the khipus kept by the community of Tupicocha in which objects and figures are embedded.[14]

The point is that just as the khipu very quickly became an instrument of various vice-regal uses and was transformed from whatever it was for the Inka into an amalgamation of European and Andean forms, so too the tocapu changed both in terms of context and form. I will leave aside the khipu, as it is the least interesting as a visual system and was one that was most useful for Spanish bureaucratic and Catholic confessional purposes.[15] The tocapu was always more performative than the khipu in the sense that it was a graphic image, therefore not an integral device as is the khipu in which the signs (knots, twists, etc.) are indissoluble from the object. Hence, the Inka tocapu appears woven into textiles, which were worn, and they were painted on adobe walls that defined the spaces of interaction such as at Tambo Colorado, or appeared on ceramics, especially *urpus* (an aryballos-shape ceramic vessel for serving corn beer), which were used in ritual feasting. These are entirely different media and different techniques for representing the same designs. That is, the tocapu was not a thing but a sign, and tocapus could appear in multiple contexts and media. As such the tocapu was much more versatile and was quickly found

Fig. 2. Raimondo di Sangro, Prince of Sansevero, "Folding colored engraved plate of alphabet/khipu with Tocapu," in *Lettera apologetica dell'Esercitato accademico della Crusca contenente la difesa del libro intitolato Lettere d'una peruana per rispetto alla supposizione de'quipu scritta alla duchessa di S**** e dalla medesima fatta pubblicare* (Naples: n.p., 1751). Houghton Library, Harvard University.

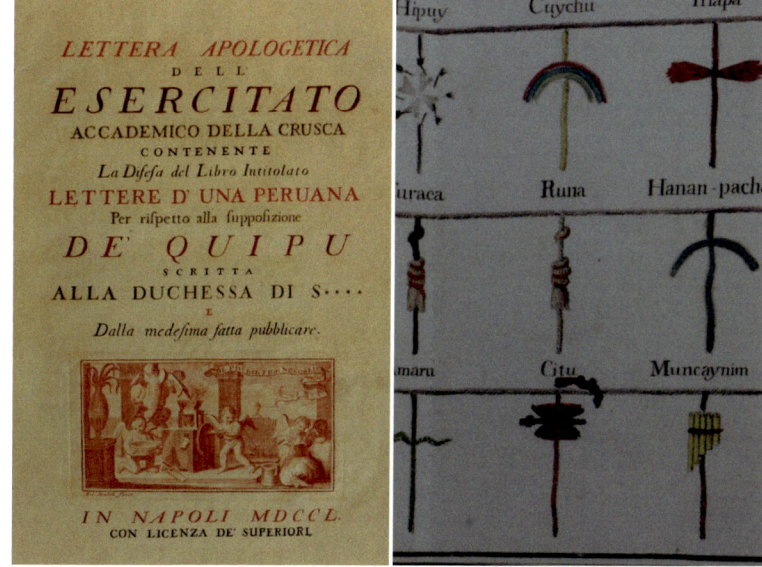

in traditional contexts where they had seldom occurred, such as being painted on *keros* (colonial wooden vessels) using *mopa-mopa,* an inlaid resin technique that seems to have come from Pasto in southern Colombia and was introduced into the southern Andes just before or immediately after the Spanish invasion. Tocapus appear on traditional *cumbi* (tapestry) woven garments such as on the most famous extant Inka uncu in the Dumbarton Oaks collection, as well as on the colonial uncu in the American Museum of Natural History that comes from Lake Titicaca and was collected by Adolph Bandelier at the end of the nineteenth century. These both display the same eccentric distribution of tocapus within a grid framework (fig. 3); however, the colonial uncu displays pairs of military figures

of the various nations of Tahuantinsuyu that are interspersed with rampant felines and the Augustinian heart at the hem. Unlike for the tocapus, there is a clear figure-ground relationship in this part of the uncu. It is also important to note that at the neck of the Bandelier uncu, the tocapus are bisected by the checkered V that separates the plain red field and the field of tocapus. We therefore are confronted with two systems of figuration that are integrated within a traditional object in which the integrity of the tocapu and whatever it might signify is intervened by the design of the neck that cuts them in half. This synthesis of European figural motifs and the geometric abstraction of the tocapu also occurs on female garments such as the *lliclla* (shawl) in which two seemingly antithetical design principles are used (fig. 4). The tocapus are arranged symmetrically in a horizontal set of registers and are linked across those registers by a defining and very recognizable diagonal using slide and rotation design principles, an Inka design phenomenon as described by Maria Ascher and Robert Ascher.[16] The converse is therefore also true; that is, the new figural style of European painting easily rendered portraits of Inka and Inka descendants wearing clothing with tocapu motifs such as in the late seventeenth-century painting of the wedding of Beatriz Coya. Most important, some of these new forms of the tocapu operate within a Christian context such as a small uncu made to dress the statue of the Christ child (fig. 5). Three systems of representation are deployed. The orb that the Christ child holds in his hand in the painting appears on either side of the uncu just above the rows of tocapus. Each orb is framed by felines, *otorongos* (jaguars) on one side and crowned rampant lions on the other. The third graphic system is the name Diego Dias, presumably the donor, written in reverse from right to left. Here, one might ask if this

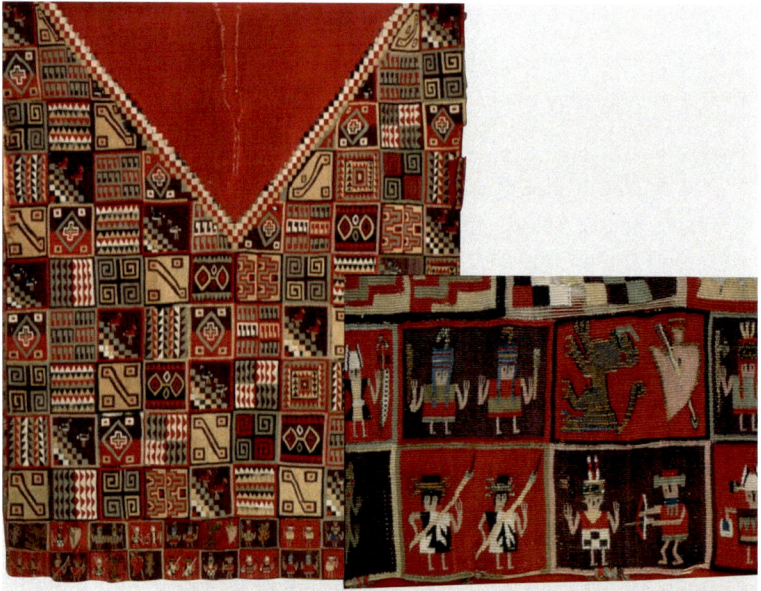

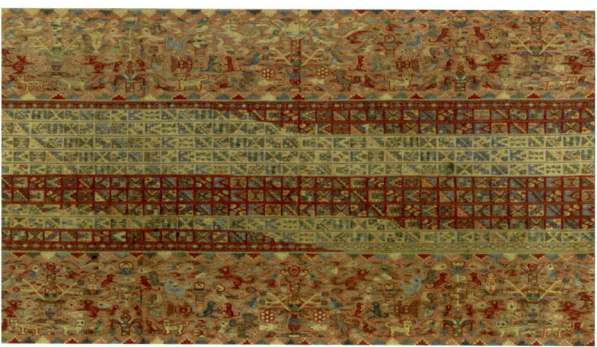

was just the weaver's mistaken understanding of the written word and how the piece was woven, but if so, then how is one to understand the horizontal rows of tocapus? Are they, too, to be viewed from left to right if there is any sense of a horizontal sequence to their relationship to the woven name, or are they to be read from right to left just as we read the alphabetic name, or is order of tocapus of no importance? That is, is there sequential disposition predicated on a predetermined order as there is for the decimal organization of the khipu? Clearly the disposition of tocapus is important on another liturgical object (fig. 6), a wooden cross now in the Ethnological Museum of Berlin, approximately a meter high and painted using the same mopa-mopa technique as used for colonial keros. No tocapu repeats on the vertical axis of the cross; they are placed along where Christ's legs, torso, and head would align. Where the vertical and horizontal of the cross meet, there is a large blossom as seen from above, presumably marking Christ's head. The tocapus on the arms of the cross are bilaterally symmetrical, mimicking or marking the bilateral symmetry of Christ's outstretched and bound arms. There are holes in the cross indicating that a sculpture of Christ's body was sometimes attached. In other words, one can trace through the layout of the tocapus the disposition of Christ's body on the cross, even when it is not present in sculptural form. But this then means that the order of the tocapus is predicated on an external organizing principle that is not intrinsic to the signs themselves, if that is what they are. Just as important, the tocapu is adaptable not only to new religious and social contexts but can be used in new materials and objects.

In these various examples one can see how tocapus were altered so as to coincide and intersect with European forms and objects in complex and divergent ways. This, I will argue,

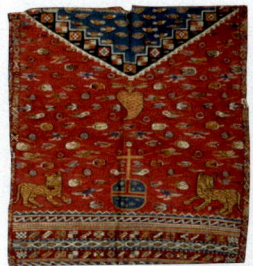 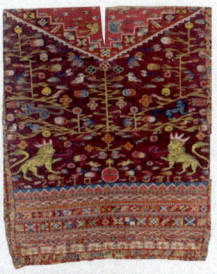

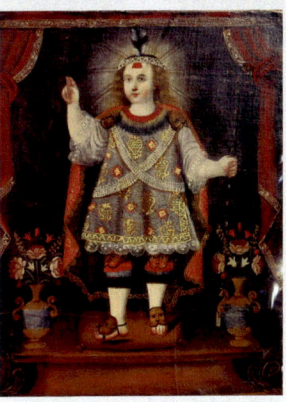

Fig. 5.

Top: Unknown artist, *Colonial Inka Uncu (front and back) for a Statue of the Christ Child.* Peru, about 1650. Approximately 40 in (101.6 cm). Museo del Inka, Cuzco (Tex-106. Ant. 729)

Bottom: Unknown artist, *Statue of the Christ Child Wearing Inka Clothing.* Cuzco, Peru, early 1700s. Oil paint on canvas. Present whereabouts unknown.

is especially true for one set of tocapus, those drawn by Guaman Poma de Ayala. This chapter will eventually focus on the tocapus that appear in Guaman Poma de Ayala's *Nueva coronica* for two reasons. First, numerous scholars have used the tocapu figures in *Nueva coronica* as a basis for believing they have found the interpretive key for the system of tocapus.[17] Second and more important, it is clear that Guaman Poma de Ayala synthesizes European and Andean systems to render his tocapus as signs whose reference is, as Urton has suggested, the notion of sign rather than to any specific meaning of each tocapu.[18]

The tocapu, as I have argued elsewhere, is a very mutable or polyvalent sign.[19] Yet despite its ubiquitous appearance, we have little information from the chroniclers or other documents that provide a means to understanding the tocapu. One can cite all of the texts that mention tocapus within a minute, and yet, as we can see, the tocapu appears on a variety of prehispanic and colonial objects, materials, and images and even expands in use after the conquest. Almost all texts associate the Inka tocapu with textiles, especially sixteenth- and seventeenth-century dictionary entries. For example, the 1586 *Diccionario Quechua-español* defines *tocapo* as "labor en lo que se brosla o texe o en vasos, tablas &c."[20] Diego González Holguín defines *tocapu* as "los vestidos de lauores preciosos, o paños de lauor texidos."[21] In Aymara, the term *tocapu* is slightly different than in Quechua as it is an adjective that can, but need not only, apply to textiles. Ludovico Bertonio's early seventeenth-century Aymara dictionary has

several entries under *tocapu,* one of which is *tocapu isi,* translated as "vestido, o ropa del Inga hecha a las mil marauillas, y assi llaman agora al Terciopelo, Telas, y Brocados &c quando quieren alabarlos" (garment, or clothing of the Inka made of a thousand marvels, and this is what they now call velvet, cloth, or brocade when they want to praise them).[22] *Isi* is the Aymara term for "vestido y cualquiera tela," so that *tocapu* refers to "ropa del Inga hecha a las mil marauillas" (Inka cloth made of a thousand marvels). The terms used by Bertonio are very similar to those used by Martín de Murúa, who wrote at almost the same time as Bertonio, and as noted above, stated that the *ñustas* wove "los vestidos del Ynga, y esculpían en ellas maravillosas labores de tocapo, que ellos dicen que significa diversidad de labores" (the dress of the Inka, and they sculpt [weave] into them works of tocapu that they say represent the diversity of embroidery).[23]

It is Pedro Sarmiento de Gamboa in his account of Inka monarchs who gives us a bit more information about the tocapus'

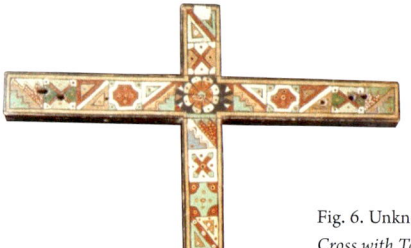

Fig. 6. Unknown artist, *Cross with Tocapus.* Peru, early 1700s. Wood with *mopa-mopa,* approximately 36 in. (91.44 cm). Ethnologisches Staatliche Museen, Berlin.

Fig. 7. *(Left)* Felipe Guaman Poma de Ayala, *Portrait of Viracocha Inca.* Ink on paper. Danish Royal Library, Copenhagen (GKS 2232 4º kvart): Guaman Poma, *Nueva corónica y buen gobierno* (about 1615), page 106 [106] *(Right)* Martín de Murúa, *Portrait of Viracocha Inca.* Watercolor on paper. In *Historia del origen y genealogía real de los reyes Incas del Pirú de sus hechos, costumbres, trajes, y manera de gobierno,* 1590–1615, folio 16v. Collection of Sean Galvin, Dublin, Ireland.

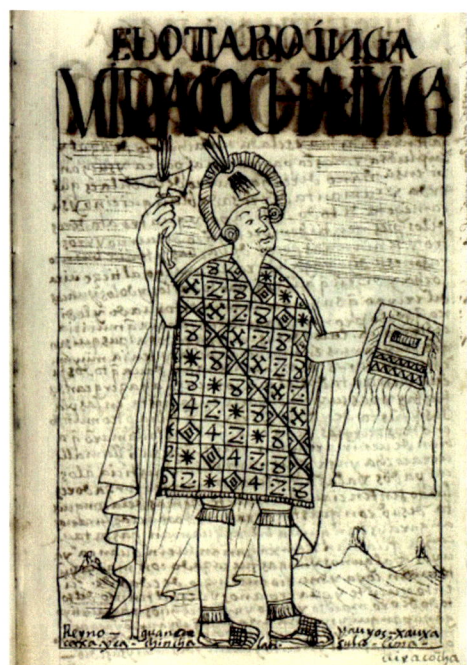
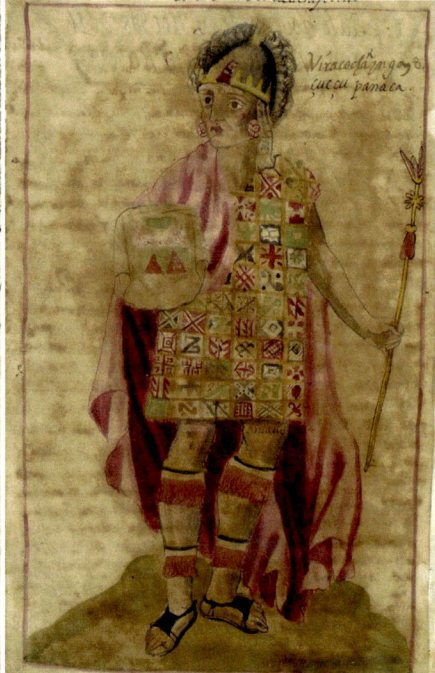

origin, which appears in his account of Inka Viracocha—and the images by Guaman Poma de Ayala and Murúa of this Inka king because their manuscripts and images are directly related to the project of Sarmiento de Gamboa and viceroy Francisco de Toledo (fig. 7). Sarmiento de Gamboa writes: "Este inga [Viracocha] fue industrioso y inventor de ropas y labores polidas, a que llaman en su lengua Uiracochatocapo, que es como entre nosotros el brocado" (This Inka was very skillful and the creator of fine clothes and designs that they call in their language Virracochatocaputha, among them is like a fine brocade).[24] Sarmiento de Gamboa's intention here is to demonstrate that the tocapu is the invention of an industrious (industrioso[25]) individual; however, this royal invention assumes a divine aspect in the account by Cristóbal de Molina, "el Cuzqueño," in his Relación de las fábulas y los ritos de los Incas, written around the year 1575. He writes that the creator of the world had two sons, one of whom was called "Tocapo Viracocha . . . quiere decir en su lengua hacedor en que se incluyen todas las cossas" (. . . which means in their language "creator," which includes all things).[26] Molina also includes two prayers to the god Viracocha, in which tocapu is referred to as an attribute of the god; the first of these is a reference to Viracocha as he who infuses life into things (Kamaq), placing everything in order and creating man and woman. The second prayer implores Viracocha for the increase of mankind.[27]

The reason to cite these texts, even though there are so few of them, is that they accord the tocapu a royal invention and a divine origin. The tocapu, then, is not merely a royal attribute, but it becomes endowed with concepts of royal invention and divine creation. These qualities are distinct from those most generally associated with the khipu. The khipu is acknowledged over and over again in the chronicles as being the instrument of record for the Inka, but it is not

marked in the literature with attributes of royal creation and divine inspiration. More important, the intimate relationship between Viracocha and tocapus also gives a precise geographic association to the tocapu: Lake Titicaca and the ruins of Tiahuanaco, both of which played a critical role in imperial origin myths of the Inka. It was here, the Inka claimed, that mankind was again created by Viracocha after the flood. The new peoples were then sent out by underground streams to emerge at the pacarina, or local place of origin.[28] These were the progenitors of all the ayllu (communities) of the world, and at Tiahuanaco they were first fashioned in stone and painted with their different ethnic dress. The monolithic sculptures of Tiahuanaco clearly served as the visual and material basis for the Inka claims. Not only did the Inka believe that Viracocha had painted these figures with the local dress of the various parts of the empire, but they recognized specific objects held in the hands of the figures, which became divine objects important to the Inkas' own imperial investiture.[29] Such a mythohistoric reading of the Tiahuanaco sculptures might allow us to suggest that the Inka also may have identified the designs on sculptures at Tiahuanaco as tocapus. Monuments such as the Ponce Monolith and El Fraile are depicted wearing a kind of short pants on which there are diagonal rows of two different cartouche-like designs. One is a rectangle within a rectangle, and the other seems to be a schematic face. Certainly, the design organization of many Wari and Tiahuanaco uncus foreshadows the tocapu arrangements and forms on Inka uncus. Similarly, the gradual breakdown of figural parts into increasingly stylized, abstract geometric arrangements also recalls the geometric abstraction of the many Inka tocapus.[30] Molina understood the tocapu as being related to Tiahuanaco and creation narratives, which suggests that such images may have inspired the formulation of these Inka myths.[31]

Aside from these texts, we have one more textual description that is a bit curious and that appears in the inventory from the Escorial of Philip II's personal possessions after his death. In the section entitled "Cosas Extraordinarias," we read the following description of an Inka uncu: "Otra camisa de yndios que dicen de cumbi [sic] texida de diversos colores y figuras, las quales son señales de armas de provincias que el ynga poseya, por donde las conocía, está apolillada y agujereada y no es de valor" (Another shirt of the Indians that they call *cumbi* woven with many different colors and figures, of which are signs of the coat-of-arms of the provinces that the Inka possessed, by which he knew them, it is moth eaten and full of holes and it is worthless).[32] I have written elsewhere what this text might mean and how it might possibly help explain the disposition of the tocapus on the Dumbarton Oaks uncu, which may also represent different territories incorporated into Tahuantinsuyu.[33]

There are equally as few early extant images of tocapus as there are texts. And almost all these images are found in the three interrelated manuscripts already mentioned, two from the manuscripts of Murúa and the one by Guaman Poma de Ayala. Most important for what shall be eventually argued about Guaman Poma de Ayala's drawings of tocapus is that the first manuscript by Murúa is not only the source for his own second manuscript but also served as the source of Guaman Poma de Ayala's *Nueva coronica*.[34] Moreover, Guaman Poma de Ayala worked on Murúa's first manuscript and produced many of the images. His hand first appears in Murúa's manuscript with a minimum gesture, adding details to Murúa's earliest images of the Inka.[35] He then provides full images for about two-thirds of the total illustrations.[36] What this

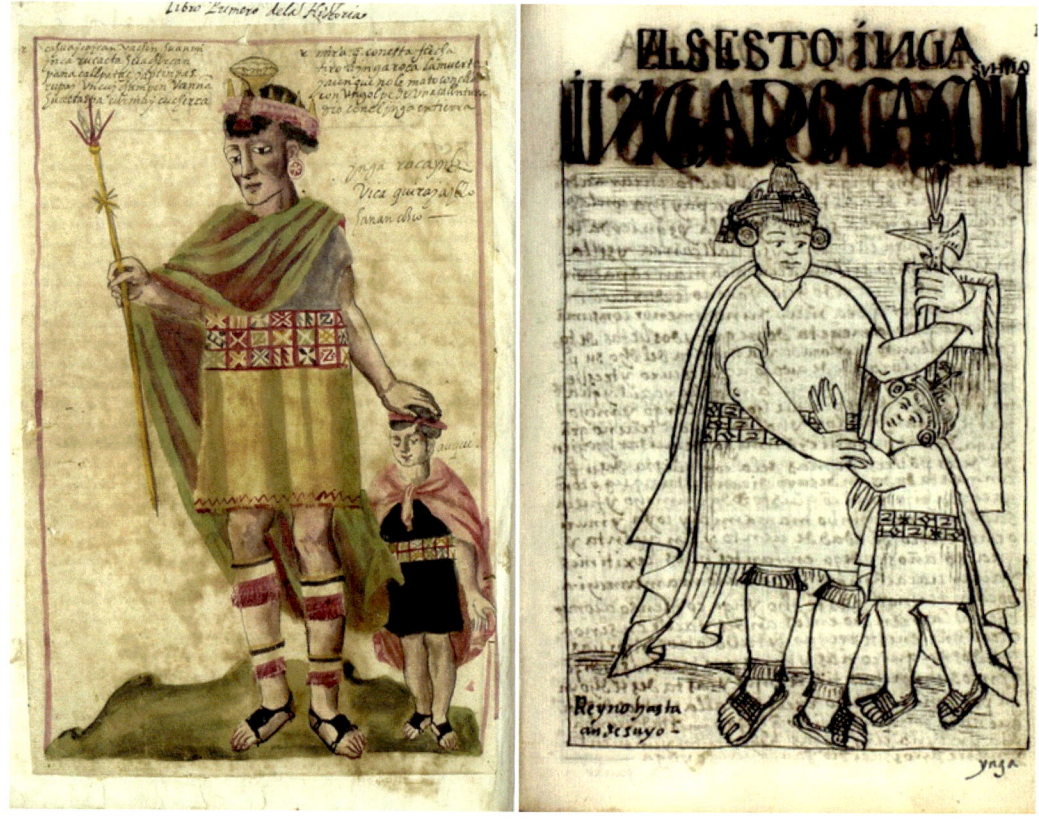

Fig. 8. *(Left)* Martín de Murúa, *Portrait of Inca Roca and Son.* Watercolor on paper. In *Historia del origen y genealogía real de los reyes Incas del Pirú de sus hechos, costumbres, trajes, y manera de gobierno,* 1590–1615, folio 14v. Collection of Sean Galvin. *(Right)* Felipe Guaman Poma de Ayala, *Portrait of Sinchi Roca and Son.* Ink on paper. DRL, (GKS 2232 4º kvart): Guaman Poma, *Nueva corónica y buen gobierno* (about 1615), page 102 [102].

implies is that there were two illustrated Murúa manuscripts that were sutured together and that Guaman Poma de Ayala worked differently in both. Guaman Poma de Ayala copied the composition of images created by Murúa in *Nueva coronica* as can be seen in a comparison of the two images of Sinchi Roca holding the hand of his young son and heir (fig. 8). This is the only Inka portrait in either manuscript in which two generations are depicted. Furthermore, Guaman Poma de Ayala copies Murúa's dedicatory letter to Philip II to address his manuscript to Philip III.[37] Most important, we know that Guaman Poma de Ayala paid close attention to the portraits of the Inka painted by Murúa in the Galvin manuscript and used what he had learned for his own drawings of the Inka in *Nueva coronica*. He not only copies their poses, gestures, and compositions, but Guaman Poma de Ayala augments his black-and-white drawings by textually describing the colors of the Inka royal uncus in *Nueva coronica*. Guaman Poma de Ayala does not base these images on some lost Inka pictorial system as Rolena Adorno suggests.[38] There is no "lost system" as Catherine Julien has asserted.[39] Rather, the portraits first found in Murúa and then copied by Guaman Poma de Ayala have their source in the portraits commissioned by Viceroy Toledo.[40] Guaman Poma de Ayala either remembered what he had seen while working with Murúa or more likely had drafts or his own copies of Murúa's texts and images. Thus, he is able to not only describe the colors as they appear in the color portraits of Murúa's first manuscript but also to copy their poses and compositions.

I will therefore focus in this chapter on the portraits of the Inka kings in the three manuscripts, because it is here that we encounter the problem that arises in the interpretation of tocapu representations, especially as they appear in the images of Guaman Poma de Ayala's *Nueva coronica*. This is because while the tocapus that appear in Murúa's images are more or less faithful representations of known tocapus that we have on Inka objects (fig. 9), as we can see in the portrait of the Inka and an uncu with the so-called key design, or two images with the *casana* design (fig. 10), including one by Guaman Poma de Ayala (fig. 11), the tocapus in the portraits of the Inka in *Nueva coronica* are generally very different even when the drawing's composition is copied from Murúa's first manuscript as in Inka Roca's portraits (see fig. 8).

They certainly are different from the tocapus on Inka royal garments (see fig. 7). Many of the royal tocapus drawn by Guaman Poma de Ayala no longer have an abstract geometric design but have instead recognizable forms such as a star, a 4, an 8, or Z and are arranged to have a strong diagonal axis, a pattern not used by Murúa. Urton suggests that because some of these forms seem to correlate to Hindu Arabic numerals, Guaman Poma de Ayala was implying "a correspondence (at some level) between what he understood the tocapu to represent for the Inka and what he knew to be the meaning, use, and power of numbers in the late sixteenth- and seventeenth-century world of colonial Peru."[41] As we shall see, at one level of analysis he is correct in that Guaman Poma de Ayala gestures through a European system toward tocapus, but he never reveals what the tocapu is or what it means. However, because Urton fixates solely on numbers as operating within arithmetic, he misses the forest for the few trees. In fact, he is even more myopic in terms of Guaman Poma de Ayala's tocapus as he only sees one species of tree. That is, he does not mention any of the other graphic signs in Guaman Poma de Ayala's tocapu images because he is not interested in anything but numbers, which are the index of "the power of numbers" for his interpretive framework. Numbers carry the symbolic weight for his argument. Hence, he does not see the overall compositional pattern of the uncus or the other non-numeric signs that also reference tocapus.

In truth, the selective reading of discrete tocapus in Guaman Poma de Ayala's drawings has been the problem for all tocapu studies that use Guaman Poma de Ayala as an explanatory source. This is because there are different forms that suggest various references. Thus Urton, Mary Frame, Gail Silverman, Peter Eeckhout, Margarita Gentile, and many others have interpreted Guaman Poma de Ayala's tocapus in various ways. For example, Frame posits that one particular tocapu represents Tahuantinsuyu and so on. Are we to understand that Guaman Poma de Ayala is using multiple systems of referentiality to create his tocapus and that they are from radically different ontological and epistemological cultural worlds? This juxtaposition or contradiction can only be sustained by eliminating what does not fit the template used. We can easily see this in the studies of Urton and Eeckhout and Danis in which the authors interpret the same tocapu according to their own radically different fancy in an a priori argument (fig. 12). Citing the same uncus

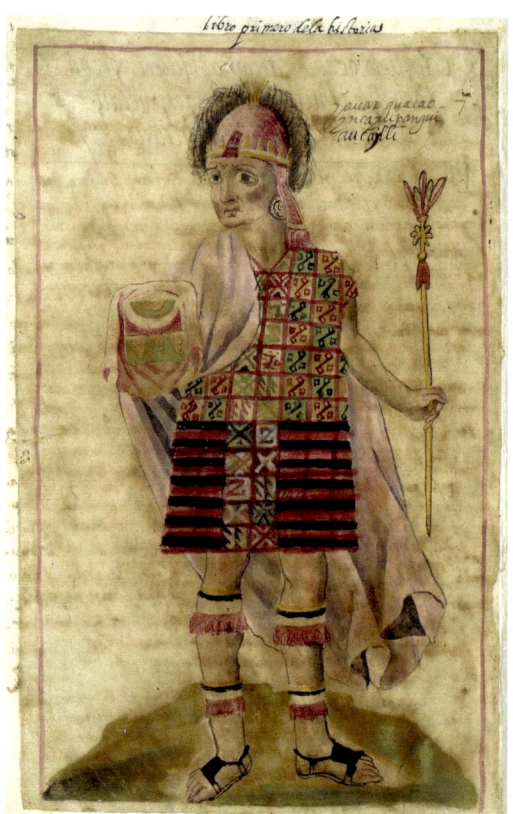

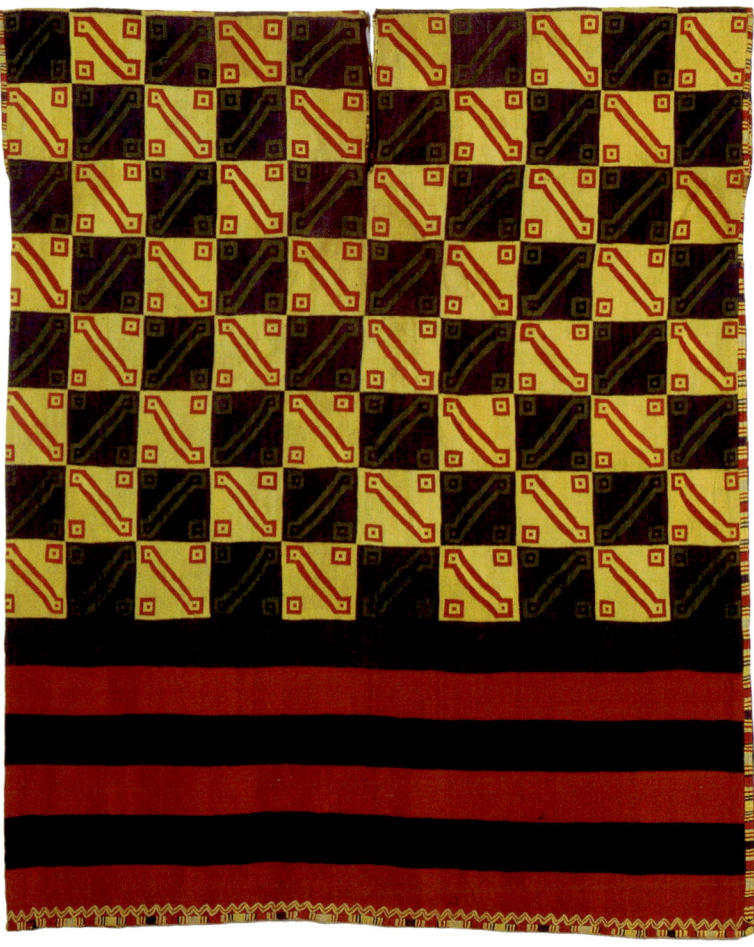

Fig. 9. (*Left*) Martín de Murúa, *Portrait of Yauar guacac Ynca Yupanqui Inca Wearing an Uncu with a "Key Design."* Watercolor on paper. In *Historia del origen y genealogía real de los reyes Incas del Pirú de sus hechos, costumbres, trajes, y manera de gobierno,* 1590–1615, folio 15v. Collection of Sean Galvin. (*Right*) Unknown artist, *Inka Uncu with Key Motif Tocapu Design.* Peru, about 1500–1532. The Textile Museum, Washington, D.C., 91.147, Acquired by George Hewitt Myers in 1932.

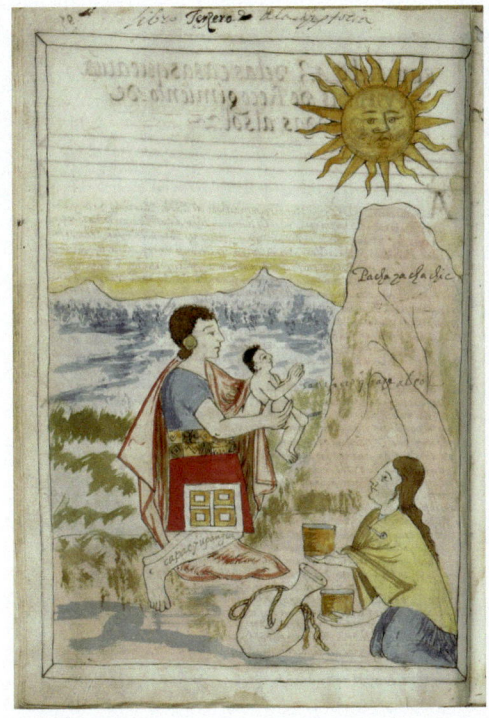

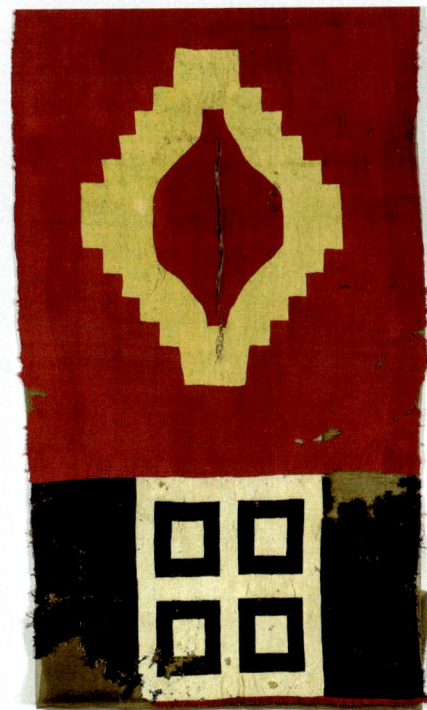

Fig. 10. (*Left*) Martín de Murúa, *Inca Wearing an Uncu with a Casana Design Making a Child Sacrifice to the Inti (the Sun)*. Watercolor on paper. In *Historia del origen y genealogía real de los reyes Incas del Pirú de sus hechos, costumbres, trajes, y manera de gobierno*, 1590–1615, folio 103v. Collection of Sean Galvin. (*Right*) Unknown artist, *Inka Uncu with a Casana Design (Tunic or Poncho)*. Peru, about 1500–1530. Catalog number A307655, Department of Anthropology, Smithsonian Institution.

and their tocapus depicted on the same Inka (Inka Yupanqui) by Guaman Poma de Ayala, these scholars draw antithetical conclusions by looking only at a select kind of sign. In the case of Eeckout and Danis, some of Guaman Poma de Ayala's tocapus are heraldic and pertain to specific kings and queens, meaning that some tocapus are not and therefore these are inconsequential to their interpretation. For Urton, they are the Inka's attraction and affinity to numbers. Moreover, color, a supposedly signifying criterion, is not of concern to these interpretations. Thus, in comparing the designs of the black-and-white drawings of Guaman Poma de Ayala with actual Inka and colonial tocapus on a variety of objects, they appear to correspond almost precisely because the color of the Inka tocapus are not reproduced, so that the black-and-white linear designs are the only signifying entities for Urton and Eeckout and Danis. They can also ignore any geometric motif that does not contribute to their interpretations.

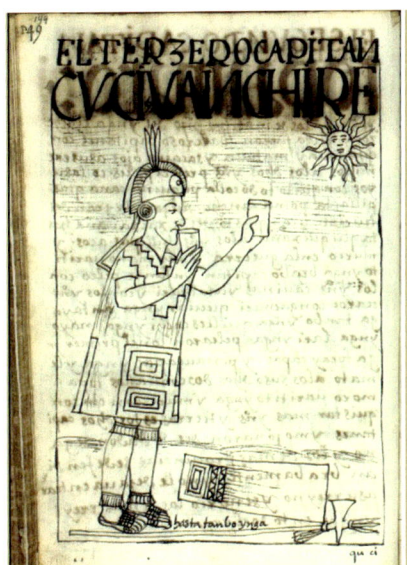

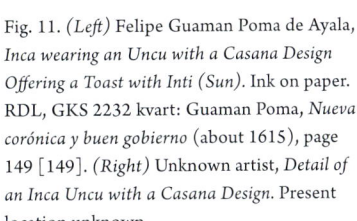

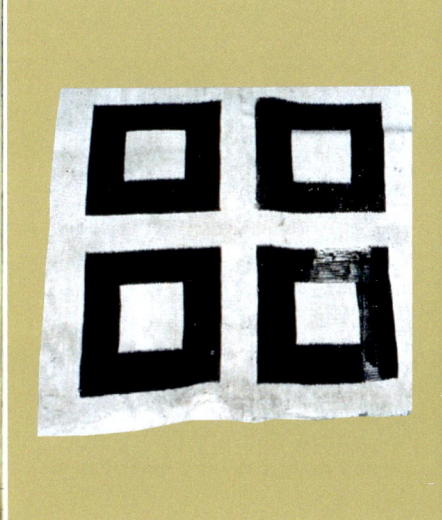

Fig. 11. (*Left*) Felipe Guaman Poma de Ayala, *Inca wearing an Uncu with a Casana Design Offering a Toast with Inti (Sun)*. Ink on paper. RDL, GKS 2232 kvart: Guaman Poma, *Nueva corónica y buen gobierno* (about 1615), page 149 [149]. (*Right*) Unknown artist, *Detail of an Inca Uncu with a Casana Design*. Present location unknown.

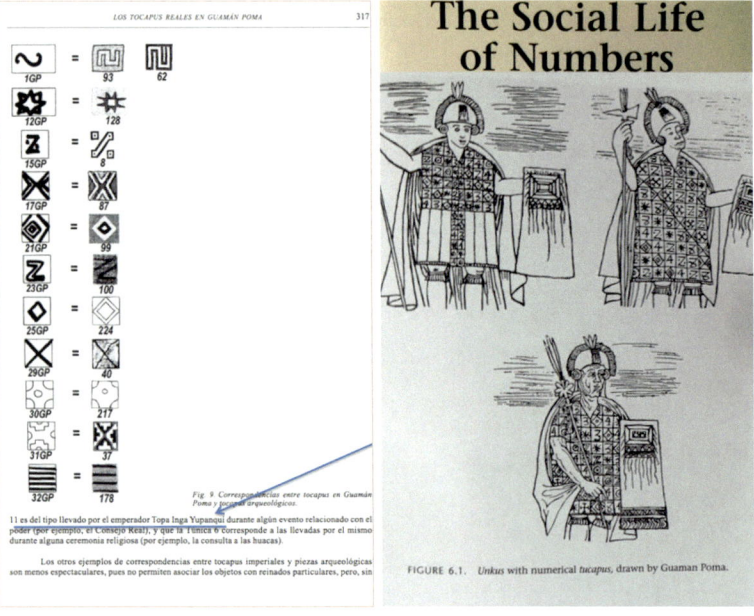

Fig. 12. Illustrations from *(Left)* Peter Eeckhout and Nathalie Danis's "Los tocapus reales en Guamán Poma: ¿Una heráldica incaica?" and *(Right)* Gary Urton's *The Social Life of Numbers: A Quechua Ontology of Numbers and Philosophy of Arithmetic* with differing interpretations of the same royal uncus with tocapus by Guaman Poma de Ayala.

Perhaps this is the case, that there are diverse references within the myriad of Guaman Poma de Ayala's tocapus, and that one can pick and choose as one likes and that was Guaman Poma de Ayala's intention. At the very least, it is obvious that Guaman Poma de Ayala has clearly shifted the ground of reference, because even when Guaman Poma de Ayala copies Murúa's image (fig. 13), such as in the portrait of Manco Capac, the tocapus are different. Guaman Poma de Ayala's tocapus are arranged in horizontal rows, and they repeat in a vertical diagonal, as opposed to how Murúa represents them in two discrete horizontal rows known as *chumpi*. This difference has to be understood as being intentional because as already mentioned, Guaman Poma de Ayala describes the colors of the dress of the Inka for his black-and-white drawings, and these descriptions, as mentioned, are based on the color in Murúa's first manuscript. Murúa himself paid close attention to Inka garments and carefully detailed them in his own watercolors.[42] He even collected them and took them with him when he returned to Spain, including what was believed to be a royal Inka uncu.[43]

The questions therefore become what is or are the sources for Guaman Poma de Ayala's drawings of tocapus in the portraits of the Inka if they are not what he saw and knew in Murúa's drawings or even the tocapus he saw on many of the Inka objects that remained or any newly made traditional forms? Why does he render them as he does? Is it pure whimsy or capitulation to the power of Western arithmetic? There seems to be an intentional change of focus on the tocapu, as Guaman Poma de Ayala does not always deviate from the tocapu designs that appear in other images he created in the Galvin Murúa manuscript and that he redrew for *Nueva coronica*. This is especially clear in the depiction of Tupac Amuru being led to Cuzco after being captured by Martin de Loyola that Guaman Poma de Ayala did for the Galvin manuscript and his *Nueva coronica*.

Codes, Ciphers, and Tocapus

Before suggesting a source and a probable explanation of why Guaman Poma de Ayala changes his tocapu forms and composition of the royal uncus in the portraits of the Inka, it is important to present a set of historical conditions concerning a different system of notation with which we can enter a path toward interpretation. This is the system of ciphers or coded writing that was used in Peru and throughout the burgeoning Spanish Empire in the sixteenth century to transmit sensitive information. The archives are full of encrypted documents from all parts of America, and manuals were published to help individuals to use ciphers. As defined by Juan Carlos Galende Díaz, cryptography consists of communicating by means of letters, signs, and numbers arranged in an order according to a key that is known only to those who possess it.[44] In the first instance it has nothing necessarily to do with writing or arithmetic.

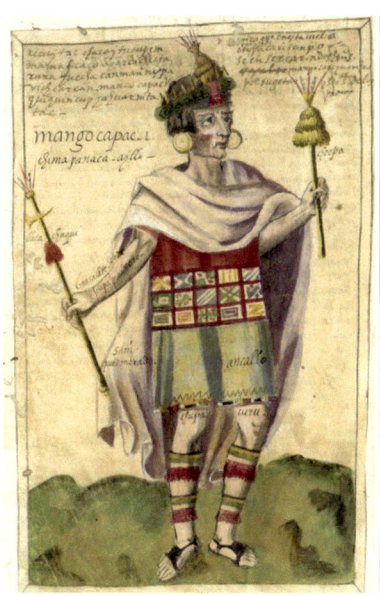
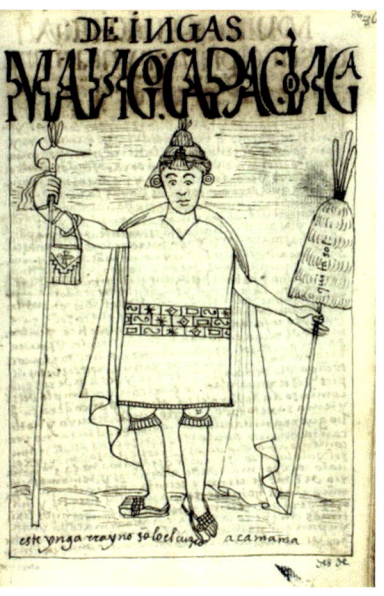

Guillermo Lohmann Villena is one of the first scholars to publish an extensive essay on the use of and forms of ciphers and codes used in colonial Latin America and Spain.[45] In it, he details the numerous uses of ciphers in sixteenth- and early seventeenth-century Peruvian documents as well as the individuals who used them such as Pedro de la Gasca, Viceroy Toledo, Sarmiento de Gamboa, and the Jesuits almost from as soon as they arrived in Peru. There are essentially three types of ciphers based on one of three principles: transposition, substitution, and hiding.[46] All three were used to different degrees in Peru and throughout the Americas and not only by Spaniards but also mestizos and Natives.

One Peruvian example that is briefly mentioned by Lohmann Villena demonstrates how widespread such ciphers were throughout the viceroyalty. It was created by José de Orozco y Gamarra who came to Peru in 1578 and participated in the suppression of a revolt in Santa Marta on the Caribbean coast. From there, he went inland, passing through Quito en route to Potosí where he hoped to make his fortune. He stayed in Quito long enough to marry the grandaughter of Atahualpa, the last Inka ruler,

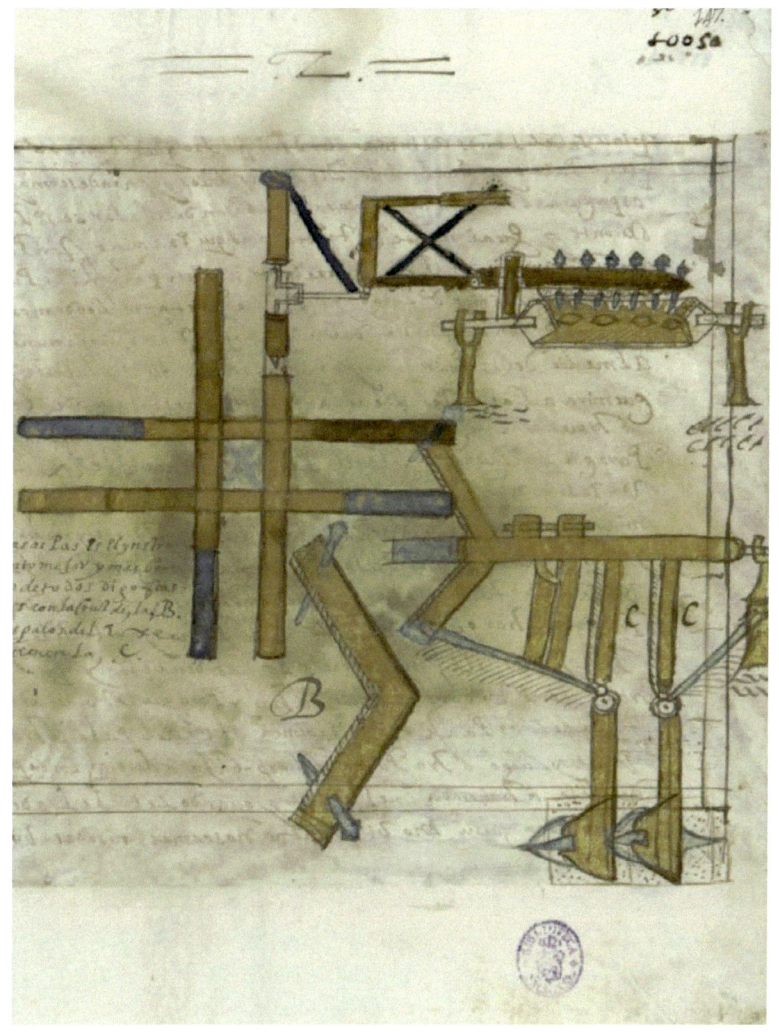

who was murdered by the Spanish. He had a son with her, named Bartholomé Inga de Orozco, who came with him to Peru, where he can best be described as having a career as a charlatan, or as Lohmann Villena calls him, "un arbitrista."[47] In 1604, he dispatched his son Bartolomé from the port of Callao with the court in Madrid as his destination. He was taking with him a document to be offered in service to the Crown, in which he provided a "new and better way" to extract silver ore at Potosí, adding a color drawing of the apparatus he had "invented" (fig. 14).[48] Worried that his plan might fall into the wrong hands, Orozco y Gamarra used a form of cryptography utilizing a complicated system of ciphers that is a series of short lines (fig. 15). The key to the cipher was separated from the document in the nineteenth century but was rediscovered by Maria Helmer in 1960, who also produced the code, or countercipher, created by Luis Valle de la Cerda after it had reached the Consejo de las Indias (Council of the Indies).[49] I am not really interested in what is encoded in the document, but rather how it is encoded. What one sees is a series of short lines seemingly placed indiscriminately on the page. But in fact, the placement and direction of the short lines is critical. The position of the line

is determined within an imaginary or invisible quadrant with squares and lines and the letters that the lines are meant to indicate; that is, the directions of the line segments but also the position in the square is relevant. Three positions are distinguished among upper vertical strokes for *b, c,* and *d.* The same applies to lower vertical strokes and left and right horizontal strokes. Two positions are distinguished for diagonal strokes at each corner (e.g., for *a* and *t*). For accurate enciphering and deciphering, it must have been necessary to apply a grid under the sheet.

This minor document is more or less interesting for its own anecdotal story, but in addition to the details of the ingenuity of the cipher itself, it demonstrates that the systems of cryptography were used by various classes of individuals at the end of the sixteenth century, including common Spaniards and descendants of Inka rulers. In reality there were a variety of different systems used by the Spaniards. The most important and unbreakable cryptograph and the one that is critical for this argument was developed by Leon Battista Alberti, detailed in his 1466 manuscript *De componendis cifris* and later published in Venice as *La cifra* in 1568. What made Alberti's system so important is that it eliminated letter frequency used in words of a language as a means of breaking and deciphering the message. Alberti's system was a polyalphabetic substitution cipher that did not just replace the plain text alphabet with a single separate alphabet but instead used multiple enciphering alphabets to create greater confusion and security. The key to Alberti's new system was a device he called a "formula." This was a cipher disk consisting of two metal disks: one a fixed outer disk, and the other a mobile inner disk attached by a common axle. In his basic description of his new cipher, he explained that he would use the outer ring of upper-case letters for his plain text as well as numbers 1 through 4 and the inner mobile ring

Fig. 15. José de Orozco y Gamarra and Bartolomé Inga de Orozco, "Secretos de las minas de Indias" (and code for decipherment), 1604. Watercolor, ink on paper. In Luis Valle de la Cerda, "Memoria de los servicios que hizo a la católica majestad de los reyes Don Phelipe II y Don Phelipe III en negocios y materia de estado y guerra en Italia, Flandes y España," 114r. Ms. 994 Biblioteca Nacional, Madrid.

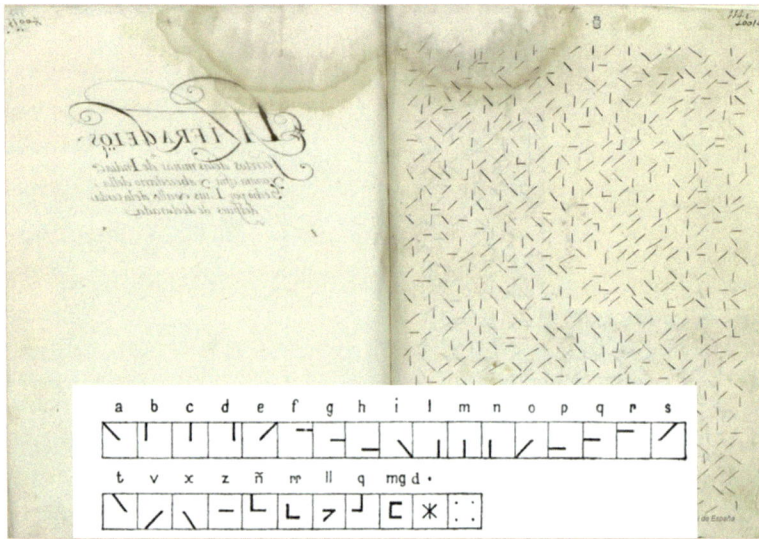

of lower-case letters for his cipher text (fig. 16).[50] This chapter is not intent on explaining Alberti's system for encoding messages but rather its dissemination through its publication first in Italy in 1568 until it reaches Peru. A major conduit for Alberti's cipher is Blaise de Vigenère's *Traicté des chiffres, ou secrètes manières d'escrire* published in 1586. In it, he describes many older ciphers and Alberti's system with illustrations in what is called the Vigenère square or Vigenère table (fig. 17). That is, he replaces the concentric round disks developed by Alberti and systematizes it with a rectangular grid. This is the best-known example of the table, but Giambattista della Porta's *De furtivis literarum notis vulgon de ziferis libri IIII* (1563) is the source for Vigenère's *Traicté des chiffres*. This work was known in Spain, as it was dedicated to Philip II. In fact, della Porta visited Philip's court in Madrid in the 1560s and presented *De furtivis* to the king.[51]

Clearly, some form of this table was already known, as we shall see, before Vigenère's *Traicté des chiffres* was published. However, his book is perhaps the most explicit on how to decipher the encoded message, and he is often credited with it. He notes that the intended receiver needs to know which row of Vigenère's table has been used to encipher each letter, so that there must be an agreed upon system of switching between rows. This is Alberti's system but what is important for this chapter is the shift from a circular format depicted by Alberti to a rectangular one by Vigenère to illustrate the system. What then becomes clearly seen in terms of the design is the relationship of the grid to the signs (letters) and the inevitable diagonal of the same letters that is visibly apparent based on the system of substitution.[52]

And how were these systems disseminated? In some cases, via their manuals of ciphers. However, unlike the French, Italian, and German theoretical treatises that were already printed in the sixteenth century, Spanish manuals only began to be printed in the mid-seventeenth century.[53] Nonetheless, Spanish manuscripts or codes about ciphers were circulating and being used extensively in America, such as by Hernán Cortés and Francisco Pizarro among the most famous examples. As we shall see, it is even possible that both Alberti's *La cifra* and Vigenère's *Traicté des chiffres* were already circulating in Spain and America within two years after the publication in France of *Traicté*.

But what does European history of cryptography have to do with tocapus and Guaman

Left: Fig. 16. Redrawn illustration of Leon Battista Alberti's "formula" as found in *De componendis cifris*, 1466. Drawn by Kyle Huffman.

Right: Fig. 17. Blaise de Vigenère, "Frontispiece and table," in *Traicté des chiffres, ou secrètes manières d'escrire* (Paris: Abel l'Angelier, 1586).

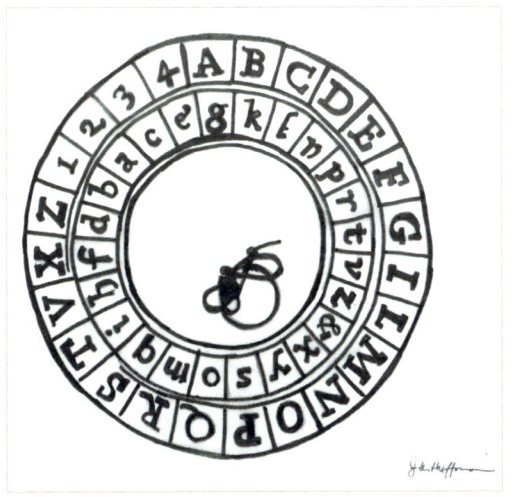

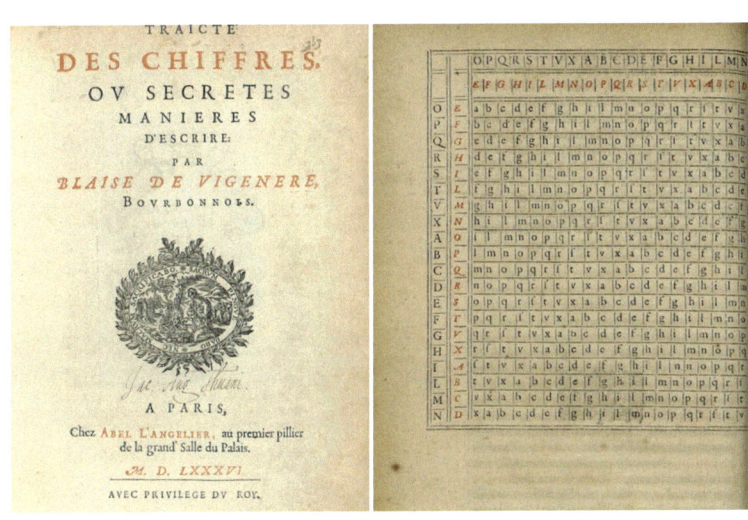

Poma de Ayala's depiction of them other than they both seem to depend on an encoded system? Alberti's *La cifra* and Vigenère's *Traicté des chiffres*[54] certainly were known in Spain, as can be seen in a plate from Gabriel Gasca y Espinosa's 1631 *Manual de avisos para el perfecto cortesano* in which he depicts a model, or "cabeza quadrante" (fig. 18).[55] The plate was no less than the "cifra cuadrada" of the encrypted system of Vigenère (see fig. 17). Whether or not Guaman Poma de Ayala fully understood the system of the polyalphabetic substitution cipher is not of real concern. What is striking is that not only do the designs differ from those in Murúa's images but also the arrangement of the symbols in Guaman Poma de Ayala's tocapus and the letters in Vigenère's table are remarkably similar, as are those in della Porta's *De furtivis*. A strong diagonal line organizes the figures within della Porta's and Vigenère's grids in the system, just as can be seen in the distribution of tocapus on the Inka's uncu as drawn by Guaman Poma de Ayala. But what could these ciphers and their pattern mean for Guaman Poma de Ayala's tocapus other than mere coincidence? After all, there are examples of tocapus arranged along a descending vertical, especially on colonial textiles and keros, as Yuri Knorozov observed.[56] However, almost none of Guaman Poma de Ayala's tocapu designs correspond to known Inka or colonial tocapu designs. Those that do appear to have a correspondence also appear in the system developed by Alberti and Vigenère. But how is it that Guaman Poma de Ayala knew about this system?

To answer these questions, it is critical to remember that Guaman Poma de Ayala, most likely through his relationship with Murúa and the Mercedarian order, had access to and used a variety of published and unpublished sources as well as the images and texts that Murúa wrote and painted.[57] One of the most important sources used by Guaman Poma de Ayala to construct

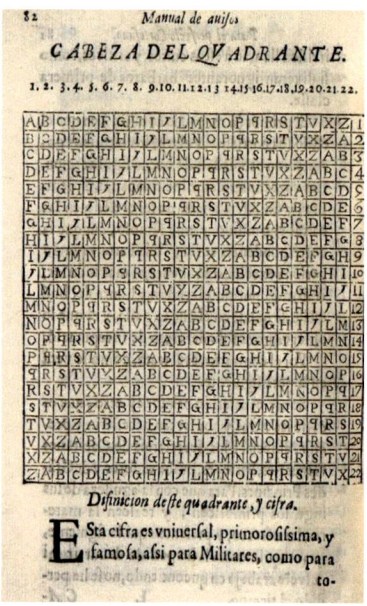

Fig. 18. Gabriel Gasca y Espinosa, "Cabeza quadrante," in *Manual de avisos para el perfecto cortesano* (Madrid: Roque Rico de Miranda, 1631).

his intersection of personal and viceregal history is, as Adorno has pointed out,[58] Diego Fernández's well-known *Primera and segunda parte de la Historia del Piru* published in 1571, a text that was first used by Murúa.[59] Both parts of Fernández's book recount the civil wars that followed the conquest, and Guaman Poma de Ayala uses Fernández's account of the rebellion of Francisco Hernández Girón in book two of the second part to structure his own account of the events. Fernández recounts how Hernández Girón arrived in Peru in 1535 with the future governor Blasco Núñez Vela. In the ensuing struggle for power between the Pizarro brothers and the Almagristas in 1537, he supported neither. Diego de Almagro was executed in 1538, and Francisco Pizarro, governor of Peru, was assassinated by Almagro's son in 1541. The next governor, Cristóbal Vaca de Castro, again had to contend with and fought Diego de Almagro el Mozo, Almagro's son, and his troops at the battle of Chupas, which was a place claimed by

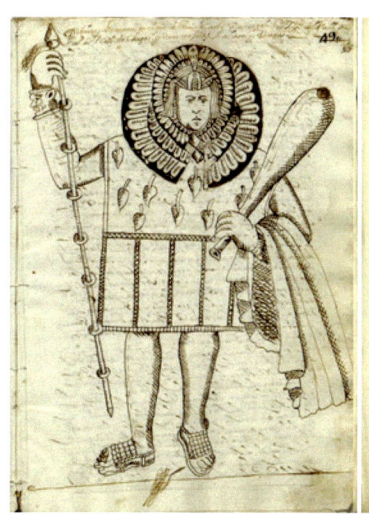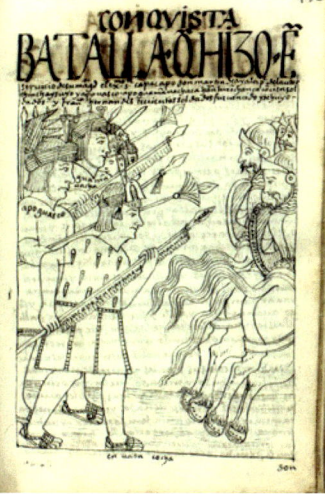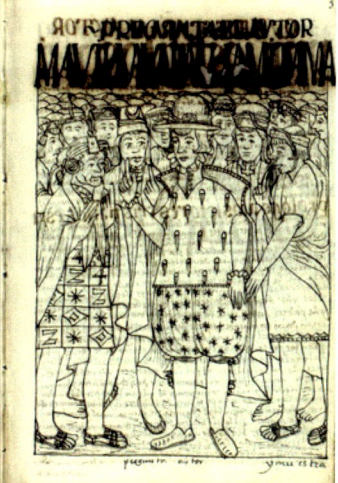

Below: Fig. 20. Felipe
Guaman Poma de Ayala,
*(Left) The Revolt of Francisco
Hernández Girón and
His Victorious Battle of
Chuquinga, (Center) Don
Martín Guaman Malque de
Ayala Leads Attack against
Francisco Hernández Girón,*
and *(Right) Francisco
Hernández Girón Taken
Prisoner.* Ink on paper. RDL,
GKS 2232 kvart: Guaman
Poma, *Nueva corónica y buen
gobierno* (about 1615), page
430 [432], 432 [434], and
434 [436].

Above: Fig. 19. *(Left)* Felipe Guaman Poma de
Ayala, *Portrait of Domingo Guaman Malque de
Aiala, Cacique Principal, Gobernador y Señor
del Valle del Pueblo de Santa Catalina de Chupa
. . ."* A 1640 copy of an original drawing by
Guaman Poma de Ayala about 1597 found
in "Expediente Prado Tello c. 1560–1640,"
folio 49r. Private collection, Lima. *(Center)*
Felipe Guaman Poma de Ayala, *Don Martín
Guaman Malque de Ayala, Leads Attack against
Francisco Hernández Girón. (Right)* Felipe
Guaman Poma de Ayala, *Author among His
Ancestors and Incas.* Ink on paper. RDL, GKS
2232 kvart: Guaman Poma, *Nueva corónica y
buen gobierno* (about 1615), page 432[434]
and 366[368].

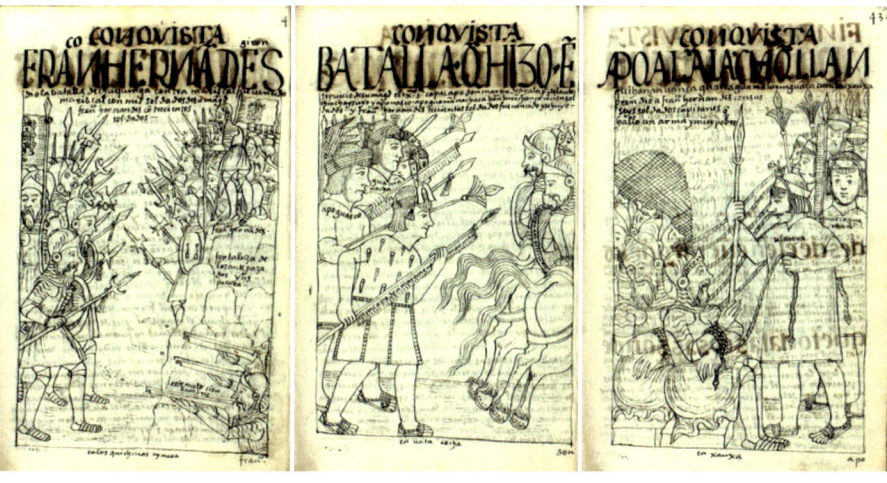

Guaman Poma de Ayala to be his ancestral home
and therefore the subject of his lawsuit for which
he produced the only colonial map of the area as
well as the portraits of his ancestors, both in the
map and in full-page drawings (fig. 19).[60]

Hernández Girón, a supporter of Núñez
Vela, fought at the battles of Añaquito and managed to escape death as his troops' defeat became
apparent. At Jaquijahuana, Hernández Girón
again took the side of the royal forces under
Pedro de la Gasca, with great success. However,
on November 13, 1553, he led a rebellion against
the Crown caused by the New Laws proclaimed
by Melchor Bravo de Saravia, the new viceroy.
Hernández Girón was eventually defeated and

on December 7, 1554, executed in Lima. As
Adorno notes, Guaman Poma de Ayala "follows
[Fernández's] account only in broadest outline,"
and most important, Guaman Poma de Ayala
asserts that the Native troops aided the Crown's
troops in an act of loyalty, whereas Fernández
and other chroniclers say they attacked both
sides.[61] More important still, the events are
depicted such that the main protagonist is his
father, Don Martín de Ayala, who appears as one
of the captains who led the Indigenous forces
against Hernández Girón and his rebellious
army (fig. 20). The title reads "Batalla que hizo
en servicio de su majestad, excelentícimo señor
capac apo don Martín de Ayala, padre del autor"

(Battle that he waged on behalf of his majesty the most excellent lord, high lord don Martín de Ayala, the father of the author). Martín de Ayala appears in the foreground with his name and title written along his spear. Here, historic loyalty and authorial presence are united in the service of the king. And according to Guaman Poma de Ayala's telling and drawing, the Native lords are those who defeat and capture Hernández Girón, as seen on page 436. And so that we understand visually who the main protagonists are and their relationship to each other, his father wears the same uncu as his grandfather, whose portrait appears in the Chupas lawsuit document and that Guaman Poma de Ayala wears in his self-portrait as author (see fig. 19). There seems to be a kind of internal genealogical dialogue that Guaman Poma de Ayala carries forth in his images, one that the intended viewer, Philip III, would have been hard pressed to follow visually.

Guaman Poma de Ayala's text and images are thus not so straightforward an account of the capture of Hernandez Girón as Fernández's account, since it is interwoven with his own personal history, as Adorno notes.[62] However, Fernández's own account is not quite as straightforward in terms of narrative as Adorno might have us believe. Rather, Fernández breaks his retelling of the historical events to explain to the reader how communication was effected between the commanders of the separated armies by using disappearing ink, codes, and ciphers. In fact, Fernández goes on for eight pages of various explanations as to how these codes and inks were used and how they worked. When describing the use of invisible ink as a means of conveying information, he recounts to the reader that "tambien se escriuio en el brazo de un indio cierto auiso: de manera, que no parecia auer alli escripto cosa alguna: y despues, fregando con carbon, ó tierra, ó con qualquier poluo, se veyan claramente las letras" (also a text was written on the arm of a certain Indian such that nothing appeared written there until later when it was rubbed with carbon, earth, or some other powder, and then letters were seen clearly).[63] The idea of inscribing an invisible message on the arm introduces the Andean body directly into the discursive arena of secret coded messages and their transmission. Among other things, one might ask what this passage might have meant to Guaman Poma de Ayala when he decided to draw texts along the arms of some of his characters? Perhaps nothing, as most text written on bodies is simply identifying names of Spaniards. But why, one might ask, is there no text written on anybody identifying who they are in the section before the conquest? This difference appears to be a conscious decision by Guaman Poma de Ayala, as some of his watercolor images of the Inka before the conquest in the Galvin manuscript have been glossed with identifying text on the bodies. Some figures even have the text written along the arms, although Guaman Poma de Ayala did not add this writing. Regardless of what such decisions were, the first text written on an Andean body depicted in *Nueva coronica* appears in the scene of Pizarro meeting with Atahualpa at Cajamarca, just before the Inka monarch's capture. The Dominican (Vincente Valverde) and two of the conquistadores (Almagro and Pizarro) are identified by their names written on their headgear. Off to Atahualpa's left appears Felipe, the go-between, whose name and position as translator are written along his sleeved arm: "Felipe Indio lengua" (fig. 21). One senses that this seemingly rather odd placement of the text is in fact in concert with Felipe's action as he raises his right arm and points upward in a deictic act of communication with his index finger in the air. The arm and gesture communicate the act of cross-cultural interaction even though no speech or translation is recorded. One of the only other images in which Guaman Poma de Ayala places text written along the arms is also a scene of an act of cross-cultural communication. A *curaca* (Andean leader of a community) rushes into the picture plane and extends his arm toward a seated *corregidor* (local magistrate) who extends toward him a goblet of wine as he drinks from the other (fig. 22). Written on the corregidor's arm is a toast of salutation to the curaca, who responds with a text written on his bare outstretched arm in anticipation of receiving the proffered goblet, "My lord, high lord I will serve you." The text only vaguely indicates what the toast means within Andean etiquette based on the reception and offering of a goblet. The sociopolitical understanding of what is transpiring along the arms both in gesture and text is veiled to all those who can't read and those who can't understand Andean social norms. In other words, this is a highly encrypted image, and those without the proper keys can have no idea what is transpiring.[64]

Only when Fernández has finished discussing the use of and meaning of ciphers does he return to the narrative of the historical events, or as he wrote at the end of the chapter on cipher and codes, "Bolviendo pues al proposito de la historia . . ." (Returning then to the historical account).[65] As one begins to enter back into the historical narrative, the reader must see in the left-hand column the table for one of the ciphers that has just been described.

What becomes clear from Fernández's text is that Andeans became very familiar with these systems, literally embodying them as their own arms were transformed into the surface onto which messages were encoded. But more important, Guaman Poma de Ayala had to have seen, at the very least, if not have read about these systems as he read about Hernández Girón with the desire to transform these events into his personal history. He therefore had to have seen the plates that appear in Fernández's book, the first two of which are based on the Albertian circular model,

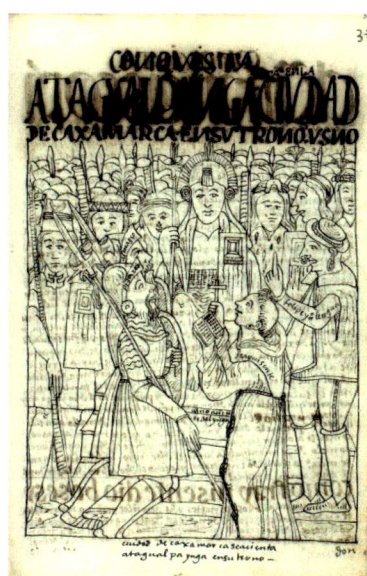

Above: Fig. 21. Felipe Guaman Poma de Ayala, *Atahualpa at Cajamarca with Pizarro and Translator Felipe.* Ink on paper. RDL, GKS 2232 kvart: Guaman Poma, *Nueva corónica y buen gobierno* (about 1615), page 384 [386].

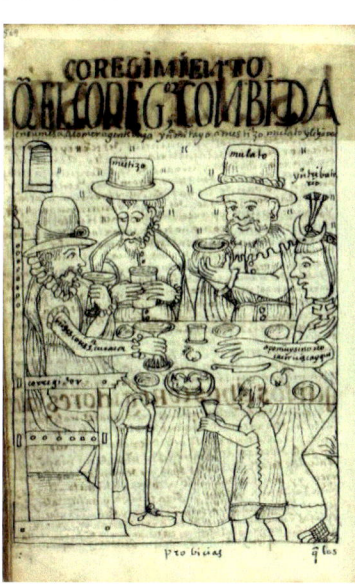

Below: Fig. 22. Felipe Guaman Poma de Ayala, *A Curaca Drinks with a Corregidor.* Ink on paper. RDL, GKS 2232 kvart: Guaman Poma, *Nueva corónica y buen gobierno* (about 1615), page 505 [509].

or "formula" (fig. 23). One can only imagine him contemplating the images in Fernández's book as he read about the ciphers, systems that he may already have experienced in reality. But here they appear as a part of history both as text and image; the first of these images appears on page 107r, and as he turned that page and searched for the continuation of the historical events, he would have been confronted with two more plates. About the first one, Fernández writes, "Es excelente primor, que hasta agora creo que nadie lo ha usado, ni Autor lo ha escipto tratando del uso desta tabla" (The first one in the diagram is excellent, and I believe that up until now no one has used it nor has written about how to use it). And about the second, he writes that "ay uno tan excelente que es como si verdaderamente fuesse invisibles" (there is one that is so good that it is as if it were invisible). This system is laid out on a grid and is similar to what appears in *Traicté des chiffres* published by Vigenère sixteen years later (fig. 24). The difference in appearance is that there is an initial vertical row of symbols in Fernández's plate. Regardless, we see in both plates a matrix into which are organized letters so that they repeat on a vertical diagonal.[66]

So, what does this digression into the sources for Guaman Poma de Ayala suggest? First, he must have at least seen these plates and surely he read about them as he extracted the details of Hernández Girón's rebellion and capture. But what does this say about his depiction of tocapus? Remember that it is very clear that Guaman Poma de Ayala is not copying the system that he saw depicted in Murúa's portraits of the Inka.[67] This becomes clear merely by comparing the tocapus in the two portraits of

Inga Viracocha, the first in Murúa's manuscript and in *Nueva coronica.*

And it is important to note that Guaman Poma de Ayala worked on the details of this image.[68] That is, he saw the tocapu designs painted by Murúa in all of the Inka portraits up close just as he saw the plates of the ciphers in Fernández's book. So, if we turn to the second to last plate in Fernández's chapter (fig. 25), we can immediately see a correspondence with the display of tocapus as worn by Viracocha in Guaman Poma de Ayala's portrait. The matrix and disposition of the letters and symbols are very similar, and this cannot be mere coincidence. I am not at all interested in trying to decipher the tocapus of Guaman Poma de Ayala, if they are decipherable at all. In fact, the form of their appearance is probably indexical rather than semantic, gesturing toward what tocapus are. But whatever the case, some of Guaman Poma de Ayala's tocapu designs appear to be very similar to symbols that appear in Fernández's plates (fig. 26). Others either seem to copy known tocapu designs or come from other sources. What is most important is their arrangement.

Why, it then has to be asked, would Guaman Poma de Ayala use such ciphers to indicate tocapus rather than depict them in any real sense by copying them from his own experience, as Murúa had done for his images? This difference between Guaman Poma de Ayala's and Murúa's

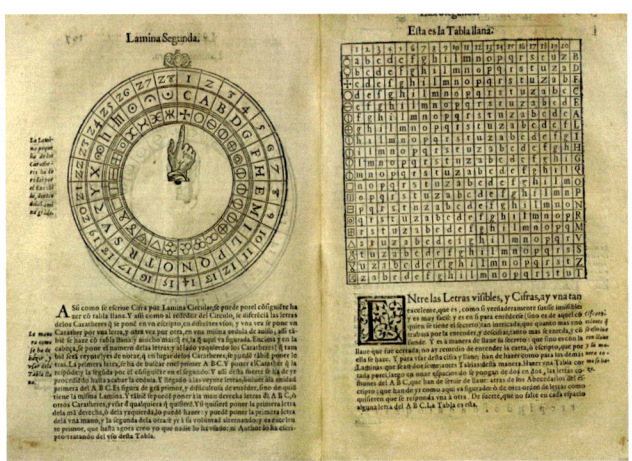

Above: Fig. 23. Diego Fernández, "El Palentino," "First plate with figure based on Alberti's *Formula,* and explanatory text." In *Primera and segunda parte de la Historia del Piru* (Seville: Casa de Hernando Diaz en la calle de Sierpe, 1571), 106v and 107r.

Below: Fig. 24. Diego Fernández, "El Palentino," "Second and third plate with figure based on Alberti's *Formula,* and table." In *Primera and segunda parte de la Historia del Piru* (Seville: Casa de Hernando Diaz en la calle de Sierpe, 1571), 107v and 108r.

models becomes ever more pertinent in terms of intention as Guaman Poma de Ayala had copied almost everything else from Murúa's Inka portraits except for color. The change must be recognized as a conscious and deliberate decision to shift the appearance of tocapus. Could it be that Fernández's printed woodcut designs simply aligned better with Guaman Poma de Ayala's own black-and-white drawings? Or was he simply intrigued by their design as he read the historical passages by Fernández? Perhaps, or is it that the cryptic tocapus are a means to suggest the tocapu system without revealing the tocapu in any true Andean sense of meaning? In fact, this occluded sense in the image is in keeping with all of Guaman Poma de Ayala's depictions of objects that concern Andean visual culture; that is, he provides an image of the instruments and objects such that we recognize what they are, but they never reveal actual symbolic reference, or as Adorno has written, "Guaman Poma de Ayala's pictures conceal more than they reveal."[69] This is certainly true for almost all Inka objects that are only schematically rendered.[70] For example, Guaman Poma de Ayala's drawings of khipus (fig. 27) show the bare minimum of elements (the so-called main cord and dependent cords) to suggest what is represented, but then they are almost always bereft of knots, the critical signifying element, whereas they are shown in the images he created for Murúa's 1590 *Historia del origen y genealogía real de los Reyes Incas del Perú* (the Galvin manuscript). Guaman Poma de Ayala certainly does not explain the system of how the khipu works, even though he claims to be a descendant of *khipucamayocs*. The lack of signifying elements is also palpable when he turns to depicting other Inka objects and media. Women are shown sitting and weaving with either their backstrap looms or before frame looms (fig. 28), yet nothing is being woven. They pass the shed stick and separate the warps with

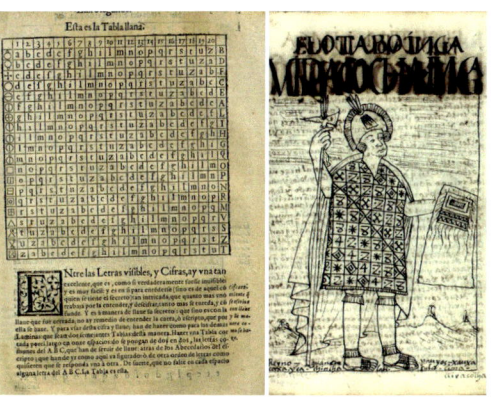

Fig. 25. (*Left*) Diego Fernández, "El Palentino," "Third plate with table." In *Primera and segunda parte de la Historia del Piru* (Seville: Casa de Hernando Diaz en la calle de Sierpe, 1571), 108r. (*Right*) Felipe Guaman Poma de Ayala, *Portrait of Inca Viracocha*. Ink on paper. RDL, GKS 2232 kvart: Guaman Poma, *Nueva corónica y buen gobierno* (about 1615), page 106 [106].

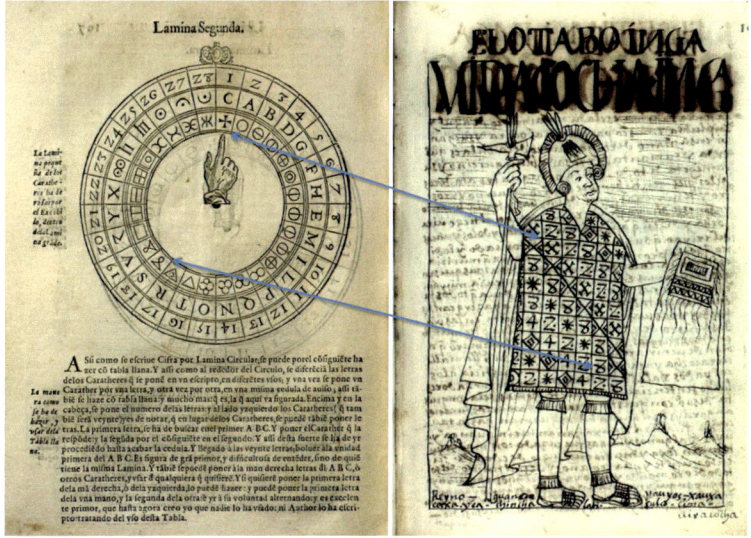

Fig. 26. (*Left*) Shared symbols in Diego Fernández, "El Palentino," "Second plate with Alberti's *Formula*." In *Primera and segunda parte de la Historia del Piru* (Seville: Casa de Hernando Diaz en la calle de Sierpe, 1571), 107v. (*Right*) Felipe Guaman Poma de Ayala, *Portrait of Inca Viracocha*. Ink on paper. RDL, GKS 2232 kvart: Guaman Poma, *Nueva corónica y buen gobierno* (about 1615), page 106 [106].

the heddle or use the comb to push down the weft, but only the warp is shown. There is no design nor is any model shown. This is radically different than the Moche ceramic drawing on a vessel in the British Museum in which not only is the partial design depicted on the warped loom but also the image being produced is depicted above both on a vessel and as a model. Vessels for ritual celebrations and toasting are depicted by Guaman Poma de Ayala, but again their barest outlines are drawn so as to merely form their shape, and their surfaces are without any designs or images (fig. 29). Of course, this is not always the case, such as in the drawings of Inka administrators, but these seem to be more signs of office without any real Andean significance. Hence the woven designs of most Inka uncus

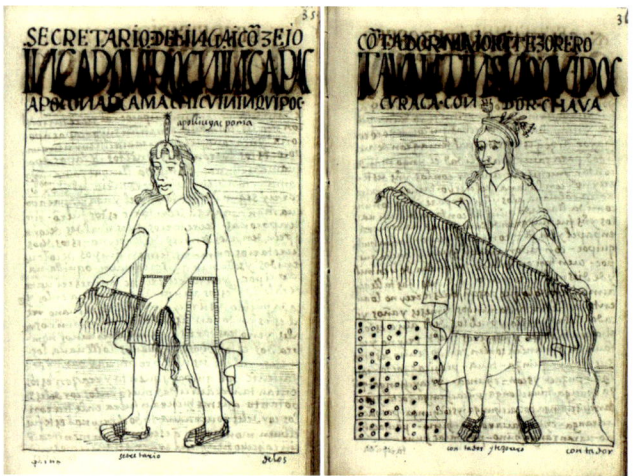

Above: Fig. 27. Felipe Guaman Poma de Ayala, *(Left) Secretary of the Inca with a Khipu* and *(Right) Chief Account of the Empire with a Khipu.* Ink on paper. RDL, GKS 2232 kvart: Guaman Poma, *Nueva corónica y buen gobierno* (about 1615), page 358 [360], and 360 [362].

Below: Fig. 28. Felipe Guaman Poma de Ayala, *(Left) Woman of 33 Years Weaving on a Backstrap Loom* and *(Right) Woman of 50 Years Weaving on a Vertical Loom.* Ink on paper. RDL, GKS 2232 kvart: Guaman Poma, *Nueva corónica y buen gobierno* (about 1615), page 215 [217], and 217 [219].

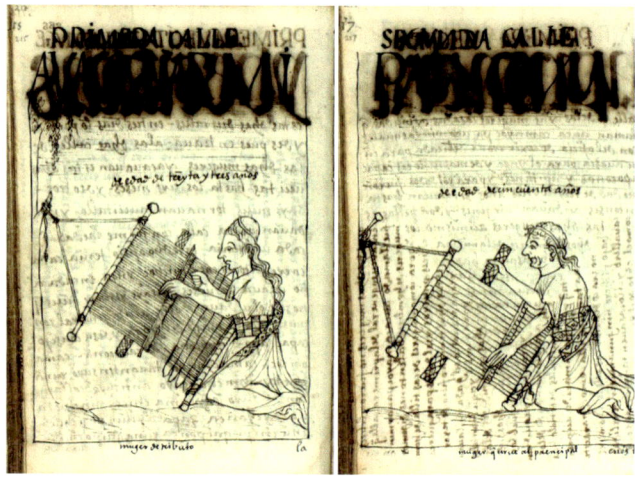

seem more cryptic than indicative of something specific, except when it comes to his own dress (see fig. 19), through which he tracks a genealogy of three generations.

The absence of iconographic specificity becomes palpable when we turn to Guaman Poma de Ayala's other drawings of colonial symbolic technology in which we see specific iconographic details in the depictions of sculpture, prints, and paintings. For example, when Andeans are depicted writing, they are shown in midsentence and we can read the text (fig. 30). Can we therefore see Guaman Poma de Ayala's tocapus as tocapus? No, it does not seem that they are transparent signs waiting for us to identify them directly, or at least not in terms of them being a key to interpreting tocapus found elsewhere. We can see them as a set of signs that by their arrangement form an index for a coded language to which we still have little access and to which Guaman Poma de Ayala gives us next to none.

I therefore end by first noting that Guaman Poma de Ayala is perhaps not without a sense of irony in his images and the relationship between text and image. He certainly extracts vengeance in text and image against his mentor Murúa both as a person and as an historian. He depicts the Mercedarian beating a woman and accuses him of trying to steal his wife and being a failed historian, writing that "comenso a escriuir y no acabo para major dezir ni comenso ni acabo" (he began to write and didn't finish, or better said, he neither began nor finished).[71] Of course, the irony here is that the manuscript (the Galvin manuscript) to which Guaman Poma de Ayala is referring and on which he participated was never finished. Rather, it served as the source for Murúa's second work, the Getty manuscript, which Murúa had indeed finished by 1615. It had been made ready for publication with a contract to have it illustrated by the most illustrious print-maker in Madrid. However, Murúa's death in 1615 brought an end to this project.

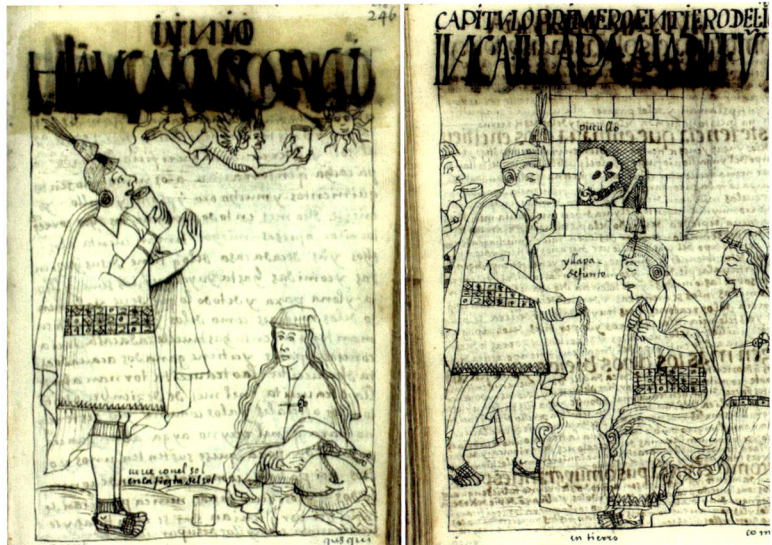

Left: Fig. 29. Felipe Guaman Poma de Ayala, *(Left) Inka Toasts with the Sun in June* and *(Right) Inka Drinks with His Ancestors.* Ink on paper. RDL, GKS 2232 kvart: Guaman Poma, *Nueva corónica y buen gobierno* (about 1615), page 246 [248] and 287 [289]

Below: Fig. 30. Felipe Guaman Poma de Ayala, *(Left) Scribe of the Town Council* and *(Right) Chief Account of the Empire with a Khipu.* Ink on paper. RDL, GKS 2232 kvart: Guaman Poma, *Nueva corónica y buen gobierno* (about 1615), page 814 [828], and 770 [784].

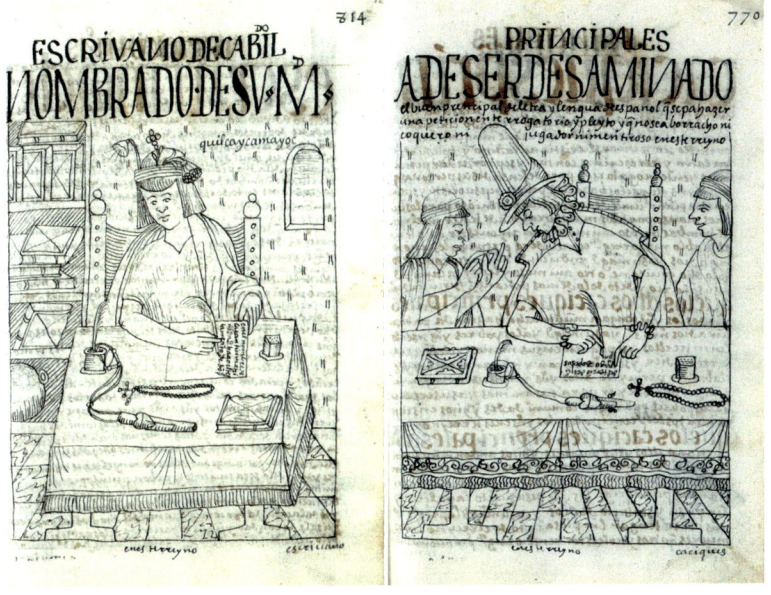

The final narrative image in *Nueva coronica* depicts the author and his son Don Francisco de Ayala as they walk with the manuscript from the Andes down toward Lima.[72] The author's youthful, well-dressed self-portrait and that of his young son belies what is claimed in his self-description as being poor and eighty years of age.[73] Father and son confidently stride across the picture plane as they lead a horse and are also accompanied by two dogs; the one behind Guaman Poma de Ayala next to the horse has the word "amigo" written above its head (fig. 31). This text is often read as the dog's name and it being Guaman Poma de Ayala's faithful companion as well as man's best friend. Indeed, that is how Sebastián de Covarrubias y Orozco begins his definition for his entry for the word "perro."[74] The lead dog, which turns and looks back and up at Francisco de Ayala, has the name Lautaro written above his head. If these are indeed portraits of Guaman Poma de Ayala's two dogs, then one might ask what it means for the author to have the last named being in his manuscript be called Lautaro. Lautaro is not a common name for a dog nor is it an innocent name in early seventeenth-century Peru. In fact, Lautaro was a very well-known and feared name

in Peru at the turn of the century. Lautaro is the Spanish name given to a Mapuche warrior (Leftraru) who had organized his people into a formidable armed resistance against the Spanish invaders. He crushed the Spanish forces led by Francisco de Valdivia in the battle of Tucapei in 1553 and almost routed them completely out of his territory before being killed in 1557.

In the only other contemporary illustrated Andean manuscript, written and illustrated by Fray Diego de Ocaña, with whom Guaman Poma de Ayala may have crossed paths,[75] one finds that Ocaña describes Lautaro as having been "criado y yanacona del mismo Valdivia" (servant and yanacona [Quechua for a kind of indentured servant] of Valdivia himself).[76] He paints his portrait and writes, "Este indio mató a la gente que fue con Villagrán, del gobernador Valdivia. Este es el traje de los indios de Chile: esta coraza es de cuero de vaca crudío. Esta arma se llama macana" (This Indian killed the troops of the Governor Valdivia that went with Villagrán. This is the dress of the Indians of Chile: this cuirass is made of cowhide. The weapon is called macana) (fig. 32). He adds at the back of the illustrated page, "Este indio Lautaro que está aquí pintado fue el que mato a toda la gente de Villagrán que fueron casi 300 hombres los muertos. Era indio muy valiente y por eso le eligieron por su capitán. Era natural del Valle de Arauco y como ellos andan ansi los he pintado para llevarlo todo" (This Indian Lautaro who is painted here was the one who killed all of the troops of Villagrán, which were almost three hundred dead. He was a very brave Indian and for that reason they elected him to be their leader. He was from the Valley of Arauco where they appear as I have painted him here).[77]

Lautaro the dog may be understood to represent the "símbolo de fidelidad" as defined by Covarrubias y Orozco in 1611, but Lautaro the man symbolizes something very different. Lautaro is the Andean who as a boy first serves the Spanish but then turns against his masters in armed resistance because the abuses by the Spanish are unrelenting. The text in *Nueva coronica* that follows this final figure narrates Guaman Poma de Ayala's travels down the Andes toward Lima where he will deliver the manuscript, and as he descends from his ancestral lands he details the travails that he witnesses as he passes through different communities.[78] One might therefore ask, is not this last image including the name Lautaro either a warning or threat and the possible antithesis of "amigo" if the manuscript's central message is ignored?

This may be laying too much interpretive apparatus to perhaps a simple image of the transmission of the manuscript, but there does seem to be the possibility of an ironic undertone of the names that Guaman Poma de Ayala gives to the two dogs: "amigo" and "Lautaro." Lautaro the warrior was at first considered a friend of the Spaniards who partially raised him and taught him to ride in combat. Guaman Poma de Ayala too was at first a friend of the Spaniards who had taught him to read and to write. And just as Lautaro took what he had learned and then used it in military defense of his people, Guaman Poma de Ayala marshals

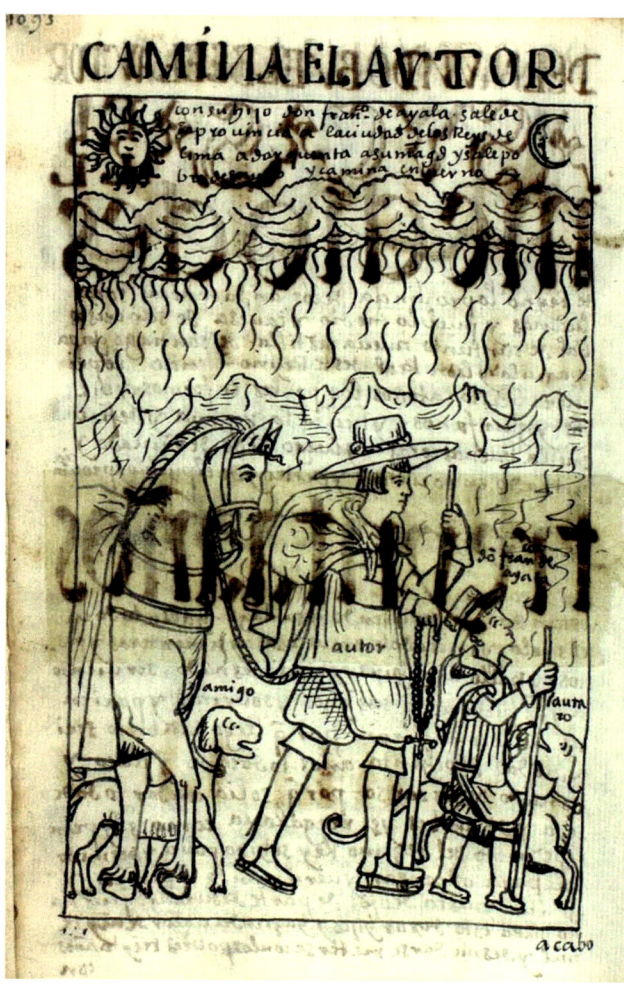

Fig. 31. Felipe Guaman Poma de Ayala, *The Author and His Son Don Francisco de Ayala Begin Their Journey to Lima*. Ink on paper. RDL, GKS 2232 kvart: Guaman Poma, *Nueva corónica y buen gobierno* (about 1615), page 1095 [1105].

his skills to create an epistolary defense of his people, and depicts himself, led by Lautaro, carrying it toward Lima where it will be sent to the king of Spain.

If there is any credibility to this interpretation, then one might therefore suggest that there is also some sense of irony in his drawings of his imperial tocapus. One might wonder that if Guaman Poma de Ayala read Fernández's discussion of ciphers and looked at the tables that seem to be the probable inspiration of his pen and ink drawings of tocapus, did he deploy their design and organization as a means to indicate the significance of the tocapus without revealing anything about them? If he did, then what might he also have thought upon reading Fernández's following words: "Entre letras visibles, y cifras, ay una tan excelente, que es, como si verdaderamente fuese invisible: y es muy fácil: y es si para entenderse (sino es aquel con quien se tiene el secreto) tan intricada que quanto mas uno trabaja por la entender y descifrar; tanto más se enreda, y confunde. Y es a manera de llave su secreto; que si no es con la llave cerrado; no ay remedio de entender la carta, o escrito, porque ella se haze" (Among visible letters and ciphers, there is one so good that it is as if it were truly invisible: it is very easy, and yet it is so intricate that if one tries to understand and decipher it (if one does not have the key), the more one becomes entangled and confused. And it is only with the key that can it be unlocked; without it there is no hope of understanding what is written).[79]

Perhaps Guaman Poma de Ayala took these words to heart as he drew the tocapus in so different a form than what he saw in Martín de Murúa's watercolors and in the world around him. Perhaps Fernández's words that accompanied the plate that may have been the source for Guaman Poma de Ayala's drawing of the tocapu uncu worn by Inka Viracocha even provided him with a sense of humor, with which he was

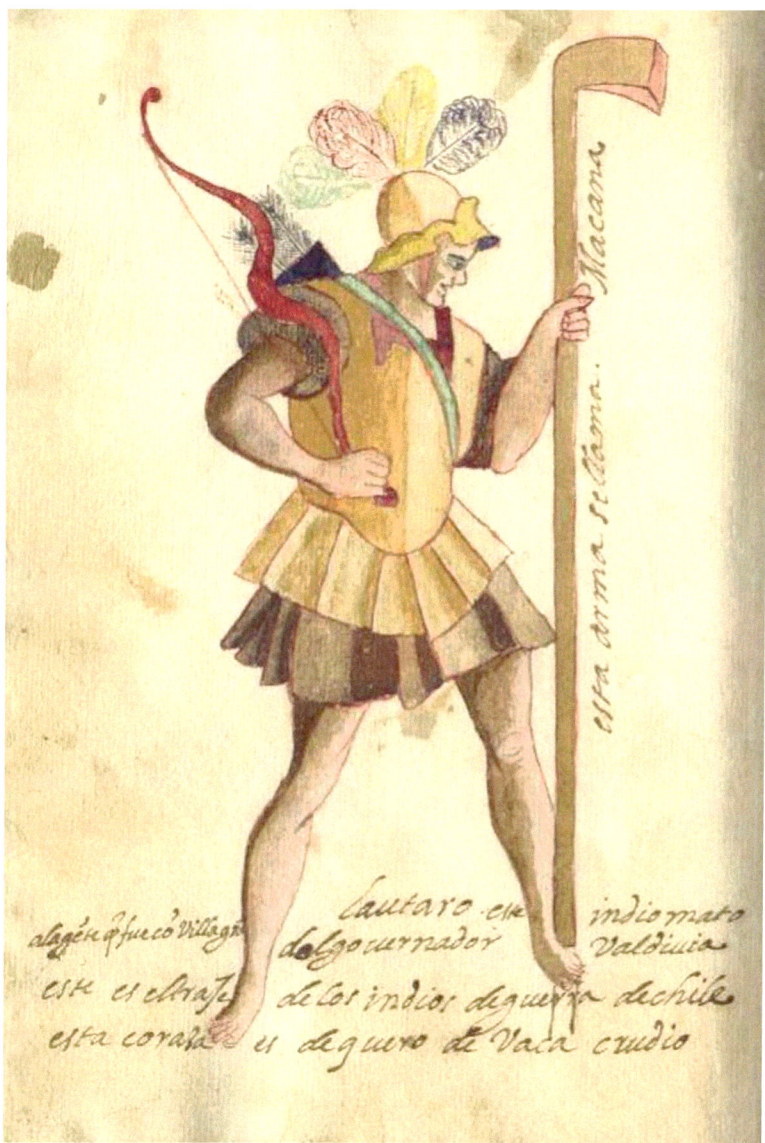

entrapping us all. Did Guaman Poma de Ayala intentionally lay a trap just as Fernández warned when he wrote about this technique and the plate "que quanto mas uno trabaja por la entender y descifrar; tanto más se enreda, y confunde . . . no hay remdio de entender" (that the more one tries to understand and decipher it, the more one is entrapped and confused . . . there is no hope of understanding.)?

✦✦✦

Fig. 32. Diego de Ocaña, *Portrait of Lautaro.* Watercolor on paper. In *Relación del viaje de fray Diego de Ocaña por el Nuevo Mundo (1599–1605)*, 1605, folio 74v. Repositorio Institucional, Universidad de Oviedo, Oviedo, Spain.

Notes

1 I will use the singular *tocapu* to designate the system as well as discrete designs within the system and the plural *tocapus* when referring to a number of specific designs. I thank Andrew Hamilton for suggesting this clarification, and any deviation from it in this chapter is a result of my own ineptitude.

2 For a bibliography and quotes suggesting that the tocapu is some form of lost writing system, see Thomas B. F. Cummins, "El *tocapu*: El nudo gordiano en los Andes," in *Sistemas de notación inca: Quipu y Tocapu: Actas del Simposio Internacional, Lima 15–17 de enero de 2009,* ed. Carmen Arellano Hoffmann (Lima: Museo Nacional de Arqueología, Antropología e Historia del Perú, 2014), 223–45.

3 The failure to achieve a systematic method of understanding what tocapus are and mean becomes palpably clear if one reads Mary Frame, "*Tokapu,* un código gráfico de los Inkas, Segunda Parte: Las configuraciones y familias de los elementos," 247–82; Paola Gonzales Carvajal, "Conexiones entre el diseños *tocapus* y diseños cerámicos diaguita del norte semiárido chileno," 283–99; José Luis Pino Matos, "El *tocapu* que narra el viaje del sol en el mes de agosto: La arquitectura inca como 'representación' calendárica del orden: Una visión dese Huánuco Pampa," 359–93; Juan Pablo Villanueva Hidalgo, "Frisos como tupaku arquitectónicos? Representaciones del tiempo y cosmovisión en la provincia Inca de Pachacamac," 301–58; and R. Tom Zuidema, "'Hacer calendarios' en quipos y tejidos: Los números y su rol en el registro simultáneo del orden socio político y calendárico andino en el Cuzco, Chuqubamaba, Collaguas," 395–445, in *Sistemas de notación inca: Quipu y Tocapu: Actas del Simposio Internacional, Lima 15–17 de enero de 2009,* ed. Carmen Arellano Hoffman (Lima: Museo Nacional de Arqueología, Antropología e Historia del Perú, 2014). See also Carmen Arellano, "Quipu y tocapu: Sistemas de comunicación inca," in *Los Incas: Arte y símbolos,* ed. Franklin Pease (Lima: Banco de Crédito del Perú, 1999), 215–26. There is no common base for or consensus of the basic methods for interpretation nor is there a consistent theoretical basis for understanding the syntactical matrix in which the tocapu operates. It would be as if every Maya epigrapher read and interpreted Maya glyphs according to their own idiosyncratic system based on personal intuitions with no relationship to language, visual order, color, context, or historical and geographic distinctions.

4 The field of Mesoamerican writing systems has expanded almost exponentially in the past fifty years, based on key colonial texts that among other things have revealed the phonetic elements of Maya glyphic writing and Aztec pictographs and a basic set of unified interpretive methods and theories. The same is true for the Aztec system of glyphs and pictographic signs. The profound differences between the state of research in Mesoamerica and the Andes concerning the understanding and decipherment of their graphic systems is clearly demonstrated by the essays concerning both areas in Elizabeth Hill Boone and Gary Urton, eds., *Their Way of Writing: Scripts, Signs, and Pictographies in Pre-Columbian America* (Washington, DC: Dumbarton Oaks, 2011).

5 The only colonial manuscript in which a tocapu design is identified in terms of what it represents occurs in Joan de Santa Cruz Pachacuti Yamqui Salcamaygua, *Relación de antigüedades deste reyno del Piru* (Lima-Cusco: Instituto Francés de Estudios Andinos y Centro de Estudios Regionales Andinos "Bartolomé de Las Casas," [1613?] 1993), 242; see Thomas B. F. Cummins, "Queros, Aquillas, Uncus, and Chulpas: The Composition of Inka Artistic Expression and Power," in *Variations in the Expression of Inka Power,* ed. Craig Morris and Ramiro Matos (Washington, DC: Dumbarton Oaks, 2007), 292–93; see also Regina Harrison, *Signs, Songs, and Memory in the Andes* (Austin: University of Texas Press, 1986), 78–81.

6 Cummins, "El *tocapu*"; Thomas Cummins and Juan Ossio, eds., *La vida y obra de Martín de Murúa* (Lima: Apus Graph Ediciones, 2019).

7 David Vicente De Rojas Silva, "Los Tocapu: Un Progama de Interpretación," *Arte y Arqueología* 7 (1981): 119–32; David Vicente De Rojas Silva, *Los Tockapu: Graficación de la Emblemática Inka* (La Paz: Producciones Cima y Colección Patrimonio, 2008); Giorgia Ficca, "Los Tocapus del Codex Galvin y de la Nueva coronica y buen gobierno: Una o más formas de escritura colonial?," *Sublevando el virreinato: Documentos contestatarios a la historiografía tradicional del Perú Colonial,* eds. Laura Laurencich Minelli and Paulina Numhauser (Quito: Abya-Yala, 2007); Rocío Quispe-Agnoli, "Cuando Occidente y los Andes se encuentran: *Qellqay,* escritura alfabética, *tokhapu* en el siglo XVI," *Colonial Latin American Review* 14, no. 2 (2005): 263–98; Gail Silverman, "Iconografía textil de Cusco y su relación con los Tocapu Inca," in *Tejidos milenarios del Perú / Ancient Peruvian Textiles,* ed. José Antonio de Lavalle and Rosario de Lavalle de Cárdenas (Lima: Integra AFP, 1999); Mary Frame, "*Tokapu:* A Graphic Code of the Inkas," in *Tejiendo sueños en el Cono Sur: Textiles andinos: Pasado, presente y futuro,* ed. Victòria Solanilla Demestre (Barcelona: Grupo d'Estudis Precolombins, 2005), 236–60; Mary Frame, "Lo que Guaman Poma nos muestra, pero no nos dice sobre *Tukapu,*" *Revista Andina* 44 (2007): 9–70; Frame, "*Tokapu,* un codigo gráfico de los Inkas," 247–82; Christiane Clados, "Neue Erkenntnisse zum *Tocapu*-Symbolsystem am Beispiel eines Männerhemdes der Inkazeit in der Altamerika-Sammlung des Linden Museum" (A Key Checkerboard Pattern Tunic of the Linden-Museum Stuttgart: First Steps in Breaking the Tocapu Code?),

Tribus: Jahrbuch des Linden-Museums, Band 56 (2007): 71–106.

8 Cummins, "El *tocapu.*"

9 Manuel Medrano and Gary Urton, "Toward the Decipherment of a Set of Mid-Colonial Khipus from the Santa Valley, Coastal Peru," *Ethnohistory* 65, no. 1 (2018): 1–23.

10 Sabine Hyland, Gene A. Ware, and Madison Clark, "Knot Direction in a Khipu/Alphabetic Text from the Central Andes," *Latin American Antiquity* 25, no. 2 (2014): 189–97; Sabine Hyland, "Writing with Twisted Cords: The Inscriptive Capacity of Andean *Khipus,*" *Current Anthropology* 58, no. 3 (2017): 412–19.

11 Enrique Fernández, S.J., ed. *Monumenta peruana VIII (1603–1604),* Monumenta Historica Societatis Iesu, vol. 128 (Rome: Institutum Historicum Societatis Iesu, 1986), 214–15.

12 Raimondo di Sangro, príncipe di Sansevero, *Lettera apologetica dell'Esercitato accademico della Crusca contenente la difesa del libro intitolato Lettere d'una peruana per rispetto alla supposizione de'quipu scritta alla duchessa di S**** e dalla medesima fatta pubblicare* (Naples: n.p., 1751). See also Thomas B. F. Cummins, "From Many into One: The Transformation of Pre-Columbian Signs into European Letters in the Sixteenth-Century," in *Sign and Design: Script as Image in a Cross-Cultural Perspective (300–1600 CE),* ed. Jeffery Hamburger (Washington, DC: Dumbarton Oaks, 2016), 96–98.

13 Hyland, Ware, and Clark, "Writing with Twisted Cords."

14 Frank Salomon, *The Cord Keepers: Khipus and Cultural Life in a Peruvian Village* (Durham, NC: Duke University Press, 2004).

15 Martti Pärssinen and Jukka Kiviharju, *Textos andinos: Corpus de textos khipu incaicos y coloniales,* vol. 1 (Helsinki: Instituto Iberomericano de Finlandia; Madrid: La Universidad de Complutense de Madrid Acto, 2004).

16 Marcia Ascher and Robert Ascher, *Code of the Quipu: A Study in Media, Mathematics, and Culture* (Ann Arbor: University of Michigan Press, 1981), 54–55.

17 Dick Edgar Ibarra Grasso, *La escritura indígena andina* (La Paz, Bolivia: Biblioteca Paceña, 1953); Yuri Knorozov, Box 13, Series 4, Folders F194–99, "Yuri Valentinovich Knorozov Papers, 1945–1998" (Washington, DC: Dumbarton Oaks); Thomas Barthel, "Viracochas Prunkgewand (TokapuStudien)," *Tribus* (Stuttgart) 20 (1971): 63–124; William Burns Glynn, *Introducción a la clave de la escritura de los Incas* (Lima: Editorial Los Pinos, 1981); Margarita E. Gentile Lafaille, "El tocapu 285: Consideraciones acerca de la llamada 'escritura incaica,'" *ARKEOS: Revista Electrónica de Arqueología PUCP* 3, no. 2 (2008); Frame,

"Tokapu: A Graphic Code of the Inkas," 236–60; Frame, "Lo que Guaman Poma nos muestra," 9–69; Peter Eeckhout and Nathalie Danis, "Los tocapus reales en Guaman Poma: ¿Una heráldica incaica?" *Boletín de Arqueología PUCP* 8 (2004): 305–23; Victoria de la Jara, "Vers le déchiffrement des écritures anciennes du Pérou," *La Nature* 3387 (1967): 241–47; Victoria de la Jara, "La Solución del problema de la escritura peruana," *Arqueología y Sociedad: Revista del Museo de Arqueología de la Universidad de San Marcos* 2, no. 8 (1970): 27–35; Victoria de la Jara, "El decifrimiento de la escritura de los Inkas," *Arqueología y Sociedad: Revista del Museo de Arqueología de la Universidad de San Marcos* 7–8 (1972): 60–77; Victoria de la Jara, *Introducción al estudio de la escritura de los Inkas* (Lima: Instituto Nacional de Investigación y Desarrollo de la Educación, 1975); Rocío Quispe-Agnoli, "Para que la Letra lo Tenga en los Ojos: *Tocapu,* Emblemas y Letreros en los Andes Coloniales del Siglo XVII," in *Lenguajes Visuales de los Incas,* BAR International Series 1848, ed. Paola González Carvajal and Tamara Bray (Oxford: British Archaeological Reports, 2008), 133–46; Gail Silverman, "Los Tocapus Incas como escritura pictórica: Lectura de un vaso ceremonial Inca," in *Sublevando el virreinato: Documentos contestatarios a la historiografía tradicional del Perú Colonial,* ed. Laura Laurencich Minelli and Paulina Numhauser (Quito: Abya-Yala, 2007); Gail Silverman, *A Woven Book of Knowledge: Textile Iconography of Cuzco, Peru* (Salt Lake City: University of Utah Press, 2008); Marie Timberlake, "Tocapu in a Colonial Frame: Andean Space and the Semiotics of Painted Tocapu," in *Lenguajes Visuales de los Incas,* BAR International Series 1848, ed. Paola González Carvajal and Tamara Bray (Oxford: British Archaeological Reports, 2008), 177–93; Gary Urton, *The Social Life of Numbers: A Quechua Ontology of Numbers and Philosophy of Arithmetic* (Austin: University of Texas Press, 1997).

18 Urton, *Social Life of Numbers.*

19 Cummins, "El *tocapu.*"

20 Anonymous, *Vocabulario y phrasis en la lengua general de los indios del Perú llamada Quichua y en la lengua española,* 5th ed., ed. Guillermo Escobar Risco (Lima: Edición del Instituto de historia de la Facultad de Letras, [1586] 1951), 84.

21 Diego González Holguín, *Vocabulario de la lengua general de todo el Perú llamada lengua Qquichua o del Inca* (Lima: Universidad Nacional Mayor de San Marcos, [1608] 1989), 344.

22 Ludovico Bertonio, *Vocabulario de la lengua aymara compuesta por el padre . . .* (Leipzig, Germany: B. G. Teubner, [1612] 1879), 357. Note: All translations are mine.

23 Martín de Murúa, *Historia General del Piru J. Paul Getty Museum Ms. Ludwig XIII 16* (Los Angeles: Getty Research Institute, [1616] 2008), 226v. I

have translated "labors" as "embroidery" based on Sebastián de Covarrubias y Orozco's 1611 entry for his third definition for the word *labor:* "labrandera, se dice de la ocupación de las mujeres de tela que hacen en ellas con la ajuja." Sebastián de Covarrubias y Orozco, *Tesoro de la lengua castellana o española* (Barcelona: Editorial Alta Fulla, [1611] 1998), 696.

24 Pedro Sarmiento de Gamboa, *Historia de los Incas* (Madrid: Biblioteca Viajeros Hispánicos, [1572] 1988), 84.

25 "Industrioso, el que tiene maña para haze lo que quiere hazer con promptitude y liberalidad." Covarrubias y Orozco, *Tesoro de la lengua castellana,* 735.

26 Cristóbal de Molina, *Relación de las fábulas y ritos de los incas* (Lima: Universidad de San Martín de Porres, [1576] 2008), 141–43.

27 Much of what is said here concerning these colonial texts and their meaning was published earlier. See Cummins, "El *tocapu.*"

28 Jeanette Sherbondy, "El regadío, los lagos y los mitos de origen," *Allpanchis* 17, no 20 (1982): 3–53.

29 Thomas B. F. Cummins, *Toasts with the Inca: Andean Abstraction and Colonial Images on Kero Vessels* (Ann Arbor: University of Michigan Press, 2002), 60–61.

30 William Conklin, "Huari Tunics," in *Andean Art at Dumbarton Oaks,* ed. Elizabeth Hill Boone (Washington, DC: Dumbarton Oaks, 1996), 2:375–98; see also Christiane Clados, "Borrowed from the Ancestors: Tiwanaku and Wari Motifs in Inca Tocapus," *Baessler-Archiv* 65 (2018/2019): 35–50.

31 Thomas B. F. Cummins, "Tocapu: What Is It, What Does It Do, and Why Is It Not a Knot?" In *Their Way of Writing: Scripts, Signs, and Pictographies in Pre-Columbian America,* ed. Elizabeth Hill Boone and Gary Urton (Washington, DC: Dumbarton Oaks, 2011), 277–317.

32 F. J. Sánchez Cantón, "Inventarios reales bienes muebles que pertenecieron a Felipe II," in *Archivo Documental Español,* 2 vols. (Madrid: Real Academia de la Historia, [1599] 1949), 1:334.

33 Cummins, "Queros, Aquillas, Uncus, and Chulpas," 282–95.

34 Tom Cummins and Juan Ossio, "'Muchas veces dudé Real Mag. açeptar esta dicha ympressa': *La tarea de hacer La Famosa Historia de los Reyes Incas de Fray Martín de Murúa,*" in *Au miroir de l'anthropologie historique: Mélanges offerts à Nathan Wachtel,* ed. Juan Carlos Garavaglia, Gilles Rivière, and Jacques Poloni-Simard (Rennes: Presses Universitaires de Rennes, 2014), 151–70; Cummins and Ossio, *La vida y obra de Martín de Murua.*

35 Thomas Cummins, "Dibujado de mi mano: Martín de Murúa como artista," in *La vida y obra Fray Martín de Murúa,* ed. Thomas Cummins and Juan Ossio (Lima: Apus Graph Ediciones, 2019), 279–304.

36 Thomas B. F. Cummins, "'I Saw it with my Own Eyes': The Three Illustrated Manuscripts of Colonial Peru: Pictures Fit for A King," in *Colors Between Two Worlds: The Florentine Codex of Bernardino de Sahagún,* Villa I Tatti 28, ed. Gerhard Wolf, Joseph Connors, and Louis A. Waldman (Florence: Kunsthistorisches Institut in Florenz, Max-Planck-Institut, 2011), 334–65; Thomas B. F. Cummins, *"Dibujado de Mi Mano:* Martín de Murúa as Artist," in *Manuscript Cultures of Colonial Mexico and Peru: New Questions and Approaches,* ed. Thomas B. F. Cummins, Emily A. Engel, Barbara Anderson, and Juan M. Ossio A. (Los Angeles: Getty Research Institute, 2014), 35–64.

37 Guaman Poma de Ayala's copying of Murúa's letter in which Guaman Poma de Ayala writes that the images are meant for the king's enjoyment is the source of Rolena Adorno's perplexity when she writes that the "historical role of Phillip III in supporting the arts is dubious." Rolena Adorno, *Guaman Poma: Writing and Resistance in Colonial Peru* (Austin: University of Texas Press, 1986), 161n2. Guaman Poma de Ayala's letter merely mimics Murúa's address to Philip II, and it is uncertain whether Guaman Poma de Ayala would have been aware of the historical differences between the two kings' support and interest in the pictorial arts. Cummins and Ossio, "'Muchas veces dudé Real Mag.'"

38 Adorno, *Guaman Poma,* 80–81.

39 Catherine J. Julien, "History and Art in Translation: The *Paños* and Other Objects Collected by Francisco de Toledo," in *Colonial Latin American Review* 8, no. 1 (1999): 35–60.

40 Thomas B. F. Cummins, "El mundo y vida de las imágenes en las páginas peruanas de los siglos XVI y XVII: El contexto virreinal de las obras de Martín de Murúa, Guamán Poma y otros," in *Escritura e imagen en Hispanoamérica: De la crónica ilustrada al cómic,* ed. Cécile Michaud (Lima: Pontificia Universidad Católica del Perú, 2015), 21–64.

41 Urton, *Social Life of Numbers,* 208.

42 Elena Phipps, Nancy Turner, and Karen Trentelman, "Colors, Textiles, and Artistic Production in Murúa's *Historia General del Piru,*" in *The Getty Murúa: Essays on the Making of Martín de Murúa's Historia General del Piru, J. Paul Getty Museum Ms. XIII 16,* ed. Thomas B. F. Cummins and Barbara Anderson (Los Angeles: Getty Research Institute, 2008), 125–26.

43 In two 1615 inventories, one at the death of Martín de Murúa and the other of the things that Martin de Murúa had sent to his brother Diego de Arangutia y Murúa, there is listed what may be his first manuscript, "un boron de su libro con algunas figuras de yndias," as well as in the second inventory

"una camisa de indio de lana de los carneros de halla de blanco, negro colorado y marillo," which may be a version of the ubiquitous checkered board or key design uncus, and then there is listed a royal uncu "una camisa delgada de lana que parece fue camisa del rey ynga." Above this attribution is written "so they say" (segun dixeron). Both documents are transcribed in Francisco Borja de Aguinagalde, *Un misterio resuelto: El autor de la* Historia General del Perú, *Fray Martín de Murúa (1566?–1615), de Eskoriatza* (San Sebastián, Spain: PHILOBIBLON, Sociedad de Bibliófilos de Guipúzcoa, 2107), 69.

44 "Criptografia consiste em comunicar por meio de letras, signos ou números, as informaçoes conseguidas pela espionagem, dispostas de tal maneira que, mesmo que o inimigo consiga interceptálas, nao consiga descobrir seu significado." Juan Carlos Galende Díaz, "Sistemas criptográficos empleados en Hispanoamérica," *Revista Complutense de Historia de América* 26 (2000): 58n1.

45 Guillermo Lohmann Villena, "Cifras y claves indianas: Capítulos provisionales de un estudio sobre criptografía indiana," *Anuario de Estudios Americanos* 11 (1954): 285–380. For a more general description of Spanish cryptography see also Juan Carlos Galende Díaz, *Criptografía: Historia de la escritura cifrada* (Madrid: Editorial Complutense, 1995).

46 Galende Díaz, "Sistemas criptográficos," 59–60.

47 Lohmann Villena, "Cifras y claves indianas," 285.

48 For a brief description of the mining technology offered by the father and son, see Jorge Cañizares-Esquerra, "Bartolomé Inga's Mining Technologies: Indians, Science, Cyphered Secrecy, and Modernity in the New World," *History and Technology* 34, no. 1 (2018): 61–70, https://doi.org/10.1080/07341512.2018.1516855.

49 Marie Helmer, "La clef du mystère (papiers chiffrés relatifs aux mines d'argent du Pérou)," *Bulletin Hispanique* 62, no. 4 (1960): 428–31.

50 Alberti describes the formula in chapters 14 and 15 of *La cifra:*

Chapter XIV. I will first describe the movable index. Suppose that we agreed to use the letter *k* as an index letter in the movable disk. At the moment of writing, I will position the two disks of the formula as I wish; for example, juxtaposing the index letter to capital *B,* with all other small letters corresponding to the capital letters above them. When writing to you, I will first write a capital *B* that corresponds to the index k in the formula. This means that if you want to read my message, you must use the identical formula you have with you, turning the movable disk until the letter *B* corresponds to the index *k*. Thus, all small letters in the cipher text will receive the meaning and sound of those above them in the stationary disk. When I have written three or four words,

I will change the position of the index in our formula, turning the disk until, say, the index *k* is under capital *R*. Then I will write a capital R in my message and from this point onward the small *k* will no longer mean *B* but *R,* and the letters that follow in the text will receive new meanings from the capital letters above them in the stationary disk. When you read the message you have received, you will be advised by the capital letter, which you know is only used as a signal, that from this moment the position of the movable disk and of the index has been changed. Hence, you will also place the index under that capital letter, and in this way you will be able to read and understand the text very easily. The four letters in the movable disk facing the four numbered cells of the outer ring will not have, so to speak, any meaning by themselves and may be inserted as nulls within the text. However, if used in groups or repeated, they will be of great advantage, as I will explain later on.

Chapter XV. We can also choose the index letter among the capital letters and agree between us which of them will be the index. Let us suppose we chose the letter *B* as an index. The first letter to appear in the message will be a small one at will, say *q*. Hence, turning the movable disk in the formula you will place this letter under the capital *B* that serves as an index. It follows that *q* will take the sound and meaning of *B*. For the other letters we will continue writing in the manner described earlier for the movable index. When it is necessary to change the setup of the disks in the formula, then I will insert one, and no more, of the numeral letters into the message; that is to say one of the letters of the small disk facing the numbers that corresponds to, let's say, 3 or 4, etc. Turning the movable disk, I will juxtapose this letter to the agreed upon index *B* and, successively, as required by the logic of writing, I will continue giving the value of the capitals to the small letters. To further confuse the scrutinizers, you can also agree with your correspondent that the capital letters intermingled in the message have the function of nulls and must be disregarded, or you may resort to similar conventions, which are not worth recalling. Thus changing the position of the index by rotating the movable disk, one will be able to express the phonetic and semantic value of each capital letter by means of twenty-four different alphabetic characters, whereas each small letter can correspond to any capital letter or to any of the four numbers in the alphabet of the stationary disk. Now I come to the convenient use of the numbers, which is admirable. (Leon Battista Alberti, *A Treatise on Ciphers,* trans. A. Zaccagnini [Turin, Italy: Galimberti, (1568) 1997].

51 Louise George Clubb, *Giambattista Della Porta, Dramatist* (Princeton, NJ: Princeton University Press, 1965), 13; Sergius Kodera, "Giambattista della Porta,"

in *The Stanford Encyclopedia of Philosophy,* ed. Edward N. Zalta (Stanford, CA: Metaphysics Research Lab, Stanford University, 2015), https://plato.stanford.edu/archives/sum2015/entries/della-porta/

For various iterations and schema as well as plates, see Giambattista della Porta, *De furtivis literarum notis vulgo, de ziferis libri IV* (Naples: Scotus, 1563), 72r–142v. For the reception of *De furtivis* in sixteenth-century Europe in general, see Gerhard F. Strasser, "Die europäische Rezeption der kryptologischen Werke Giovanni Battista Della Portas," *Morgen-Glantz: Zeitschrift der Christian Knorr von Rosenroth-Gesellschaft* 18 (2008): 85–112.

52 As one might imagine, the world of cryptography is vast, and the internet is filled with material from which I have had to draw in the days of pandemic and quarantine, unable to go to Widener Library. I have used the Wikipedia page on Alberti's system as well as the French Wikipedia page on Vigenère, following sources that were used by the entries. My descriptions of the two cryptographic systems are an amalgamation of these sources as I have no interest in actually trying to understand and describe them myself.

53 Lohmann Villena, "Cifras y claves indianas," 288n3.

54 Lohmann Villena, "Cifras y claves indianas," 288–89n3.

55 Gabriel Gasca y Espinosa, *Manual de avisos para el perfecto cortesano* (Madrid: Roque Rico de Miranda, 1631).

56 Knorozov, Folder F196.

57 Adorno, *Guaman Poma,* 13–35; Cummins and Ossio, "'Muchas veces dudé Real Mag,'" 151-70.

58 Adorno, *Guaman Poma,* 16.

59 Martti Pärssinen, "Otras fuentes escritas por los cronistas: Los casos de Martín de Murúa y Pedro Gutiérrez de Santa Clara, *Histórica* (Lima) 13, no. 1 (1989): 45–65.

60 Felipe Guaman Poma de Ayala, *Y no hay remedio,* ed. Elías Prado Tello and Alfredo Prado Prado (Lima: Centro de Investigación y Promoción Amazónica, [1594-1646] 1991).

61 Adorno, *Guaman Poma,* 170.

62 Adorno, *Guaman Poma,* 16.

63 Diego Fernández, "El Palentino," *Primera and segunda parte de la Historia del Piru* (Seville: Casa de Hernando Diaz en la calle de Sierpe, 1571), 105v.

64 Cummins, *Toasts with the Inca,* 328–29.

65 Fernández, *Historia del Piru,* 109r.

66 If Guaman Poma de Ayala was inspired by the diagrams printed in Fernández, diagrams which ultimately derive from Alberti's system, there is irony in the fact that one of the individuals who tried

to interpret the tocapu, Thomas Barthel, was an experienced German cryptologist during World War II. Barthel, "Viracochas Prunkgewand (TokapuStudien)," 63–124. As a cryptologist, Barthel must have known of Alberti's system, which was really indecipherable until the nineteenth century without the key. If Barthel did see any correspondence with Guaman Poma de Ayala's images, he certainly never mentions it in his discussion of tocapus. Barthel's work on tocapus was paralleled by his nemesis, the famous Maya epigrapher Yuri Knorozov, who also must have known of this Albertian system. Regardless, neither scholar in the end produced any real advance in the understanding of tocapus.

That they both worked on tocapu decipherment is in part a result of their mutual interests as well as perhaps their antagonistic intellectual relationship. Barthel was diametrically and vociferously opposed to Knorozov's idea that Maya glyphs could be phonetic. It is perhaps no coincidence that between 1970 and 1973, or just after Barthel published his 1971 study, Knorozov also began to look at the tocapus on keros as supplied by Victoria de la Jara, and he had copies of her publications. De la Jara, "Vers le déchiffrement," "La Solución del problema," and "El decifrimiento." De la Jara corresponded with both scholars and used their letters as corroborative evidence for her own unsubstantiated interpretations. Knorozov obtained a facsimile edition of Guaman Poma de Ayala's *Nueva coronica* and studied his tocapus on the portraits of the Inka and on the figures in the months of the Inka calendar. Knorozov copied those parts of the tocapu patterns that appeared to be essential, in that they form the basis for repetitions, and filled in some repetitions partially, in pencil. Each drawing is accompanied by a brief description of what is happening in each scene. Furthermore, he meticulously recorded numerical peculiarities such as the number of rows/columns of the tocapus or number of rays of the sun depicted and occasionally copied graphic elements found outside the tocapu (e.g., headdress).

In several of his drawings, Knorozov identified a single tocapu, in which he discerned the origin of symmetry. For example, the tocapus that appear in Guaman Poma de Ayala's drawing for "December" are laid out a symmetrical pattern to the left and right of the fourth tocapu; or, in the case of "April," symmetry begins at the first tocapu and goes to the bottom and to the right. Knorozov considered mirror symmetry to be a strong organizing principle and assumed that the diagonal repetition of symbols has a downward orientation. Several of his drawings show that he considered this symmetry as a general organizing principle.

Knorozov noted that the successful decipherment based on previous research requires a point of reference being essential to attaining a solution. For example, having just a bilingual document such as the Rosetta stone was not enough; it was the presence of a proper name, "Ptolemy," that could be consistently identified that made the decipherment of Egyptian writing possible and plausible. Knorozov thus wrote that his own decipherment of Maya writing (positing that Diego de Landa's Maya list of glyph correspondences was actually a syllabary) only become plausible because of the association of a word with a corresponding image in the Dresden codex. For tocapus, Knorozov therefore decided to dedicate a great deal of attention to the iconography of surrounding images that are on colonial keros and Guaman Poma de Ayala's drawings, for these could offer such a point of reference, if one were to match a grapheme with a recurrent iconographic element, such as a dog's tail as he mentions. The difference in regard to Maya glyphs is, of course, the highly geometric overall structure of the tocapu, which Knorozov attempted to solve by considering the tocapu as an abstract transformation of an animal head to a geometric design. A similar approach has more recently been used by Mauiuz Ziólkowski et al. and Silverman, but without any citation of Knorozov's unpublished research. Mauiuz S. Ziólkowski, Jaroslaw Arbas, and Jan Szmenski, "La Historia en los queros: Apuntes acerca de la relación entre representaciones figurativas y los signos 'tocapus,'" in *Lenguajes Visuales de los Incas,* BAR International Series 1848, ed. Paola González Carvajal and Tamara Bray (Oxford: British Archaeological Reports, 2008), 163–76; Gail Silverman, *The Signs of Empire Inca Writing, Volume 1* (Cuzco: Editorial Kopy Graf E.I.R.L., 2012). I thank Elena Iourtaeva for her translation of and comments about the Knorozov documents.

67 There are patterns of tocapus within a grid that are arranged so as to have a diagonal created by repeating figures, such as the tocapu on a colonial lliclla (see figure 4), as well as on colonial keros. This similarity does not explain why Guaman Poma de Ayala decided to radically change the tocapu designs of the Inka portraits from what he had seen in Murúa's portraits nor does it account for his use of certain symbols that do not appear in any other form of tocapu.

68 Cummins, "Dibujado de mi mano," 298–302.

69 Adorno, *Guaman Poma,* 89.

70 Cummins, "Queros, Aquillas, Uncus, and Chulpas."

71 Felipe Guaman Poma de Ayala, *El primer nueva coronica y buen gobierno* (Danish Royal Library, Copenhagen [GKS 2232 4°], 1615), 1080 [1090]. Complete digital facsimile edition of the manuscript, with a corrected online version of Felipe Guaman Poma de Ayala, *El primer Nueva corónica y buen gobierno,* ed. John V. Murra and Rolena Adorno, Quechua translations by Jorge L. Urioste, 3 vols. (Mexico City: Siglo Veintiuno, [1615] 1980), www.kb.dk/elib/mss/poma/.

72 The image initiates the eighteen folios that chronicle Guaman Poma de Ayala's journey to Lima that were a late addition to the manuscript. Rolena Adorno, "Guaman Poma and His Illustrated Chronicle from Colonial Peru: From a Century

of Scholarship to a New Era of Reading." A new introduction to the web publication of *Nueva coronica y buen gobierno,* May 2002 (website). Accessed June 10, 2020. http://wayback-01.kb.dk/wayback/20101108104655/http://www2.kb.dk/elib/mss/poma/presentation/index-en.htm.

73 Guaman Poma de Ayala's written words about himself are almost always taken as statements of fact while his self-portraits are seen as idealizations, and so it is suggested that he was too old to have even drawn the images in *Nueva coronica.* Augusta E. Holland, *Nueva coronica: Tradiciones artísticas europeas en el virreynato del Perú* (Cuzco: Centro de Estudios Regionales Andinos "Bartolomé de Las Casas," 2008), 127–33. As Adorno has pointed out, the dates of his birth can vary by at least fifteen to twenty years and one must therefore not fixate on the age he assigns to himself. Adorno, "Guaman Poma and His Illustrated Chronicle."

74 "Perro, Animal conocido y familiar, símbolo de fidelidad y de reconocimiento a los mendrugos de pan que le echa su amo." Covarrubias y Orozco, *Tesoro de la lengua castellana o española,* 816. For whatever reason, Covarrubias y Orozco has no entry for the word *amigo.* González Holguín's Quechua entries for amigo are extensive, extremely complex, and go well beyond the range of a European language definition of friend, and include the entry "Amigo de perros. Allccoman sonco." González Holguín, *Vocabulario de la lengua general de todo el Perú,* 405.

75 Cummins, *Toasts with the Inca,* 173–75.

76 Diego de Ocaña, *Un viaje fascinante por la América Hispana del siglo XVI* (Madrid: Studium, [1608] 1969), 112–13.

77 Ocaña, *Un viaje fascinante por la América Hispana,* 112–13.

78 One would really have to wait another 158 years for a similar itinerary of travel and critique as written by Concolorcorvo [pseud.], *El lazarillo de ciegos caminates desde Buenos Aires hasta Lima* (Gijón [Lima]: Imprenta de Rovada, 1773).

79 Fernández, *Historia del Piru,* 108r. This text seems to paraphrase what Blaise de Vigenère says about the table he invents: "si sont bien les beaux usages d'icelle, car il embrouille tout cela, et ceux qui se sont meslez de l'interpreter en une confusion d'orchemes, et infinité de revolutions d'alphabets, laborieux et embrouuillez ce qui se peut, et avec tout cela inutiles; des fort peu d'industrie au reste et invention; la ou ceste table peut servir por tout." Blaise de Vigenère, *Traicté des chiffres, ou secrètes manières d'escrire* (Paris: Abel l'Angelier, 1586), 50. Alberti also mentions the intent to "confuse the scrutinizer" (see note 50 above) and so may be the Latin source for the French and Spanish texts.

ANTONIO URQUÍZAR-HERRERA

The Meaning of Objects from the Indies in Early Sixteenth-Century Castilian Households

At the beginning of the sixteenth century, the Spanish arrival in the Indies was no more than a rumor for most Europeans. The first objects, and the first people, that traveled from the Indies to Europe were the earliest testimony to that arrival in what some thought may—at that stage it was still unclear—turn out to be a new route to the Indies, and, in fact, a new continent that would later become known as America.[1] Throughout the sixteenth century, hundreds of objects of all kinds arrived in Europe from the Americas. Sometimes their journey ended in the coffers and chambers of noble palaces. Some of these objects, however, traveled around Europe and were exhibited at parades and festivals, while other particularly remarkable pieces were central to the most sophisticated courtly *Wunderkammern*. In this regard, these American objects played a key role in the second half of the sixteenth century in places such as Habsburg Austria and Medici Florence, which has been documented in literature on collections. More recently, reference has been made to the relevance of the American objects possessed by the Spanish Crown during the reigns of Charles V and Philip II, along with interest in the shipments of Hernán Cortés from 1519 onward.[2]

For the last century, historians have focused on analyzing the novelty of these objects in Europe, as well as their capacity to embody otherness or exoticism.[3] However, as I sought to express in a previous 2011 article on the topic, I believe that the idea of continuity should receive more attention.[4] On one hand, the material, spatial, and conceptual proximity between American objects and other objects in humanist chambers should be analyzed.[5] On the other hand, the insertion of American objects in the temporal chain of the genealogical gallery of a prince or nobleman should also be considered. In addition, this chapter investigates the reasons behind the conservation, or destruction, of American objects in Spain. I believe that a comparison with the fate of different kinds of objects and references to other nobiliary collecting habits could prove to be enlightening.

Previous research has focused on the princely collections of the mid-sixteenth century. In this context, I believe the arrival of the first American objects in the late fifteenth and early sixteenth centuries deserves careful consideration. The early reception of American objects, their social dissemination, and the comparison to later catalogues of American objects in Europe could be matters of great interest.

The literary sources on Christopher Columbus's arrival in the Americas and his return to Europe are widely known. For example, among others are Columbus's own letters and those of Pietro Martire d'Anghiera, and the memoirs of Bartolomé de Las Casas. All these texts emphasize the evidentiary role that goods from the Indies played in building the Americas' image.[6] Also well-known are the first descriptions of La Española (Hispaniola) highlighting the role of *rescates*[7] and paying special attention to the people, clothes, weapons, and animals encountered there. Columbus himself expounded in his journal on how the Indians swam across to the Spanish boats and "brought us parrots and cotton thread in balls, and javelins and many other things," while some years later, among other references, Las Casas referred to rescates and the exchange of American goods.[8] One generation later, Columbus's son, Hernando Colón, continued the trend in his father's biography, writing with a perspective that spread a favorable image of the Americas in Europe. In this instance, the meeting with the Indians in the Americas as well as Columbus's accountability to the Spanish monarchs on his return were both made visible through the description of the same catalogue of objects.[9] After Columbus returned to the Iberian Peninsula, news spread of this new world. Whether it was at the Catholic monarchs' court or on the streets of Lisbon, Seville, or Barcelona, conversations referred to cannibals and their bows, Caribbean gold and pearls, and the islands' fauna, particularly parrots. Las Casas, who witnessed Columbus's arrival in Seville, underlined how people filled the streets to see Columbus, the Indians, and the parrots and gold that he had brought.[10] In his opinion, when displaying all these novelties to the Catholic monarchs and the Castilian and Aragonese nobility in Barcelona, Columbus had the air of a "senator of the Roman people."[11]

Martire d'Anghiera's letters and other texts about the Americas focused on the description of three kinds of objects that somehow summed up the representation of the New World. Bows exemplified the technical and cultural gap, gold illustrated the available treasures, and feathers evoked both otherness and proximity. Why proximity? Apparently, feather ornaments were seen as symbols with similar meanings in the Americas and Europe. Feather ornaments were exotic but not strange to the late medieval and Renaissance humanistic literary tradition (including many iconographical references to Roman crests). Feather crests had a long tradition of use as signs of nobility, as well as political and military might and success in fifteenth-century battles and tournaments in Spain and throughout Europe.[12] Together, these objects created the identity of the Americas and, as we will see, American bows, gold, and feathers were all spoils and triumphs.

Sources show that objects like those brought back by Columbus soon became of interest not only in Spain but also all over Europe.[13] In Spain, a 1497 letter from Don Íñigo López de Mendoza, second Count of Tendilla, expressed his gratitude to Juan Sánchez de la Puebla for "the things from the Indies that you sent to me, which gave me great pleasure."[14] Although there are no further references to the objects Tendilla received, his indication of "pleasure" is quite illustrative of the reception of these goods in the context of courtly magnificence and curiosity.[15] As we will see, that reference to pleasure can be found in other similar examples.

In 1507, the inventory of Don Juan de Guzmán, third Duke of Medina Sidonia, appraised the possessions that he had treasured in previous years.[16] In this case, the list offered a precise description of the catalogue of objects that were arriving from the Americas at that time, as well as their location in the palace.

In connection to this inventory, we can recall Kate Holohan's recent reference to a 1502 journey to America undertaken by a group of Franciscan friars, sent from Seville by Cardinal Francisco Jiménez de Cisneros to evangelize the continent.[17] A few months later, some of these friars returned to Spain with objects that included well-known American idols, which Cisneros donated to the University of Alcalá. A closer look at the source for that voyage (a sixteenth-century biography of Cisneros by his secretary Juan de Vallejo) shows that the first port of call on the return trip was Sanlúcar de Barrameda—a village under the rule of the Medina Sidonias and site of their ancestral home. The voyage subsequently continued to Seville, where the Medina Sidonias were then living. This closer look also reveals that the catalogue of American objects arriving in Sanlúcar and Seville in 1502 matches some of the supposedly American items in the 1507 Sevillian inventory of Don Juan de Guzmán. Furthermore, Vallejo offered an interesting description of the interpretative context of those objects. On their arrival in Seville, "the monarchs and court (and here we must include Don Juan) derived great pleasure."[18] Again, the words are those of the Count of Tendilla.

From the 1507 inventory, we know that Guzmán owned a set of fabrics, ornaments, jewelry, weapons, and furniture from the Indies. The inventory also includes European musical instruments, clocks, historical and mythological tapestries, maps, drawings, and a humanist library. There were other expensive and exclusive objects that were produced in the Americas but in a European fashion, such as "the rich silver altarpiece with its doors . . . that has in the middle the image of Our Lady, who has twenty-six small and large pearls, and eight sapphires and seven large and small rubies, with two pieces of mother-of-pearl, a Saint George, and another image of Our Lady."[19]

The ball from the Indies, the bell, the crown, the animal figures, the feather objects, the cotton skirts and fabrics, the *tirador* (spear-thrower), the hammock—all these non-European objects in Seville were placed in a foreign environment, devoid of their original function. Once in Seville, the skirts were no longer used to cover the body, nor was the hammock used for sleep. Interestingly, Vallejo felt the hammocks to be such a strange artifact that they needed an explanation: "He also brought some of the beds where the Indians sleep, which were completely made of cotton. They are called hammocks and are like the thick blankets that we have here, and are very soft, and they are hung from thick and strong ropes, made by them, and they sleep in this way, as do their wives and children" (fig. 1).[20]

The inventories contained the same objects mentioned in the texts about the Americas. This did not happen by chance. The descriptions, the rumors, and the pieces all traveled together in the same ships. "The snake [*sierpe*] from the Indies" that was listed in the 1532 postmortem inventory of the first Marquis of Tarifa, Don Fadrique Enríquez de Ribera, can be equated to the interest that Las Casas, among many other authors, expressed in the description of the idols representing snakes that they had encountered in the Americas.[21]

For their part, the Medina Sidonia family's small collection of artifacts from the Americas was intended to illustrate the news of the continent across the ocean (still considered to be the "Indies") and was placed next to other non-European testimonies of African barbarians and, we are told, Moriscos. We can imagine that these pieces had been brought together to show the breadth of the known world and the privileged position of the Medina Sidonias, who were involved in both the African and American routes.[22] The "many new things from those lands," which Vallejo explicitly mentioned, were objects

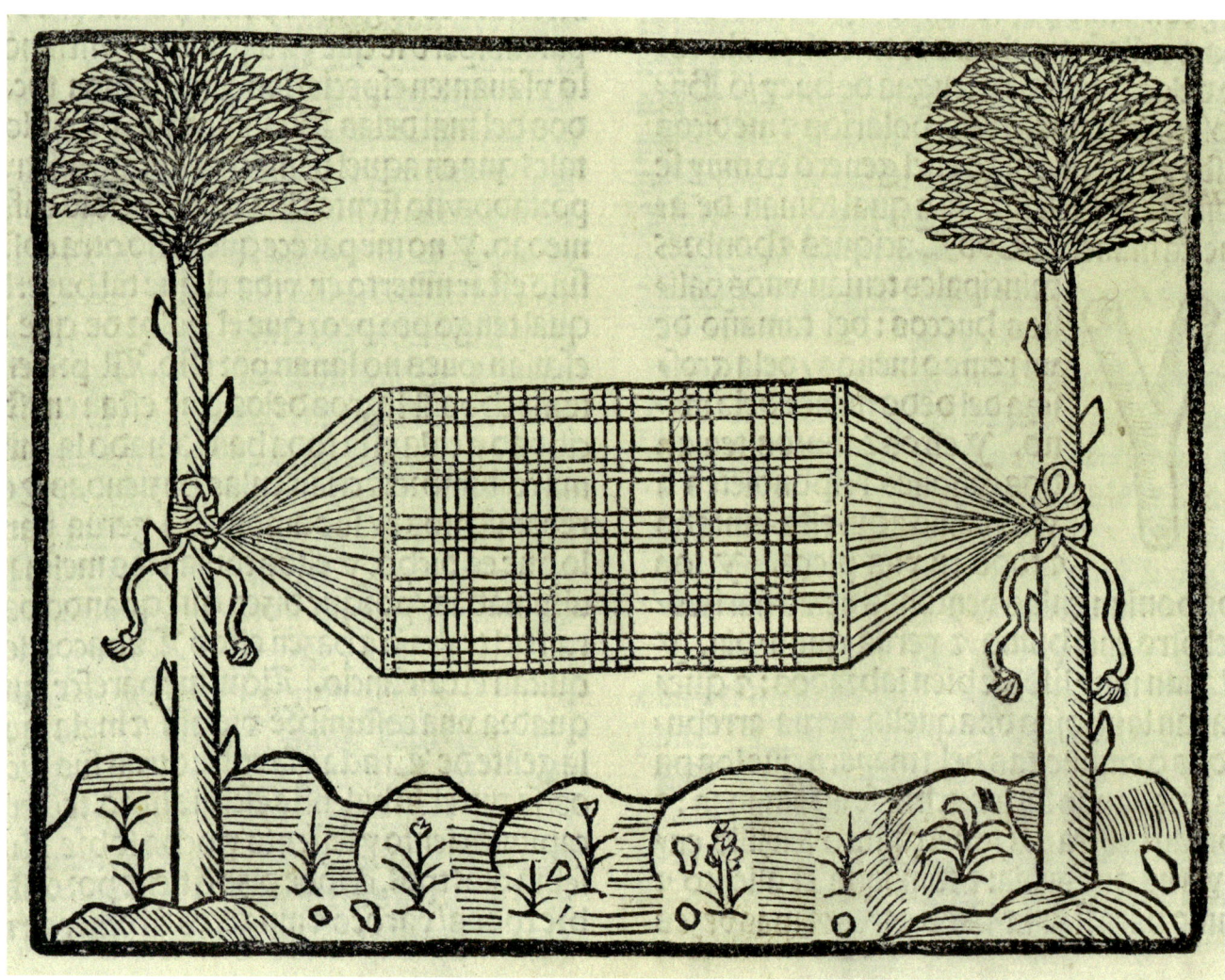

Fig. 1. Hammock. Gonzalo Fernández de Oviedo y Valdés, *La historia general de las Indias* (Seville: Juam Cromberger, 1535).

that other Europeans knew only from hearsay or reading.[23] The Medina Sidonias and other Spanish families (the Alcalás, also in Seville, for instance, or the Mendozas) were able to exhibit them in their own homes as early as the turn of the sixteenth century.[24]

Triumphs and Memories

American objects, like any other collected items, could convey different meanings in different contexts. Peter Mason has rightly pointed out how European collectors were guided by ingrained habits and by how "exotic objects could, therefore, come to function within aristocratic contexts which were very different from their original setting."[25] By placing my research question in the field of noble collections, I then propose that the social and dynastic interpretation of collections must be considered. As has been commented, early modern social treatises, early modern history books, and other texts frequently read by the nobility offer numerous clues as to how the objects in the collections were interpreted in social terms.[26] The notion of the visual "signs of distinction" is a topic central to this literature. Following the classical tradition of Roman triumphs and insignia, these signs were commonly spoils obtained through the military victories of the ancestors, or iconographical emblems extracted from them. Ferdinand II of

Aragon's funeral in Brussels (1516) exhibited spoils from his military victories in the Iberian Peninsula and the Mediterranean, including several Moorish flags and spears from Granada. In this context, characters dressed "in the Indian fashion" also appeared, covered with feathers that acquired the same emblematic value relative to triumph.[27] Other ceremonial parades in Spain and Europe showed similar features in relation to the Indies.[28] The virtues of the prince and the family could be embodied in these signs that gave visibility to the social position of their lineage. That was clearly the role of the Indian objects identified as swords, shields (*rodelas*), chainmail vests, crowns, or flags (*pabellón*) that were stored in Simancas Castle by Charles V, along with other American clothes, feather fabrics, jewels, and other similar goods of Morisco origin related to the conquest of Tunisia.[29] Described in particular detail were the shields in Charles V's postmortem inventory.[30]

We should note the importance of Charles V's court in the revival of the classical concept of spoils. Following a similar pattern, another fine example in the Habsburg courts is the Ambras armory, where early viewers of the Mexican treasures perceived the pieces in connection to the military conquest of the Americas (despite commonly mistaken attributions of origin).[31] Albrecht Dürer's famous commentaries on the Americana he saw in Brussels in 1520 not only revealed the wonder and *ingenium* of foreign lands but also recognized and highlighted the military nature of "two rooms full of armor of the people there," including weapons, harnesses, darts, and shields.[32] Charles V's 1558 funerary monuments in Valladolid and Mexico showed portraits of Atahualpa and Moctezuma "with their Indian insignia of the bow and the arrow."[33] At the end of the century, paintings of the conquest of Mexico and the presentation of American objects at the Medici armory emphasized the idea of trophy.[34]

In this context, it is then reasonable to believe that those American weapons, hunting supplies, and insignia that were placed in noble houses could have been interpreted from a nobiliary perspective. I consider Alessandra Russo's notion of the heraldic language of the Cortesian descriptions of his shipments to be both accurate and evocative.[35] Although literature on Americana in early modern Europe has not often commented on this fact, in my opinion, the tradition of using such insignia must have played a role in creating an interpretative framework for American objects in noble households. Let us begin by recalling the case of Cortés, who himself offers numerous clues in this regard (fig. 2). While Columbus could be seen as an explorer who enriched the monarchs by opening trade routes, Cortés presented himself as a soldier who expanded the territory of the empire through conquests that brought military triumphs. In his *Cartas de relación,* Cortés did not so much seek to describe this difference, nor was he solely concerned with showing the wealth of the new territory, but he did use recognizable symbols to give visibility to military victories of those involved. Unlike the rescates mentioned at the beginning of his first *relación,* which continued the Columbian model, there was a greater emphasis placed on trophies in later text. In this sense, the fact that his shipments contained a significant number of weapons can also be interpreted as a desire to make evident the nature of conquest.[36] However, although the inventory of the goods that Cortés left in Seville at his death showed neither American objects nor memorabilia from the conquest, the situation in Mexico was quite different.[37] The inventory of the house in which Cortés lived during his retirement in Cuernavaca suggests that he exhibited reminders of his military life there among tapestries and *guadamecíes* (embossed leather hangings) with heroic themes, although (at

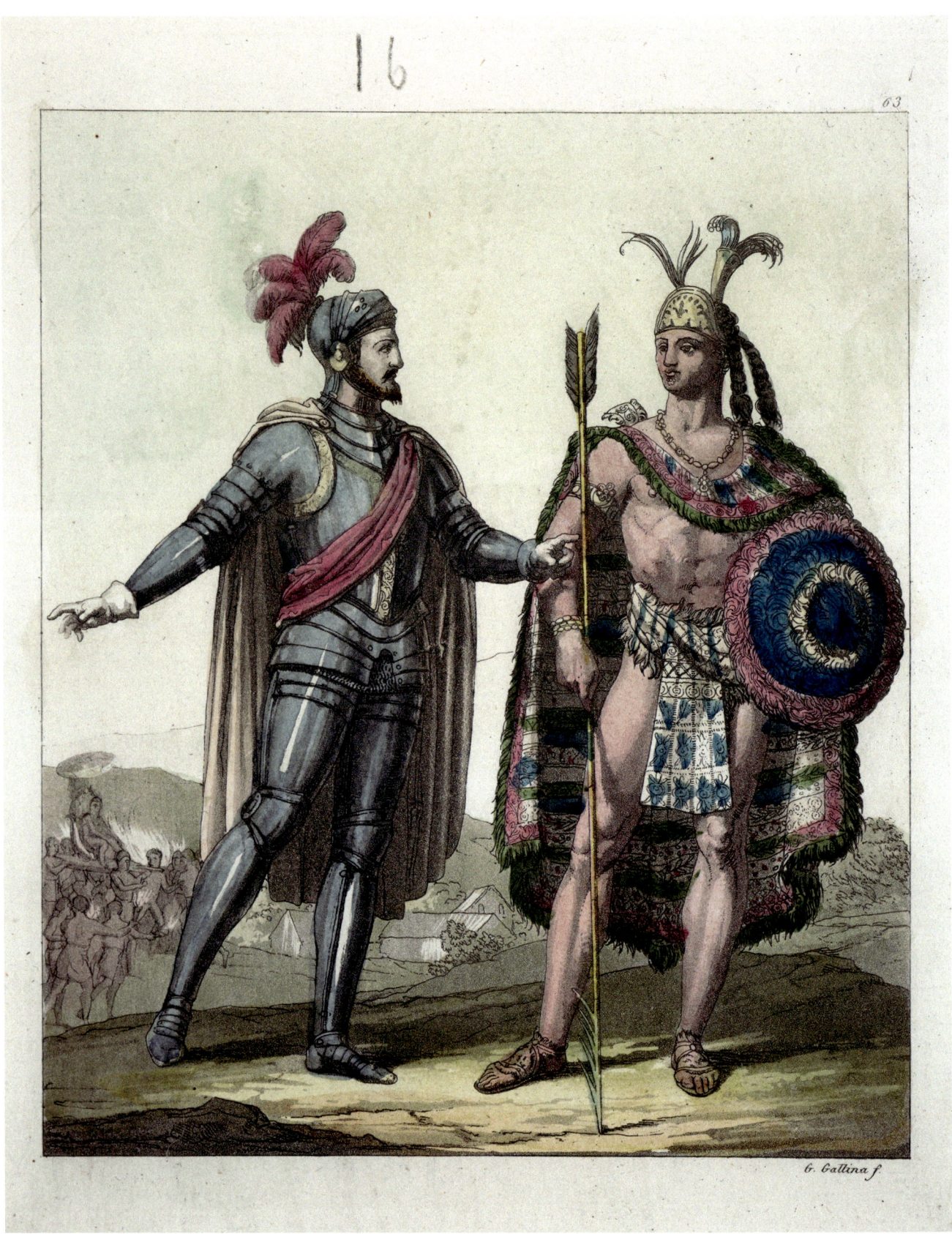

least in the inventoried part of the house) these were personal memorabilia rather than trophies taken from the enemy: several swords, one *jaez* (harness), and one *mochila* (backpack).[38] It is also important to remember how the letter of arms granted by Charles V in 1529 specified that the coat of arms had to represent, among other things, three crowns for "the three kings of the city of Tenochtitlan that you defeated" as well as a representation of that city in memory of its taking.[39] Unfortunately, the drawing of Cortés's coat of arms contained in the letter represented those crowns in the European fashion and made Tenochtitlan look like a Christian European city.[40] The only feathers in the drawing were the usual European crests surrounding the helmet on top of the coat. However, spoils were, undoubtedly, valued as evidence of nobility.

In this sense, it is interesting to see how Cortés's shipments (as well as the objects listed in them) appeared recurrently in a large number of the narratives about the events of the conquest, from Cortés's *Cartas de relación* to later texts. This was true of historiographical texts written soon after the actual events, such as the books of Bernal Díaz del Castillo and Francisco López de Gómara, but it also applied to later, part fictional accounts, such as those by Gabriel Lasso de la Vega.[41] Even more important are the administrative documents of the time, of which *Cartas de relación* can be considered an example, that show us how some of these objects occupied a central place in the political and judicial articulation of the conquest. Charles V's expected one-fifth share of the Mexican spoils is a case in point, appearing recurrently in Cortés's *Cartas de relación,* in the *juicio de residencia* to which he was subjected,[42] and in many other documents,

such as a well-known letter of 1523 in which the emperor himself took an interest.[43] Indeed, when Cortés described the capture of Tenochtitlan in his third relación, he went into detail about the distribution of the trophies and the delivery of the king's one-fifth share to the emperor's treasurer. Here, he writes, "Among the pillage obtained in that city, we acquired many golden shields and feathers and plumages and such wonderful things that cannot be explained in writing or understood if they are not seen."[44] The text itself points to the way in which these objects symbolized actual experiences. Feather head-dresses and jewels were ethnographic ornaments with an economic exchange value, but they were also the hoard from a conquest that acquired value through the appropriation of the distinctive signs of the warrior. Sometime later, Lasso de la Vega's imagination would see an enemy adorned during combat, wearing "a braggart plumage . . . in different bright colors, blue, yellow, white and red, pearls, and emeralds."[45]

Bernal Díaz del Castillo's respected voice described Aztec weapons as "coats of arms and inventions," clearly in connection to the classical tradition of the symbolic interpretation of spoils (fig. 3).[46] Other later authors, like José de Acosta, suggest similar associations.[47] Diego de Velázquez, who was Cortés's main opponent, tried to denounce Cortés's illegitimate ambition, describing how he (and Pedro de Alvarado) had agreed to be dressed as Indian nobles, bedecked in jewels, gold, and feathers. Among other jewels, Cortés also received a headdress that consisted of "a head like a dragon, of gold, and on the outside there were rich feathers and rings of gold and silver, and birds, with legs, and feet, and beaks, and eyes of gold, and the body and wings of rich feathers, which the Indians like a lot, and many stones of great value to them."[48]

In this context, it might also be the case that those nobles in Spain who had received Cortés's

Opposite: Fig. 2. Gallo Gallina, *Encounter of Hernán Cortés and Moctezuma.* Italy, about 1850. Hand-colored engraving on paper, 6½ × 5½ in. Denver Art Museum: Gift of the Collection of Frederick and Jan Mayer, 2000.353.

feather shields and who saw Cortés arriving in Toledo in 1528 "as a great Lord" (to quote López de Gómara), carrying Indians, American animals, feather shields, blankets, and other curiosities, were reminded of the Roman tradition of visible signs of nobility.[49] The American feather shields that were sent to the Spanish sixteenth-century churches came in the wake of the previous arrival of Islamic spoils from the reconquest.[50] Similarly, the shields located in noble cabinets could be found alongside Islamic spoils and were part of genealogical galleries and iconographic programs related to military virtues.[51]

Christoph Weiditz was another witness to Cortés's arrival in Toledo in 1528.[52] The representations of Indians contained in his *Trachtenbuch* are widely known,[53] but his commentaries in the margins of the drawings also help us understand their interpretation in that context (fig. 4). At the sight of the Indians depicted in the manuscript, Weiditz expresses interest in the objects that they had brought with them. He states, "Thus, the Indians go, have costly jewels let into their face," "thus, they go in India with their arms two thousand miles away, where gold is found in the water," "this is also the Indian manner, how they have brought wood jugs with them out of which they drink," and "this is an Indian, a noble of their kind."[54] The later commentary is particularly interesting. In identifying that Indian as a noble, Weiditz probably reproduced ideas he was exposed to in Charles V's court. This Indian was probably not an Aztec noble.[55] However, in my opinion, his beholders thought that the feathers on the standard could be identified as insignia.

Once in Europe, a social reading was projected onto these non-European objects simply because they were seen in a princely or nobiliary context, inside family palaces as part of a larger group of genealogical objects. For example, a nutmeg (probably from the East Indies) owned by the sixth Duke of Medina Sidonia, Don Juan Alonso de Guzmán, had "a silver setting with a coat of arms." In that situation, we can expect an added genealogical meaning of the object.[56] Furthermore, we should note that such social and ideological readings were undoubtedly fostered by the fact that these objects were presents or conquest spoils. Not only Cortés (and Díaz del Castillo) spoke a lot about the role of these

Fig. 3. Unknown artist, *Feather fan or Insignia*. Mexico, about 1520–30. Feathers, cane, and pigment. Weltmuseum Wien, Vienna, Austria.

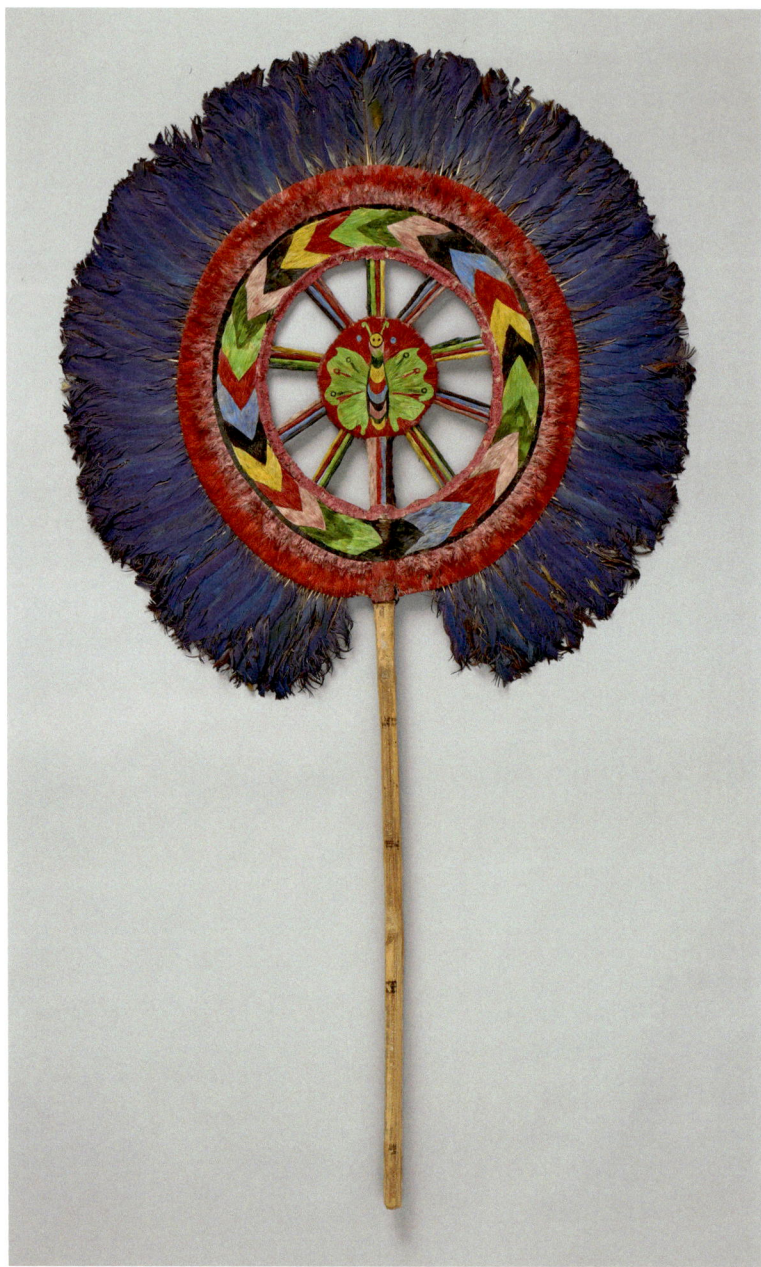

objects in the theater of conquest. Similar stories about Pizarro's triumphs and spoils circulated in Europe after the first Peruvian objects arrived in Seville in 1538.[57] The Habsburgs exhibited the family triumphs all over Europe and in Spain, from the early shipments of Cortés's objects to Philip II's collection of Inca treasures in Madrid.[58] The new Spanish nobility who had obtained their titles in the conquest of the Americas built the public image of their lineage through the memory of these events and made use of American iconography, which in some cases included the proud exhibition of blood links with the Indian elites, as in the case of the Toledo Moctezuma family in Cáceres (fig. 5).[59] The old Spanish noble houses, either by imitation or by participation in the political programs of the Crown, also introduced the Americas into their residences.

Two 1706 engravings show the endurance and the wide European circulation of these sixteenth-century ideas on the value of spoils.[60] Both of them represent views of the Dutch collection of Levinus Vincent (fig. 6). Although that collection focused on natural curiosities and had a clear scientific purpose, the Americana had a distinctive profile as it was displayed in the form of spoils.

Silver Settings

As sixteenth-century viewers had acknowledged, the economic appraisal of American objects was a relevant part of their common appreciation. That appraisal could either entail precise figures, as we can see in the inventories, or it could rest on the general perception of wealth that the rarity of the goods and the skills of the craftsmen could produce. In both cases, the materiality of the American objects was closely related to their exchange value. In this context, it is interesting to see how several objects of little material value received silver settings that enhanced their monetary appreciation in Europe. This was a common

trend. Among many examples, Don Juan Alonso de Guzmán's aforementioned nutmeg acquired "a silver setting with coats of arms."[61] Its material value rested mostly on its half ounce of silver.[62] Similar examples can be found in countless inventories in sixteenth- and seventeenth-century Spain, Florence, and Munich.[63] Alongside the noble house's humanistic involvement, the need for a supplementary economic value that could enrich the cultural appreciation of the objects was a familiar occurrence in this context. The concept of "Cortesian objects," which Russo coined to name the early sixteenth-century American production of hybrid objects, is also related to this idea.

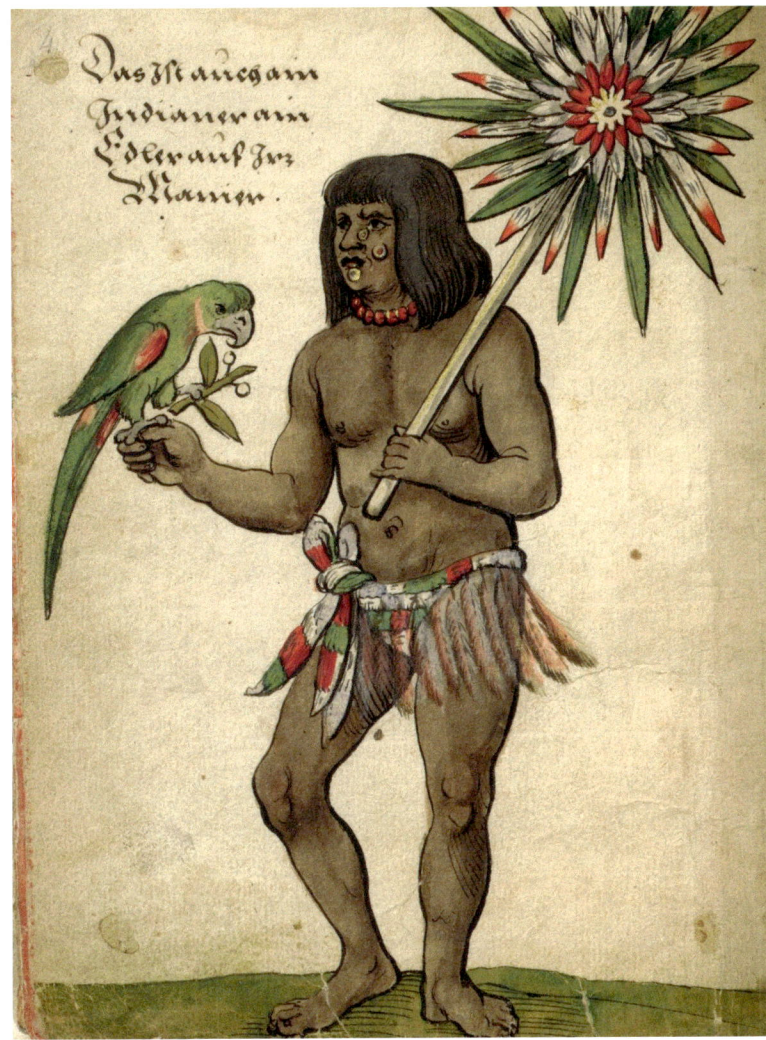

Fig. 4. Christopher Weiditz, *An Indian Noble*, about 1528. Watercolor on paper. Germanisches Nationalmuseum, Nuremburg, Germany.

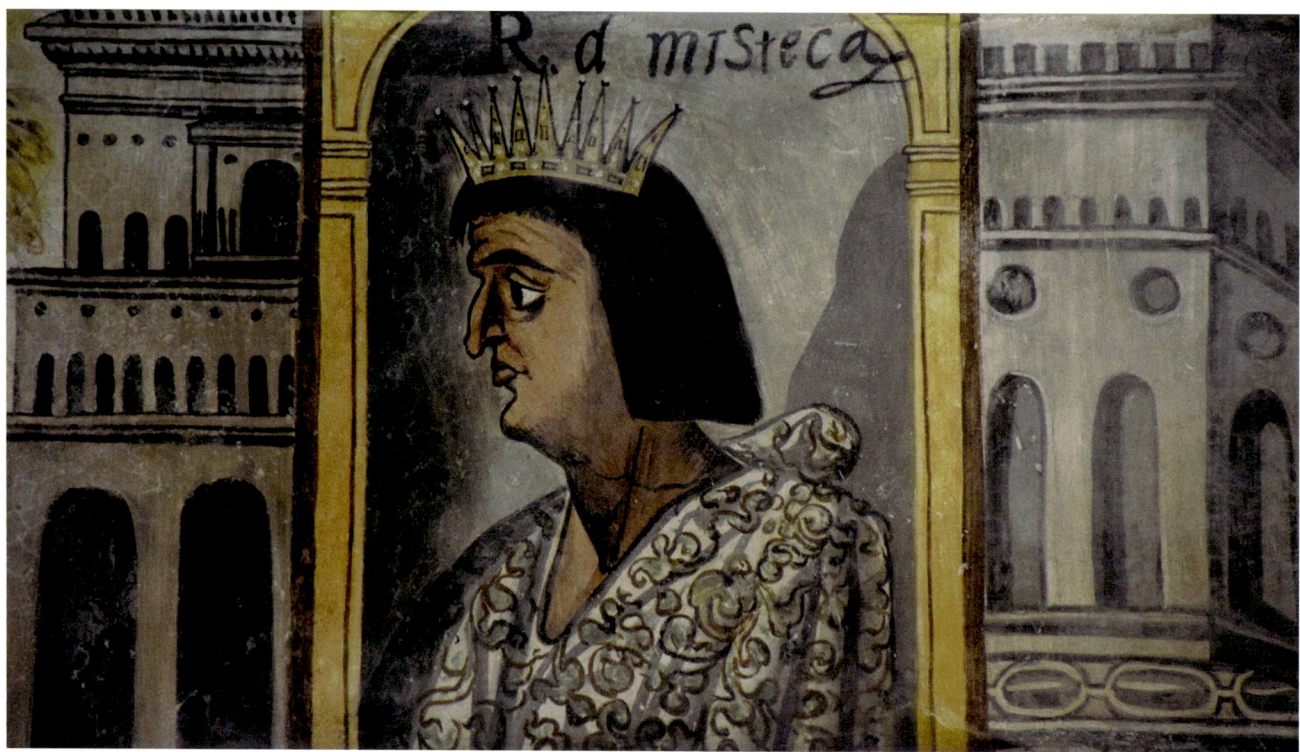

Fig. 5. Unknown artist, *Portrait of a Mexica King* (detail). Cáceres, Spain, about 1580. Mural. Palacio Toledo Moctezuma, Archivo Histórico de Cáceres, Ministerio de Cultura.

Sources like the historian Pietro Martire d'Anghiera stressed the economic value of the objects sent from the Americas as evidence of the wealth awaiting conquest. Literature has commonly remarked on that fact. On one hand, classical sources on the concept of spoils explained how the exhibition of conquered treasures enhanced the triumph in Rome. On the other hand, the emphasis on the richness of the objects created a link to other basic concepts of noble culture, such as the idea of magnificence or the social and political value of the exchange of presents. As Martire d'Anghiera stated, the first Mexican presents sent by Cortés "came from provincial villages, but the most recent ones came from the hoard of the powerful King Montezuma, from the nobility of his court and from the great temples of his Gods."[64] It is not by chance that the catalog of objects that he highlighted, namely clothes and jewels, perfectly matched the humanistic repertoire of magnificence that made visible the power of princes, nobles, and the church. In

this regard, the luxurious nature and artistic value of the new objects coming from Mexico were obviously closer to the expectations of the nobility (i.e., to the noble habit of presenting objects in exchange for favors) and to its collecting interests than those first tools and fabrics that arrived from the Caribbean in Columbus's day.[65]

In the second half of the sixteenth century, a great number of the inventories of the Spanish nobility contained American goods that were owned in the spirit of collecting.[66] However, primitive tools, like the Indian bow and arrows present in the house of the Marquis of Zahara, became progressively rare.[67] In this period, most of the objects showed hybrid alterations that enriched their value. There was also a clear interest in materials with value in and of themselves, such as ivory, coral, mother-of-pearl, or semiprecious stones. In a similar context to the porcelain from the East Indies, this was the period of jewelry and small luxury items, such as spoons and mother-of-pearl boxes. In addition, the ships from the Americas also brought tables, buffets, chairs, and other exotic wooden furniture that appear in multiple inventories. A perfect example of that trend can be found, again, in the 1558 postmortem inventory of Don Juan Alonso de Guzmán. The nutmeg with his coat of arms was part of a complete humanist cabinet filled with portraits, paintings, books, musical instruments, jewels, and mother-of-pearl curiosities, as well as a number of rare items, such as "a little black girl with her mouth open and a dog pulling her ear," which may have been a painting.[68] The comparison between the 1539 and the 1553 inventories of the Medici household shows similar changes in the nature of American goods.[69]

Parrots, which had initially amazed the conquistadors, still preserved their awe at the end of the sixteenth century. However, their multicolored feathers were interpreted, at times, in a jeweled medium, as can be seen in the "golden parrot adorned with diamonds" in the Count of Castellar's 1580 inventory.[70] Other goods shared a similar fascination, such as the spices that were enclosed in silver spice ships for the sake of ostentation.[71] The feathers moved from ritual headdresses to Christian religious representations, such as the "little altarpiece with its Indian feather doors with a descent from the cross carved in the round, and the workmanship . . . considered to be worth a *ducado* and a half," in the inventory of the Marquis of Tarifa.[72] The silver that adorned Cortés's Aztec ornaments could still be found, but now in different forms, such as the "silver brazier with a candlestick made from *palo de las Indias,* which weighted three *marcos* with its stick and all," in the inventory of the counts of Urueña[73] or "a tray and dish of the Indies" in the Duke of Alcalá's inventory.[74]

Vanishing Goods

In early modern Spain, American hammocks were of no practical use for noble life.[75] The

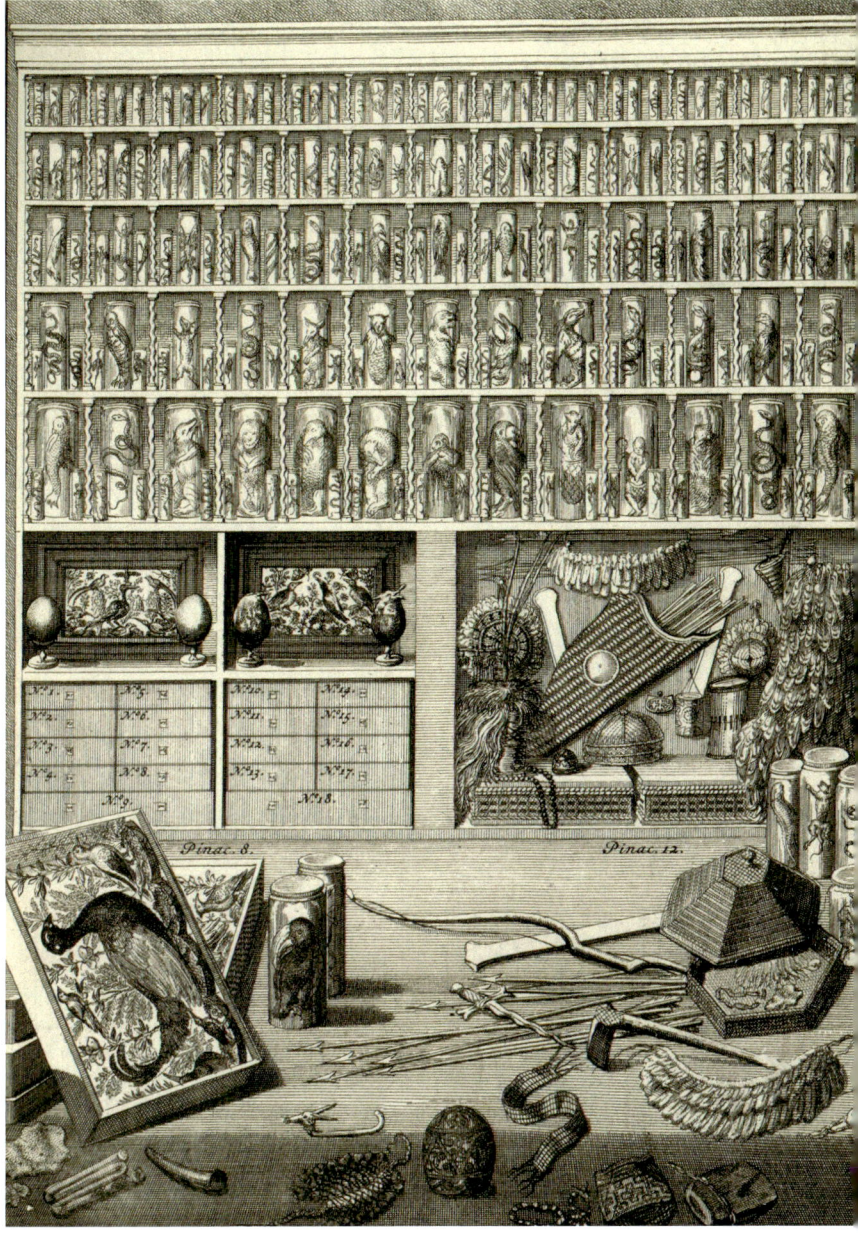

Fig. 6. Levinus Vincent, illustration from *Wondertooneel der nature* (Amsterdam: François Halma, 1706).

hammocks in early sixteenth-century noble cabinets were simply exhibited as curiosities from a new world. Once the Americas became better known, hammocks were only retained in their condition as furniture, albeit still useless for noble purposes and as such were thrown away.

On the death of Charles V in 1558, his inventories contained hundreds of objects. Around half of them were precious stones and pieces of gold, while several other dozen were Americana:

feather objects, shields, fans, crests, headdresses, jewels, weapons, and clothes. Most of Charles V's goods were sold following the German legal tradition. Philip II, for instance, had to buy his father's armory.[76] Several authors who have written about the collections of American objects in Europe have remarked on the vanishing of most of the American goods that arrived in Spain: "Practically nothing escaped destruction in Spain."[77] Many have explained this fact by commenting on "Spain's indifference to the fate of New World artifacts and its quick willingness to convert the cultural spoils of conquest into financial gain."[78] Charles V's auction of Americana is often referred to as a good example of this Spanish attitude of indifference to the fate of New World artifacts for monetary gain.

This willingness to forfeit Americana in exchange for money certainly existed. The economic exchange value of jewels and any objects containing precious stones, gold, and silver was always carefully considered. Cortés's shipments systematically listed the weight and value of all goods, as did Charles V's postmortem inventories.[79] Jewelry was commonly melted for extracting gold and silver on both sides of the Atlantic Ocean. Cortés did the same when collecting taxes.[80] Indeed, the practice was established in Europe, where monarchs and nobles had long been selling jewels or melting silver services down whenever cash was required.

Nevertheless, not all of Charles V's American goods vanished. As elsewhere, some of the most relevant ones were sent to other European courts as valuable political presents often intended to stress dynastic connections, in what must be understood as a sign of appreciation rather than disdain.[81] In 1520, Cortés sent a gold cup to Francisco de los Cobos, the emperor's powerful *secretario*. In a letter to his father, Cortés explained that he expected the secretary to appreciate it "because it is a new thing given that has been made by the hand of the people of this land, and I gave it to him more for its novelty than for its price."[82]

It is very important to note that when Charles V retreated to the Yuste monastery, he took with him a number of pieces related to the Americas: maps and "two big paper books where different trees, plants, and people and other things from the Indies are painted," as well as feather clothes, including "a feather blanket from the Indies, covered in black taffeta" and "three feather quilts from the Indies, two of them red with borders in yellow and brown, and the other all in brown."[83] This set of items was small but sufficient to embody the representation of the new continent as part of the empire. Indeed, the set was smaller than the group of weapons he had also taken to Yuste: a couple of daggers, a sword, a crossbow, and a harquebus.[84] After the emperor's death, all the goods at Yuste were moved to Valladolid and Madrid and were sold. Some of them, like Charles V's beloved painting of the Trinity by Titian (*The Glory,* now at the Museo del Prado), were bought by his son, the new King Philip II (in this case, for 75,000 *maravedíes,* or 200 ducados).[85] Prominent members of the court and the Spanish nobility bought other goods, such as jewels and tapestries. One of the Indian feather quilts was bought (for 7 ducados) by Don Diego Hurtado de Mendoza, who was one of the most prominent sixteenth-century Spanish collectors and brother to the viceroy of New Spain, Antonio de Mendoza. Again, the other five quilts were bought by Philip II (for 10, 12, and 17 ducados), who also acquired the two illustrated Indian books (for 45,000 maravedíes, which is 120 ducados). Despite the difference in the economic appraisals, Philip II undoubtedly wanted these American items to remain within the family, as happened with *The Glory* or the armory. Another feather quilt was bought by Philip II "for the service of Most Serene Prince Carlos," by then the designated successor to the Crown.[86]

A few years later, during the reign of Philip II, Francisco de Toledo referred to the creation of a Museum of Americana in Madrid. Although probably misinterpreted,[87] this statement should at least be a clear indication as to the value that American objects could acquire in the context of the "memories of the glories of other kingdoms that Your Majesty has in his armory and chamber."[88]

The terms of the interpretation of noble collections as social signs shed some light on the disappearance of the first American objects in Spain. The Crown retained what it considered convenient to preserve the memory of the Habsburg conquest of the Americas. As for the nobility, although some houses had received American objects in the sixteenth century, only a very small number of them had had direct involvement with the military events in the Americas. In general terms, there was no direct connection between the American goods and the memory of the virtues of the ancestors of these noble houses. Thus, there was no great interest in their conservation. However, the comparison with the fate of Islamic objects is interesting. Which noble houses preserved Islamic objects down the centuries? In general, those that possessed objects related to events involving family ancestors.

Trends for and against conservation coexisted in common usage in every noble house in early modern Spain. On the one hand, many kinds of objects were frequently protected by entailments (*mayorazgos*), including works of art or historical weapons. On the other hand, cash was needed, and most of the movable properties of each generation were sold after the death of the head of the house.[89] In almost all cases, there was no reason to include American objects in the mayorazgos, with the possible exception of the descendants of the few conquistadors who reached entitled nobility in the sixteenth century.[90]

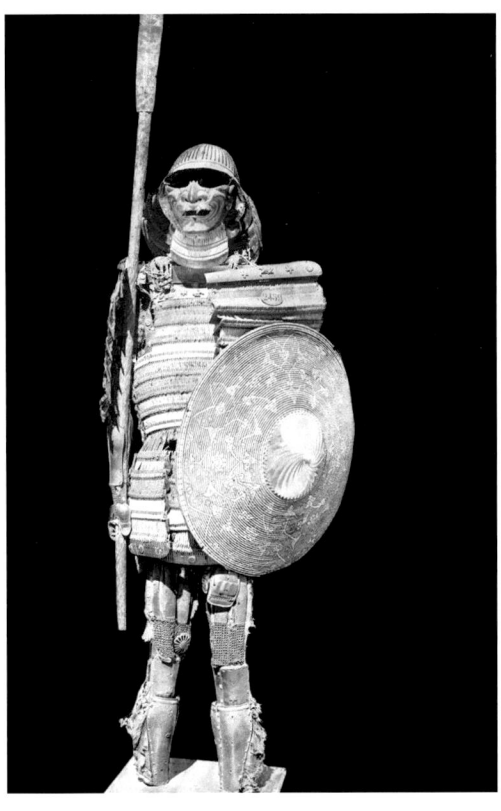

Fig. 7. Jean Laurent, *Chinese Armor at the Spanish Royal Collection,* before 1884. Ministerio de Educación, Cultura y Deporte, Instituto del Patrimonio Histórico, Madrid, Archivo Ruiz Vernacci, VN-06442. The pieces of the armor were in fact Japanese and American.

The sale of most of Charles V's American goods was part of this general pattern. However, the arrival of new American artifacts at different moments of the sixteenth, seventeenth, and eighteenth centuries was another aspect of the same pattern of circulation. As James Amelang has pointed out, American goods continued to arrive and to be seen in the private realm of the palaces of the Spanish nobility.[91] Therefore, it cannot be said that the vanishing of the first sixteenth-century items was due to a lack of interest. There was interest in the Americas, in American luxury products, and, when those in question had undertaken military or political service to the Crown in the Americas, there was interest in American insignia. This applied to spoils, such as the weapons of three Indian kings (likely spoils of Moctezuma) described by Diego de Cuelbis in the Royal Armory, that were exhibited in combination with three sets of Japanese armor (fig. 7), an unexpected combination of objects which, as

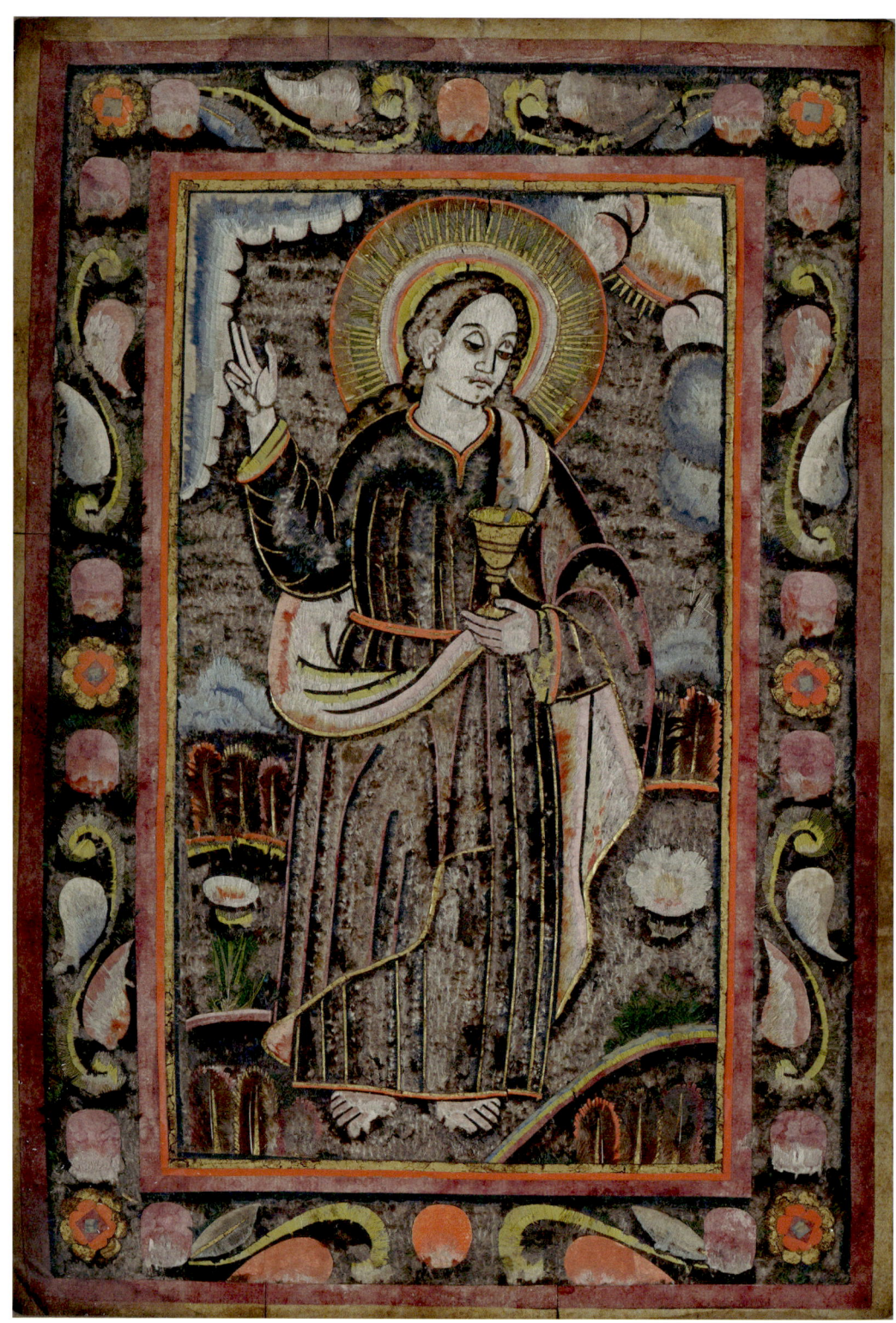

Fig. 8. Unknown artist, *St. John the Evangelist*. Mexico, 1600s.
Feathers glued on paper, mounted on copper, 30¼ × 9³⁄₁₆ in.
Denver Art Museum: Gift of the Collection of Frederick and
Jan Mayer, 2013.389.

Álvaro Soler de Campos suggested, showcases the interest in American artifacts.[92] Furthermore, the American objects (including chocolate) that were brought or sent back to Spain by sixteenth- and seventeenth-century viceroys in memory of their appointment is good evidence of this interest.[93] The dukes of Alburquerque, who have been recently studied, are a case in point.[94]

Quite another matter is the fate of these objects after one or two generations in Spain. The luggage of the Sicilian and Neapolitan Spanish viceroys was also full of local memorabilia. Unlike American goods, a sizeable share of Italian artifacts can still be found in Spanish palaces, churches, and museums. What was the difference between American and Italian artifacts, for example? Not only materiality. Besides magnificence and other political, social, or dynastic reasons, the many paintings and statues from Italy were also treasured with regard to "fine arts," a concept that was (and still is) the most important idea in the narrative of collecting in Western society.[95] The comparison with the fate of tapestries is also interesting in this regard. Tapestries, the richest of objects in noble households, were considered art pieces in the sixteenth century, but in the eighteenth this artistic appreciation declined, at which point many of them disappeared. With regard to the first American objects, only feather paintings (fig. 8) could properly claim this artistic recognition, as many early sources stated, but all of them show that the recognition was not equal to that of paintings and did not last as long.[96]

To conclude, this idea can be illustrated by the example of the 1637–39 sale of the goods of Don Fernando Afán de Ribera, third Duke of Alcalá, former viceroy in Naples and Sicily and governor of Milan, as well as one of the main collectors of Italian painting in seventeenth-century Spain.[97] The House of Alcalá went bankrupt after the unexpected death of the duke during a diplomatic mission to Germany, and different

sales of his goods took place in Seville and Genoa, where his wife awaited him with the embassy luggage. The comparison of the fate of Alcalá's American objects with his European paintings is quite telling. While his inheritor, the Duke of Medinaceli, bought the library and a whole set of classical antiquities such as family portraits and paintings attributed to Velázquez, Perugino, Dürer, Titian, Bassano, and Ribera, Medinaceli ignored two "images of feather." Instead, they were traded in a public auction to a man named Rodrigo de Abreu for the price of six reales, the same price paid in that auction for a single "canvas of a Venus, all cracked and broken."[98] Moreover, "a stone snake that was broken" was recorded among many other items in a section of objects that were "wrecked and mistreated by time."[99] This may well have been the same *sierpe* of the Indies" that, as I have noted, warranted a dignified section on its own in the 1532 inventory of Don Afán de Ribera's ancestor Don Fadrique Enríquez de Ribera, the first Marquis of Tarifa. Concurrently, the Genoa auction comprised dozens of paintings, jewels, weapons, scientific instruments, and a single hammock, which might have been in the family since the early sixteenth century and was still considered an artifact worthy of taking to an embassy. Why, then, did a certain "Caballero Pinelo" (probably a member of the Sevillian elite like Rodrigo de Abreu) buy it for 40 reales?[100] What happened to it afterward? We do not know, just as we have no knowledge of what happened to the jewels, weapons, or scientific instruments also sold in Genoa or the feather paintings sold in Seville. All of this deserves further investigation. By contrast, thanks to research conducted by scholars such as Jonathan Brown, Richard Kagan, Vicente Lleó, and more recently David Mallén, we do know that many of the paintings held by the Duke of Alcalá in Seville are still hanging on different walls throughout Europe.[101]

✛ ✛ ✛

Notes

Many thanks to Nicola Stapleton for her thorough revision of the English. This study was carried out in the framework of the "PoLeNo—Políticas en tránsito para la legitimación nobiliaria: memoria e historia del coleccionismo y las escenografías domésticas de la nobleza española (1788–1931)" HAR2015-66311-P Research Project, financed by the Spanish Ministry of Science, Innovation and Universities/AEI/UE Feder Funds.

1 See Peter Mason, "From Presentation to Representation: *Americana* in Europe," *Journal of the History of Collections* 6, no. 1 (1994): 1–20.

2 See, among others, Miguel Morán and Fernando Checa, *El coleccionismo en España: De la cámara de maravillas a la galería de pinturas* (Madrid: Cátedra, 1985); Peter Mason, *Infelicities: Representations of the Exotic* (Baltimore: Johns Hopkins University Press, 1998); James S. Amelang, "The New World in the Old? The Absence of Empire in Early Modern Madrid," *Cuadernos de Historia de España* 82 (2008): 147–64; Alessandra Russo, "Cortés's Objects and the Idea of New Spain: Inventories as Spatial Narratives," *Journal of the History of Collections* 23, no. 2 (2011): 229–52; Cristina Hernández Castelló, "Objetos de Indias en las cámaras mendocinas a finales de la Edad Media," *Estudios de Historia de España* 18, no. 1–2 (2016): 185; Kate Holohan, "Collecting the New World at the Spanish Habsburg Court, 1519–1700" (PhD diss., New York University, 2015), 62; and Christian F. Feest, "European Collecting of American Indian Artifacts and Art," *Journal of the History of Collections* 5, no. 1 (1993): 4.

3 For a very interesting archival insight that documents the limits of that exoticist explanation, see Nuno Senos, "De todas as partes do Mundo: Conclusão," in *De Todas as Partes do Mundo: O Patrimônio do 5º Duque de Bragança, D. Teodósio I,* ed. Jessica Hallett and Nuno Senos (Lisbon: Tinta-da-China, 2018), 372–73; and Nuno Senos, "The Empire in the Duke's Palace: Global Material Culture in Sixteenth-Century Portugal," in *The Global Lives of Things: The Material Culture of Connections in the Early Modern World,* ed. Anne Gerritsen and Giorgio Riello (London: Routledge, 2016), 137–39.

4 Antonio Urquízar-Herrera, "Imaginando América: Objetos indígenas en las casas nobles del Renacimiento andaluz," *Historia y Genealogía* 1 (2011): 205–21.

5 Russo, "Cortés's Objects," 229–52.

6 For a recent review of the wide bibliography on this topic, see Bethany Aram and Bartolomé Yun-Casalilla, eds., *Global Goods and the Spanish Empire, 1492–1824: Circulation, Resistance and Diversity* (London: Palgrave Macmillan, 2014), 23. See also Friedrich Polleross, "América en las artes plásticas," in *El teatro descubre América: Fiestas y teatro en la Casa de Austria (1492–1700),* ed. Andrea Sommer-Mathis, Teresa Chaves Montoya, Christopher F. Laferl, and Frederich Polleross (Madrid: Fundación Mapfre, 1992), 271–326.

7 *Rescates* have been traditionally interpreted as forced barters with which it was intended to obtain objects of high value and wealth from the Indians.

8 All English translations of foreign-language texts and documents are my own unless otherwise noted. Bartolomé de Las Casas, *Historia de las Indias* (Madrid: Imprenta de Miguel Ginesta, 1875), 1:296. Among many other examples on the first arrival in La Española, see also Las Casas, *Historia,* 1:313, 319, 393, 438. A later shipment of pearls and gold to the Catholic monarchs is described in Las Casas, *Historia,* 2:353. See also the descriptions in Columbus's letters announcing the arrival in the Indies, such as the one to Luis de Santángel printed in 1493 and rapidly translated into other European languages. Richard H. Major, *Select Letters of Christopher Columbus, With Other Original Documents Relating to his Four Voyages to the New World* (London: Hakluyt Society, 1847).

9 See, for instance, the Italian edition, Hernando Colón, *Historie del S. D. Fernando Colombo* (Venice: Francesco de' Franchesci Sanese, 1571), 51v–52r, 150r–v. See also Andrés de Bernáldez's echo of the descriptions of La Española. Andrés de Bernáldez, *Historia de los Reyes Católicos* (Seville: Imprenta de D. José María Geofrin, 1870), 362.

10 See Las Casas, *Historia,* 1:477; see also 462, 464, 472, 478.

11 See Las Casas, *Historia,* 1:478.

12 See Noel Fallows, *Jousting in Medieval and Renaissance Iberia* (Woodbridge, UK: Boydell Press, 2011), 95–97.

13 Among many references, see Polleross, "América en las artes plásticas," 289–307.

14 Tendilla had previously loaned money to Sánchez de la Puebla, probably to be invested in American trade. Aurelio García López, "La correspondencia del conde de Tendilla: Nuevos datos sobre el mecenazgo de la familia del Cardenal Mendoza," *Wad-al-Hayara* 22 (1995): 83, 96. See also Hernández Castelló, "Objetos de Indias," 185. This Juan Sánchez de Puebla might be connected to a Juan Sánchez de Puebla who has been documented in the log book of the Castilian late fifteenth-century fleet in Seville. See Eduardo Aznar, "La experiencia marítima: Las rutas y los hombres de mar," in *Andalucía 1492: Razones de un protagonismo,* ed. Antonio Collantes de Terán Sánchez and Antonio García-Baquero González (Seville: Algaida, 1992), 148.

15 See Hernández Castelló, *Poder y promoción artística: El conde de Tendilla, un Mendoza en tiempos de los Reyes Católicos* (Valladolid, Spain: Universidad Valladolid, 2017); and Antonio Urquízar-Herrera, *Coleccionismo y nobleza: Signos de*

distinción social en la Andalucía del Renacimiento (Madrid: Marcial Pons, 2007), 44.

16 Postmortem inventory of Don Juan de Guzmán, third Duke of Medina Sidonia (Seville, 17 August 1507; Duke's house in the San Miguel parish in Seville). Archivo Ducal de Medina Sidonia (hereafter ADMS), Leg. 931, fols. 22v–23r, Sanlúcar de Barrameda.

17 Holohan, "Collecting the New World," 62.

18 Juan de Vallejo, *Memorial de la vida de Fray Francisco Jiménez de Cisneros,* ed. Antonio de la Torre (Madrid: Imprenta Bailly-Baillere, 1913), 45.

19 See Urquízar-Herrera, *Coleccionismo y nobleza.*

20 Vallejo, *Memorial de la vida,* 45. Another description of the hammocks can be found in Las Casas, *Historia,* 1:310.

21 Postmortem inventory of Don Fadrique Enríquez, first Marquis of Tarifa. Archivo General de Andalucía (hereafter AGA), Section Alcalá (ducado), Leg. 16–39 (Seville, 1 May 1532), Seville. See, for instance, Las Casas, *Historia,* 4:355, 359.

22 On the ambiguous meaning of "Indies" and the use of the words "moriscos" and "moreschi" to refer to American objects in Spain and Italy, see Detlef Heikamp, *Mexico and the Medici* (Florence: EDAM, 1972), 10; Anthony A. Shelton, "Cabinets of Transgression: Renaissance Collections and the Incorporation of the New World," in *The Cultures of Collecting,* ed. John Elsner and Roger Cardinal (Cambridge, MA: Harvard University Press, 1994), 201–3; and Jessica Keating and Lia Markey, "'Indian' Objects in Medici and Austrian-Habsburg Inventories," *Journal of the History of Collections* 23, no. 2 (2011): 286–88. See also Russo, "Cortés's Objects," 237; Senos, "De todas as partes," 362; and Senos, "The Empire," 132.

23 Vallejo, *Memorial de la vida,* 45.

24 On the American objects in the 1505–32 Alcalá inventories, see Urquízar-Herrera, "Imaginando América." On the general Spanish situation, see also Morán and Checa, *El coleccionismo en España,* 129–38; and Holohan, "Collecting the New World." See also Hernández Castelló, "Objetos de Indias," 173–88.

25 Mason, *Infelicities,* 83; and Mason, "From Presentation to Representation," 10. The aristocratic collection was a frequent context for American objects all over Europe. See also Shelton, "Cabinets of Transgression," 199; Heikamp, *Mexico and the Medici,* 34; and Holohan, "Collecting the New World," 69. On the adaptation of exotic objects in the European mindset, see also Shelton, "Cabinets of Transgression," 201; Benjamin Keen, *The Aztec Image in Western Thought* (New Brunswick, NJ: Rutgers University Press, 1971), 55; Tzvetan Todorov, *La conquête de l'Amérique: La question de l'autre* (Paris: Éditions du Seuil, 1982); and

Stephen Greenblatt, *Ces merveilleuses possessions: Découverte et appropriation du Nouveau Monde au XVIe siècle* (Paris: Belles Lettres, 1996).

26 See Antonio Urquízar-Herrera, "Teoría de la magnificencia y teoría de las señales en el pensamiento nobiliario español del siglo XVI," *Ars Longa* 23 (2014): 93–111; and Antonio Urquízar-Herrera, "'Making Invisible Things Visible and Palpable': Visual Marks of Nobility in Early Modern French Social Theory and the Embodiment of Social Estates in Collections, 1550–1650," *Word & Image* 31, no. 3 (2015): 386–97.

27 See Elisa Ruiz García, "Aspectos representativos en el ceremonial de unas exequias reales (a. 1504–1516)," *En la España Medieval* 26 (2003): 276–77. See also Polleross, "América en las artes plásticas," 280.

28 See, among many examples, the presence of an Indian cacique and some of his subjects among the characters of the Burgos reception of Anna of Austria on the occasion of her marriage to Philip II in 1571. *Anonymous, Relación verdadera, del recibimiento, que la muy noble y muy mas leal ciudad de Burgos . . . hizo a la Magestad Real de la Reyna nuestre señora, doña Anna d'Austria . . .* (Burgos, Spain: Phillipe de Junta, 1571). See also Pilar Varela Ledo, *Relación verdadera del recibimiento que la ciudad de Burgos hizo a la reina doña Anna de Austria en 1570* (A Coruña, Spain: Sielae, 2016), 156. Without references to the Spanish case, see Suzanne Boorsh, "America in Festival Presentations," in *First Images of America: The Impact of the New World on the Old,* vol. 1, ed. Fredi Chiappelli (Berkeley: University of California Press, 1976), 500–15. See also Deanna MacDonald, "Collecting a New World: The Ethnographic Collections of Margaret of Austria," *Sixteenth Century Journal* 33, no. 3 (2002): 649.

29 Fernando Checa Cremades, dir., *Los inventarios de Carlos V y la familia imperial,* vol. 1 (Madrid: Fernando Villaverde, 2010), 320–23, 328. See also Russo, "Cortés's Objects," 241; Mason, *Infelicities,* 83; and Holohan, "Collecting the New World," 75–126. On the other hand, it must be admitted that the armory of Valladolid, which was a key symbolic space for Charles V, did not contain any American pieces. In any case, the symbolic importance of Simancas for the lineage is clear. Objects that were very relevant to the history of the lineage were placed there, like "the sword they say that was from the Catholic King." Checa Cremades, *Los inventarios de Carlos V,* 267–79, 330. See also Carina L. Johnson, *Cultural Hierarchy in Sixteenth-Century Europe: The Ottomans and Mexicans* (Cambridge: Cambridge University Press, 2011), 97.

30 "Six bucklers *[rodelas]* from the Indies, different each one from the others; one of them had several turquoise stones and a gold cordon around it, which was removed and weighted in five marcos, and it was put in a cloth and given to the said Juannin and Fransois; and the other buckler that has two

turquoise moons garnished in gold, that is below. And the other that has on one side a half moon of gold with a cordon around, and a figure on the other side. The other three bucklers are different, one of them has some gold on it, and they were placed in a coffer, and the best two were wrapped in their canvas covers. The two bucklers are similar to *adargas* [leather shields from Spanish Islamic origin] and have feathers around. The gold points in the middle are missing from some of these bucklers." Checa Cremades, *Los inventarios de Carlos V,* 323.

31 Christian F. Feest, "Vienna's Mexican Treasures: Aztec, Mixtec, and Tarascan Works from 16th Century Austrian Collections," *Archiv für Völkerkunde* 44 (1990): 11.

32 Albrecht Dürer, *Memoirs of Journeys to Venice and the Low Countries* (Auckland, New Zealand: Floating Press, 2010), 56.

33 Polleross, "América en las artes plásticas," 300.

34 Giovanni Cipriani, "Il mondo americano nella Toscana del Cinquecento: Collezionismo e letteratura," *Miscellanea storica della Valdelsa* 98, no. 283 (1992): 234; Heikamp, *Mexico and the Medici,* 20–22; Lia Markey, *Imagining the Americas in Medici Florence* (University Park: Pennsylvania State University Press, 2016), 93–117. On Italy and the Americas, see also the recent Elizabeth Horodowich and Lia Markey, eds., *The New World in Early Modern Italy, 1494–1750* (Cambridge: Cambridge University Press, 2016).

35 Russo, "Cortés's Objects," 241–43; and Alessandra Russo, *The Untranslatable Image: A Mestizo History of the Arts in New Spain, 1500–1600* (Austin: University of Texas Press, 2014), 26–29, 56–57, 175–76. See also Mason, *Infelicities,* 83.

36 Hernán Cortés, *Cartas de relación,* ed. Ángel Delgado Gómez (Madrid: Castalia, 1993), 108–110, 128, 132, 138, 140, 149–50, 209–11, 230–33, 259, 429, 438, 458, 649–50.

37 Antonio Muro Orejón, *Hernando Cortés: Exequias, almoneda e inventario de sus bienes* (Seville: Escuela de Estudios Hispano-Americanos, 1966), 64–73. See also Russo's argument on the American meaning of Cortés's possession of a volume of the treatise *De sphaera.* Russo, "Cortés's Objects," 245.

38 The inventory of Cortés's main house in Mexico City is not known, and the one in Cuernavaca was not complete, so it is possible he might have kept American spoils there following the Islamic spoils tradition of the Spanish nobility after the wars of Granada. José Luis Martínez, ed., *Documentos cortesianos* (Mexico City: UNAM, 1990), 4:352–432.

39 Martínez, *Documentos cortesianos,* 1:331–32.

40 For a reproduction of the document containing a drawing of the coat of arms, see Muro Orejón, *Hernando Cortés,* 47. See also Martínez, *Documentos cortesianos,* 3:53–54.

41 See, for instance, Francisco López de Gómara, *Historia general de las Indias* (Zaragoza, Spain: Agustín Millán, 1552), 1:15r, 92v, 93r; and Gabriel Lasso de la Vega, *Elogios en loor de los tres famosos varones don Jaime Rey de Aragón, Don Fernando Cortés Marqués del Valle y don Álvaro de Baçán Marqués de Santa Cruz* (Zaragoza, Spain: Alonso Rodríguez, 1601), 41r, 48v–49r, 52r. On the impact of López de Gómara in European literature on American objects, see Keating and Markey, "'Indian' Objects," 292.

42 The *juicios de residencia* were evaluations of the performance of public officers after their terms.

43 Martínez, *Documentos cortesianos,* 1:275.

44 Cortés, *Cartas de relación,* 429–30, and also 139, 149. See also the declarations of Bernardino Vázquez de Tapia and Juan de Burgos at the *juicio de residencia.* Martínez, *Documentos cortesianos,* 2:36, 43–44, 55–57. See also Martínez, *Documentos cortesianos,* 1:173, 183–85, 194, 205–6, 232–40, 275.

45 Gabriel Lasso de la Vega, *Mexicana* (Madrid: Luis Sánchez, 1594), 54r.

46 "They also had many cotton weapons, that were padded on the outside and very richly ornamented with feathers of different colors in the manner of coats of arms and inventions." Bernal Díaz del Castillo, *La conquista de Méjico* (Madrid: Atlas, 1943), 26.

47 José de Acosta, *Historia natural y moral de las Indias* (Madrid: Dastin, 2002), book 4, chap. 37, 285.

48 Martínez, *Documentos cortesianos,* 1:205. See Russo, *Untranslatable Image,* 56–57.

49 López de Gómara, *Historia general de las Indias,* 1:93v. On the presence of López de Gómara in Toledo in 1528, see María del Carmen Martínez Martínez, "Francisco López de Gómara y Hernán Cortés: Nuevos testimonios de la relación del cronista con los marqueses del Valle de Oaxaca," *Anuario de Estudios Americanos* 67, no. 1 (2010): 275. See also Glen Carman, *Rhetorical Conquests: Cortés, Gómara, and Renaissance Imperialism* (West Lafayette, IN: Purdue University Press, 2011); and Nora Edith Jiménez, *Francisco López de Gómara: Escribir historias en tiempos de Carlos V* (Zamora: Colegio de Michoacán, 2001).

50 Hernán Cortés's 1522 shipment of feathers and jewels to different Spanish chapels, churches, and monasteries clearly followed the previous pattern of the donation of Islamic spoils that had been set during the wars against Islam in the Iberian Peninsula. As is well known, that shipment did not arrive to Spain because it was captured by pirates. Martínez, *Documentos cortesianos,* 1:242. On the connection between the conquest of Islamic Spain and the conquest of the Americas, see, among others, Serge Gruzinski, *What Time Is It There? America and Islam at the Dawn of Modern Times* (Cambridge: Polity, 2010), 126.

51 See Antonio Urquízar-Herrera, "Islamic Objects in the Material Culture of the Castilian Nobility: Trophies and the Negotiation of Hybridity," in *Jews and Muslims Made Visible in Christian Iberia and Beyond, 14th to 18th Centuries: Another Image,* ed. Borja Franco Llopis and Antonio Urquízar-Herrera (Leiden: Brill, 2019), 187–212.

52 Polleross, "América en las artes plásticas," 276.

53 Christoph Weiditz's *Trachtenbuch* is a sixteenth-century costume book representing a number of characters seen in Spain at that time. See Elizabeth Hill Boone, "Seeking Indianness: Christoph Weiditz, the Aztecs, and Feathered Amerindians," *Colonial Latin American Review* 26, no. 1 (2017): 42.

54 This English translation has been taken from Hill Boone, "Seeking Indianness," 42, 44.

55 Hill Boone, "Seeking Indianness," 42–44.

56 Postmortem inventory of Don Juan Alonso de Guzmán, sixth duke of Medina Sidonia. ADMS, Leg. 942 (Sanlúcar de Barrameda 26 November 1558). On Don Juan Alonso de Guzmán, see Urquízar-Herrera, *Coleccionismo y nobleza,* 132–40.

57 See, for instance, Pedro de Cieza de León's descriptions of the treasures in Cajamarca and Cusco. Pedro de Cieza de León, *Descubrimiento y conquista del Perú* (Madrid: Zero, 1984), 198–200, 228. See also Shelton, "Cabinets of Transgression," 196.

58 See Holohan, "Collecting the New World," 174–202. In France, François I acted similarly with the Canadian objects sent by Jacques Cartier, as well as with the Brazilian objects sent by Nicolas Durand de Villegagnon, André Thevet, and Jean de Léry. See Antoine Schnapper, *Le géant, la licorne et la tulipe: collections et collectionneurs dans la France du XVIIe siècle* (Paris: Flammarion, 1988), 180.

59 Little is yet known about the American goods in the Spanish palaces of the conquistadors, and this topic deserves further research. See some early works on the iconographical programs of the buildings: Salvador Andrés Ordax, "El palacio de Moctezuma, en Cáceres," *Memorias de la Real Academia de Extremadura de las Letras y las Artes* 1 (1983): 83–105; Salvador Andrés Ordax, "Los frescos de las Salas Romana y Mejicana del Palacio Moctezuma de Cáceres," *Norba-Arte* 5 (1984): 98–106; and Pilar Mogollón and Antonio Navareño, "Palacio del marqués de la Conquista en Trujillo," *Memorias de la Real Academia de Extremadura de las Letras y las Artes* 1 (1983): 83–105. For a relevant American example of the use of military iconography in the construction of the public image of the conquistadors, see, for instance, the well-known facade of the Montejo Palace in Mérida, Mexico.

60 Levinus Vincent, *Wondertooneel der nature* (Amsterdam: François Halma, 1706), n.p. See Mason, *Infelicities,* 87; and Feest, "European Collecting," 4.

61 Similar examples of enriched nutmegs are found in the Munich inventory of 1598. See Peter Diemer, ed., with Elke Bujok and Dorothea Diemer, *Johann Baptist Fickler: Das Inventar der Münchner herzoglichen Kunstkammer von 1598* (Munich: Bayerische Akademie der Wissenschaften, 2004), 56–57. There was a coconut from the Maldives mounted in silver in Don Teodósio I of Bragança's Portuguese inventory of 1563. See Senos, "De todas as partes," 362; and Senos, "The Empire," 139.

62 Postmortem inventory of Don Juan Alonso de Guzmán, sixth Duke of Medina Sidonia. ADMS, Leg. 942 (Sanlúcar de Barrameda 26 November 1558).

63 Also in Seville, the first Marquis of Tarifa, Don Fadrique Enríquez de Ribera, possessed a similar wooden bucket that was adorned with a silver setting. Postmortem inventory of Don Fadrique Enríquez, first Marquis of Tarifa. AGA, Section Alcalá (ducado), Leg. 16-39 (Seville, 1 May 1532). See also Lauran Toorians, "The Earliest Inventory of Mexican Objects in Munich, 1572," *Journal of the History of Collections* 6, no. 1 (1994): 64; and Keating and Markey, "'Indian' Objects," 293–96.

64 Pietro Martire d'Anghiera, *Cartas sobre el Nuevo Mundo* (Madrid: Polifemo, 1990), 126. Letter 779 to the bishop of Cosenza (1523).

65 See Juan Miguel Serrera's study of the provenance of the Mexican tables in the Medina Sidonia family inventory of 1568. Juan Miguel Serrera, "Notas sobre la presencia durante el siglo XVI de muebles mexicanos en el palacio sanluqueño de los duques de Medina Sidonia," in *Andalucía y América en el siglo XVI* (Seville: Escuela de Estudios Hispano-Americanos, 1983), 2:437–51.

66 See Urquízar-Herrera, "Imaginando América"; and María Paz Aguiló Alonso, "El coleccionismo de objetos procedentes de ultramar a través de los inventarios de los siglos XVI y XVII," in *Relaciones artísticas entre España y América,* ed. Enrique Arias (Madrid: CSIC, 1990), 117.

67 Other examples are the "bow of the Indies with six arrows and a bone thimble and gloves" sold in the *almoneda* (auction) of Don Luis Ponce de León, Marquis of Zahara. Archivo Histórico de la Nobleza, Fondo Osuna, Leg. 1639/1-74 (Marchena, 1610), Toledo; and in the Indian clothes of Doña Isabel Osorio, wife to Don Diego de Carvajal, Lord of Jódar. AGA, Section Casa Ducal de Alba, Jódar, Leg. 19 (33) (Jódar, 1546).

68 Postmortem inventory of Don Juan Alonso de Guzmán, sixth Duke of Medina Sidonia. ADMS, Leg. 942 (Sanlúcar de Barrameda 26 November 1558). See also Urquízar-Herrera, *Coleccionismo y nobleza,* 132–42; and Urquízar-Herrera, "Imaginando América."

69 See Heikamp, *Mexico and the Medici,* 34–38.

70 Postmortem inventory of Don Juan de Saavedra, Count of El Castellar. AGA, Section Señorío de El Viso, Leg. 2-23 (Seville, 12 July 1580). On the arrival of parrots, see Toorians, "Earliest Inventory," 64–65.

71 See Bethany Aram, "Taste Transformed: Sugar and Spice in the Sixteenth-Century Hispano-Burgundian Court," in Aram and Yun, Global Goods, 125.

72 Postmortem inventory of Don Fernando Enríquez de Ribera, fourth Marquis of Tarifa, and his wife. AGA, Section Alcalá (ducado), Leg. 16-40 (Seville, 23 July 1590).

73 Inventory of the goods received by Doña María Girón in bequest of her parents Don Pedro Girón and Doña Mencía, counts of Urueña. Archivo Histórico de la Nobleza, Fondo Osuna, Leg. 1512 (1544).

74 Inventory of the goods of the Duke of Alcalá that were sold after his death. AGA, Section Alcalá (duchy), Leg. 17-002 (Genoa, 19 May 1637).

75 On André Thevet sleeping in a hammock while in the Americas, see Mason, Infelicities, 64.

76 Checa Cremades, Los inventarios de Carlos V, 49–50.

77 Heikamp, Mexico and the Medici, 8.

78 Shelton, "Cabinets of Transgression," 188. Heikamp has also claimed that "in Spain, after Charles V everything pre-Columbian—heathen—had to be annihilated." Detlef Heikamp, "American Objects in Italian Collections of the Renaissance and Baroque: A Survey," in First Images of America: The Impact of the New World on the Old, vol. 1, ed. Fredi Chiappelli (Berkeley: University of California Press, 1976), 456. See also Todorov, La conquête, 169. On the other hand, as Elke Bujok points out, non-European ethnographica in early modern inventories have in fact been lost at a higher rate than European artifacts all over Europe. Elke Bujok, "Ethnographica in Early Modern Kunstkammern and Their Perception," Journal of the History of Collections 21, no. 1 (2009): 18. See also Holohan, "Collecting the New World," 116–26.

79 See, for instance, Martínez, Documentos cortesianos, 1:232.

80 Martínez, Documentos cortesianos, 1:486. See also, María del Carmen Martínez Martínez, ed., Hernán Cortés: Cartas y memoriales (León, Spain: Universidad de León; Junta de Castilla y León, 2003), 152.

81 See MacDonald, "Collecting a New World," 654. See also Feest, "Vienna's Mexican Treasures," 34. Among many other examples, see, for instance, the boat from the Indies that arrived in Livorno in 1572. Many of the curiosities that it carried were presented by the Medici to different Italian and European relations. Toorians, "Earliest Inventory," 61. See also Ezio Bassani, "Il colezionismo esotico dei Medici nel cinquecento," in Le Arti del Principato Mediceo, ed. Candice Adelson (Florence: SPES, 1980), 58.

82 Martínez Martínez, Hernán Cortés, 106. Quoted from a 1520 letter from Cortés to his father at the Archivo General de Simancas, Consejo Real, 588-7, fols. 1r–3r.

83 Checa Cremades, Los inventarios de Carlos V, 288. See also Holohan, "Collecting the New World," 44, 75–126, especially 85 and 116. In López de Gómara's narration, feather covers were a relevant part of the goods that Cortés brought with him to his introduction to Charles V. López de Gómara, Historia general de las Indias, 92v.

84 Checa Cremades, Los inventarios de Carlos V, 290–91, 300–1.

85 Checa Cremades, Los inventarios de Carlos V, 368.

86 Checa Cremades, Los inventarios de Carlos V, 502–3, 531. See also Holohan, "Collecting the New World," 118–20.

87 Toledo may not have used the exact term "museum," but the conscious display of objects as evidence of the New World is clear. See Holohan, "Collecting the New World," 174–80. See also Amelang, "The New World in the Old?," 147–64; and Isabel Yaya, "Wonders of America: The Curiosity Cabinet as a Site of Representation and Knowledge," Journal of the History of Collections 20, no. 2 (2008): 179.

88 Holohan, "Collecting the New World," 177. That idea was not far from the arrangement of weapons and feathers that could be found in Flicker's inventory of the Munich Kunstkammer. See Bujok, "Ethnographica," 22–23.

89 The Medina Sidonias are, again, a particularly fine example of that. See Urquízar-Herrera, Coleccionismo y nobleza, 101.

90 As Bujok points out, in most cases American objects in Europe did not arouse interest in the context of their provenance. Bujok, "Ethnographica," 20.

91 Amelang, "New World in the Old?," 149.

92 Álvaro Soler de Campos in conversation with the author, October 25, 2018. See also Holohan, "Collecting the New World," 223. A few photographs by Jean Laurent reproduce the look of the figures in 1868. Fototeca del Patrimonio Histórico, VN-06442, VN-06804, and VN-06894.

93 Irene Fattacciu, "The Resilience and Boomerang Effect of Chocolate: A Product's Globalization and Commodification," in Aram and Yun, Global Goods, 259.

94 Francisco Montes, Mecenazgo virreinal y patrocinio artístico: El ducado de Alburquerque en la Nueva España (Seville: Real Maestranza de Caballería de Sevilla, 2016), 226–50. Also, the counts of Alba de Liste. See Holohan, "Collecting the New World," 50; and Amelang, "New World in the Old?," 151.

95 See Feest, "European Collecting," 1–2; and Holohan, "Collecting the New World," 32. See also Feest, "The Collecting of American Indian Artifacts in Europe, 1493–1750," in *America in European Consciousness, 1493–1750,* ed. Karen Kupperman (Chapel Hill: University of North Carolina Press, 1995), 342–60.

96 A recent and systematic review of the topic can be found in Alessandra Russo, Gerhard Wolf, and Diana Fane, eds., *Images Take Flight: Feather Art in Mexico and Europe* (Chicago: University of Chicago Press, 2015).

97 Jonathan Brown and Richard L. Kagan, "The Duke of Alcalá: His Collection and Its Evolution," *Art Bulletin* 69, no. 2 (1987): 231–55; Vicente Lleó, *La Casa de Pilatos: Biografía de un palacio sevillano* (Seville: Editorial Universidad de Sevilla, 2017); and, offering the documents of the Seville sales, David Mallén, "La colección artística del III Duque de Alcalá: Nuevos documentos," *Ars Longa* 26 (2017): 111–30.

98 Mallén, "La colección artística," 118–19, 125, 127–29. Original documents in the Protocolos archive of Seville, Real Audiencia, 29339. This Rodrigo de Abreu might be connected to the Rodrigo de Abreu who was a notary in Seville in 1627 and member of an elite local family. See Diego Ortiz de Zúñiga, *Discurso genealógico de los Ortizes de Sevilla* (Cádiz, Spain: Pedro Ortiz, 1670), 144.

99 See Mallén, "La colección artística," 129.

100 The same 40 reales paid for the hammock also bought, for instance, "a painting of Zaragoza," a "painting of a fish," and a sword, while a drawing attributed to Raphael was sold for 209 reales, "a big painting of Saint Francis with an angel" for 1,050, "a painting of Saint Lawrence" attributed to Titian for 1,200, a box with mathematical instruments for 244, an astrolabe for 778, and "a small gold box with a jacinth on the lid" for 900. Postmortem inventory of the third Duke of Alcalá, AGA, Section Alcalá (ducado), Leg. 17-002 (Genoa, 19 May 1637).

101 Brown and Kagan, "The Duke of Alcalá"; Lleó, *La Casa de Pilatos;* and Mallén, "La colección artística."

RAFAEL RAMOS SOSA

Sculpture at Home in Baroque Lima

In contrast with painting from the viceroyalty of Peru, which has been the subject of numerous studies, the role of sculpture and its use in domestic settings is still understudied. Undeniably, judging from old inventories, it is evident that there were more paintings than sculptures in the average Peruvian home. The possible cause for this disparity is perhaps the fact that paintings were less expensive than sculptures.

To study household contents of private houses and noble residences, we usually rely on written documents: inventories, letters of dowry, and wills. By their nature, these source documents determine not only the type of houses that we are able to study but also restrict in some ways the social and economic levels of their owners and inhabitants—generally members of the upper classes of the colonial society. However, there are a few cases pertaining to households that are more modest and to their owners who, though belonging to lower strata of society, also made wills or left written inventories.

In the case of Lima, the former capital of the viceroyalty of Peru in South America, there are several studies of domestic architecture that include some information about furnishings, in particular those written by María Dolores Crespo

Rodríguez and Antonio San Cristóbal Sebastián. Crespo Rodríguez, for example, included in her book an addendum on furniture, paintings, and sculptures, as well as other types of objects, such as costumes that were used in the home. Although *Arquitectura doméstica de la Ciudad de los Reyes (1535–1750)* is not an exhaustive

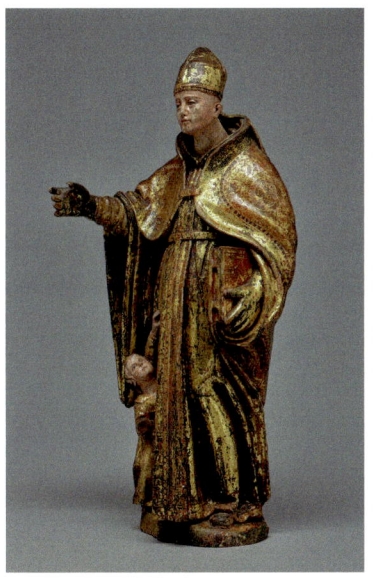

Fig. 1. Unknown artist, *Saint Thomas of Villanueva*. Peru, 1600–50. Cedar with *estofado* (wood, gesso, paint, and gold leaf), 25 × 12½ × 7½ in. Denver Art Museum: Gift of Mr. and Mrs. John Critcher Freyer for Frank Barrows Freyer Collection, 1974.339.

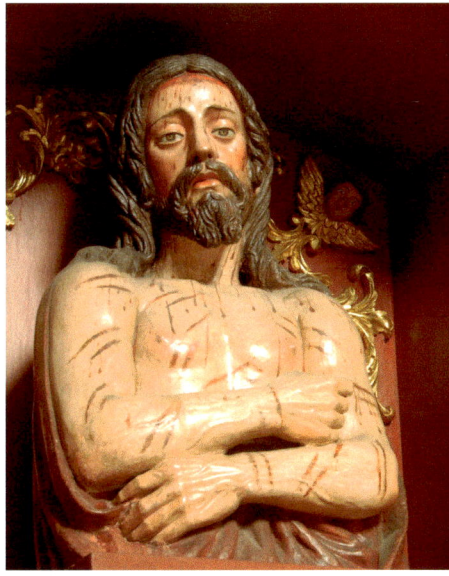

Fig. 2. Unknown artist, *Ecce Homo*. Peru, 1600s. Ceramic and paint, 27½ × 17¾ in. Monastery of Mount Carmel, Lima, Peru.

63

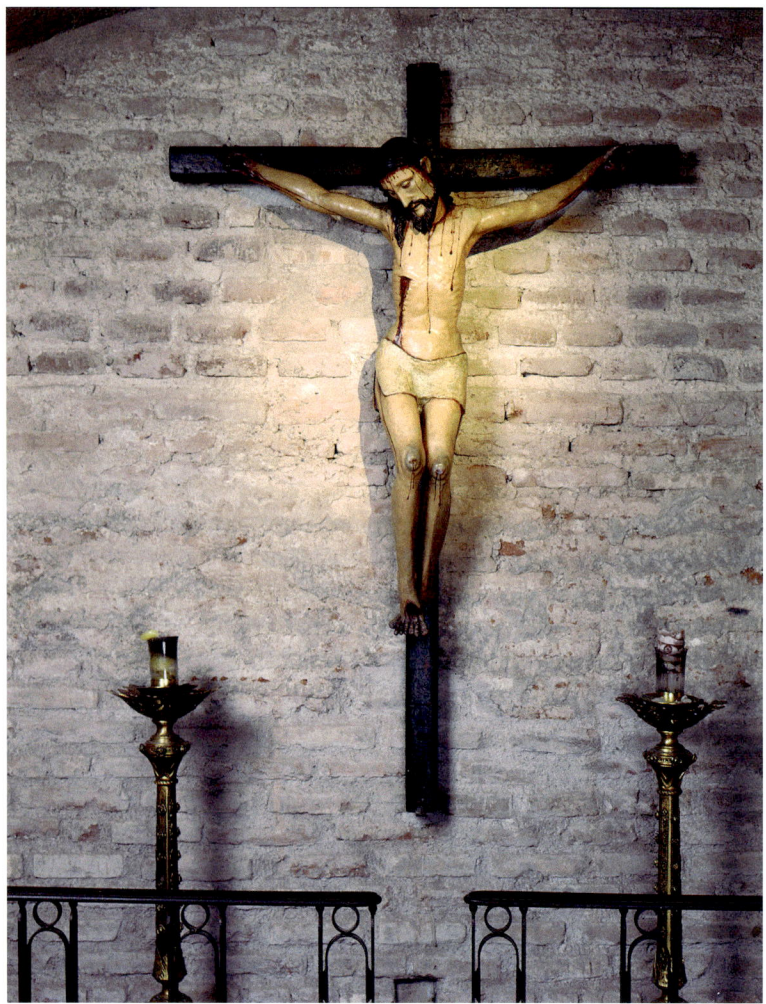

Fig. 3. Unknown artist, *Cristo de los Favores*. Peru, late 1500s. Maguey, overall height 49 in. Sanctuary of Santa Rosa, Lima, Peru.

scenes; views of cities; and landscape, genre, and still-life paintings. Domestic sculpture was usually of religious character, perhaps due to its function in daily life, as it was generally made use of in the rooms where it was placed. However, as we shall see, small-format sculpture featuring decorative and profane subjects was also present in domestic environments, particularly toward the end of the Spanish era. Although sculpture was relatively scarce, there are some cases where the artist's name appears in old documents, especially with high-quality works. This type of evidence leads us to deduce that owners not only appreciated the devotional aspect of a sculptural work but also its artistic value.

Sculpture Materials and Origins

Domestic sculpture in Lima was usually executed in polychrome wood, very much like the works found in churches and other religious spaces (fig. 1). However, small sculptures made of other materials, some of them identified with Peruvian material culture traditions, are also mentioned in historic documents. Polychrome ceramic sculpture, for example, often appears in inventories, and few pieces of this type survive today. One of the most significant existing examples is an *ecce homo* in the collection of the Monastery of Mount Carmel in Lima (fig. 2). "A glazed earthenware bull" listed in one document indicates that other types of sculptures, in this case linked to specific artisanal traditions, were also used at home. This later type probably was frequent but rarely is mentioned in inventories.[2]

A material widely used in Peruvian sculpture, especially in the Andes, was the maguey plant. Maguey was cheap and easy to work with, a material whose technique of manufacture originated in the Indigenous workshops of the Andes. The maguey is a type of cactus plant from which a fibrous material is extracted. Coarse pieces of this material were used to make a structural core that

study, the different sources consulted during her research produced a great deal of interesting information. Documents generally comprise listings of household objects, which unfortunately rarely include information on where the objects were located within the house or how they were used.[1]

As I have already pointed out, in contrast with the overall abundance of paintings of different formats in the various inventories consulted, sculpture is found in a lesser number, and the works typically range from medium to small in size. Regarding the subject matter of paintings, I have found a greater variety of themes, which are predominantly religious; however, they also include other subjects, such as mythological

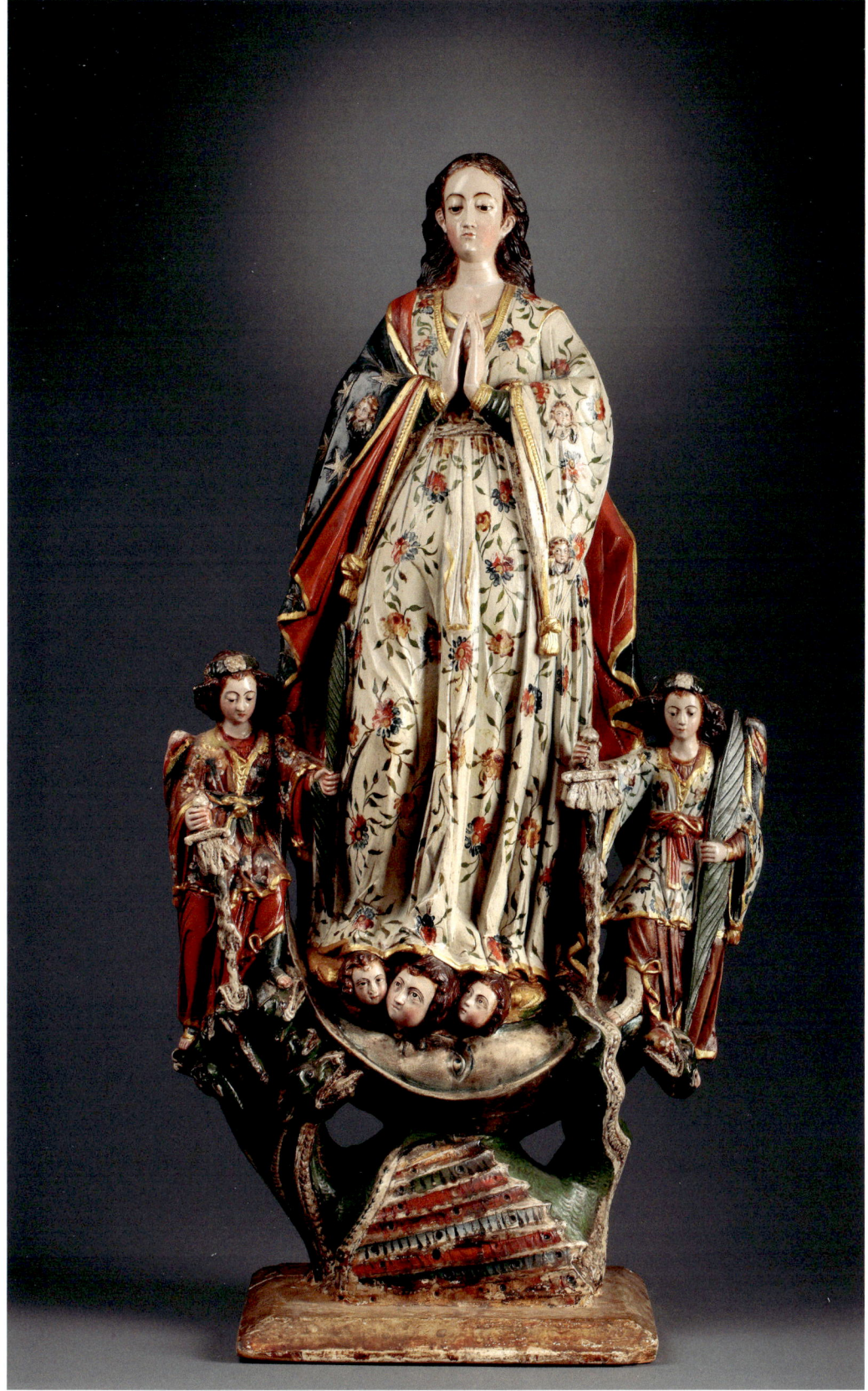

Fig. 4. Unknown artist, *Inmaculada Apocalíptica.* Peru, 1600s. Huamanga stone, paint and gold leaf, 23¼ × 11⅞ × 4½ in. Private collection, Lima, Peru.

was then covered with glued cloth and a paste made from the plant. In sculpture, the clothing, face, and hands were made either of wood or sometimes also with maguey paste. This type of sculpture was not common in Lima during the sixteenth or early seventeenth century; however, starting in the late seventeenth century, and particularly during the following century, we see an increasing number of pieces in local inventories. A remarkable example of the technique is the *Cristo de los Favores* (fig. 3), a crucifix dating from the late sixteenth or early seventeenth century to which Saint Rose of Lima had a great devotion.[3]

Another popular material used in sculpture was Huamanga stone, which is a type of fine alabaster quarried in the eponymous city (later renamed Ayacucho) halfway between Lima and Cuzco. The off-white color of this slightly translucent stone emulated more expensive ivory, and its fine texture allowed gilded and polychrome finishes. In addition to statues, bas-relief alabaster plaques were also popular. According to documents, sculptures and objects made of Huamanga stone were very common in Lima households beginning in the sixteenth century, becoming increasingly popular during the following centuries (fig. 4). In addition to religious pieces, sculptures of secular subjects were produced as well, especially during the late eighteenth century and throughout the following century (figs. 5 and 6). Many examples of Huamanga stone sculpture are kept in museums, such as the Denver Art Museum (figs. 7 and 8), as well as private collections and monasteries.[4]

In general, local artists produced the sculptures found in Lima households; however, as the city was the capital and seat of the viceregal court, pieces that arrived from other locations are also listed in inventories. Certain documents include pieces that came from the Iberian Peninsula, especially works that came from Sevillian workshops; Quito, seat of one of the most remarkable sculpture schools in the New World (figs. 9 and 10); Naples, in particular small figurines such as depictions of Jesus as a child; and China, for small works in ceramic or ivory.[5]

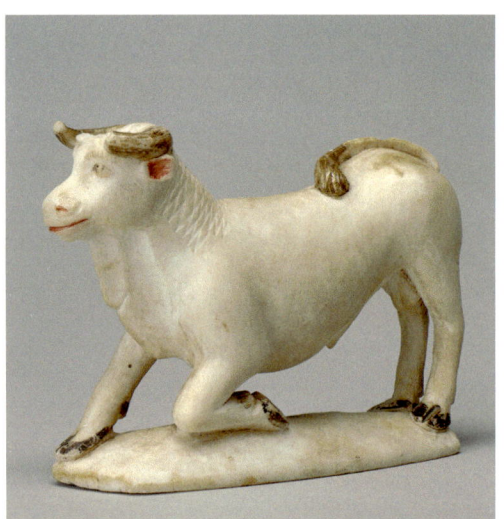

Fig. 5. Unknown artist, *Figure of Kneeling Bull.* Peru, 1700s. Huamanga stone and paint, 3 × 1¼ × 4½ in. Denver Art Museum: Gift of Engracia Freyer Dougherty for Frank Barrows Freyer Collection, 1972.259.

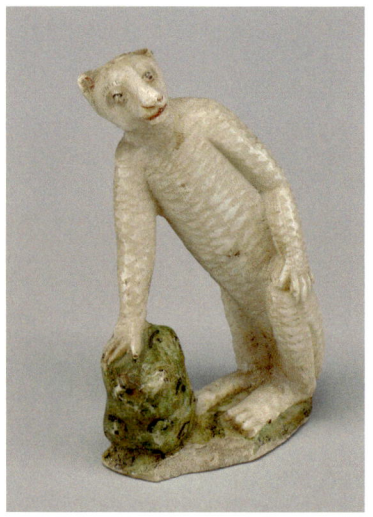

Fig. 6. Unknown artist, *Bear Figure.* Peru, 1700s. Huamanga stone and paint, 4¼ × 2⅝ in. Denver Art Museum: Gift of Frank Barrows Freyer II for the Frank Barrows Freyer Collection, 1969.362.

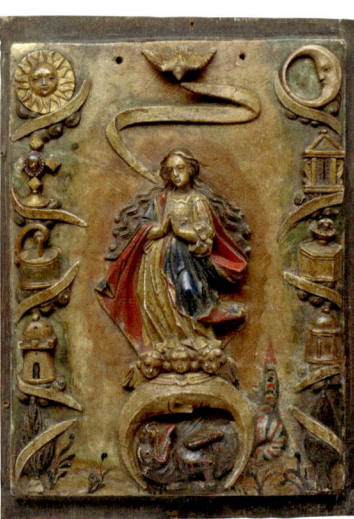

Fig. 7. Unknown artist, *The Immaculate Conception.* Peru, 1700s. Huamanga stone, paint and gold leaf, 11 × 8 in. Denver Art Museum: Gift of Mr. and Mrs. Morris A. Long, 1983.397.

Locations of Sculpture in the Home

Inventories rarely specify the place or room in which artwork was found; however, when a location was specified, the oratory (chapel) and the bedroom are the rooms where sculptures of high artistic or sentimental value were most frequently found. In upper-class households, sculptures are at times listed in the *estrado* (ladies' sitting room) and the *sala* (main sitting room). I would like to point out three areas or rooms that, in addition to their natural use as domestic spaces devoted to certain activities, also functioned as spaces that were more intimate. In these spaces, art had a plurality of uses that reflected both the owners' personal taste and their personal devotion to the church. These spaces are oratories, bedrooms, and libraries.

Oratories

In upscale houses, or those of clergymen, there was often a room used as a chapel or oratory for families and personal piety. These oratories were furnished with numerous devotional paintings and sculptures of various kinds. For example, according to the will of Cipriano de Medina, the rector of the University of San Marcos (1622) in Lima, several unusual sculptures from his oratory are listed. He writes, "We declare that in our oratory there is an image of Our Lady of the Thorn made in Seville by the hand of Juan Martínez Montañés, and an ivory ecce homo with its ebony display case with a plate glass window."[6] The inventory made after his death in 1635 also recorded an ivory "Christ at the Column."[7]

In the 1622 inventory of Don Francisco Verdugo, the bishop of Huamanga, numerous furniture items, silver objects, and fine textiles are listed, as well as several paintings and sculptures. Among these objects, the inventory states that there is also the following:

A large altarpiece of Our Lady with the Sleeping Child and Saint John, two hundred pesos. . . .

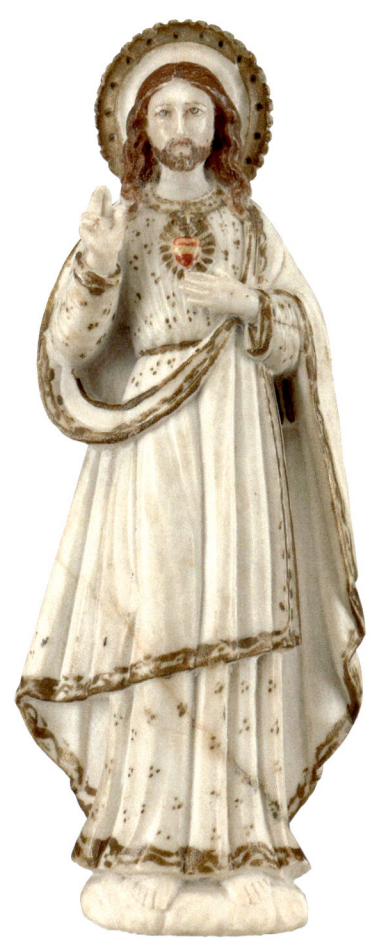

Fig. 8. Unknown artist, *Christ Showing Sacred Heart.* Peru, 1700s. Huamanga stone, paint and gold leaf, 7¼ × ¾ × 2 in. Denver Art Museum: Gift of John Critcher Freyer for Frank Barrows Freyer Collection, 1971.431.1–2.

A Crucifixion, not very large, with Our Lady and Saint John, one hundred and thirty pesos. . . . An ivory crucifix, with its ebony cross with silver ends, two hundred and fifty pesos. . . . A carved Child Jesus, at his feet a snake, the world and death, veneered in ebony with its plate-glass window, one hundred and fifty pesos.[8]

In this same vein of owners with sophisticated taste and a penchant for the work of the great Sevillian master sculptor Juan Martínez Montañés was the rich merchant Gonzalo Arias. In 1650, he stated,

In the oratory of my house [there is] an image of Our Lady of the Immaculate Concepción with its pedestal that should be one vara tall with its gold and enameled silver crown of which I have had and is by Montañés. Likewise two full-length angels with

their pedestals of two-thirds [of a vara tall] with candlesticks in their hands, and a full-length Baby Jesus with its base that depicts the triumph over death, the demon, and the flesh, which all four seem to me to be by Montañés.[9]

There is also a mention of an ivory Christ with a silver base that came from the estate auction (*almoneda*) of Don Diego Fernández de Córdoba, who was the Marquis of Guadalcázar and viceroy of Peru.[10]

In the house of Diego de Alvarado in the valley of Huambacho in 1649, there is a mention of "a statue [*imagen de bulto*] of Our Lady of the Presentation, one vara and three-fourths tall with a crown, and another the same of the Child Jesus." There is also a record of "two earthenware sculptures of Our Lady and Saint Hyacinth,"

an "earthenware Child Jesus with his tunic of chambray [fine cotton cloth]; an earthenware Saint John with his silver diadem; a glazed earthenware bull; twelve little earthenware angels, half of them silvered and the other half with color." In addition, this inventory also includes a "maguey Crucifix one vara tall." I include these listed objects to demonstrate that easy-to-work materials, such as ceramic or maguey, were also used (not just the usual polychrome wood) for their medium as well as for their affordability.[11]

In 1670, there is documentation that at the house of *alférez* (second lieutenant) Pedro de Meresilla, there was a very well-furnished oratory with numerous paintings and sculptures. This oratory included a painting of the Virgin of the Rosary, portraits of the deceased and his wife, and paintings depicting Saint Francis, Saint Dominic, the Immaculate Conception, and Saint John the Baptist, the latter two adorning each side of the oratory. On top of the central canvas were three other paintings of God the Father, Saint Peter, and Saint Paul. There was also a damask canopy housing a sculpture of a crucifix, which was placed over the altar. Meresilla also owned numerous carved Huamanga stone sculptures, including two statues of the Child Jesus and their bases, two others of the same subject but smaller, and a statue of Saint Joseph with the Christ Child on a carved pedestal (fig. 11). In this collection, he also had a sculpture of the Immaculate Conception, two small statues of Saint John the Baptist and Saint Anthony of Padua, another smaller sculpture of Saint Joseph with the Child, a small statue of Saint Francis, and "a little cradle with a Jesus of Huamanga stone." In addition to the aforementioned objects, the oratory also had sacred ornaments and vessels.[12]

The oratory of Pedro de Valdés (1670) housed an ivory crucifix of two-thirds of a vara high with its cross of ebony (fig. 12), a statue of

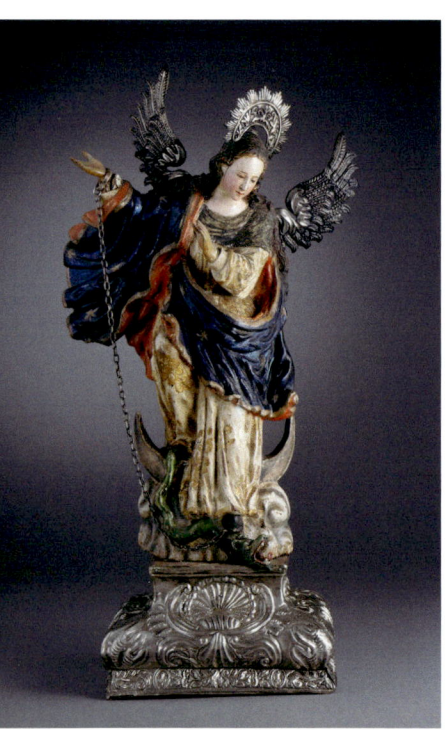

Fig. 9. Unknown artist, *Virgin of Quito*. Ecuador, about 1750. Wood, gesso, paint, silver, gold and silver leaf, 17½ × 9½ × 6½ in. Denver Art Museum: Gift of Mr. and Mrs. John Pogzeba, 1974.265.

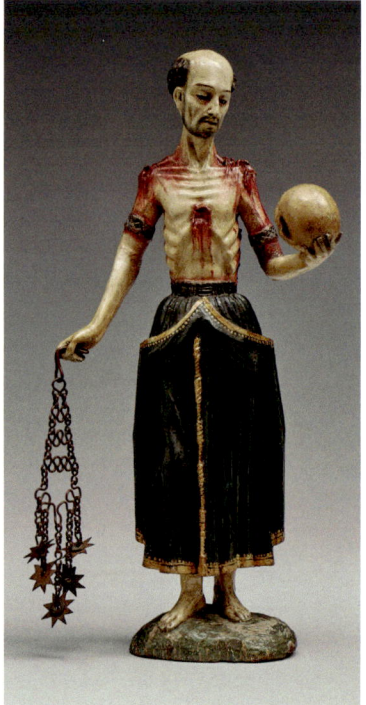

Fig. 10. Unknown artist, *St. Peter of Alcantara Penitent*. Ecuador, early 1700s. Wood, gesso, glass, metal, and paint, 12 × 6 × 3½ in. Denver Art Museum: Gift of the Stapleton Foundation of Latin American Colonial Art, made possible by the Renchard family, 1990.332.

Our Lady of Loreto with the Child Jesus, three small and two large sculptures of the Christ Child, and a sculpture of Saint Joseph, probably made of wood. To complete the group was another Saint Joseph carved in Huamanga stone.[13]

Bedrooms

Although we can assume that some of the pieces listed in inventories were located in the bedrooms, it is not common to specify in old documents where objects were found. However, bedrooms were one of most lavishly decorated rooms in a house and frequently were embellished with paintings, sculptures, reliquaries, and incense burners as well as all sorts of furniture and personal use objects. In a 1670 inventory of the bedroom of a deceased woman, there are records of "sixteen small paintings of different

devotions, old, which are hung in the bedroom of the deceased lady" that are listed. Also mentioned are

a work of the Holy Christ Crucified, which the said deceased had at the headboard of her bed, a small silver holy water font, and three painted plates that the said deceased had at the headboard of her bed: one of Our Lady of the Immaculate Conception, one of the Lord Saint Joseph and Child Jesus, and another of Our Lady with Child Jesus in her chest. Huamanga stone panel with Christ carrying the cross on his back, small, which the said deceased had at the headboard of her bed.[14]

This inventory gives us an approximate idea of how bedrooms were furnished with paintings and small sculptures, since bedrooms were

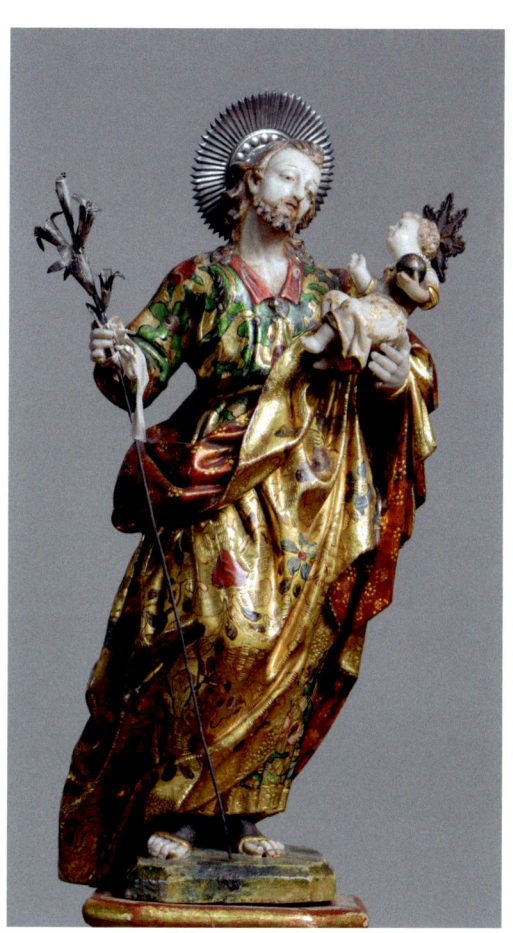

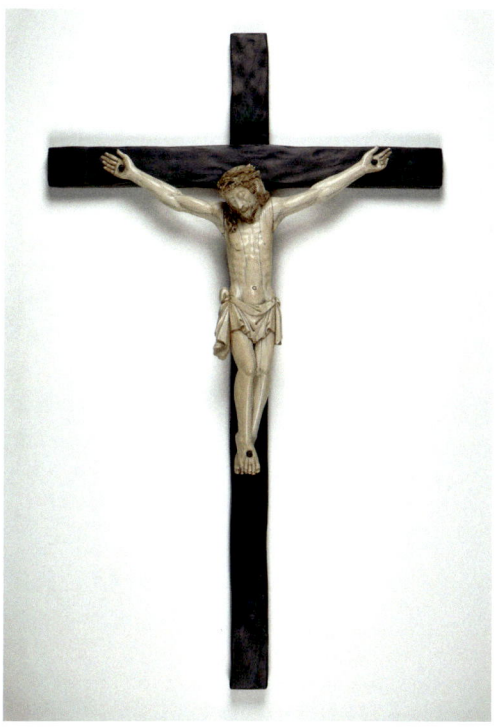

Fig. 12. Unknown artist, *Christ on the Cross*. India or Philippines, 1600s. Wood, ivory, and paint, 51 × 39 in. Denver Art Museum: Gift of the Collection of Frederick and Jan Mayer, 2015.547A–C.

Left: Fig. 11. Unknown artist, *San José con el Niño*. Peru, 1700s. Huamanga stone, paint, gold leaf and silver. Monastery of Nazarenas, Lima, Peru.

sanctuary spaces, as can be seen from these records.

Libraries

The chronicler Pedro Ramírez del Águila, in his 1639 account of the city of La Plata (Sucre), commented that

There are many libraries in this city that are simultaneously curious and copious, where both theologians and jurists can be found, and are valued at four thousand, six thousand, eight thousand, and ten thousand pesos. They are adorned with rich plates and paintings, with fine earthenware vessels, flasks, flowers of gold and silk, bouquets, jewels and reliquaries, and all other kinds of curiosities. The contents of which are displayed and polished for the intellectuals that attend them, who respectively are as present in Salamanca or Alcalá; among these are the convents, the listeners, the lawyers, the prebendary, and other ecclesiastics.[15]

Fig. 13. Unknown artist, *Baby Christ*. Peru, 1700s. Huamanga stone and paint, 3 × 3¼ × 7¾ in. Denver Art Museum: Gift of Frank Barrows Freyer II, 1969.361.

It was common within libraries to house a great variety of different types of objects that seemed to coexist with books. This suggests a tendency among intellectuals to create spaces of subjective and personal intimacy, in which, together with

the study of and the intellectual work with books, it was possible to engage in literary experiences, explore personal pastimes, contemplate artworks, and search for spiritual solace. We foresee in this type of space an antecedent of later museum collections.[16]

Types and Subjects

As can be seen in the various inventories consulted, a small or medium-size crucifix was possibly the most common and frequent type of sculpture found in households. A Christ on the cross placed on top of the altar, or a larger version of the same hung on the wall above it, under a canopy, always presided over the oratory. Along with wooden crucifixes, ivory ones are frequently listed in upper-echelon houses. Carved from an expensive material, those costly works of exquisite craftsmanship were imported from the Philippines or Europe. Many examples of this type of sculpture survived and can be admired today in museums (such as the museum of the Cathedral of Lima), in some convents, and in private collections. Less common were metal crucifixes, however, even though some of this type have been found in documents, such as the inventory of Leonor de Mujica from 1730, which lists "a bronze Christ of half a vara long on its cross of more than half a vara long."[17]

Another frequent subject of domestic sculpture was the figure of the Child Jesus in diverse types (fig. 13), of which the most popular was the standing statue (fig. 14). Although the origin of this type of sculpture dates from the end of the Middle Ages, it really blossomed during the Renaissance and further developed in the Baroque age. This was the kind of ideal image for personal piety, mostly because sculptures were embellished with fine fabric clothing, which were changed according to the liturgical festivities of the year or the taste of the owners, encouraging reverence and interaction with

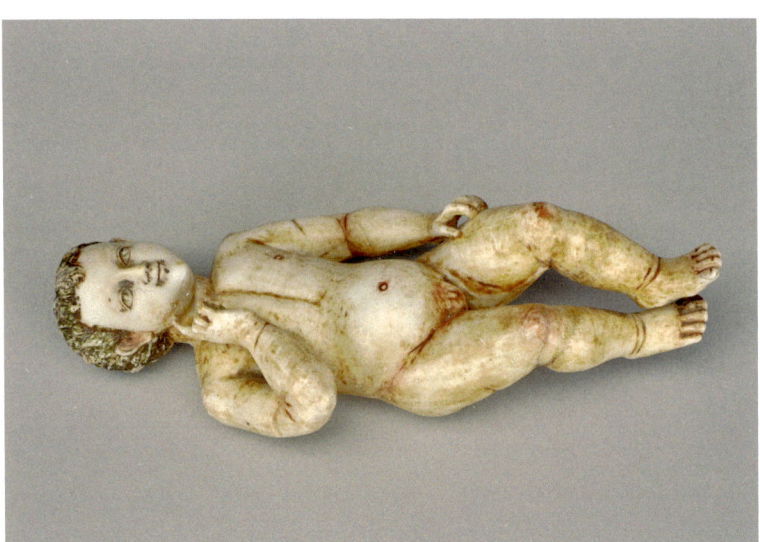

a sacred sculpture. Juan Martínez Montañés's 1606 *Niño Jesús del Sagrario* is perhaps the model that served to inspire sculptors across Spanish America, as copies and versions by disciples and followers were exported from Seville to the Americas and the Philippines (fig. 15). In historic documents, there are households that list up to half a dozen Christ Child sculptures made in materials such as wood, ivory, wax, or Huamanga stone. These medium-size images could be displayed in plate-glass cases, such as the ones that still today can be seen in some convents and monasteries.[18]

Between Church and Home and Vice Versa

The vitality of religious sculpture during the colonial era was overtly manifested in church interiors as well as during the busy processions of Holy Week. In addition, that omnipresent public manifestation reached private homes in the form of small sculptures for personal devotion. However, with some images, the opposite was true—a sculpture intended for private domestic use would eventually arrive in a church and serve for public devotion. For example, in the 1660s, the Lima-born venerable member from the Society of Jesus, Father Francisco del Castillo, one of the most charismatic priests in town, who often preached standing on top of a table in the Plaza del Baratillo holding a crucifix in hand, participated in one case of reverse migration. In his autobiography, Father Castillo narrates that Doña Úrsula Calafe, a generous lady from Lima, gifted to the Society of Jesus resources to build the Chapel of the Desamparados (Forsaken). This wealthy woman had in the oratory of her house an image of the Virgen del Pilar de Zaragoza (Our Lady of the Pillar). Father Castillo asked her to also bestow that holy statue upon the Society of Jesus, as he wanted to refurbish it into another devotion, that of the

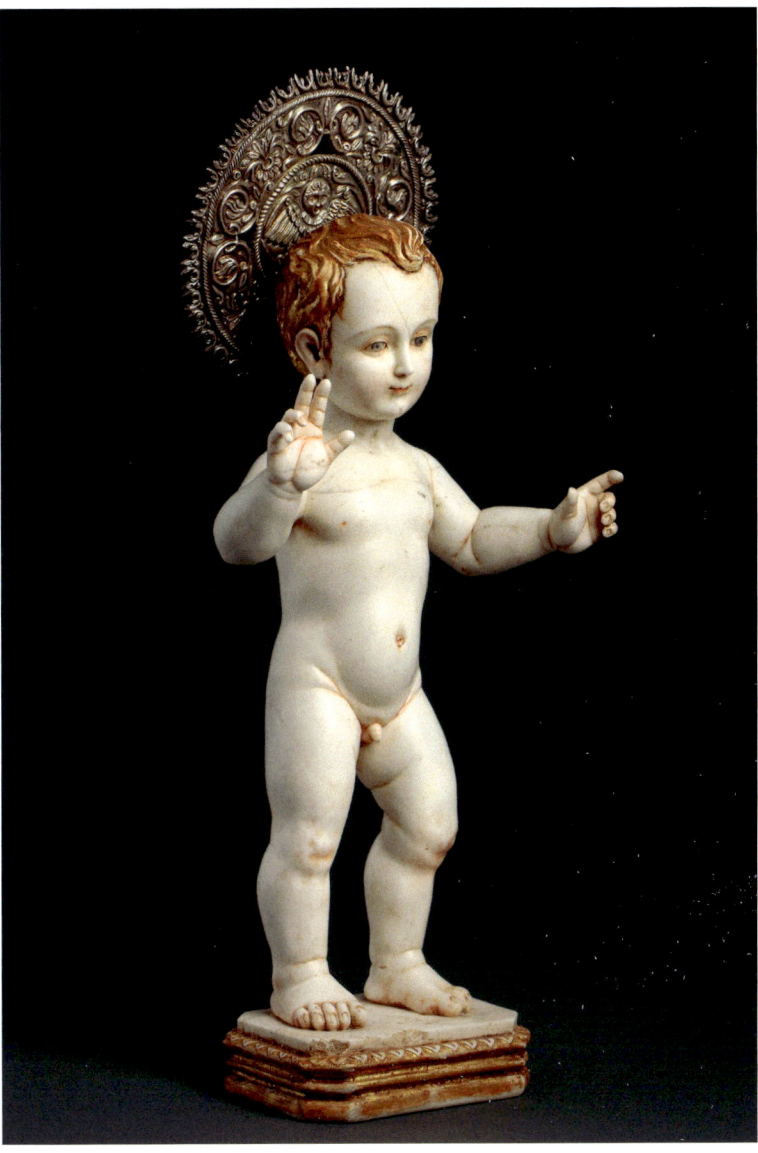

Virgen de los Desamparados (Our Lady of the Forsaken), and place the image in the newly built chapel. He wrote,

I took her [the Virgin] to a very important and talented master in the art of sculpture called Tomás de la Parra, a very virtuous and exemplary man. I asked him to use that image to make me another of Our Lady of the Forsaken with the Baby Jesus in the left hand and with the right hand holding a silver bouquet per scepter, and with two holy innocent children on both sides; the master made the image

Fig. 14. Unknown artist, *Niño Jesús Bendiciendo*. Peru, 1600s. Huamanga stone, paint, gold leaf and silver, 21⅝ × 8⅝ × 5½ in. Private collection, Lima, Peru.

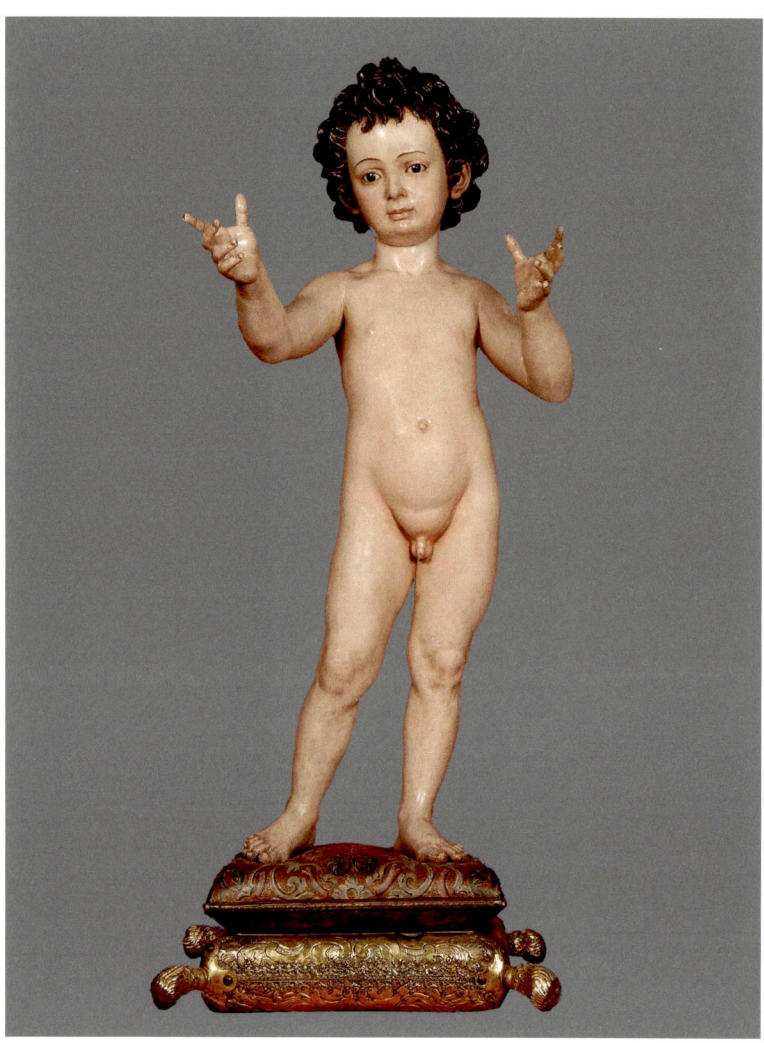

Fig. 15. Juan Martínez Montañés, *Niño Jesús del Sagrario.* Spain, 1606. Polychrome wood, 35¾ × 14¹⁵⁄₁₆ × 15 in. Archicofradía Sacramental del Sagrario de la Catedral, Seville, Spain.

with such perfection and beauty that it seemed that the angels had made it, as they did in Valencia.[19]

Another example of a sculpture that transferred from a private home to a church is that of the image of Our Lady of Aránzazu, a sculpture brought from Spain at the expense of the wealthy merchant Juan de Urrutia. This devout man commissioned a statue of the Virgin to ultimately be placed in his name in the altarpiece in the church of San Francisco in Lima. Our Lady of Aránzazu arrived at the port of Lima on July 31, 1646, and was received with artillery salvo in a ceremony presided over by Urrutia in the company of other faithful and members of the Franciscan order. A

few days later, the sculpture was taken to Urrutia's house and placed on top of an altar that was set up in a richly decorated room on the top floor. There, the Virgin was unveiled and hymns and prayers were sung in her honor. To celebrate, the rich merchant organized a bullfight in the square in front of his house, with illustrious guests, including the son of the viceroy and other important city authorities, attending the event. Special guests participated in the celebrations from the balconies of the neighboring houses. After several weeks of family and neighbors worshipping the image at Urrutia's house, the Virgin was moved to the cathedral, where the Franciscans took custody of the statue. From the cathedral, the Virgin was moved in procession to the chapel at the church of the convent of San Francisco. Celebrations culminated with a solemn mass in her honor.[20]

Concluding Thoughts

In this approach to sculpture in Lima domestic interiors, we can appreciate that the rich "life of religious images" was present in many aspects of daily life, not only in churches and spaces of public worship but also in the intimate and personal spaces of family life. Sculpture is a manifestation of the humanized religiosity characteristic of the Catholic Baroque in which the images exist and take on a life of their own as objects of devotion and a means of approaching God. In this short chapter, we have also seen cases in which a family sculpture becomes an image of public worship in a church.

As discussed, the most common sculpture subjects were crucifixions, images of the Immaculate Conception or the Virgin with the Child, and the Child Jesus in various iconographies. At the same time, other types of small artisanal and decorative sculptures appeared that became more widespread during the eighteenth century. It is also worth reiterating the importance of sculpture made with local materials, such as the maguey and the Huamanga stone, in both domestic and general contexts. Finally, because Lima was the capital of the most important Spanish viceroyalty at this time, as well as the seat of a viceregal court, local holdings of high-quality small and medium-sized sculptures were remarkable, either because of the materials from which they were made, or because of the artists who made them. Often works found in Lima were created in other important artistic centers in the Americas or in Europe. Clearly, collectors placed value on aesthetic and artistic qualities in addition to the religious significance of the sculptures.

✚ ✚ ✚

Notes

1 María Dolores Crespo Rodríguez, *Arquitectura doméstica de la Ciudad de los Reyes (1535–1750)* (Sevilla: Diputación Provincial, 2006), 297–340; Antonio San Cristóbal Sebastián, *La Casa Virreinal Limeña De 1570 a 1687.* (Lima, Peru: Fondo Editorial del Congreso del Perú, 2003).

2 Archivo General de la Nación, Lima, Perú (hereafter AGN) Sección Protocolos notariales, Escribano Juan de Carvajal, no. 255, 1649, 18 v.

3 Ramón Mujica Pinilla, *Los Cristos de Lima: Esculturas en madera y marfil, s. XVI–XVIII* (Lima, Peru: Banco de Crédito, 1991), 44–45; and Rafael Ramos Sosa, "Reflexiones y noticias sobre escultores y ensambladores indígenas en Bolivia y Perú, siglos XVI y XVII," in *Barroco Andino: Memoria del I encuentro internacional,* ed. Norma Campos Vera (La Paz, Bolivia: Viceministerio de Cultura; Unión Latina, 2003), 245–56.

4 Natalia Majluf and Luis Eduardo Wuffarden, *La piedra de Huamanga: Lo sagrado y lo profano* (Lima, Peru: Museo de Arte de Lima, 1998).

5 Rafael Ramos Sosa, "Escultura napolitana en Hispanoamérica: Testimonios e imágenes," in *Sculture e intaglio lignei tra Italia meridionale e Spagna, dal Quattro al Settecento,* ed. Pierluigi Leone de Castri (Naples: Artstudiopaparo, 2015), 211–20.

6 All translations are my own unless otherwise stated.

7 AGN, Martín Ochandiano, no. 818, 474–79, 494.

8 Crespo Rodríguez, *Arquitectura doméstica,* 349–52.

9 Antonio Holguera Cabrera, "Gonzalo Arias: Una aproximación crítica al coleccionismo limeño durante el siglo XVII," in *Coleccionismo, mecenazgo y mercado artístico en España e Iberoamérica,* coord. Antonio Holguera Cabrera, Ester Prieto Ustio y María Uriondo Lozano (Seville: Universidad de Sevilla y SAV, 2017).

10 AGN, Martín Ochandiano, no. 1287, 1166–81; and Holguera Cabrera, "Gonzalo Arias," 15–29.

11 AGN, Juan de Carvajal, no. 255, 17. I thank Javier Chuquiray for this documentary reference.

12 AGN, Marcelo Antonio de Figueroa, no. 664, 168; and Crespo Rodríguez, *Arquitectura doméstica,* 310n44.

13 Crespo Rodríguez, *Arquitectura doméstica,* 310n44.

14 Crespo Rodríguez, *Arquitectura doméstica,* 310n43, 336n213.

15 Pedro Ramírez del Águila, *Noticias políticas de Indias y relación de la ciudad de La Plata* (Sucre, Bolivia: Ed. Jaime Urioste, 1978), 58–59.

16 Rafael Ramos Sosa, "Concurso de artes y letras: Aspectos artísticos del Siglo de Oro en Charcas," *Anuario de estudios Bolivianos* 14 (2008): 397–415.

17 AGN, Pedro Espino Alvarado, no. 281, 554–5. I thank Antonio Holguera for this documentary reference.

18 Rafael Ramos Sosa, ed., *El Niño Jesús y la infancia en las artes plásticas* (Seville: Archicofradía Sacramental del Sagrario, 2010).

19 Francisco del Castillo, *Un místico del siglo XVII, autobiografía del Venerable padre Francisco del Castillo de la Compañía de Jesús* (Lima, Peru: Ed. Rubén Vargas Ugarte, 1960), 75.

20 Rafael Ramos Sosa, *Arte festivo en Lima virreinal, siglos XVI y XVII* (Seville: Junta de Andalucía, 1992), 256–57.

DONNA PIERCE

Material Matters
Global Trade at the Edge of the Spanish Colonial Empire

I n the era of global trade, imported goods came to serve as status symbols by testifying to their owners' ability to acquire objects from many areas. However, in some cases, they were preferred because of the materials from which they were made. This chapter will focus on the two most prevalent of all Asian imports to colonial Latin America: porcelain and silk. Both were manufactured from materials that made them far superior to their competitors. The kaolin clay that was used in porcelain allowed the vessels to be harder and thinner than any other form of ceramic, including their closest rival: the lead, and tin, glazed earthenware now known as Talavera, or majolica. Fine silk was produced in Europe, but Asian silks often were finer and woven with exotic patterns. In documents of the colonial period, Asian goods would generally bear a higher value than their closest rivals, indicating that the material mattered.

With the conquest and occupation of the Philippines in 1565, Spain finally had its own trade route to Asia, and by 1579 the famous galleon fleets began to sail annually from Manila to Acapulco laden with trade goods.[1] In Acapulco, the goods were off-loaded onto mules for the long journey overland either to Mexico

City for local consumption and distribution within New Spain, or to the east coast where they were again loaded onto ships for the trip across the Atlantic to Spain.[2] The initial peak of Asian trade (1570–1620) coincided with the first silver booms in Mexico, making it possible for colonists to purchase the precious materials at the trade market established in the main plaza of Mexico City known as the Parián, after the market of the same name in the Chinese area of Manila.

Asian goods are mentioned in travelers' comments and other documents such as dowries, wills, and estate inventories. Most writers in Latin America referred to the objects generically as "from China" (much like we use "Asia" today), or occasionally as "from Japan." This makes it difficult today to discern the actual source, even though we know goods also came to the Americas from India, Southeast Asia, Malaysia, Indonesia, and, of course, the Philippines, where a large contingent of Asian craftsmen (known as sangleys) had settled specifically to produce goods for the galleon trade.

Asian objects were interspersed within colonial households along with objects from other areas and ones produced locally.[3] In colonial homes, imported status objects were concentrated in two main areas: the *estrado* area of the

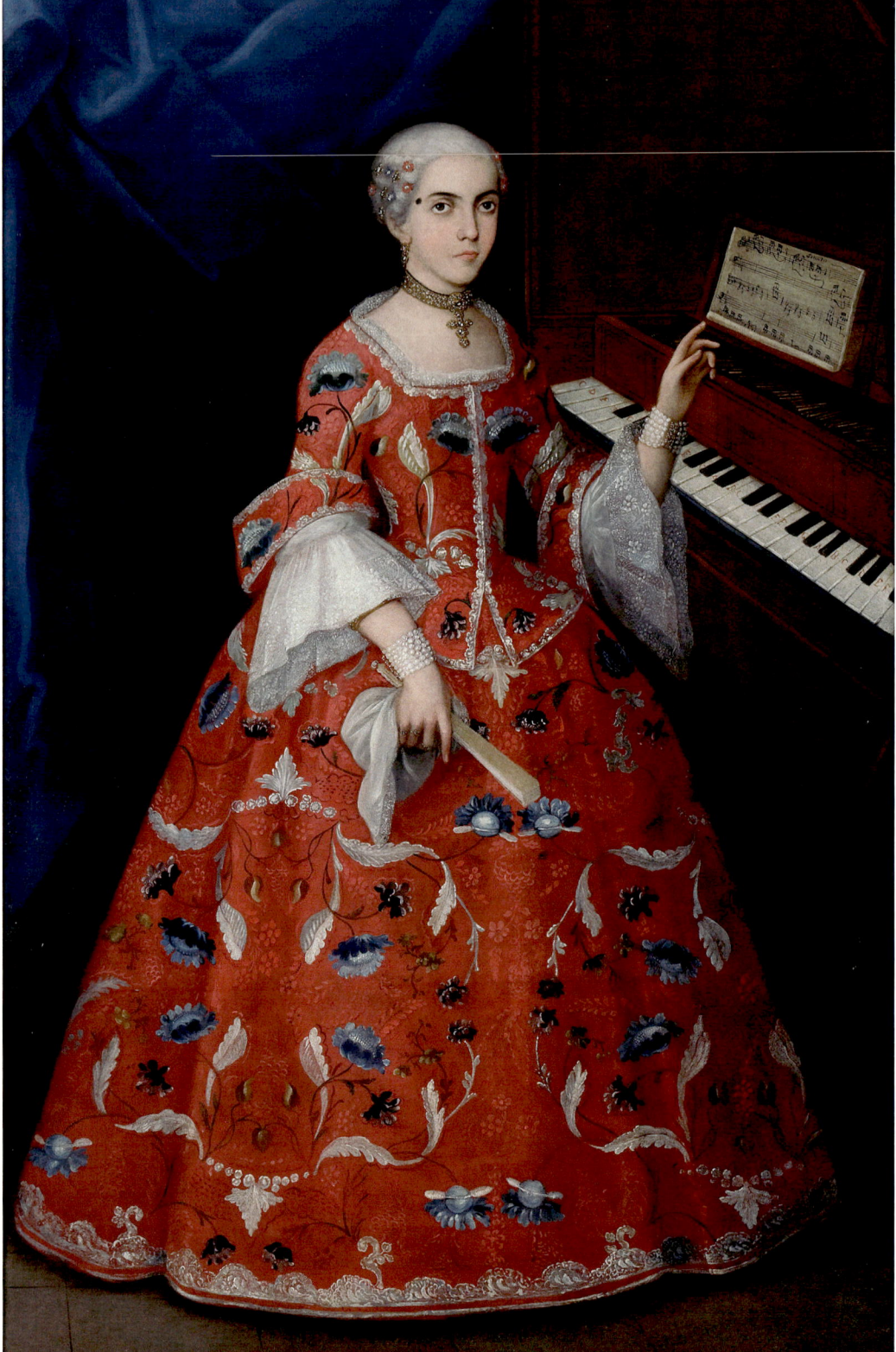

Fig. 1. Unknown artist, *Young Woman with a Harpsichord*. Mexico, 1735–50. Oil paint on canvas, 72¼ × 50⅞ in. Denver Art Museum: Gift of the Collection of Frederick and Jan Mayer, 2014.209.

salon and in master bedrooms. Similar in usage to the drawing room of Anglo and Anglo-American homes, the salon was usually a long room with a raised platform at one end generally reserved for women. Known as an estrado, the low platform preserved the Spanish Muslim custom of sitting on or near the floor.[4] Women sat on low stools or seat cushions, often made of imported Asian silk, and drank chocolate, frequently from Chinese porcelain cups.[5] In upper-class households, master bedrooms were furnished with beds that were often canopied with luxurious silks from China. An example appears in a Mexican inventory from 1650 as "a bed of West Indian ebony with bronze fittings, three coverlets, and an orange Chinese canopy."[6] Such elaborate canopied beds were not restricted to the urban centers, and examples are described in remote areas. Apparently, all types of people aspired to own Asian goods, and some lower-class families seem to have had a few articles of silk clothing and one or two pieces of low-quality porcelain.

In addition, in Latin America, status was often defined as much by behavior and appearance as by aristocracy, or wealth, or race.[7] As a result—and in spite of repeatedly legislated sumptuary laws—the appearance of wealth or well-being was desirable among all classes and in all areas, however remote. In short, people often wore their wealth (fig. 1). Indeed, travelers to the Americas from Europe often commented on the extensive use of Asian silks among all classes. In the 1620s in Mexico, the British Dominican friar Thomas Gage claimed, "Both men and women are excessive in their apparel, using more silks than stuffs and cloth."[8] Gage described Black and mulatto women in Mexico wearing skirts and headcloths of silk along with "sleeves . . . of Holland or fine China linen, wrought with colored silks" (fig. 2).[9] He also described well-off Indian women wearing *huipiles* (a prehispanic type of overblouse worn by Native women) made

from "fine linen brought from China, which the better sort wear with a lace about."[10]

Portraits reflect this phenomenon, often depicting both men and women clothed in what may be Chinese silks. Although silk fabrics were imported from Spain and made in Mexico from both locally produced silk and imported silk thread, the tremendous quantity, quality, and affordability of Asian silks was visible. The viceroy of Peru described them as early as 1594 when he wrote to the king stating that Chinese silks and other textiles are so cheap that Indian chieftains and even commoners are using them

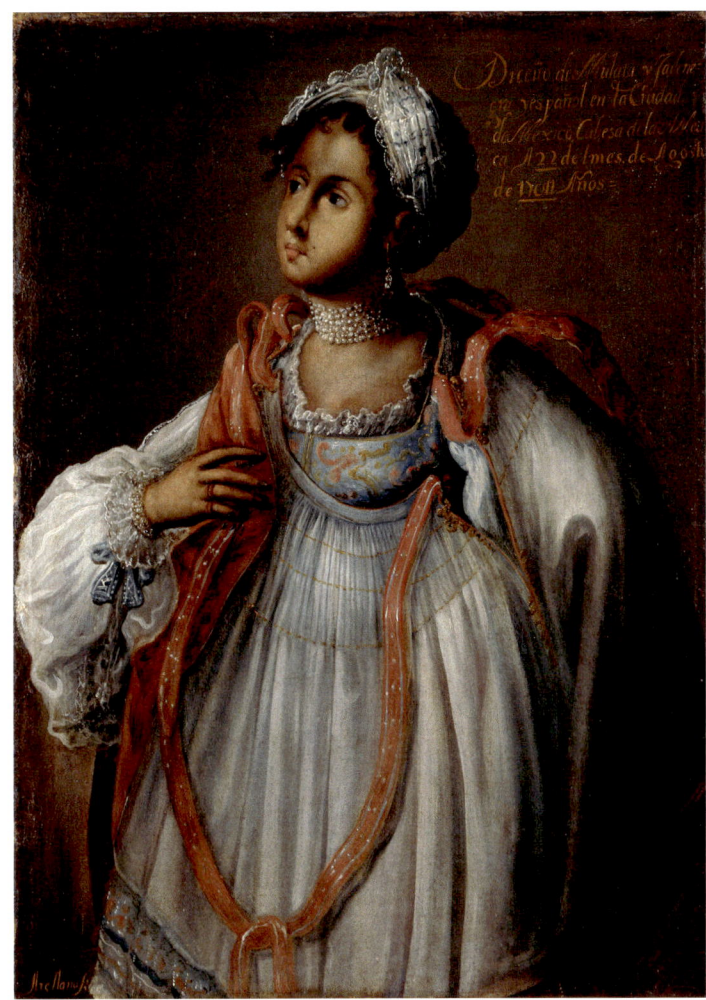

Fig. 2. Manuel de Arellano (active 1691–about 1722), *Diseño de Mulata (Rendering of a Mulatta)*. Mexico, 1711. Oil paint on canvas, 46¾ × 36⅛ in. Collection of Frederick and Jan Mayer.

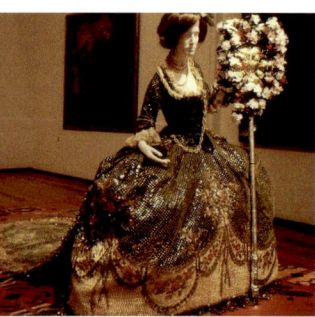

Fig. 3. *Woman's dress.* Mexico, 1600s–1700s. Velvet, silk and metallic thread, sequins. Collection of Museo Nacional de Historia, Mexico City.

for clothing instead of cloth of local manufacture.[11] Surviving articles of clothing demonstrate this splendor, including a green velvet court dress decorated with silver thread and sequins believed to have belonged to the wife of one of the viceroys and surviving today in the collection of the Museo Nacional de Historia in Mexico City (fig. 3).[12] Although Spanish velvet makers were active in Mexico as early as the 1540s, velvet was also regularly imported from China, as were sequins,[13] possibly including those seen here as well as ones sent to provincial regions of New Spain where dressing in fine fabrics also was common.

As a case study, this chapter will look at the importation and use of Asian porcelains and silks in one of the most remote and inaccessible areas of the Spanish territories: the northern province of New Mexico. Over 1,800 miles north of Mexico City, it was landlocked and reachable only by overland travel. Written documents and modern archaeological excavations evidence the presence of Asian porcelain and silks in the capital city of Santa Fe, as well as in remote villages and missions in Indian pueblos from settlement in 1598 into the nineteenth century. Since few intact artifacts survive from colonial New Mexico, archaeological fragments and written descriptions are matched here with similar extant objects or ones seen in paintings from central Mexico.

New Mexico (1598–1680)

The first Spanish settlement in New Mexico was located next to San Juan Pueblo. Known as San Gabriel, it was occupied from 1598 to 1617. When it was excavated in the 1960s, several sherds of Chinese porcelain were located, all high-quality pieces.[14] In particular, a small sherd decorated in red overglaze enamels on one side and blue underglaze on the other has been identified as an example of the high-end luxury ware known by the Japanese word *kinrande* (gold

brocade), referring to the gilt decoration used in medallions or elsewhere on the sides of vessels.[15]

Although usually not surviving in archaeological contexts, examples of textiles brought to San Gabriel are reflected in the belongings of a Spanish woman who moved there in 1600.[16] According to the expedition inventory, Francisca Galindo's wardrobe included nine dresses of velvet, satin, and silk taffeta, in bright colors including red, green, and yellow, trimmed with lace cuffs and starched ruffs, and fastened with gold buttons. In fact, several gilt brass buttons were excavated at San Gabriel. Francisca also brought a headdress and necklace of pearls with her to New Mexico. Although only one skirt is specifically described as Asian, it is probably safe to assume that at least some of the other silks in her wardrobe and household furnishings were Asian in origin.

In addition, Francisca had a bedspread, a bed canopy, and seat cushions, probably for the estrado, all made of embroidered red silk.[17] At least three other settler families brought silk bedclothes to New Mexico.[18] Since the settlers lived in an abandoned adobe Indian pueblo with its traditionally small rooms, these silk-canopied beds must have seemed out of place. Indeed, Francisca, her husband, and other settlers ran away in 1601 and were later punished for abandoning the settlement when they arrived in Mexico City.

In spite of the early mutiny of some settlers, others remained, determined to make New Mexico a permanent settlement. In 1610, the new governor moved the capital to present-day Santa Fe and initiated construction of *casas reales* (royal buildings); the surviving section is now known as the Palace of the Governors. Modern archaeological excavations and historic documents reveal that Asian porcelains and silks were used there as well. For example, a bed was described there in 1662 in the bedroom of Teresa de Aguilera de Roche, wife of governor Bernardo López de Mendizábal, as furnished with "a bedspread from China of embroidered yellow silk" and "a canopy of silk from China."[19] She also owned five yellow silk cushions, which were most likely for the estrado. Teresa also had a small chest with the supplies for making and drinking chocolate—which she and her husband enjoyed every afternoon at three o'clock. Her chocolate chest included at least one Chinese porcelain chocolate cup. In 1974, dozens of Chinese porcelain sherds were excavated from the Palace of the Governors, all dating before 1680.[20] Four sherds bear designs in what appear to be abraded gold leaf: two from a cup with fern designs in gold on a solid cobalt-blue background and two other sherds from a cup with red and green overglaze. All four of these date before 1644.[21]

Monks and nuns often owned vessels of porcelain as well. Gage described his reception in Veracruz, Mexico, in 1625 by the prior of the Dominican monastery: "His chamber was richly dressed . . . his tables covered with carpets of silk; his cupboards adorned with several sorts of China cups and dishes."[22] This was true in New Mexico as well, where sherds of porcelain have been found in excavations at virtually all mission sites in Indian pueblos. Some of the most recently excavated examples come from the Pueblo of San Lázaro (fig. 4).[23] One of the earliest pueblos to be missionized, a church was under construction at San Lázaro by 1613. However, unrest and frequent raids by Apaches caused the pueblo to be virtually abandoned by 1680 when the various Pueblo groups united in rebellion, driving the Spanish entirely out of New Mexico for thirteen years. Without Spanish military protection, it was too dangerous to live there, so the native Indians never returned to San Lázaro.

Thirty porcelain sherds have been located at San Lázaro to date, representing a rather large sampling since only about 1 percent of the pueblo has been excavated. The historical context of San Lázaro provides very precise dates for these sherds; that is, between missionization in 1613 and abandonment in 1680. One sherd depicting a horse and rider (fig. 5) was excavated from the historic-era kiva and has been matched by experts to a vase from the Chongzhen period (1628–1644) in the collection of the Princessehof National Museum of Ceramics in the Netherlands (fig. 6).[24] Another sherd from a cup or small bowl depicts a duck or goose (fig. 7), often seen in garden scenes on

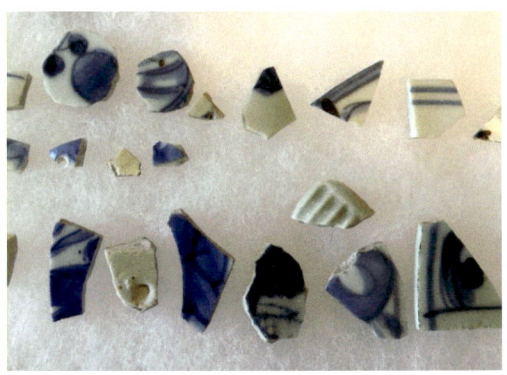

Fig. 4. Unknown artists, *Sherds of porcelain*. China, Ming dynasty, before 1644. Excavated from San Lázaro Pueblo, New Mexico. Collection of Forrest Fenn, Santa Fe, New Mexico.

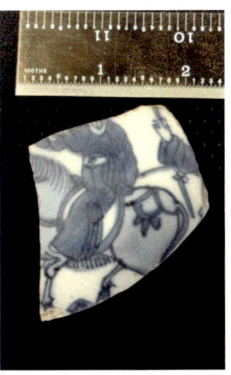

Fig. 5. Unknown artist, *Sherd of porcelain*, China, Ming dynasty, before 1644. Excavated from the historic kiva at San Lázaro Pueblo, New Mexico. Private collection.

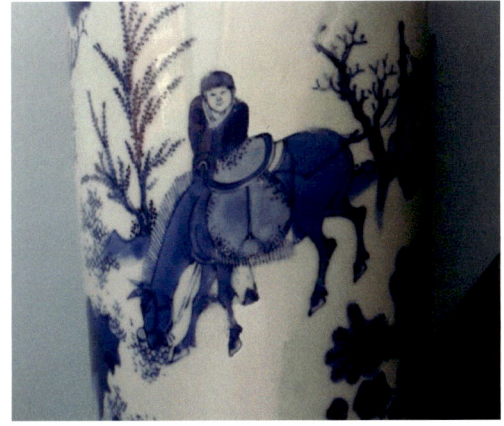

Fig. 6. Unknown artist, *Porcelain vase* (detail). China, Ming dynasty, Chongzhen period (1628–1644). Collection of Princessehof National Museum of Ceramics, Netherlands (on loan from the Ottema Kingma Foundation), NO 901.

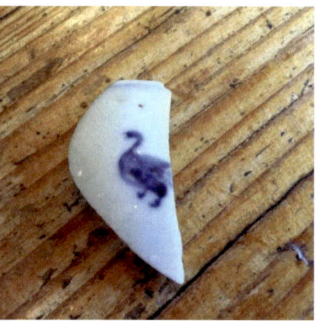

Fig. 7. Unknown artist, *Sherd of porcelain*. China, Ming dynasty, before 1644. Excavated at San Lázaro Pueblo, New Mexico. Collection of Forrest Fenn, Santa Fe, New Mexico.

Fig. 8. Unknown artist, *Soup plate with geese*. China, Ming dynasty, Wanli period (1573–1620). Porcelain with cobalt underglaze, 14¼ in. (36.2 cm) diameter. Metropolitan Museum of Art, New York, Rogers Fund, 16.93.

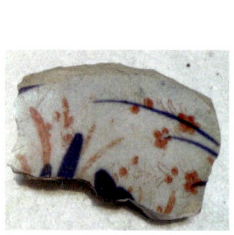

Fig. 9. Unknown artist, *Sherd of porcelain*. China or Japan, late 1600s–early 1700s. Excavated at San Lázaro Pueblo, New Mexico. Collection of Forrest Fenn, Santa Fe, New Mexico.

Ming porcelain, such as the soup plate from the Wanli period (1573–1628) in the collection of the Metropolitan Museum of Art in New York (fig. 8). A rather large sherd from San Lázaro with blue underglaze and red overglaze designs (fig. 9) presents something of a mystery since it represents a type believed to date after 1680, but San Lázaro was entirely abandoned by 1680. In addition, some experts believe it to be Japanese, rather than Chinese, which is curious since Japan was closed off to direct trade with Spain and Portugal in 1639. Not only do these sherds elicit questions within the scholarly community of Asian arts but also beg the question of who exactly owned the porcelain at San Lázaro? Did it all belong to the priest and the handful of other Spaniards believed to have lived at the pueblo?

Or, did the Pueblo Indians also value and acquire the material?

New Mexico after Resettlement (1693–1821)

After New Mexico was resettled by the Spanish in 1693, and throughout the remainder of the colonial period, wills and estate inventories mention Asian porcelain and textiles in private homes, and they generally bear a higher value than other fabrics or ceramics.[25] As for textiles, Luisa Gómez del Castillo (Lujan) had "a new cape of Chinese silk lamé with silver trim" in 1721, while Margarita Martín had a skirt of "red Chinese silk" in 1744.[26] When Antonio Durán, a mestizo blacksmith from Taos, was killed by Plains Indians in 1748, he left to his

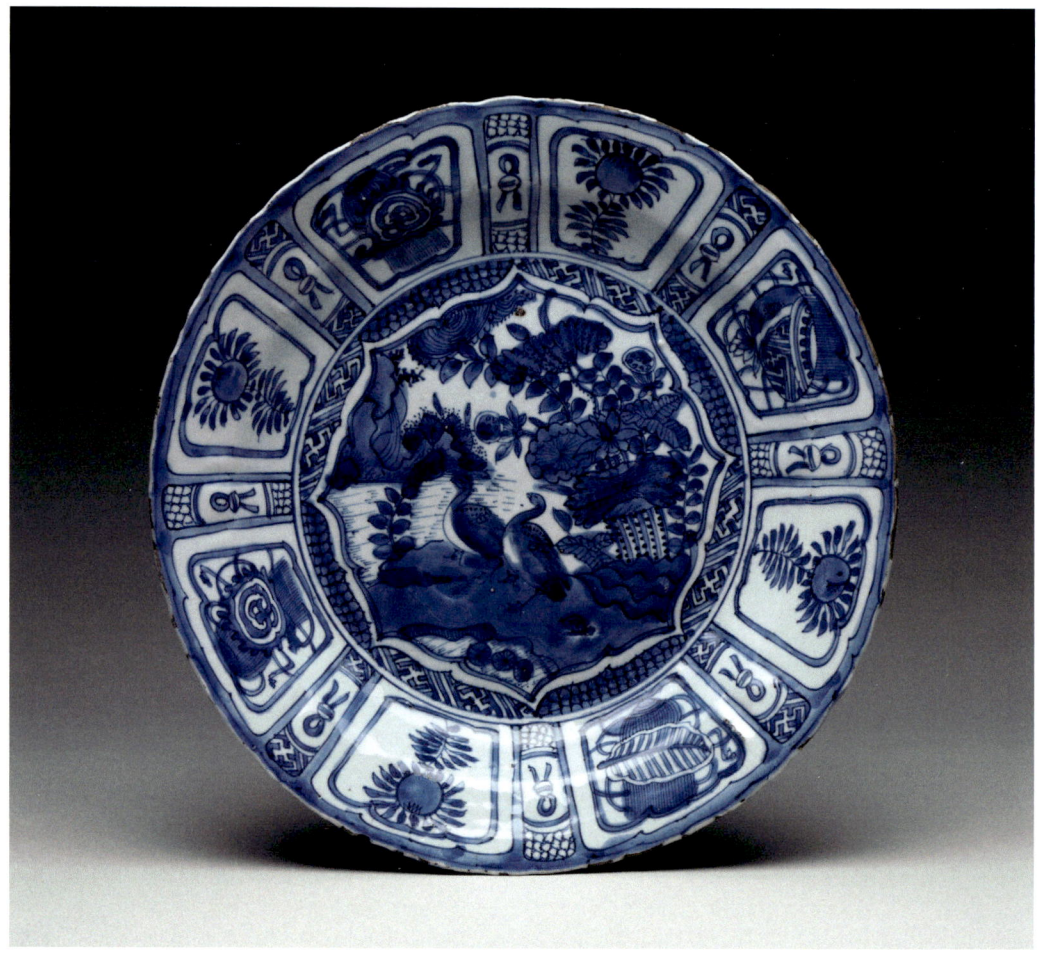

only daughter "10 yards of red Chinese silk bolt cloth" and "6 yards of ribbon from China woven with gold and silver."[27] Although very few wills of Native Americans survive, that of Juana Galbana of Zia Pueblo in 1753 lists "a cape of silk taffeta" but does not specify it as Asian.[28] In 1762, Nicolasa Lujan owned a "short cape of black velvet from China" and "one fine kimono" (*quimono fino*).[29] Although we do not know exactly what type of garment this refers to, there are a total of six other kimonos listed in colonial New Mexican documents,[30] and we know from a ship manifest that Japanese kimonos were brought from Manila to Acapulco in 1736.[31]

The only example of a colonial textile to survive from New Mexico is an elegant three-piece man's suit of silk fabric with gold-thread buttons and trim (fig. 10).[32] When it was conserved at Hampton Court Palace in London in the 1980s, the staff there dated it between 1690 and 1720 based on construction techniques and cut. Textile experts identified the fabric as a combination of Chinese and European silks. Now discolored by time, they believed the pants and jacket to have been of cream-colored silk with the waistcoat of red silk.

Estate inventories from New Mexico also itemize Chinese porcelain with chocolate cups, plates, and the deeper soup plates (see fig. 8) among the most frequently listed items. Most people owned two or three of each, but when Juan Montes Vigil of Santa Fe died in 1762, he had nine plates, five soup plates, and eight cups of Chinese porcelain; in 1776, Gertrudes Armijo of Taos owned a dozen cups and six bowls of porcelain.[33] Occasionally other vessels are mentioned such as a large "vase [*tibor*] from China" in the 1721 dowry of Luisa Gómez, and a bottle of Chinese porcelain owned by her mother, Juana Lujan, in 1762.

Margarita Martín of Rio Arriba, north of Santa Fe, owned "six medium-sized plates of

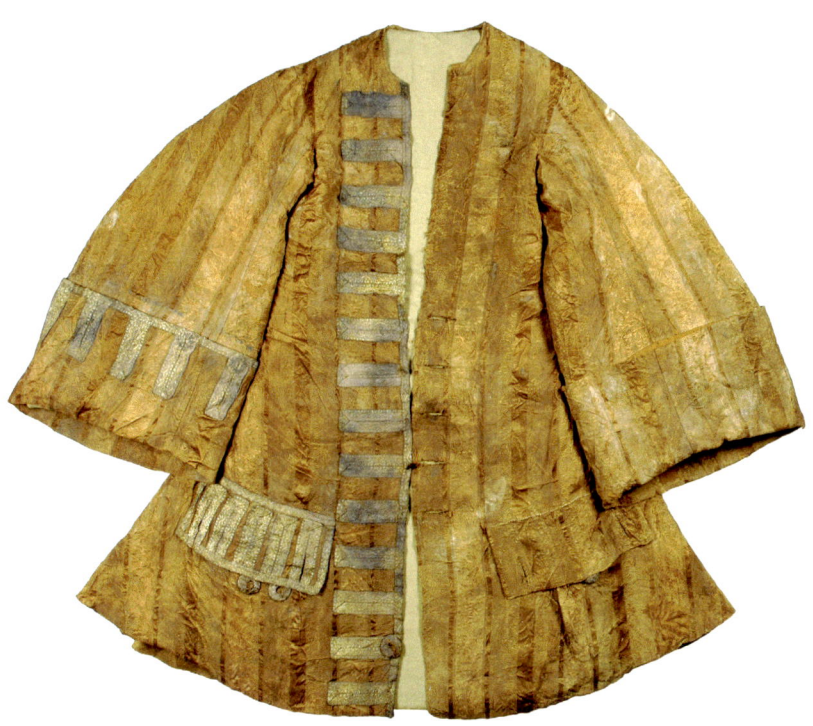

Chinese porcelain," which were valued at three pesos each for a total of eighteen pesos, more valuable than her high wooden four-poster bed at ten pesos, or even her painted chest imported from Michoacán at twelve pesos.[34] Many people owned both Chinese porcelain and Mexican majolica. In 1748, the Chinese chocolate cups owned by Antonio Durán de Armijo were valued twice as much as his majolica ones,[35] whereas in 1780, Manuel Montes Vigil's porcelain chocolate cups were valued more than five times his majolica ones.[36]

Local Materials and Art

Additional evidence for the presence of Asian goods in colonial Latin America is seen in local art forms and chinoiserie materials produced in imitation of Asian arts.[37] The influence of Asian fabrics on local textile production in New Spain—whether direct or via chinoiserie fabrics from Europe—is well-known but not well explored by scholars.[38] In addition to family or cottage industries, larger textile factories,

Fig. 10. Unknown artist, *Man's jacket*. Mexico or New Mexico, about 1700. Silk, gold, and silk thread braid, 89¾ × 38⅜ in. Museum of International Folk Art on long-term loan from the Archdiocese of Santa Fe (A.1987.75.1v), Santa Fe, New Mexico.

or *obrajes,* were established from early on as well. In 1569, a hundred English sailors were abandoned on the east coast of Mexico by the English privateer John Hawkins.[39] After being force-marched to Mexico City, some of them were sentenced to card wool alongside Indian workers in a factory in Texcoco. Miles Philips, who had been Hawkins's thirteen-year-old cabin boy, apprenticed himself to a silk weaver in Mexico City. Mexican textile production thrived, in particular in the towns of Puebla, Campeche, Querétaro, Oaxaca, and Mexico City, as well as on the northern frontier in New Mexico. Documentation on some Mexican factories survives in archives along with a handful of sample books, such as the one in the collection of the Brooklyn Museum with samples of silk and cotton fabrics.[40] Fabrics imported from Mexico are noted in New Mexican documents.

Asian motifs in the distinctive decorative arts of New Mexico have long been noted,[41] but how those influences arrived in New Mexico—whether directly from actual Asian goods or via chinoiserie objects from Europe or Mexico—has never been studied. In exploring this topic, we should not underestimate the ability of decorative arts and even utilitarian objects to be transmitters of artistic ideas and motifs. As we know, Asian goods, particularly textiles and porcelains, were prevalent in New Mexico, making them able to transmit motifs that would have been available for makers of other forms of decorative arts to appropriate. As we will see, paintings and sculptures of saints made in New Mexico often depict what may be Asian or Asian-inspired fabrics, and Asian inspiration in individual works of textile art

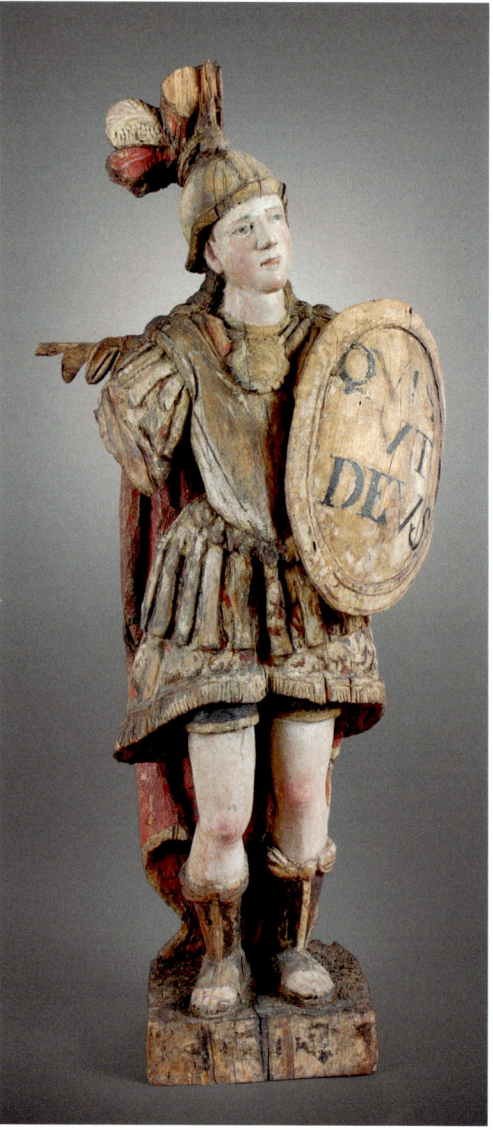

Fig. 11. Bernardo Miera y Pacheco, *Saint Michael.* New Mexico, 1774–76. Wood, gesso, gold leaf, paint. From Zuni Pueblo altar screen. Zuni Pueblo Visitors' Center, Zuni, New Mexico.

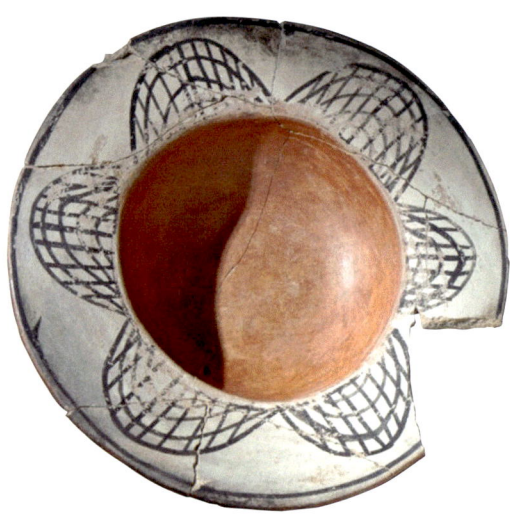

Fig. 12. Tewa Indian artist, *Earthenware soup plate,* Cuyamungue, New Mexico, 1600s. Tewa polychrome. Collections of the Museum of Indian Arts and Culture / Laboratory of Anthropology, Santa Fe, New Mexico (1955/11).

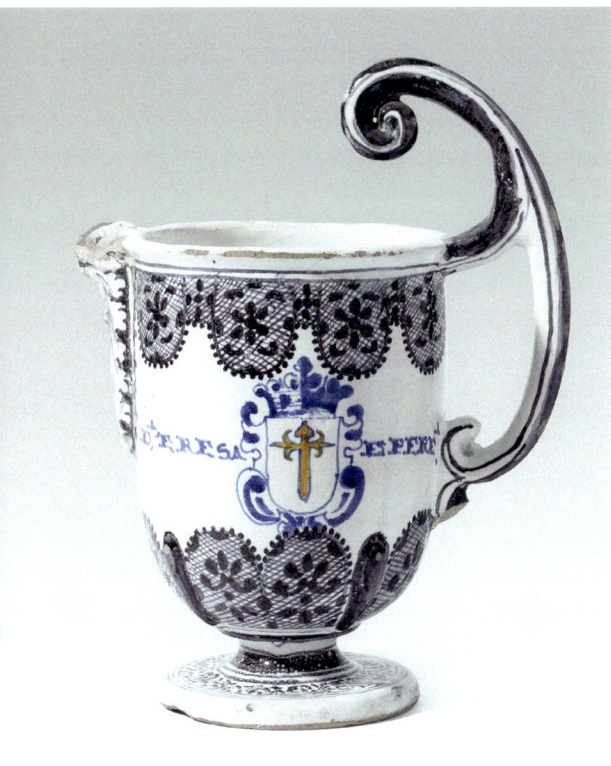

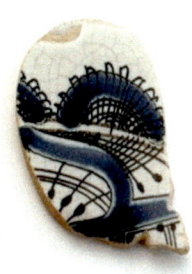

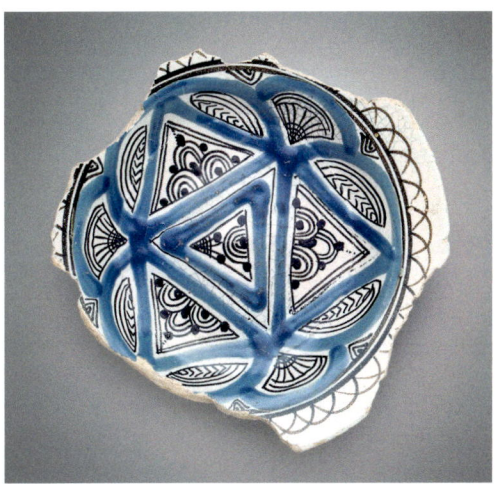

is often apparent, notably in the local embroideries of New Mexico.[42] The source material for these could have been imported artworks, prints, or engravings, but it just as easily could have also been the fabrics themselves in New Mexico, as indicated by the archaeological and documentary records. At times, this influence may have been indirect, transferred via chinoiserie materials made in Europe or Mexico but still ultimately Asian in inspiration.

Religious art had been imported to New Mexico from central Mexico from the early colonial period but was soon produced locally as well.[43] The difficulty of acquiring canvas, gold leaf, and oil paints on the frontier resulted in the use of locally made paints on pine panels and cottonwood carvings. Although artists are mentioned in documents from the early 1600s on, no extant works of art can be associated with them. The identity, much less the biography, of many New Mexican artists is unknown. Captain Bernardo Miera y Pacheco (1714–1785) is the earliest New Mexican artist identified by name whose surviving works of art can be connected to him.[44] Born near Burgos, Spain, in 1714, he moved to New Mexico in 1754. He is listed in documents of the period as a sculptor and painter as well as a rancher-farmer, soldier, mathematician, and cartographer.

In New Mexico, Miera y Pacheco adopted at least one material from the Pueblo Indians. He was commissioned to make art for various Pueblo mission churches, including a large altar screen at Zuni, which no longer survives in situ, but the columns and one statue are extant (fig. 11).[45] Miera y Pacheco would have lived in the pueblo temporarily during construction and probably would have hired and trained assistants from the pueblo population. In the process, he learned from the Indians of Zuni how to make a

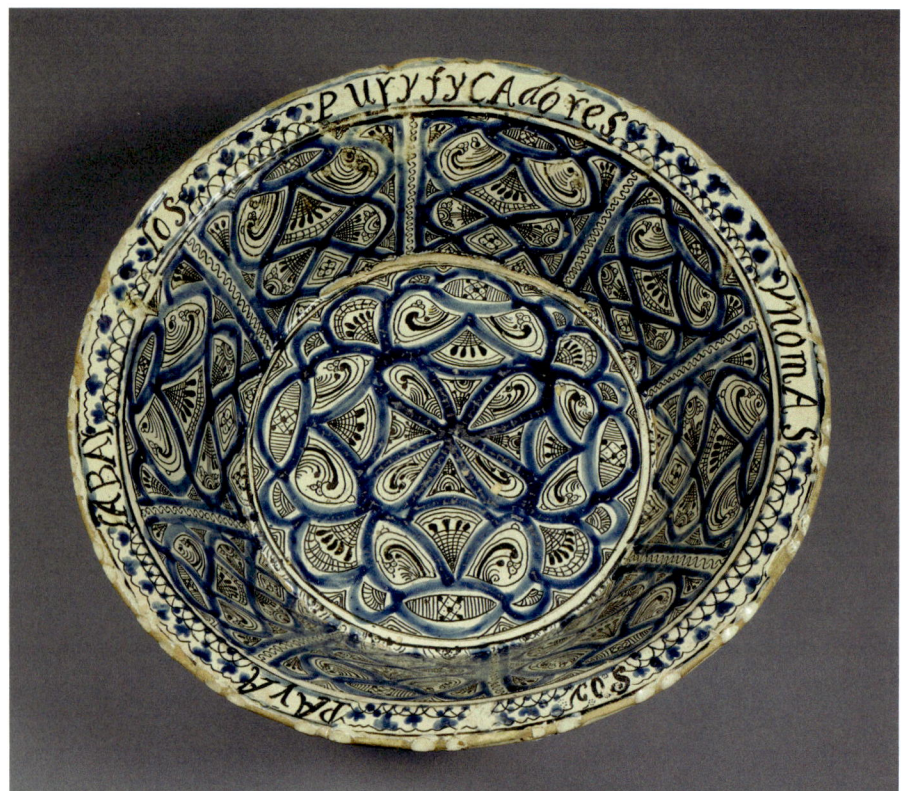

Left: Fig. 16. Master Potter "A", *Basin (lebrillo)*. Mexico, about 1650. Majolica, 20¾ in. diameter. Metropolitan Museum of Art, New York, Gift of Mrs. Robert W. de Forest, 1912 (12.3.1).

Below: Fig. 17. Unknown artist, *Porcelain sherds*. China, before 1644. Excavated from the Palace of the Governors, Santa Fe, New Mexico. Collections of the Museum of Indian Arts and Culture / Laboratory of Anthropology, Santa Fe.

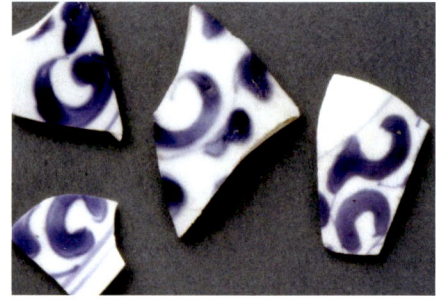

blue paint from a local mineral (azurite). Miera y Pacheco used the Pueblo-style blue paint himself in conjunction with imported oil paints, as it has recently been identified through chemical testing on the large statue of Saint Michael, which originally was made for the Zuni altar screen.[46] Miera y Pacheco was so taken with the qualities of this paint that he advocated its exportation to Mexico for profit by the government.[47] Later artists in New Mexico followed his example, often using imported pigments alongside paints made from local vegetal and mineral materials similar to those used by the Pueblo Indians, including the blue paint now known as "Zuni blue."

In New Mexico, the Pueblo Indians continued their long tradition of making unglazed pottery after the Spanish came to the area. Archaeological evidence from Spanish home sites corroborates wills and inventories, documenting a mix of Chinese porcelain, Mexican majolica, and Native Pueblo ceramics, indicating that all three were used in most Spanish households.[48] Within a matter of years after Spanish settlement, Pueblo potters began to imitate the shapes of imported vessels. Soup plates (fig. 12), footed cups, goblets, and candlesticks all became popular new forms.

In an example of international and cross-cultural artistic exchange, some Pueblo ceramic vessels (including fig. 12) used new scalloped decorations in imitation of a popular seventeenth-century Spanish bobbin lace design, which had been appropriated from clothing first into majolica made in Spain (fig. 13), and then into a type of Mexican majolica, now known as Puebla Polychrome (figs. 14–15).[49] Initially, the tall, scalloped patterns are also reminiscent of—and often in the same location as—the vertical lotus petal panels around the side walls of Chinese export porcelain (see fig. 8), conflating European and Asian motifs. In Puebla

Polychrome examples, at first the lace patterns still resemble the actual scalloped lace designs but soon are broken down into fragments of lace motifs (fig. 16).[50] In addition, black dots are inserted into Puebla Polychrome lace patterns to represent the knots used in lace production.

Mexican majolica with these scalloped patterns was imported by Spanish settlers to New Mexico, where it is found in both Pueblo and Spanish archaeological sites that predate 1680 (see figs. 14–15). Probably for Spanish patrons, some Native ceramicists adapted the scalloped lace patterns in their more linear Indigenous decorative manner (see fig. 12).[51] The soup plate form and the scalloped lace/lotus petal motifs around the side walls could have been appropriated either from Mexican chinoiserie majolica or directly from Chinese porcelain examples imported to New Mexico. In the Native-made piece here (see fig. 12), we see that a new form,

the soup plate, unknown in pre-Spanish New Mexico, was inspired by Chinese or Mexican examples. At the same time, the materials of lace and ceramics, from Europe, inspired a new type of scalloped decoration on an object made from local materials and technique of manufacture.

And finally, in addition to the local materials that New Mexican artists incorporated into their artwork, they also adopted individual motifs inspired by Asian objects. For example, scrolls in the shape of the letter C were prevalent in Asian art and were appropriated in the arts of Europe and the Americas, including New Mexico, particularly among the rocaille motifs of the rococo style. In New Mexico, the motif spread originally through the exportation of Chinese porcelains, such as the chocolate cups excavated from the Palace of the Governors (fig. 17), as well as pieces from San Lázaro (see fig. 4, lower right) and other New Mexican sites. Asian and Asian-inspired fabrics also depicted the C-scroll motif, as seen in surviving fabrics and paintings

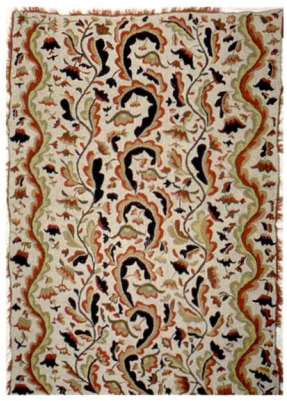

Fig. 18. Unknown artist, *Colcha embroidery bedspread.* New Mexico, about 1790. Wool embroidery on handspun, handwoven plain weave wool *(sabanilla).* Museum of Spanish Colonial Art, Santa Fe, New Mexico, Gift of Mary Cabot Wheelwright (1958.41).

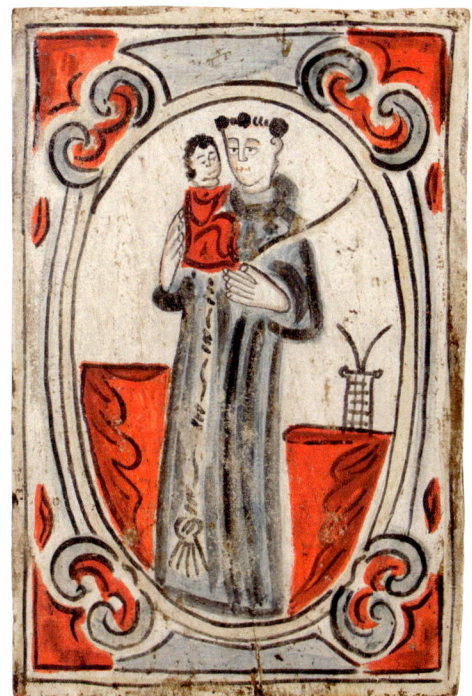

Fig. 19. Molleno (active 1800–1850), *Saint Anthony.* New Mexico, about 1800. Pine, gesso, water-based paints, 10¹³⁄₁₆ × 7½ in. Museum of International Folk Art, Santa Fe, New Mexico, bequest of Charles D. Carroll (A.1971.31.41).

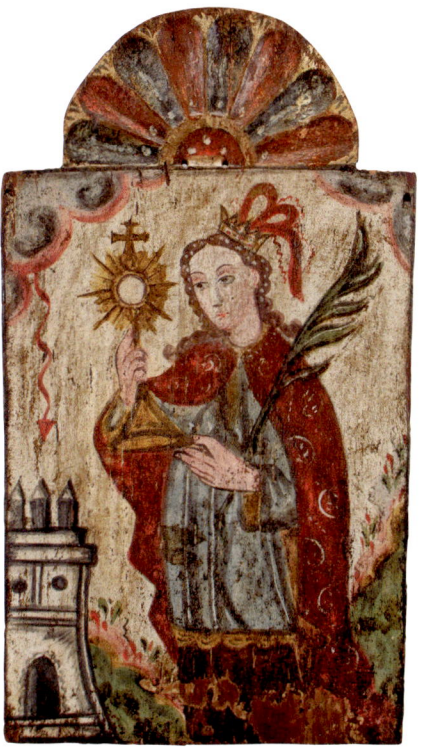

Fig. 20. Laguna santero (active 1785–1810), *Saint Barbara.* New Mexico, late 1700s–early 1800s. Pine, gesso, and water-based paint. Museum of International Folk Art, Santa Fe, New Mexico, IFAF Collection (FA.1968.22.82).

from Mexico. In New Mexico, the C scroll was reproduced in locally made embroidered bedspreads (fig. 18) and altar frontals. It was also used frequently on painted wood altar screens, altar furnishings, sculptures, and small paintings (fig. 19). In fact, the C-scroll motif sometimes appears in the appropriate location on the capes and gowns of images of saints (fig. 20).

In sum, motifs and shapes seen in the highly desired Asian materials of porcelain and silk were reproduced in New Mexico with local materials such as native earthenware ceramics, local woods painted with local mineral and plant-based paints, and embroideries made from locally spun and dyed wools and cottons. In the process, a lively new local tradition developed in colonial New Mexico that merged materials and motifs from disparate origins on the northernmost edge of the Spanish Empire.

✚ ✚ ✚

Notes

At the 2010 Mayer Center symposium, I gave a paper on the topic of Asian trade goods in colonial New Mexico that was published as "'At the Ends of the Earth': Asian Trade Goods in Colonial New Mexico, 1598–1821," in *At the Crossroads: The Arts of Spanish America and Early Global Trade, 1492–1850: Papers from the 2010 Mayer Center Symposium at the Denver Art Museum,* ed. Donna Pierce and Ronald Otsuka (Denver, CO: Denver Art Museum, 2012), 155–82. This chapter is the sequel to that essay. Here, I have briefly reviewed the earlier paper with materiality in mind, added new research, and then expanded it in a different direction by looking at ways imported materials inspired local artists as well as how local materials were utilized to create new art forms.

1 William Lytle Schurz, *The Manila Galleon* (New York: Dutton, 1939), remains the best overall source on the topic. See also Francisco Santiago Cruz, *La nao de China* (Mexico City: Jus, 1962); Carmen Yuste López, *El comercio de la Nueva España con Filipinas, 1590–1785* (Mexico City: Instituto Nacional de Antropología e Historia, 1984); Marina Alfonso Mola and Carlos Martínez Shaw, eds., *El galeón de Manila* (Madrid: Aldeasa, 2000); and more recently, works by Mariano Ardash Bonialian including *El Pacífico hispanoamericano: Política y comercio asiático en el Imperio Español (1680–1784)—La centralidad de lo marginal* (Mexico City: El Colegio de México,

Centro de Estudios Históricos, 2012) and *China en la América colonial: Bienes, mercados, comercio y cultura del consume desde México hasta Buenos Aires* (Mexico City: Instituto Mora, Consejo Nacional de Ciencia y Tecnología, 2014).

2 Portions of this chapter are adapted from Donna Pierce, "By the Boatload: Receiving and Recreating the Arts of Asia," in *Made in the Americas: The New World Discovers Asia,* Dennis Carr, Gauvin A. Bailey, Timothy Brook, Mitchell Codding, Karina H. Corrigan, and Donna Pierce (Boston: Museum of Fine Arts, 2015), 52–73; and Donna Pierce, "Popular and Prevalent: Asian Trade Goods in Northern New Spain, 1590–1850," in "Beyond Silk and Silver," ed. Dana Leibsohn and Meha Priyadarshini, special issue of *Colonial Latin American Review* 25, no. 1 (2016): 77–97, http://dx.doi.org/10.1080/10609164.201 6.1180786. See also Donna Pierce, "From Global to Local: The Diaspora of Asian Decorative Arts in Colonial Latin America," in *Picturing Commerce in and from the East Asian Maritime Circuits, 1550–1800,* ed. Tamara H. Bentley (Amsterdam: Amsterdam University Press, 2019), 127–58.

3 Gustavo Curiel, "Customs, Conventions, and Daily Rituals among the Elites of New Spain: The Evidence from Material Culture," in *The Grandeur of Viceregal Mexico: Treasures from the Museo Franz Mayer,* Héctor Rivero Borrell Miranda, Gustavo Curiel, Antonio Rubial García, Juana Gutiérrez Haces, Peter C. Marzio, and David B. Warren (Mexico City and Houston: Museo Franz Mayer and Museum of Fine Arts Houston, 2002), 23–43; and Gustavo Curiel and Antonio Rubial García, "Los espejos de lo propio: Ritos públicos y usos privados en la pintura virreinal," in *Pintura y vida cotidiana en México: 1650–1950,* Gustavo Curiel, Fausto Ramírez Rojas, Antonio Rubial García, and Angélica Velázquez Guadarrama (Mexico City: Fomento Cultural Banamex, Conaculta, 1999), 49–153.

4 For information on the use of the *estrado* in Spain, see José Gabriel Moya Valgañón, Sofia Rodríquez Bernis, Casto Castellanos Ruiz, María Paz Aguiló Alonso, and Juan José Junquera Mato, *Mueble español: Estrado y dormitorio* (Madrid: Consejería de Cultural, Dirección General de Patrimonio Cultural, 1990); and Grace Hardendorff Burr, *Hispanic Furniture from the Fifteenth through the Eighteenth Century* (New York: Archive Press, 1964). For Colombia, see María del Pilar López Pérez and Carlos Bejarano Calvo, *En torno al estrado: Cajas de uso cotidiano en Santafé del Bogotá, siglos XVI al XVIII* (Bogotá: Museo Nacional de Colombia, 1996). For Venezuela, see Carlos F. Duarte, *Museo de Arte Colonial de Caracas "Quinta de Anauco"* (Caracas: Ediciones de la Asociación Venezolana Amigos del Arte Colonial, 1979). For Mexico, see Carmen Aguilera, Elisa Vargas Lugo, Marita Martínez del Río de Redo, Jorge Loyzaga, Luis Ortiz Macedo, Teresa Castelló Yturbide, Manuel Carballo, María Cecilia Martínez López, and Fernando Sánchez Martínez, *El mueble mexicano: Historia, evolución e influencias*

(Mexico City: Fomento Cultural Banamex, 1985); and Curiel, "Customs, Conventions, and Daily Rituals." And for New Mexico, see Donna Pierce, "Furniture," in *Spanish New Mexico: The Spanish Colonial Arts Society Collection,* vol. 1, ed. Donna Pierce and Marta Weigle (Santa Fe: Museum of New Mexico Press, 1996), 62–79; and Robin Farwell Gavin, "*La Sala del Estrado:* Women's Place in the Palace," *El Palacio* 115, no. 4 (Winter 2010): 48–55.

5 For general information on Chinese porcelain in Mexico, see Jean McClure Mudge, *Chinese Export Porcelain in North America* (New York: Clarkson N. Potter, 1986); George Kuwayama, *Chinese Ceramics in Colonial Mexico* (Los Angeles: Los Angeles County Museum of Art, 1997); Etsuko Miyata Rodríguez, "Early Manila Galleon Trade: Merchants' Network and the Market in Sixteenth- and Seventeenth-Century Mexico," in *Asia and Spanish America: Trans-Pacific Artistic and Cultural Exchange, 1500–1850: Papers from the 2006 Mayer Center Symposium at the Denver Art Museum,* ed. Donna Pierce and Ronald Otsuka (Denver, CO: Denver Art Museum, 2009), 37–57; Clara Bargellini, "Asia at the Missions of Northern New Spain," in Pierce and Otsuka, *Asia and Spanish America,* 191–99; and, most recently, Meha Priyadarshini, *Chinese Porcelain in Colonial Mexico: The Material Worlds of an Early Modern Trade* (London: Palgrave Macmillan, 2018). For New Mexico, see Patricia Fournier, "Ceramic Production and Trade on the Camino Real," in *El Camino Real de Tierra Adentro,* vol. 2, ed. Gabrielle G. Palmer and Stephen L. Fosberg (Santa Fe, NM: Bureau of Land Management, 1999), 160–172; David V. Hill and John A. Peterson, "East Meets West on the Camino Real," in Palmer and Fosberg, *El Camino Real de Tierra Adentro,* 147–52; Pierce, "'At the Ends of the Earth'"; and Pierce, "Popular and Prevalent."

6 Manuel Toussaint, *Colonial Art in Mexico,* trans. and ed. Elizabeth Wilder Weismann (Austin: University of Texas Press, 1967), 168.

7 Michael A. Brown, "Portraits and Patrons in the Colonial Americas," in *Behind Closed Doors: Art in the Spanish American Home, 1492–1898,* ed. Richard Aste (New York: Brooklyn Museum, 2013), 127–55; and James Middleton, "Reading Dress in New Spanish Portraiture," in *New England / New Spain: Portraiture in the Colonial Americas, 1492–1850: Papers from the 2014 Mayer Center Symposium at the Denver Art Museum,* ed. Donna Pierce (Denver, CO: Denver Art Museum, 2016), 101–46.

8 Thomas Gage, *Thomas Gage's Travels in the New World,* ed. J. Eric S. Thompson (Norman: University of Oklahoma Press, 1985), 68.

9 Gage, *Travels,* 69.

10 Gage, *Travels,* 221.

11 Woodrow Borah, *Early Colonial Trade and Navigation between Mexico and Peru* (Berkeley: University of California Press, 1954), 121–22; and George Kuwayama, "Chinese Porcelain in the Viceroyalty of Peru," in Pierce and Otsuka, *Asia and Spanish America,* 165–74.

12 Virginia Armella de Aspe, Teresa Castelló Yturbide, and Ignacio Borja Martínez, *La historia de México a través de la indumentaria* (Mexico City: Inversora Bursatíl, 1988), 56–65.

13 Elena Phipps, "The Iberian Globe: Textile Traditions and Trade in Latin America," in *The Interwoven Globe: The Worldwide Textile Trade, 1500–1800,* ed. Amelia Peck (New York: Metropolitan Museum of Art, 2013), 28–45.

14 Florence Hawley Ellis, *San Gabriel del Yungue as Seen by an Archaeologist* (Santa Fe, NM: Sunstone Press in conjunction with the Florence Hawley Ellis Museum of Anthropology, 1989); and Florence Hawley Ellis, *When Cultures Meet: Remembering San Gabriel del Yungue Oweenge: Papers from the October 20, 1984 Conference Held at San Juan Pueblo, New Mexico* (Santa Fe, NM: Sunstone Press, 1987). The recovered artifacts are on long-term loan from San Juan Pueblo to the Maxwell Museum of Anthropology, University of New Mexico, Albuquerque.

15 Personal communication, Linda Shulsky Pomper, Research Associate, Metropolitan Museum of Art, New York, April 1992, April 1993, March 2015, August 2016. See also Linda R. Shulsky, "Chinese Porcelain in New Mexico," *Vormen uit Vuur* 153, no. 3 (September 1994): 13–18; Pierce, "At the Ends of the Earth'"; and Pierce, "Popular and Prevalent."

16 George P. Hammond and Agapito Rey, *Don Juan de Oñate: Colonizer of New Mexico, 1595–1628,* 2 vols. (Albuquerque: University of New Mexico Press, 1953), 1:522–548. See also Pierce, "'At the Ends of the Earth'"; and Pierce, "Popular and Prevalent." Francisca was from Puebla, Mexico, while her husband, Antonio Conde de Herrera, was from Jerez de la Frontera, Spain. They came to New Mexico with their extended families including Francisca's three sisters and her husband's father and son from a previous marriage. See David H. Snow, *New Mexico's First Colonists: The 1597–1600 Enlistments for New Mexico under Juan de Oñate, Adelante and Gobernador* (Albuquerque: Hispanic Genealogical Research Center of New Mexico, 1998), 18, 41, 50, 62–63.

17 Cordelia Thomas Snow, "'A Headdress of Pearls': Luxury Goods Imported over the Camino Real during the Seventeenth Century," in *El Camino Real de Tierra Adentro,* vol. 1, ed. Gabrielle G. Palmer (Santa Fe, NM: Bureau of Land Management, 1993), 69–76.

18 Hammond and Rey, *Don Juan de Oñate,* 1:252–53, 523–27. See also Pierce, "Popular and Prevalent."

19 Inquisition investigation, Archivo General de la Nación, Mexico City, Inquisición 593, expediente 1, f. 60; and Investigation of López de Mendizábal by his successor, Archivo General de la Nación, Mexico City, Concurso de Peñalosa, v. 1, ff. 395–400

(ff. 396v–397r). Note: All English translations from archival documents are my own unless otherwise stated. See Pierce, "'At the Ends of the Earth'"; and Pierce, "Popular and Prevalent."

20 Cordelia Thomas Snow, "A Brief History of the Palace of the Governors and a Preliminary Report on the 1974 Excavation," *El Palacio* 80, no. 3 (October 1974): 1–22. The recovered artifacts are in the collection of the Laboratory of Anthropology, Museum of New Mexico, Santa Fe.

21 Personal communication, Linda Shulsky Pomper, Research Associate, Metropolitan Museum of Art, New York, April 1992, April 1993, March 2015, August 2016. See also Linda R. Shulsky, "Chinese Porcelain in New Mexico." In Pierce, "From Global to Local," I incorrectly identified these pieces as kinrande. I apologize to Linda Shulsky Pomper for my error.

22 Gage, *Travels,* 34.

23 Some of these sherds are owned by private collector Forrest Fenn; others are in another private collection. As yet they are unpublished except for one group photo of some (but not all) of the pieces, along with majolica and glass sherds, in Forrest Fenn, *The Secrets of San Lázaro Pueblo* (Santa Fe, NM: One Horse Land and Cattle Co., 2004), pl. 169.

24 Personal communication, Linda Shulsky Pomper, Research Associate, Metropolitan Museum of Art, New York, March 2015, August 2016.

25 These unpublished wills and estate inventories are located in the New Mexico State Records Center and Archives in Santa Fe, Spanish Archives of New Mexico (hereafter, SANM) I and II.

26 Luisa Gómez de Castillo Lujan: Dowry inventory included in estate settlement, 1762, Juana Luján, Santa Cruz, SANM II: 556. The dowry of her daughter, Luisa Gómez del Castillo, is included in the will of Juana. See also Richard Ahlborn, "The Will of a New Mexico Woman in 1762," *New Mexico Historical Review* 65, no. 3 (July 1990): 315–55; and Margarita Martín: Estate inventory, 1744, Margarita Martín, Santa Cruz, SANM I: 530.

27 Estate inventory, 1748, Antonio Durán de Armijo, San Gerónimo de Taos, SANM I: 240.

28 Estate inventory, 1753, Juana Galbana, Zia Pueblo, SANM I: 193.

29 Estate inventory, 1762, Juan Montes Vigil, Santa Fe, SANM I:1055.

30 According to Carmen Espinosa, these were "kimonos del Japón." Carmen Espinosa, *Shawls, Crinolines, Filigree: The Dress and Adornment of the Women of New Mexico, 1739–1900* (El Paso: Texas Western Press, 1970), 17. However, the phrase "del Japón" does not appear in the original documents. Other wills and inventories also mention "kimonos," but again the country of origin is not specified, with one exception: the 1704 estate inventory of governor Diego de Vargas mentions a "new purple kimono

from China." Two kimonos are listed in the inventory of the estate of María Gertrudes Armijo, Taos, March 26, 1776, SANM I: 48; two more in the estate inventory, 1780, Manuel Montes Vigil, Abiquiu, SANM I: 1060; and one in the estate inventory, 1832, María Micaela Baca, Santa Fe, SANM I: 144.

31 Pablo Guzman-Rivas, "Reciprocal Geographic Influences of the Trans-Pacific Galleon Trade" (PhD diss., University of Texas at Austin, 1960), 60.

32 See Pierce, "Popular and Prevalent," 87–89.

33 Estate inventory, 1762, Juan Montes Vigil, Santa Fe, SANM I: 1055; and 1776, María Gertrudes Armijo, Taos, SANM I: 48.

34 Margarita Martín, SANM I: 530.

35 Antonio Durán de Armijo, SANM I: 240.

36 Manuel Montes Vigil, SANM I: 1060.

37 For a discussion of chinoiserie production in Europe, see Hugh Honour, *Chinoiserie: The Vision of Cathay* (London: John Murray, 1961). For colonial Mexico, see Gustavo Curiel, "Perception of the Other and the Language of 'Chinese Mimicry' in the Decorative Arts of New Spain," in Pierce and Otsuka, *Asia and Spanish America,* 19–36; and Sonia I. Ocaña Ruiz, "De Asia a la Nueva España via Europa: Lacas asiáticas y achinadas en el siglo XVIII," in *Anales del Instituto de Investigaciones Estéticas* 39, no. 111 (2017): 131–188.

38 In fact, Latin American colonial textile production in general is not yet well published. Some exceptions include Armella de Aspe, Castelló Yturbide, and Borja Martínez, *La historia de México;* Dilys E. Blum, "Textiles in Colonial Latin America," in *The Arts in Latin America, 1492–1820,* ed. Joseph J. Rishel and Suzanne Stratton-Pruitt (Philadelphia, PA: Philadelphia Museum of Art, 2006), 146–54; Gridley McKim Smith, "Dressing Colonial, Dressing Diaspora," in Rishel and Stratton-Pruitt, *Arts in Latin America,* 155–63; Elena Phipps, Johanna Hecht, and Cristina Esteras Martín, *The Colonial Andes: Tapestries and Silverwork, 1530–1830* (New York: Metropolitan Museum of Art; New Haven: Yale University Press, 2004); and, most recently, Phipps, "The Iberian Globe." See also contributions by social and economic historians such as Jan Bazant, "Evolution of the Textile Industry of Puebla, 1544–1845," *Comparative Studies in Society and History* 7, no. 1 (October 1964): 56–69; Manuel Miño Grijalva, *Obrajes y tejedores de Nueva España, 1700–1810: La industria urbana y rural de una economía colonial* (Mexico City: El Colegio de México, 1998); and Manuel Miño Grijalva, "El camino hacia la fábrica en Nueva España: El caso de la 'Fábrica de Indianillas' de Francisco de Iglesias, 1801–1810," *Historia Mexicana* 34, no. 1 (July–September 1984): 135–48.

39 Rayner Unwin, *The Defeat of John Hawkins: A Biography of His Third Slaving Voyage* (London: Readers Union/Allen and Unwin, 1960); Job Hortop, *The Rare Travails of Job Hortop* (London: William

Wright, 1591); and for Miles Philips's account, see Richard Hakluyt, *Principal Navigations, Voyages, Traffiques, and Discoveries of the English Nation (1589)*, vol. 14, ed. Edmund Goldsmid (Edinburgh: Goldsmid, 1884–90).

40 Reproduced and discussed in Diana Fane, ed., *Converging Cultures: Art and Identity in Spanish America* (New York: Brooklyn Museum and Harry N. Abrams, 1996), 100–101.

41 The first to note this was E. Boyd, *Popular Arts of Spanish New Mexico* (Santa Fe: Museum of New Mexico Press, 1974), references throughout.

42 Donna Pierce, "The Active Reception of International Artistic Sources in New Mexico," in *Transforming Images: New Mexican Santos In-Between Worlds*, ed. Claire Farago and Donna Pierce (University Park: Pennsylvania State University Press, 2006), 44–57.

43 Much has been published on the colonial art of New Mexico, but the most useful sources remain Boyd, *Popular Arts of Spanish New Mexico*; and William Wroth, *Christian Images in Hispanic New Mexico: Taylor Museum Collection of "Santos"* (Colorado Springs: Taylor Museum of the Colorado Springs Fine Arts Center, 1982). See also Larry Frank, *New Kingdom of the Saints: Religious Art of New Mexico, 1780–1907* (Santa Fe, NM: Red Crane Books, 1992); Donna Pierce, "Saints in New Mexico," in Pierce and Weigle, *Spanish New Mexico*, 1:29–59; Marie Romero Cash, *Santos: Enduring Images of Northern New Mexican Village Churches* (Boulder: University Press of Colorado, 2003); and Charles Carrillo and Thomas J. Steele, *A Century of Retablos: The Dennis and Janis Lyon Collection of New Mexican Santos, 1780–1880* (Manchester, VT: Hudson Hills Press, 2007). Two recent publications address the hybridity of these works: Claire Farago and Donna Pierce, eds., *Transforming Images;* and William Wroth and Robin Farwell Gavin, eds., *Converging Streams: Art of the Hispanic and Native American Southwest* (Santa Fe, NM: Museum of Spanish Colonial Art, 2010).

44 Josef Díaz, ed., *The Art and Legacy of Bernardo Miera y Pacheco: New Spain's Explorer, Cartographer, and Artist* (Santa Fe: Museum of New Mexico Press, 2013). See also John L. Kessell, *Miera y Pacheco: A Renaissance Spaniard in Eighteenth-Century New Mexico* (Norman: University of Oklahoma Press, 2013).

45 Robin Farwell Gavin and Donna Pierce, "The Altar Screens of Bernardo Miera y Pacheco," in Díaz, *Art and Legacy,* 63–102.

46 Chemical analysis conducted on the surviving statue of St. Michael revealed azurite blue paint. Jia-sun Tsang, unpublished treatment report, Conservation Analytical Laboratory Examination Report and Treatment Proposal, Paintings Conservation Department, Smithsonian Institution, CAL # 5286, March 26, 1991; and Jia-sun Tsang,

personal communication, 1995. See also Gavin and Pierce, "Altar Screens," 81–87, note 16.

47 H. Bailey Carroll and J. Villasana Haggard, trans. and eds., *Three New Mexico Chronicles: The Exposición of Don Pedro Bautista Pino, 1812; The Ojeada of Lic. Antonio Barriero, 1832; and the Additions by Don José Agustín de Escudero, 1849,* Quivira Society Publications Vol. 11 (Albuquerque, NM: Quivira Society, 1942), 2:99. In his exposition on the natural resources of New Mexico, Pino states, "There are soils of various colors—blue, green, yellow, white, red. In the Zuni pueblo, there is to be found a soil of an azure or Persian blue color which Don Bernardo de Miera, a mathematician and painter, has asserted could be made into a useful commercial product because it furnishes a perfect paint of that color." Carroll and Haggard, *Three New Mexico Chronicles*, 2:99. See also Gavin and Pierce, "Altar Screens," note 15.

48 Personal communication, Cordelia Thomas Snow, Archaeological Records Management Section of the Historic Preservation Division of the State of New Mexico, Laboratory of Anthropology, August 2016. See also the excellent article, Cordelia Thomas Snow, "Objects Supporting Ideas: A Study of Archaeological Majolica and Polite Behavior in New Mexico, 1598–1846," in *Inscriptions: Papers in Honor of Richard and Nathalie Woodbury,* ed. Regge N. Wiseman, Thomas C. O'Laughlin, and Cordelia T. Snow, Papers of the Archaeological Society of New Mexico 31 (Albuquerque: Archaeological Society of New Mexico, 2005), 187–197.

49 For discussion of majolica in general and Puebla Polychrome in particular, see John M. Goggin, *Spanish Majolica in the New World: Types of the Sixteenth to Eighteenth Centuries,* Yale University Publications in Anthropology 72 (New Haven: Yale University Department of Anthropology, 1968); Florence C. Lister and Robert H. Lister, *Andalusian Ceramics in Spain and New Spain: A Cultural Register from the Third Century B.C. to 1700* (Tucson: University of Arizona Press, 1987); Margaret Connors McQuade, *Talavera Poblana: Four Centuries of a Mexican Ceramic Tradition* (New York: Americas Society, 1999); and Robin Farwell Gavin, Donna Pierce, and Alfonso Pleguezuelo, eds., *Cerámica y Cultura: The Story of Spanish and Mexican Mayólica* (Albuquerque: University of New Mexico Press, 2003). The most comprehensive source on Mexican majolica remains Enrique A. Cervantes, *Loza blanca y azulejo de Puebla,* 2 vols. (1939; repr., Puebla, Mexico: Gobierno del Estado de Puebla, Secretaria de Cultura, 1987).

50 For examples, see Cervantes, *Loza blanca y azulejo,* 1:97, 101, 105, 107; Lister and Lister, *Andalusian Ceramics,* 238–239; and Gavin, Pierce, and Pleguezuelo, *Cerámica y Cultura,* 264–265.

51 Donna Pierce, "Mayólica in the Daily Life of Colonial Mexico," in Gavin, Pierce, and Pleguezuelo, *Cerámica y Cultura,* 265.

JONATHAN TAVARES

Adapting European Arms to the Americas
The Material Culture of Conflict in Colonial New Spain, 1500–1800

The material culture of arms and armor in the early colonial Americas has received little scholarly attention.[1] This void is perhaps relative to the scarcity of verifiable extant objects. Much of the imported arms and armor were produced of iron and steel, which was either reused or repurposed as a scarce material or corroded in the extreme climate. Organic materials—leather, textiles, and wood—were also used in abundance and similarly were subject to rot and decay. In one of the few general studies on the topic, Harold L. Peterson premised that the new environment faced by the Europeans forced rapid and gradual adaptations unique to the setting.[2] Through an examination of a series of rare surviving objects and written historical accounts, this chapter will build on Peterson's argument to explore the consumption, adaptation, and production of Spanish colonial arms and armor in Latin America. The objects and materials surveyed here include crossbows, steel armor, leather, ironwork, and firearms.

Crossbows

Crossbow fragments are among the earliest extant arms that were excavated in the 1960s and 1970s from shipwrecks of Spanish galleons off the coast of Texas. A trade convoy from Veracruz to Spain was hit by a massive storm in 1554, and three ships ran aground on a sandbar near the Padre Islands. Most of the uncovered artifacts are now housed in the Corpus Christi Museum of Science and History in Texas.[3] Although the crossbow fragments are all heavily corroded and rotted, several essential elements are remarkably intact, such as parts of the wooden stocks (body of the crossbow), steel bows, horn nut (portion that holds the drawn string), wedges to secure the bow, and an iron draw lever (fig. 1). The pieces are comparable to a contemporaneous Spanish military crossbow from a noble Valencian family armory that is now in the collection of the Art Institute of Chicago (fig. 2). The size and proportions of the bows match, and the stocks of the Padre Island crossbow fragments were fitted with brass or iron plates, inlaid flush with the wood in an identical pattern to those on the Art Institute's crossbow. The carbon steel bows of the Padre Island pieces would have taken two hundred to three hundred pounds of draw weight to pull back the string and would have been capable of shooting bolts thirty to fifty yards at point blank range.[4] These fragments document a mid-sixteenth-century uniquely Spanish use of military crossbows, at least fifty years after they

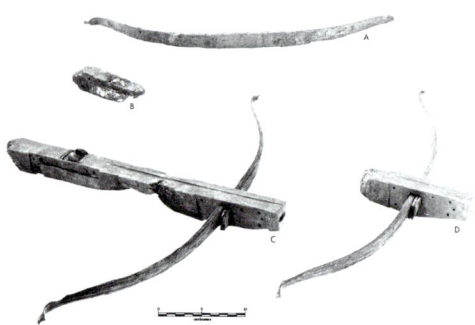

Fig. 1. Fragments of crossbows from a Spanish wreck off the coast of the Padre Islands, Texas. Spanish, before 1554. Corpus Christi Museum of Science and History.

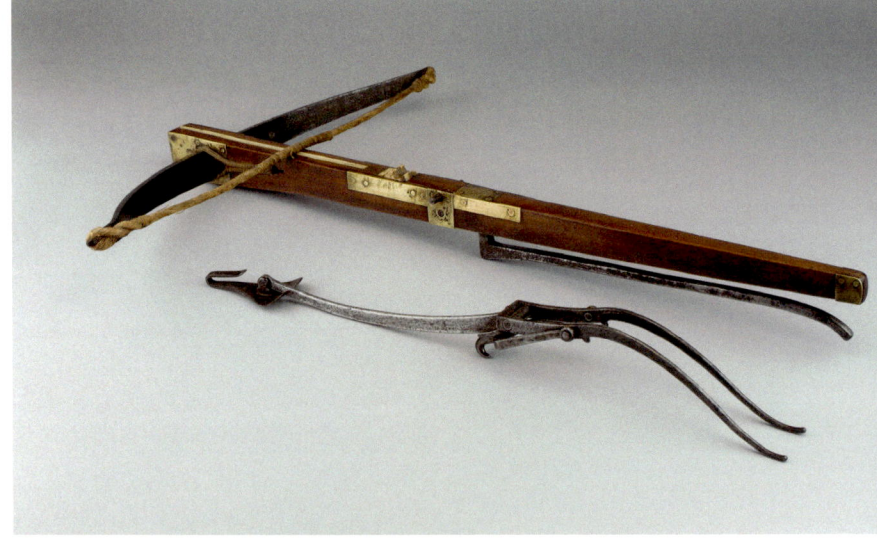

Fig. 2. *Crossbow.* Spanish, 1530–60. Steel, iron, brass, fruitwood, bone, and hemp. Art Institute of Chicago 1982.3073.

had been supplanted by firearms and gone out of general use in the rest of Europe. Earlier in the sixteenth century, in an account of the failed Panfilo de Narváez expedition to Florida (1527), Álvar Núñez Cabeza de Vaca describes scavenging the metal parts of crossbows to make nails for a boat to return to Mexico City.[5] At the end of the century, crossbows are listed among the armaments taken by Juan de Oñate on his 1597 expedition into present-day New Mexico.[6]

Why did the Spanish continue to use crossbows for quite so long after firearms became much more common? Long after a supply of gunpowder either spoiled, due to humidity and moisture, or ran out, there had been no means or infrastructure to produce more, and crossbows continued to be viable distance weapons. In his 1568 account of his experiences under Hernán Cortés decades earlier, Bernal Díaz del Castillo describes the replenishment of supplies:

Cortés therefore issued a circular notice to all the districts of our alliance in the neighborhood of Tezcuco, to send him each within the space of the next eight days, eight thousand arrow heads [crossbow bolt heads] made of copper; also an equal number of shafts, of a particular wood. By the expiration of the given time the whole number was brought, executed to a degree of perfection which exceeded the pattern. Captain P. Barba who commanded the crossbowmen ordered each of his soldiers to provide themselves with two cords and nuts . . . for one of the last ships which came from Castile had brought out a supply of the materials to make cords, and also powder.[7]

Copper was a metal found in abundance in the Americas, and Native production could ensure a lasting supply of copper bolt heads, whereas gunpowder was less viable to reproduce at this early stage. Copper crossbow bolt heads have been discovered at Blanco Canyon in Texas and Piedras Marcadas Pueblo in New Mexico, possibly encampments from Francisco de Coronado's 1540 expedition.[8] Scientific analysis of the lead isotopes in the copper crossbow bolts from these two sites reveals that they were produced from related alloy and probably from ore mined in Mexico.[9]

The archaeological evidence from these two Coronado sites also reveals a number of lead shots from arquebuses (smooth-bore barreled firearms) that demonstrates their presence alongside the crossbows. Indeed, Coronado's roster of equipment and weapons lists nearly an equal number of both, twenty to twenty-five each. In terms of efficiency, the time required to load and fire a crossbow or arquebus were roughly the same, fifteen to thirty seconds. Both are also mentioned in the published account by an anonymous Portuguese gentleman who accompanied Hernando de Soto on his 1539 Florida expedition:

Those people [the Natives of Florida] are so warlike and so quick that they make no account of foot soldiers; for if these go for them, they flee, and when their adversaries turn their backs they are immediately on them. The farthest they flee is the distance of an arrow shot. They are never quiet [standing still] but always running and crossing from one side to another so that the crossbows or the arquebuses can not be aimed at them; and before a crossbowman can fire a shot, an Indian can shoot three or four arrows, and very seldom does he miss what he shoots at.[10]

This passage describes a form of effective Native guerrilla warfare against the Spanish and Portuguese soldiers, who were more accustomed to open field engagements with infantry and cavalry formations. Crossbows and firearms were more effective under cover, which necessitated wearing either mail or steel plate armor. Over the course of the seventeenth century, there was a gradual shift from using both crossbows and firearms to relying entirely on firearms as distance weapons.

Mail and Plate Armor

Archaeological and documentary evidence reveals a pervasive use of steel mail and plate armor throughout the sixteenth century. Similar to the staying power of the crossbow in the Americas, mail armor was worn well into the seventeenth century, when it was in sharp decline in Western Europe. Steel plate armor more effectively deflected percussive blows; however, the steel mesh rings that made up mail armor had the advantage of being extremely flexible, could be made into garments, and the openwork of the links also allowed for ventilation, which was crucial in hot climates. For this reason, Iberian men-at-arms wore mail in place of and in combination with plate armor in the warmer Mediterranean throughout the sixteenth century.

The openwork of mail was not impervious, but the advantages must have outweighed the disadvantages, considering the hundreds of pieces of mail recorded brought to the Americas. The Portuguese man-at-arms in the de Soto expedition relates that Florida Natives used stone or bone arrowheads that often broke apart when hitting armor. The cane or reed could also splinter and "enter through the links of mail and are more hurtful."[11] Coronado's muster roll lists a total of nearly sixty mail shirts, various breaches, thigh defenses, sleeves, and collars.[12] Much later, the muster rolls of the 1597 Oñate expedition continue to list over a hundred mail shirts, some thigh defenses, breaches, and steel breastplates (corselets).[13] Some mail is described as coarse, and some fine, referring to the size of the riveted rings. Tailoring was a mark of quality on mail shirts, which could have as many as three or four different sizes of rings. Thicker or denser rings would make up collars and cuffs, while more open rings on sleeves would relieve some weight and allow for greater ease of movement. A fine shirt might have several hundred thousand rings and weigh up to fifteen pounds or more. Considering the masses of mail used by Coronado's men, it is no wonder that archaeological fragments have been discovered in several sites.[14]

The earliest archaeological discovery of mail from Spanish expeditions was made in the 1880s, near Paint Creek in central Kansas, consisting of a patch of heavily corroded mail of about two and a half inches in length.[15] Some have speculated that it was part of a trapper, a form of horse armor, but the small size of the piece does not allow for such a clear identification. The rings are thick and robust, with rivets closing the ends, and are entirely in keeping with fifteenth- to sixteenth-century European mail manufacturing. In 1959, more fragments (a few rings) were excavated at Paint Creek in middens, Native trash heaps. Around Cow Creek near the town of Saxman in Kansas, larger fragments of mail, the largest about 7½ × 2½ inches, were discovered in 1960 and 1974 (fig. 3).[16] Dating these finds precisely is impossible; however, judging by the Native pottery sherds from the same levels, the Cow Creek fragments appeared no earlier than the late fifteenth century and no later than the early eighteenth century. Plains archaeologist Waldo Wendel theorized that these fragments might represent "plunder from a destroyed expedition rather than stray pieces."[17] Mail shirts or items recorded in the Coronado and Oñate muster rolls might have been found or acquired by Natives, who may have kept or traded them over a long period of time. This is mentioned in various legends and eyewitness accounts of Plains warriors, such as the famous Comanche chieftain Iron Jacket (Pohebits-quasho), who wore an allegedly Spanish mail shirt that had been passed down to him by ancestors.[18] Several pueblo sites in New Mexico have also revealed mail fragments, which deserve further collective study.[19]

Very few fragments of steel plate armor have been found. One of the most telling is the excavated remains of a sallet that was discovered in the 1950s at the site of Yunque Pueblo (San Gabriel), which was made the first capital of present-day New Mexico by Oñate in 1598. The settlement was later abandoned in the seventeenth century in favor of the new capital, Santa Fe. The sallet was a type of light, open-faced helmet commonly used by archers, crossbowmen, and gunners throughout Western Europe in the fifteenth century (fig. 4). The San Gabriel sallet, with its shallow-boxed raised bowl, is distinctive and related to Spanish archers' sallets that usually featured flared brims, as seen in an intact example from about 1500, formerly in the Spanish castle of Guadamur in the province of Toledo and now in the collection of the Art Institute of Chicago (fig. 5). If the San Gabriel sallet was used by Oñate's troops at the end of the sixteenth century, the helmet would have been quite antique, nearly a century old. Wearing old armor was perhaps very common in New Spain, since serviceable steel armor, however unfashionable, was still an important resource. Ironically though, the helmet's preservation could owe to being discarded in the settlement's trash heap.

The San Gabriel helmet is very different from the traditional combed or pointed morions most popularly associated with the Spanish conquistador. Nevertheless, from the period of Christopher Columbus to Cortés, this sallet form was more commonly used by earlier conquistadors. One of the few examples of the traditional pointed morion or cabasset helmet form, which may have been used in New Spain, is in the Peabody Essex Museum in Salem, Massachusetts. It was given to the museum in 1821 by Samuel Curson of Havana, and a nineteenth-century paper label glued to the side

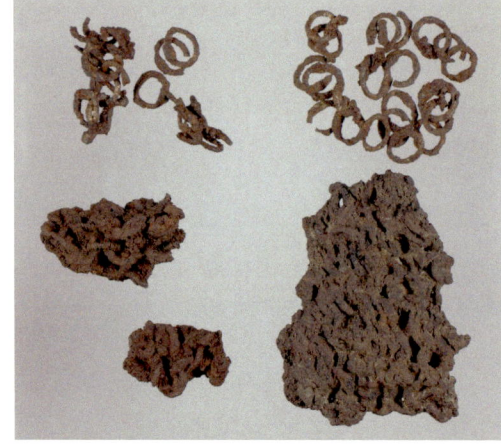

Fig. 3. Fragments of mail discovered in Cow Creek near the town of Saxman, Kansas. Western Europe, probably 1500s. Iron, the largest patch about 7½ × 2½ in. Kansas State Historical Society.

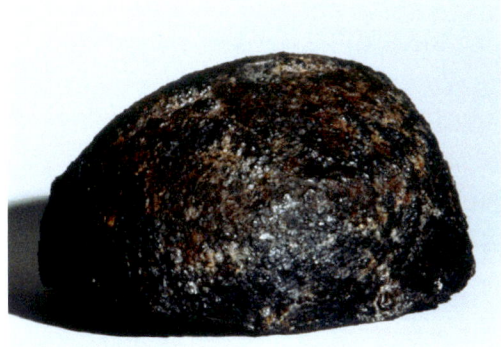

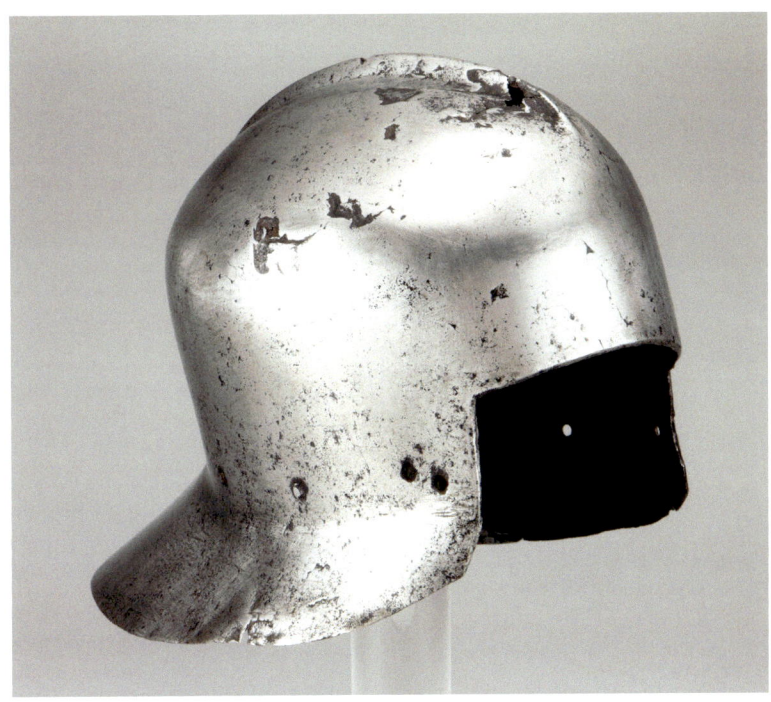

Fig. 4. *Helmet* (archer's sallet). Probably Spain, about 1500, discovered in the 1950s at the site of the Yunque Pueblo (San Gabriel). New Mexico History Museum, Palace of the Governors, Santa Fe (9773.45).

Fig. 5. *Helmet* (archer's sallet). Spanish, about 1500. Steel. Art Institute of Chicago, 1982.2471.

of the helmet bowl notes: "A Ancient Spanish H[elmet] found in Mexico and probably u[sed] by some of the followers of Cortez."[20] The helmet is well preserved, has never been in the ground, and retains its bands of etched decoration. It is a high-quality, munitions-grade officer's morion, produced around 1580–90 in Milan, a major armor-making center for centuries. As a part of the Spanish Empire in the late sixteenth century, Milanese armorers equipped all from the king to the common soldier, and morions were made in the thousands. The tall, almond-shaped bowl and horizontal brim of the Peabody Essex morion form approximated a steel version of the late sixteenth-century hat. Lost on the helmet are the additional cheek pieces and lining. The highly serviceable open-faced helmet provided glancing surfaces to ward off arrows, swords, club blows, and even musket or arquebus shots to some extent.[21] In Europe, helmets went out of fashionable use after the first half of the seventeenth century, and the same was presumably true for troops in the Americas. As gunshots became more powerful and commonplace, the helmets were less likely to afford the protection required, and their usefulness was outweighed by their discomfort in hot and humid environments.

Leather and Ironwork

In response to the unfamiliar climate in New Spain, the soldiers adapted and adopted more Native forms of armor made of textile, fibers, and leather. The strongest evidence for this comes from Coronado's muster roll that lists forms of body armor differentiated from Spanish or Castilian armor: "native armor," "buckskin coats," and "armor of this land." In the context of the mid-sixteenth century, this probably meant coats or padded caps of woven, braided, quilted, and layered cotton and bast (plant stalk) fibers with leather. For instance, on Coronado's roll, Juan de Villegas is listed with "armor of the country and for the head of double thickness."[22] Aztecs and other peoples of the Americas used quilted or padded armor known as an *ichcahuipilli* (cotton shirt), none of which survive from this period.

In the *Relación de las cosas de Yucatán* (1566), Bishop Diego de Landa briefly describes ichcahuipilli as "jackets of cotton, quilted in double thicknesses, which were very strong."[23] Based on Coronado's roll, it has been argued that Native weapons and armor were far more common than imported Spanish armor both among Spanish men-at-arms and the many Natives who journeyed with them.[24] The cotton armor afforded good protection against arrows and obsidian bladed weapons while having the advantage of relative light weight and breathability.

However, the use of cotton for defensive garments was not entirely unfamiliar to the Spanish.

Since at least the twelfth century in Europe, cotton was used to fashion padded defensive garments such as gambesons, or aketons, that were lightweight and breathable. By the sixteenth century, doublets, which were made of quilted wool and linen and padded with imported Mediterranean cotton, were worn under coats of mail or plate and used as a light form of armor on their own as well. The use of cotton armor vanished in the sixteenth century, while heavy leather coats for cavalry (buff coats) continued to be worn in the seventeenth century. In colonial America, a tradition of buckskin armor—long coats of leather and fiber called *cueras*—carried

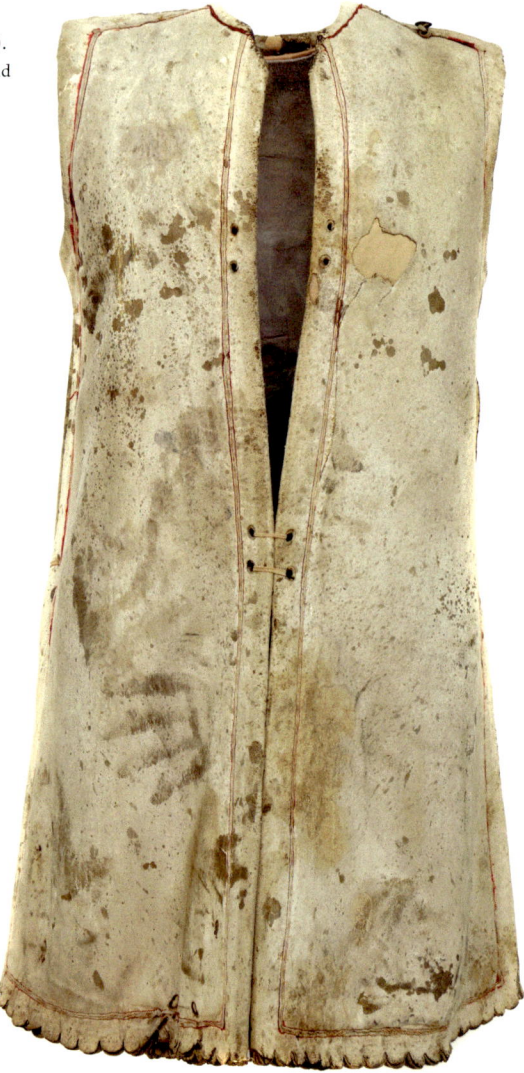

Fig. 6. *Cuera* (leather coat). Colonial New Spain, second half of the 1700s. Museo del Ejército, Toledo, Spain (43090).

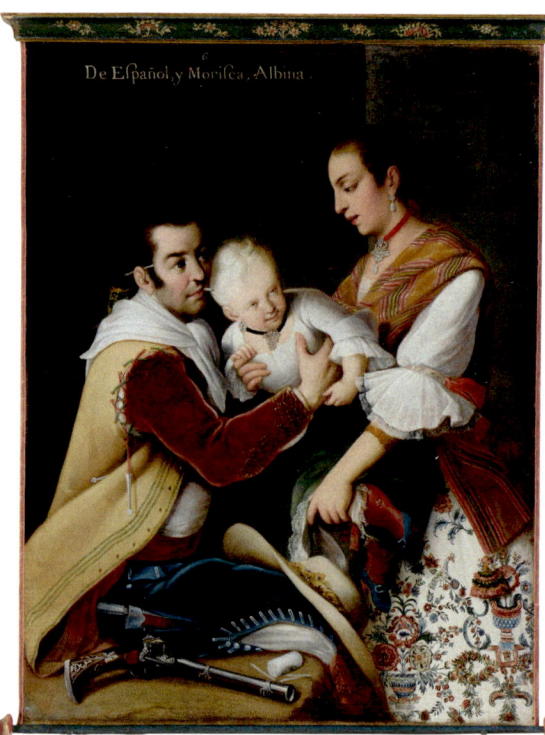

Fig. 7. Miguel Cabrera, 6. *From Spaniard and Morisca, Albina Girl (6. De español y morisca, albina)*. Mexico, 1763. Oil on canvas, 51⅝ × 41⅜ in. Los Angeles County Museum of Art, purchased with funds provided by Kelvin Davis in honor of the museum's 50th anniversary and partial gift of Christina Jones Janssen in honor of the Gregory and Harriet Jones Family (M.2014.223).

on well into the eighteenth and nineteenth centuries with the mounted *soldados,* or *dragones, de cuera.* Beginning in the seventeenth century, the dragones, or cavalrymen, protected the frontiers and presidios up and down New Spain and the interior provinces from modern-day Texas, New Mexico, and Arizona to California. Wearing large leather coats, they were outfitted like no other troops in Spain or any of its colonies. It is difficult to determine to what extent the cuera was developed from either European buff leather coats or Native forms.

Only one cuera, from among hundreds produced and used over a century, is known to survive from the second half of the eighteenth century, which is in the Museo del Ejército in Toledo, Spain (fig. 6). This cuera was preserved in the noble family of the Conde de la Cortina: an ancestor is said to have worn it as an officer in New Spain and returned to Spain with it.[25] The coat consists of several layers of buckskin and is ornamented with red cloth appliques, much of which is now lost and best preserved along the center back. The rectangular pattern of the coat has pairs of holes along the sides for laces or points that were tied to form a large, open-sided vest. The shape is much less tailored than European antecedents, and while the angular form of the shoulders recalls images of the Native ichcahuipilli armor, the construction of multiple layers of buckskin is unique to this type of coat armor. A 1763 casta painting in the Los Angeles County Museum of Art depicts a *dragón de cuera* wearing such a coat with points attaching red velvet sleeves that are trimmed with metallic thread embroidery at the cuff (fig. 7). These coats were not only protective but, like much of eighteenth-century military culture, also indicative of rank through relative differences in material adornment. Further analysis of this surviving cuera is necessary to better understand this sophisticated example of later leather armor.

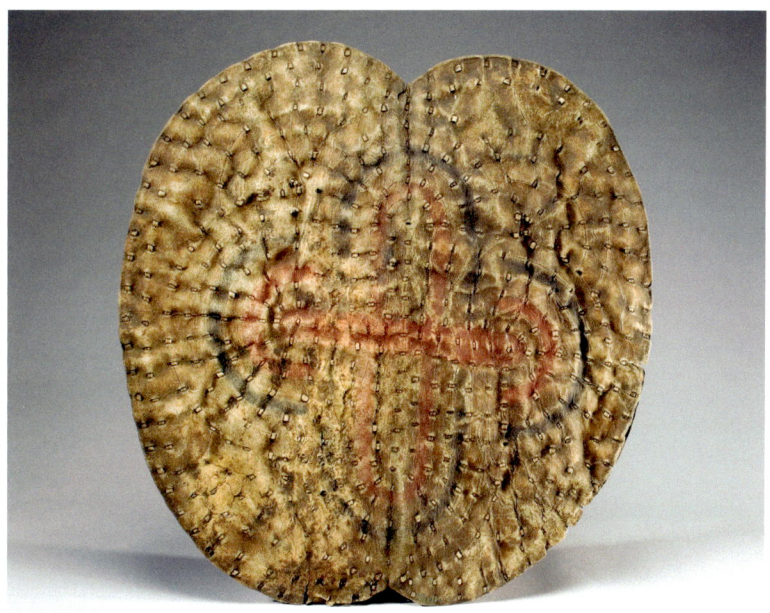

The hybrid nature of the dragones' equipment extends to another unusual article of layers of leather, the *ardaga,* or shield. These were derived from leather shields used by Arab, North African, or Berber light cavalry. These North African shields were transplanted to Spain during the Nasrid dynasty (thirteenth century) and remained in use well into the sixteenth century.[26] The ardaga's form is characterized by a double kidney or heart shape with handles made of two cords of leather on the inside. In New Spain, like the cuera, the ardaga was made using a Native layering technique that kept the pieces of leather together with lacings of hide, often forming elaborate crosses or a motif that resembles Solomon's knots. The precise origin and meaning of the latter remains unclear, though Helmut Nickel points out that it resembles the Aztec glyph for gold.[27] Several ardagas survive, including one in the Denver Art Museum that dates to the eighteenth century (fig. 8). Many surviving eighteenth- and nineteenth-century examples are painted with the arms of Spain.

There are a number of contemporary images of the dragones de cuera wearing their cueras,

Fig. 8. *Adarga* (shield). Mexican, probably 1700s. Leather and paint, 21 × 21 in. Denver Art Museum: Gift of James Economos, 1973.216.

using ardagas, and riding horses equipped with leather armor (trappers) to protect the neck and flanks of the beast from arrows. For instance, the bull-hide paintings of the last stand of Commandant Pedro de Villasur in 1720 represent Natives and Spanish dragones fighting other Natives and French troops.[28] The figures are readily identifiable according to the distinctive equipment associated with either tribe or country. The horses, reintroduced into the Americas by the Spanish, were an important and precious means of transportation, as the next presidio or settlement was often hundreds of miles away through harsh and hostile environments. Protecting a horse often made the difference between life and death. While in much of Europe horse armor gradually fell out of military use by the mid-sixteenth century, in Spain, to this day, picadors (mounted bullfighters) continue to use leather padded horse armor to protect them from gorging bull horns. Those used by the dragones were perhaps related, though no leather horse armor from New Spain is known to have survived.

A bizarre piece of scale armor in the Nebraska History Museum may be a hitherto unknown form of horse armor used by some unit of dragones de cuera, perhaps in the eighteenth century (fig. 9). Although this piece has traditionally been identified as a gorget (neck defense for a human), the dimensions of the piece seem more likely to be that of a peytral (defense for the breast of a horse).[29] In the 1870s, US cavalry surgeon Charles Styer gifted elements of armor to Captain John Gregory Bourke. Styer alleged that these elements, consisting of a breastplate, backplate, and helmet, were discovered encasing the bones of a supposed Spanish soldier in the arid lands between the Rio Grande and Pecos Rivers, an area also referred to as the Staked Plains. Today, the only extant pieces are the patch of scale armor and an iron helmet with a front brim. Bourke lost the breast- and backplate to theft, which also unfortunately robs

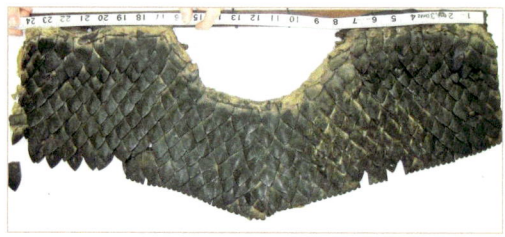

Fig. 9. Fragment of a scale armor (probably a peytral or defense for a horse's breast). Probably colonial New Spain, possibly 1700s–early 1800s. Iron, leather, and cotton twill. Nebraska History Museum, Lincoln.

modern scholars of more diagnostic clues to the relative age of the pieces. The breastplate was described as having brass rivets lining the sides, possibly a typical eighteenth- or early nineteenth-century European dragón breastplate. The iron baseball-cap-like helmet does indeed support this assertion, as it resembles a typical dragón helmet of the eighteenth century, albeit without any of its leather or fabric covering.

The chevron-shaped patch of scale armor has a lateral width of twenty-six inches and is made of over 302 scales, of which 280 were produced of smelted iron, rolled to uniform thickness, and stamped out into fishlike scales in a swage block. Flat or rectangular scales line the base of the piece, demonstrating that this is a finished edge, and that the piece must be largely intact. All the scales are riveted to a fibrous woven tape that is stitched to a cotton twill textile. Along the two ends are a few remains of leather strapping attached by iron screws and treaded washer-shaped nuts.[30] The chevron shape does suggest a neck defense, but with a dragón breastplate, such a piece seems largely superfluous and cumbersome. As a horse's peytral, the leather strappings could have fastened to either side of the saddle or further extensions. Scale armor is not efficient for joint movement over a human upper body, though for a horse it would remain suspended straight down and above the withers or joint above the legs and requires less flexibility.

Scale armor was generally unknown in Europe since antiquity and the late Middle Ages, while evidence indicates an established and advanced production of munitions-grade scale armor made in volume to outfit a unit of dragones. Several hundred other scales of identical form have been excavated in New Mexico, six of which are in the collection of the Metropolitan Museum of Art in New York City.[31] The iron used to make the scales was produced in a bloomery-smelting furnace, indicating that they were made before the more efficient industrial processes of the nineteenth century.[32] The production source of the smelted iron remains unclear, though it is reasonable to surmise that they were made in Mexico.

Ironwork production in Mexico must have existed and perhaps even thrived at the end of the seventeenth and into the eighteenth centuries. Aside from the extensive processes required to produce scale armor, there is further evidence in a unique expression of blacksmith art in New Spain, the forging of massive cruciform stirrups. The T- or cross-shaped stirrups appear to be entirely unique to New Spain and seem unrelated to any traditional Spanish form. They are characterized by two long, flat, side wings; a foot hole; and a long bent flange under the foot. These tours de force of forging seem impractical for riding and weighed as much as a considerable two and a half pounds each. A pair of stirrups in the Art Institute of Chicago are signed "Morales," dated 1732, and are elaborately pierced and chiseled with scrolling foliage inhabited with beasts (fig. 10). The decorative workmanship is relative to Spanish and central and southern Italian ironwork found on cup-hilted rapiers, knives, and firearm furniture or mountings from the seventeenth century. On stirrups, this ornamentation was adapted into a completely new form. In the Biblioteca Histórico Militar of Barcelona, a watercolor of an eighteenth-century officer from the "Interior Lands" or militia portrays the extent of the finery of a wealthy militiaman, parading in fine horse trappings and elaborate stirrups (fig. 11). The surviving iron stirrups give testament to a distinct material culture of the conspicuous consumption of these hacienda-owning militiamen that is largely lost. There is much potential for further research into this unique and complex aesthetic.

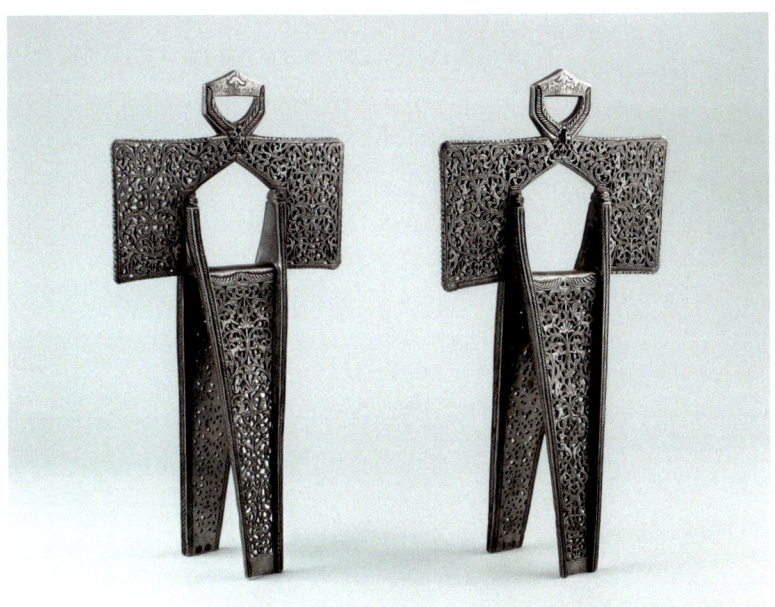

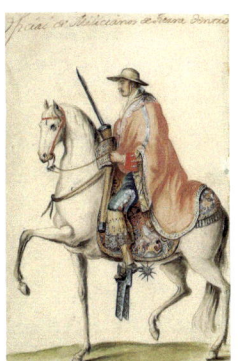

Fig. 11. Unknown artist, *Depiction of an Officer of the Militia of the Interior Lands (Oficial de milicianos de tierra dentro)*. Colonial New Spain or Spain, 1700s. Watercolor and ink on laid paper. Biblioteca Histórico Militar de Barcelona.

Fig. 10. Master Morales, *Pair of stirrups*. Mexico, dated 1738. Iron. Art Institute of Chicago 1982.2207a-b.

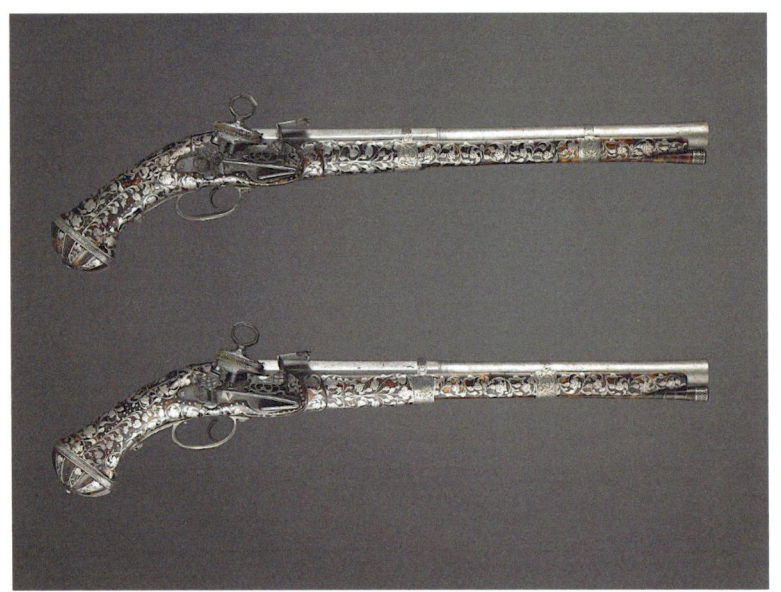

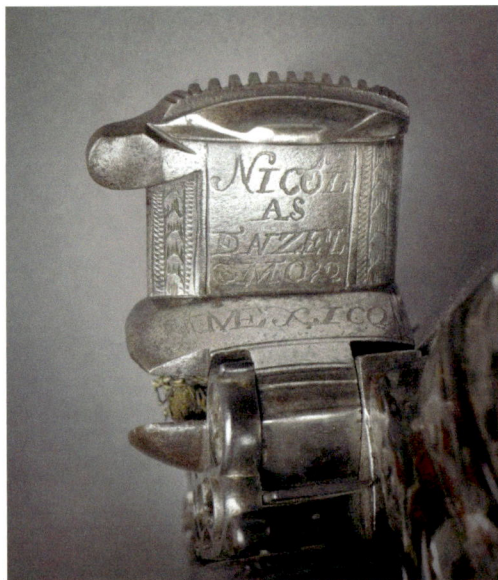

Fig. 12. Nicolas de Anzelmo, *pair of flintlock (patilla) pistols*. Mexico, dated 1692. Steel, silver, wood, tortoiseshell, and leather. Private collection.

Fig. 13. Detail of fig. 12, of the steel or frizzen of the flintlock pistol.

Firearms

One last example of arms speaks to the ambitious level of craftsmanship New Spain had reached in its Native production, just before the turn of the eighteenth century: a pair of tortoiseshell and silver overlaid bandolier (sash) pistols (fig. 12). These deluxe pistols are the earliest known signed and dated firearms made in Mexico. Engraved on the front face of the steel (frizzen) portion of the lock (the part that is struck by a flint when fired) are "De Anzelmo" and "Mexico." On the barrel, the date 1692 is engraved (fig. 13). Comprehensive research notwithstanding, a Nicolas de Anselmo (or Anzelmo) is recorded born in Mexico City in the district of Santa Veracruz in 1628 and is further recorded married to an Antonia Ruiz in 1666. Nicolas de Torres, an official gunsmith, or *arcabucero,* is listed as one of the witnesses.[33] This signing of the pistols demonstrates a certain pride in craft, and documentary reference to an official gunsmith in Mexico suggests that gunsmithing was practiced in New Spain at the highest level of skill and

must have been established for at least one full generation if not before the end of the seventeenth century.

The pair of pistols are most unique among a typical Spanish patilla, or miquelet (the Spanish and Mediterranean variant of flintlock ignition systems), in that they are entirely veneered in tortoiseshell with a ground of foil gilding over a native species of Florida dogwood. Oral tradition has linked the pistols to the viceroy of New Spain, but they may have been for Don Diego de Vargas (1643–1704), governor of the territories of Santa Fe de Nuevo México (1690–96, 1703–4), whose will gives to his son "two pairs of pistols, a bandolier of Anselmo."[34] The bandolier perhaps describes pistols of a certain type that are fitted with clips along their sides to fix onto the long, broad leather or textile belt that crossed diagonally over the torso. The year 1692 engraved on the pistols is the year de Vargas gained power as governor after famously taking back Santa Fe and the lands lost to the Pueblo Revolt of 1680. If these pistols were de Vargas's, they could have been presentation pieces given by Crown officials in recognition for regaining the lost territory. While these ideas are largely shrouded in speculation, the extraordinary use of materials and elaborate degree of decoration places these pistols in an august category reserved for the wealthiest and most prestigious.

The pair of firearms is yet another curious blend of influences on New Spain's material culture, such as the use of tortoiseshell that was influenced perhaps by objects traded with Southern India and East Asia. In seventeenth- and eighteenth-century New Spain, tortoiseshells were worked into caskets, frames, screens, and cabinets with silver mounts. Few tortoiseshell-stocked pistols are known, and most were produced in Augsburg and the Netherlands in the early seventeenth century and are unrelated to the pistols in question. Indeed, if Anzelmo had not signed "Mexico" on the lock, it would have been assumed that the metal fittings were made in Ripoll, a major center of Spanish firearms

production for centuries. Born in Mexico, Anzelmo may have learned his trade from his father, who himself perhaps emigrated from Ripoll or was familiar with the highly skilled art of gunsmithing from Ripoll. The revelation posed by these pistols is not only that New Spain had the ability to create such fine pieces of workmanship but also that scores of unsigned and hitherto unidentified colonial arms were made before and after these masterworks. This pair of pistols provides a window into a unique culture of arms that deserves the collaborative efforts of researchers, archaeologists, and object-based historians to situate in a more comprehensive global context.

Conclusion

At the beginning of the sixteenth century, Spanish conquistadors invaded the Americas armed with crossbows, firearms, cannons, horses, steel armor, and swords. This material culture of European conflict is encapsulated in a depiction of the arrival of Cortés in Veracruz that now

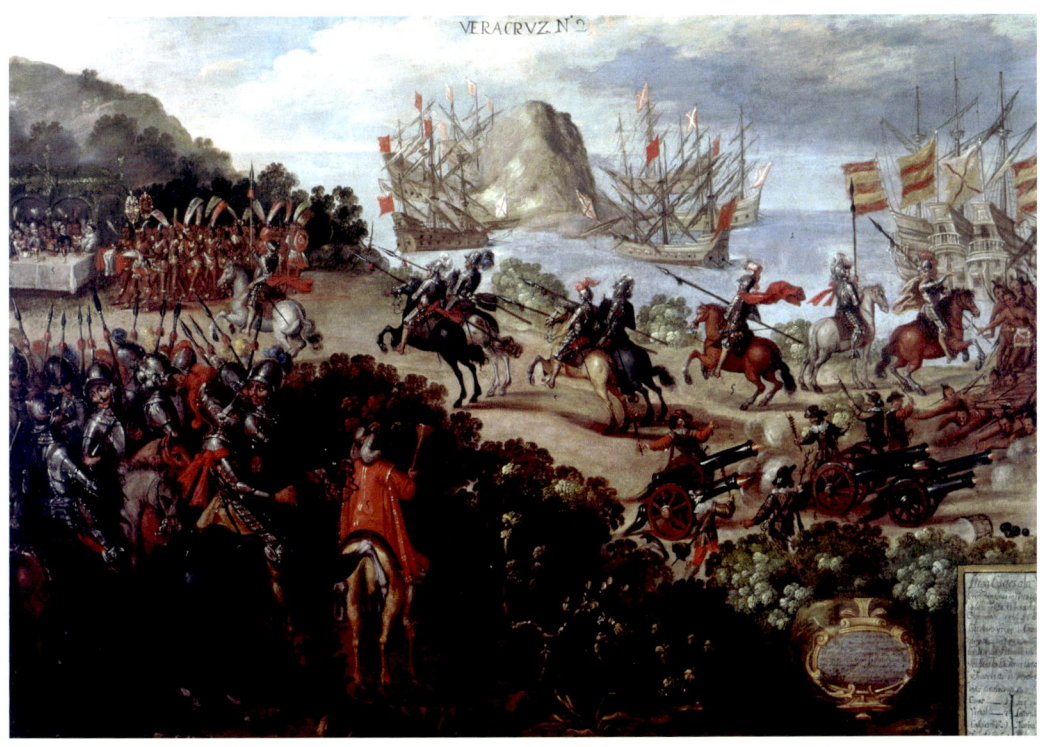

Fig. 14. Unknown artist, *The Arrival of Cortés in Vera Cruz and the Reception by Moctezuma's Ambassadors.* Colonial New Spain, second half of the 1600s. Oil on canvas, 47.2 × 78.7 in. Library of Congress (091.00.00), Jay I. Kislak Collection.

hangs in the Library of Congress (fig. 14). Painted by an anonymous colonial Mexican artist, the composition is teeming with blasting cannons and rearing horses, all strategically on parade to instill shock and awe in the Aztec dignitaries. It is a seventeenth-century allegory of Spanish military might, a fantastical image produced over a hundred years after the apocryphal event, one image of eight that presents a narrative of the triumphant conquistador. At the center of this narrative is an arms race that the Spanish prided themselves on winning. In reality, much of the steel and iron succumbed to the new environment, and the Spanish were forced to adopt and adapt more lasting native resources and forms.

From importation, to adaptation, and finally to hybrid and unique local production, the story of colonial Latin American arms and armor is both illusive and complex in its origins and influences. The few objects that survive, often in disconnected contexts, offer more questions than answers. The above examples provide only an alluring glimpse of a material narrative that is central in the history of New Spain yet rarely touched on. This research relied on a scant overview of a handful of known extant objects and published sources. Fundamental questions remain about such basic things as the evidence for the first iron smelting and gunpowder production in the Americas. Answers may perhaps be found in unsearched period accounts, ship manifests, and muster roles in the General Archives of the Indies in Seville. Also awaiting attention are colonial household inventories and administrative documents in local holdings. There is an abundance of archival work yet to be explored, to make up for the paucity of objects, to continue to draw links, to make major discoveries, and to formulate a fuller understanding of the material culture of arms and armor in the colonial Americas.

✝ ✝ ✝

Notes

1 The subject of Spanish American colonial arms and armor for the sixteenth and seventeenth centuries is touched on by Harold L. Peterson, *Arms and Armor in Colonial America 1526–1783* (Harrisburg, PA: Stackpole Company, 1956). Picking up where Peterson leaves off, illustrating known military examples of arms in private and public collections, is Sidney B. Brinckerhoff and Pierce A. Chamberlain, *Spanish Military Weapons in Colonial America 1700–1821* (Harrisburg, PA: Stackpole Books, 1972).

2 Peterson, *Arms and Armor,* 3.

3 Doris L. Olds, *Texas Legacy from the Gulf: A Report on Sixteenth Century Shipwreck Materials from the Texas Tidelands,* Texas Memorial Museum Misc. Papers 5; Texas Antiquities Committee Publication 2 (Austin: Texas Memorial Museum, 1976). On the crossbows that were discovered and their analysis, see J. Barto Arnold III, David R. Watson, and Donald H. Keith, "The Padre Island Crossbows," *Historical Archaeology* 29, no. 2 (June 1995): 4–19.

4 I am grateful to Jens Sensfelder for his knowledge of comparative draw weights and ranges for European crossbows.

5 Peterson, *Arms and Armor,* 7.

6 Peterson, *Arms and Armor,* 8.

7 Bernal Diaz del Castillo, *The True History of the Conquest of Mexico, By Captain Bernal Diaz del Castillo, One of the Conquerors, Written in the Year 1568,* trans. Maurice Keatinge (London, 1800), 280.

8 Alyson M. Thibodeau, John T. Chesley, and Joaquin Ruiz, "Lead Isotope Analysis as a New Method for Identifying Material Culture Belonging to the Vázquez de Coronado Expedition," *Journal of Archaeological Science* 39, no. 1 (January 2012): 58–66, doi:10.1016/j.jas.2011.07.025.

9 Thibodeau, Chesley, and Ruiz, "Lead Isotope Analysis," 5.

10 Knight of Elvas, *True Relation of the Hardships Suffered by Governor Hernando de Soto & Certain Portuguese Gentlemen during the Discovery of the Province of Florida: Now Newly Set Forth by a Gentleman of Elvas,* trans. James Alexander Robertson (DeLand: Florida State Historical Society, [1557] 1933), chapter 8, http://www.floridahistory.com/elvas-1.html, accessed May 31, 2019.

11 Knight of Elvas, *True Relation.*

12 Juan de Cuebas, *The Muster Roll and Equipment of the Expedition of Francisco Vázquez de Coronado,* trans. Arthur S. Aiton (Ann Arbor, MI: William L. Clements Library, 1939).

13 Original documents translated and edited by George P. Hammond and Rey Agapito, *Don Juan de Oñate, Colonizer of New Mexico, 1595–1628,* (Albuquerque: University of New Mexico Press, 1953), 5:226–85.

14 Waldo R. Wendel, "Chain Mail in Plains Archeology," *Plains Anthropologist* 20, no. 69 (August 1975): 187–96.

15 This fragment of mail is kept in the Kansas Museum of History by the Kansas Historical Society, Topeka (74.70).

16 Wendel, "Chain Mail in Plains Archeology," 193.

17 Wendel, "Chain Mail in Plains Archeology," 195.

18 Peter Bleed, Lindsay Long, Jessica Long, Madeleine Roberg, and David Killick, "Scale Armor on the North American Frontier: Lessons from the John G. Bourke Armor," *Plains Anthropologist* 60, no. 235 (August 2015): 216.

19 Mail rings have been discovered in New Mexico at the Santiago Pueblo, the Sevilleta Pueblo, and other various localities that were poorly documented. Charles Haecker, email message to author, March 26, 2019. One other fragment of mail that has come to be known and associated with the Coronado expedition is a mail glove consisting of a thumb and two fingers. This is said to have been found in Blanco Canyon near Floydada, Texas, and given to the Floydada County Museum in 1990. It is my belief, though not examined, that it is a fake produced from a modern twentieth-century butcher's mail glove to protect the thumb and two fingers of the off hand. The piece has little or no corrosion, unlike all other known excavated fragments, is made of butted not riveted rings, and is tailored in the round in a fashion not practiced for gloves in the sixteenth or seventeenth century.

20 Peabody Essex Museum, helmet (M4486). Information provided by Karina Corrigan, email message to author, July 15, 2019.

21 On the development and use of the morion, see Jonathan Tavares, "The Morion: Helmet of the Early Modern Soldier" (master's thesis, Bard Graduate Center, 2006).

22 Cuebas, *Muster Roll,* 15.

23 Friar Diego de Landa, *Yucatan Before and After the Conquest,* trans. and with notes by William Gates (New York: Dover Publications, 2012), chapter 29. Note: Gates points out a translation error where the word "tabb" used by de Landa has been thought to mean salt and implied that the cotton was soaked in brine (salted water) to harden it; Gates argues that the word is tab, describing rather that it was quilted and has nothing to do with brine.

24 According to Richard Flint, as much as 90 percent of the European portion of the expedition used Native arms and armor. Richard Flint, *No Settlement, No Conquest: A History of the Coronado Entrada* (Albuquerque: University of New Mexico Press, 2008), 62.

25 Later generations presented the *cuera* to the Spanish army in the nineteenth century. Gérman Dueñas Beraiz, curator at the Museo del Ejército (Army Museum) in Toledo, Spain, in email message to author, June 19, 2019. This coat and the equipment of the *dragones de cuera,* or presidio soldiers, is the subject of a forthcoming article by Beraiz for the *Anales del Museo de América*.

26 Helmut Nickel, "About the Adarga: A Shield of Two Faiths, Three Continents, Four Cultures and Seven Centuries," in *The Armorer's Art: Essays in Honor of Stuart Pyhrr,* ed. Donald J. LaRocca (Woonsocket, RI: Mowbray Publishing, 2014), 13–24.

27 Nickel, "About the Adarga," 22.

28 These are also known as the Segesser hide paintings, after the Swiss family that had possession of the hides since the mid-eighteenth century and sold them to the New Mexico History Museum in Santa Fe in 1988.

29 Bleed et al., "Scale Armor," 201. See also Hugh C. Rogers and Donald J. LaRocca, "A New World Find of European Scale Armor," *Gladius* 19 (1999): 225.

30 On the construction of the scale armor, see Bleed et al., "Scale Armor," 202–8.

31 Metropolitan Museum of Art (1998.366.1-6). See Rogers and LaRocca, "A New World Find," 221–30.

32 Bleed et al., "Scale Armor," 213.

33 Archivo General de la Nación, Instituciones Coloniales, Regio Patronato Indiano, Matrimonios (069), Vol. 194. I am grateful to Tatiana Seijas for finding this entry.

34 The original will of Diego de Vargas is housed at the New Mexico State Records Center and Archives in Santa Fe. A photostat copy is in the library of the University of Arizona: Diego de Vargas will (MS 064), Special Collections.

GABRIELA SIRACUSANO

Materiality between Mind and Hands
Some Approaches to Native Creativity in Colonial South America

In 1653, after many years wandering around the Americas, Jesuit priest Bernabé Cobo, regarding his ethnographical inquiries about the people of America—the Americas—would declare:

They display such limited use of logic and such sense-lessness that it seems as if they go around stupefied, without thinking about anything. Often, in order to investigate this matter myself, when I see them sitting still or sitting down, I ask them in their own language what they are thinking about. To this they ordinarily answer that they are not thinking about anything. I used to know an intelligent, bilingual Indian who was a tailor. Once while he was sewing, the Indian was asked by a friend of mine what he was thinking about. The Indian answered by asking how he could think about anything while working. In truth, this, I think, is what causes the Indians to do so well at any mechanical trade which they decide to learn. Their attention is not distracted to some other thing; rather all their faculties are employed exclusively in the task at hand.[1]

Pensar en nada, "to think about nothing." With this statement, Cobo is creating the argument for the belief of a certain way of reasoning and feeling that, in his perspective, turned the Native people of the Americas into a kind of automaton. His interpretation of this is their wandering around without any reasonable purpose, standing with their eyes open as if looking nowhere, or just moving their hands automatically to paint, carve, or hold an object while fixating their gaze on it. Imagination, invention, creativity, and ingenuity were qualities Cobo did not identify in their practices, not to mention the possibility of concentration or even mental evasion from their controlled activities! Although he accepted some nations were ahead of others concerning ability and ingenuity, he did not doubt himself in attributing ignorance and corruption of morals to all of them, with drunkenness—one of the ingredients of the ancient topic of paganism—as one of the origins. In the Americas, this topic would gain momentum when explaining or justifying evangelic actions. But the Jesuit priest also associated this mindless performance with their proficiency in the mechanical arts, and by the seventeenth century in Spain, Sebastián de Covarrubias would conceive of ingenuity as a natural force of understanding that could be applied to any liberal or mechanical practice developed by reason and speech.[2] Of course, Cobo's opinion was not the only one on this subject. Many years before him, José de Acosta would show his admiration of Andean ingenuity and industry in creating things such as fortresses and temples, "as seen in Cuzco, . . . where there are stones of immense grandeur that cannot be thought how they were cut, brought, and settled where they are."[3] When talking about the *khipus*, the mnemotechnic objects created by the Inka, Acosta would declare:

These Indians will take these grains, and will put one here, the other there, and eight who knows where: they will take one grain from here, they will exchange three of them from there, and in fact they come to have this sum very much precise without making any mistake. . . . If this is not ingenuity, and if these men are beasts, judge whoever wants, but what I judge as true is that in what they dedicate [themselves to], they give us great advantages.[4]

We also know how Felipe Guamán Poma de Ayala himself would try to explain to the king of Spain the fact that despite the lack of invention, ornament, and polished style in the writing of his *El primer nueva corónica y buen gobierno* (The First New Chronicle and Good Government), he offered him a variety of paintings "drawn by my hand and ingenuity"—the marriage between hand and mind that Cobo did not believe in.[5]

Between these two antagonistic concepts regarding Native people—that is, the assessment of their inventiveness but also the suppression of any intellectual activity within local communities—stood another skill. That skill was the capacity to imitate, or rather copy, art forms. Now, this "talent" granted to those who painted or carved any image would be the counterpart of the lack of originality, together with the presence of certain negative qualities that would be understood as inherent to Native people such as being rough and clumsy in their understanding (qualities that for the common Native people would also be linked to laziness and drunkenness, as I mentioned).

For decades, discourses about Spanish American art history were based on many of these parameters. While it is now possible to see how new theoretical and conceptual approximations anchored in the acceptance of otherness, the diversity of divergent and simultaneous aesthetics, and the untranslatability of the visual/textual regimes of one culture to another have allowed us to trace a new critical-aesthetic cartography on these productions, many written and visual tales are still weighed down with these preconceptions. Most of the time this manifests in the assignment of qualities such as "naivety" or "simplicity" to their beauty, or they are simply dismissed as extremely pious and given space in the curatorial realms of ethnographic and colonial museums but are not allowed to appear next to the artifacts, paintings, and sculptures in the "fine arts" museums of the world. Fortunately, this is changing every day. Ticio Escobar, who is the founder of the Museo del Barro of Asunción, Paraguay, is thinking about how to begin to reverse these curatorial dynamics in the art historical canon. He asks, "How can the edge of the aesthetic be defined in cultures that blend pure beauty with the bustle of the cult, the prosaic pursuits of food, and the complicated exercise of the social pact?"[6]

Now, can the archaeology of the material dimension and the anthropology of matter help to defuse these preconceptions? When I speak of archaeology of the material dimension, I mean the possibility of inquiring, of investigating the materiality of the aesthetic objects from an interdisciplinary perspective. Going through this process of investigation functions as an attempt to understand results that arise from the application of analytical methods and techniques derived from sciences such as chemistry and physics as the evidence and testimony of a network of cultural practices that made them possible. Even the work of those that has been placed under the magnifying glass of the most complex and sophisticated analytical equipment, and has been previously seen as irrefutable, must be interpreted in the new light of this cultural network, a meeting between weft and warp that is impossible to recognize without the intervention of other social sciences and conservation. It is for this reason, and especially as an art historian, that I appeal to these two specific terms that evoke the action of two disciplines that are not my own: archaeology and anthropology, the first as a science that studies human practices through material remains, and the second as a science anchored on the gaze of human behavior and human material and symbolic productions. Humanity and materiality: these are two sides of an equation that should never be blurred or lost sight of while scholars perform their tasks. To initiate interdisciplinary historical-artistic research based on the archaeology of the material dimension and on the anthropology of the matter, materiality must then be understood as a document of the past. This allows us to position ourselves differently in front of these artifacts and gives us the ability to identify the creative processes that took place during their creation.

Returning to the original question: can an archaeology and an anthropology of matter contribute to overcoming those prejudices regarding the place given to the creativity and intellectual ingenuity in the fabrication of the artifacts by diverse local social actors in colonial South America?

Searching for Creativity in Colonial South America

For several years, our team has been developing various research agendas around the sacred sculpture *Our Lady of Copacabana* (Bolivia; fig. 1) by Francisco Tito Yupanqui. Regarding his creative process in 1583, I have on many occasions mentioned how he—a rough and clumsy

yet good Christian, according to the written sources—was seeking a license in Potosí that would allow him to carve and paint images without any restrictions.[7] These written sources show how he started wandering and visited many churches in order to find a good model; that is, the best prototype to copy from. After many days, he found the one that fit his expectations at the Santo Domingo church, which housed the sculpture of the Virgin of the Rosary, a sixteenth-century Spanish image. The Augustinian chronicler Ramos Gavilán describes this moment as such: "He put his eyes on her with strange attention, wishing that the idea of the

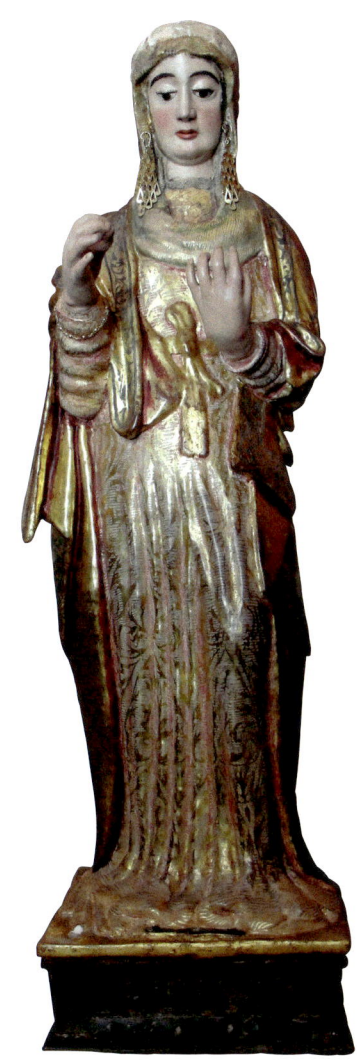

Fig. 1. Francisco Tito Yupanqui, *Our Lady of Copacabana.* Bolivia, 1583. Polychrome wood, maguey, glued fabric, and paper, 39⅝ × 11¼ × 12⅝ in. Basilica of Our Lady of Copacabana, Copacabana, Bolivia.

original image could be imprinted in his mind, so that afterward, and due to its prototype and look, he could give birth to his so beloved work."[8] This statement describes a very precise moment, that of the *invenzione,* of creativity, at which this rough Native artist would define the conceptual model of the image he wanted to create by means of an operation that would involve not only mechanical but also intellectual skills.

Regarding these mechanical and technical skills, recent research our team has completed has allowed us to discuss in depth the materials and techniques that Tito Yupanqui selected and used for the fabrication of *Our Lady of Copacabana,* thanks not only to multiple analytical techniques but also to a thorough contrast between these signifiers and those coming from the textual and visual worlds (fig. 2). This research allows scholars to identify the use of Spanish traditional polychrome technique and how it was combined with local materials that have particular religious significance or other meaning such as atacamite and lapis lazuli pigments.[9] This also allows the comparison between the techniques and materials utilized to create the Virgin and those

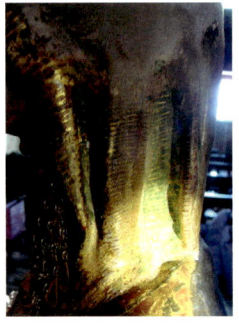

Fig. 2. Detail of the veil of the *Our Lady of Copacabana.*

Fig. 3. Hernández Galván y Francisco de Vargas, *Retablo of Ancoraimes.* Bolivia, 1500s. Polychrome wood, approximately 16 × 13 ft. Bolivia.

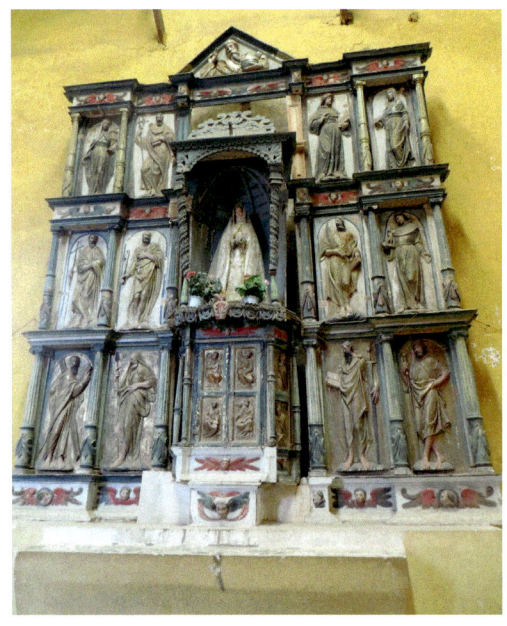

used in the retablo, or altarpiece, in a church in Ancoraimes, Bolivia (fig. 3), which supposedly Tito Yupanqui worked on by day with a Spanish painter called Vargas while painting the sculpture by night. The results were astonishing. Both the sculpture and the retablo have the same exact technique and presence of atacamite.[10]

While on the subject, I would like to pay specific attention to the imagination that is implicated in the process of creating these works and how it can be tracked with visual and material choices. Here, I want to discuss the specific attitude toward attention and mnemonic operations, the desire not to make a common copy but to produce a new, original image by actively appropriating some features of a model, which could imply putting them in contrast with one's own cultural expectations. This refers to a mental and manual accommodation of one's own and foreign technical traditions and aesthetics applied within a new representational horizon. Also, this act seems to display a physical instant of immobility, of stillness while observing the model: that "strange attention," an immobility that, in terms of European symbolic and iconographic gestures, had frequently stood as a symbol of melancholy, inspiration, and creativity. But in the New World, that same immobility would embody negative attitudes toward local creators.

Creativity in the Guarani Jesuit Missions

There must have been many intimate and non-shareable moments that occurred in many Native workshops. The Native artisans were not expected to develop their own vision but rather to create good copies from models brought to them from Europe. But as we will see, that was not always what happened. For example, in the Complejo Museográfico Provincial Enrique Udaondo of Luján in the province of Buenos Aires—the largest museum collection in Argentina—there is a small canvas of a portrait of the Virgin Mary (fig. 4). Until 1992, on the opposite side of the canvas there was a handwritten script that read "J. M. Kabiyú, fecit, Itapúa, 1618." Itapúa was the location of one of the Jesuit reductions in the Guaraní territories.[11] Seeing as how one, if not the main, purpose of the Jesuit order in the Americas was to create the kingdom of God on Earth, according to Spanish royal plans, there were certain influences in everyday practices. The manufacturing of images at the Jesuit province of Paracuaria was especially heavily influenced by this purpose or goal but also aided in solidifying the order's purpose: making sure everything led to the exaltation of the triumph of faith in pursuit of eternal salvation.

It is well known how the diverse Native peoples of the region took part in this process, and the historically written sources and local art historiography have often pointed out Natives' ability to copy as a characteristic feature. Father Antonio Sepp, one of the first Jesuit missionaries in Paraguay, would recognize that Native people "imitated like monkeys everything they see." He would also admit that "these poor devils are like artisans so skilled and with so much facility to learn that although it may look incredible and sound like a fable . . . everything they have in front of their eyes they can make very easily."[12]

However, let us return to the Virgin Mary portrait. In 1969, Jesuit Father Guillermo Furlong would say that although an unknown Native person—J. M. Kabiyú—was mentioned on the back,[13] it was "more than probable" that the French coadjutor brother Louis Berger "had much to do with its composition" and that the Indian must have been his pupil.[14] Josefina Plá would later attribute it to Father José Brasanelli, another well-known Jesuit artist, moving the painting's chronology to a later date.[15] Much later, Bozidar Darko Sustersic would agree and

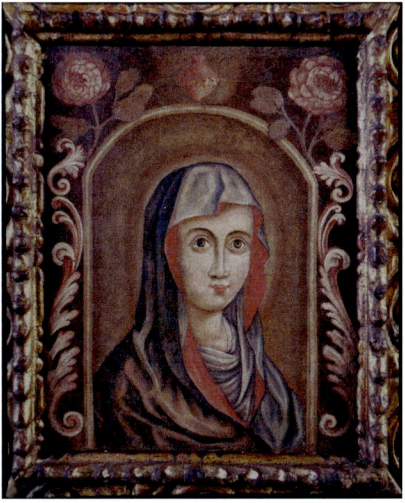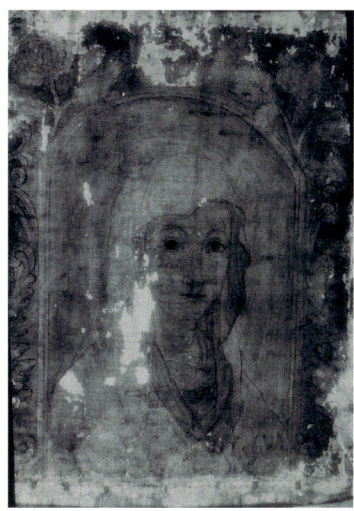

attribute this painting to the skillfulness of Brasanelli, even though he understood that the signature of Kabiyú indicated a Native contribution.[16] Thus, the question must be posed: is the identification of two different artisans enough to explain what is happening here?

At the beginning of the 1990s, the scholar Héctor Schenone would offer yet another interpretation. In 1992, the Tarea Foundation, a private foundation devoted to the conservation and restoration of art, was established in Argentina.[17] It focused on carrying out investigations on hundreds of paintings, including the Virgin Mary portrait discussed here, and was led by Schenone. Due to the foundation's efforts, it was discovered that the signature on the wood was almost a copy of an original manuscript inscription on the reverse side of the canvas. The difference was in the name: Habiyú instead of Kabiyú. Schenone paid attention to the dating, attribution, and iconography of the piece. He noted that the calligraphy seemed to be later than 1618, as well as the fact that "at the same time . . . the image of the heart of Mary, located in the upper part of the painting, [referred] to a devotion created by San Juan Eudes fifty years later."[18] He also noted that in Guaraní, the name Habiyú stands for *velludo* (hairy)

Left: Fig. 4. J. M. Kabiyú, *Portrait of Virgin Mary.* Jesuit Guaraní Missions, Itapúa, Paraguay, 1618. Oil paint on canvas, 7⅞ × 7⅛ in. Complejo Museográfico Provincial Enrique Udaondo, Luján, Argentina.

Right: Fig. 5. Transmitted light and infrared light photograph of the *Portrait of Virgin Mary* (fig. 4).

and *lanudo* (shaggy), which was probably the painter's nickname.

In addition, if we consider that Itapúa was founded in 1615, Schenone suggested that it was quite improbable that only three years later a painting workshop was up and running in the mission, despite Berger's presence. During the restoration of the Virgin Mary portrait, another element was discovered that added to our understanding. A photograph taken with transmitted light and infrared film revealed the presence of an underlying preparatory drawing (fig. 5). While Sustersic would attribute it to Berger, noting a difference between this drawing "of evident European hand" and the schematic and frontal painting done by a skilled Native painter, Schenone surmised it was an action performed by a Native painter "skilled in handling brushes and also a very good drawer."[19] Finally, Sustersic also pointed out something very interesting when he suggested that "he who made it must have been an expert in body painting, who was a sculptor and also a mask painter." Sustersic concludes this due to the frontal representation of the Virgin, as well as the emphasis given to her

Fig. 6. Unknown artist, *Trinity.* Jesuit Guaraní Mission of Trinidad, 1700s. Polychrome wood, approximately 59 × 87 × 39 in. Museo de La Plata. Universidad Nacional de La Plata, Province of Buenos Aires, Argentina.

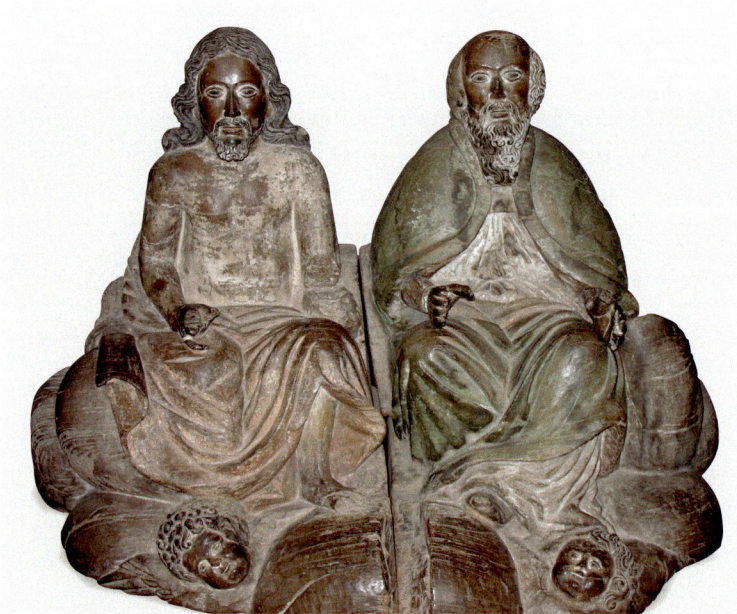

gaze by her big eyes and the relationship with the spectator.[20]

Now, when we observe the painting and its underlying drawing, many of these comments seem reasonable. The sketch shows a fine and subtle line that defines a delicate portrait while the painting displays a different poetic, reminding us of Mary's Byzantine-style portrait from the Valencia model, as Schenone would suggest, but that, as we will see, also embodied many local gestures.

What seems clear is that we are seeing the result of an action that cannot be explained only by inventive copying, translation, or the application of certain style categories. If the image was produced by a Guaraní or even by the Jesuit Berger, what we have here is a dynamic practice moved by mental, sensorial, material, and aesthetic gears every time an image emerges within the edges, the borders of different immeasurable cultural epistemologies, no matter how controlled it is. No one could have avoided this mechanism from the very first moment they got to know each other's cultural habits—an adaptation, an internal movement that demanded an intersection and exchange of knowledge, expertise, mental representations, material traditions, and ritual and religious practices, as well as social ones, belonging to different cultural horizons. A certain kind of invisible mobility provided the opportunity to choose, negotiate, approve, or even reject and challenge the other's choices, to the extent possible and of course always taking into account the inequality of the relationship. To try to understand this operation, we need to identify the material conditions that made the creation of these images in the missions possible.

The Paraguay Jesuits missions' inventories after their expulsion list many objects of different genres, from which we can infer not only the trades and materials involved but also the knowledge that was necessary to reach the mentioned goals: the creation of images and liturgical and paraliturgical objects that would strengthen the power of God in those lands.[21]

In general, the records emphasize the work and spaces of the carpenters, retablo makers, sculptors, painters, lathe turners, and silversmiths, as well as for those who made musical instruments. They show the presence of adzes, hammers, brushes for moldings, files, pincers, gouges, compasses, squares, lancets, brushes and tongs, grinding stones, steelyards, and scales, which made up the basic tools, all coming from the European tradition. As for the raw materials necessary for producing the images, the records reveal the presence of cedar wood, glass, canvas, bars of lead and silver, gold and silver sheets and powders, oils and gums, resins such as incense and turpentine, wax, paper, alum, and gypsum, as well as boxes and jars of colors from Castile: indigo, red carmine (the common one and one the painters name "Italian"), vermilion, *azarcon* (minium), "blue powders," verdigris, Prussian blue, shades from Italy, white, "yellow color" and orpiment, *almagre* (hematite), and Armenian bole.[22] By way of comparison, in the inventories of the missions of Loreto, San Pedro, Santa Ana, San Francisco de Borja, San Joaquin, and San Martín of the Moxos and Chiquitos missions in Bolivia, the materials mentioned are blue powders, white, "aseyte" ([sic] *aceite*; oil), plaster, "orpiment for the paintings of the Church," resins, "vermellon," "a parcel of Cuzco of colors," brazilwood, magnesium, orpiment, and bole.[23] That is, a palette as varied as that which could be found in any Spanish or Italian workshop; or in other words, the presence of a material tradition rooted in the names of Pliny, Heraclio, Theophilus, and many others. As for literature about art, the Jesuit inventories tell us about the use of *Arte de la pintura* (Art of Painting; 1649) by Francisco Pacheco, *El museo pictórico y escala óptica* (The Pictorial Museum and Optical Scale; 1715–24) by Antonio Palomino, *De' secreti del*

reuerendo donno Alessio Piemontese (The Secrets of Alexis of Piedmont; 1555), and Bernardo Montón's *Secretos de artes liberales y mecánicas* (Secrets of Liberal and Mechanical Arts; 1734). These manuals and books of secrets, published in quartos or in octavos and rooted in an ancient hermetic tradition, enabled a rather fast and synthetic transmission of recipes for making color or applying certain techniques.[24] In 1769, the second story of a Jesuit mission office showed the presence of two copies of *Secretos de artes liberales y mecánicas.*[25]

The cultural-historical and chemical analysis we have been doing since 2004 on many Guaraní Jesuit collections in Argentina and Paraguay held by such places as the Museo de La Plata (fig. 6), the Udaondo Museum of Luján, the Museo de Arte Hispanoamericano Isaac Fernández Blanco of Buenos Aires (fig. 7), the Museo del Barro of Asunción, and some smaller ones located near their missions enabled us to identify some of the ways all these materials were used. Saint Gregory Magnus (fig. 8) and Saint Leon Pope (fig. 9), two eighteenth-century sculptures carved out of cedar, or Guaraní *ygary,* that belonged to the Trinidad mission reveal the presence of copper resinate and malachite for the greens of their pluvial coats; traces of real hair; ochre over a mixture of gold and silver powders on their stoles; lead white; minium; vermilion; and hematite, all over a calcium sulfate preparation layer (though in some cases we found calcite). Another piece coming from the Trinidad mission is a niche that contained a tabernacle used for keeping the consecrated host (fig. 10). Its material dimension shows the presence of Verona green earth and Kassel earth (obviously imported by the Jesuits) and Prussian blue and indigo.[26] Father José Sánchez Labrador in his manuscript "Paraguay Natural Ilustrado" (Natural Paraguay Illustrated), written between 1771 and 1776, had included recipes for the Prussian blue that "today has

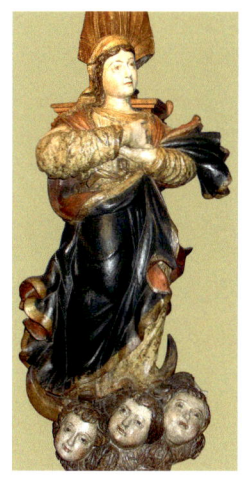

Fig. 7. Unknown artist, *Immaculate Conception.* Jesuit Guaraní Missions, 1700s. Polychrome wood, 33½ × 19⅛ × 14⅜ in. Museo de Arte Hispanoamericano Isaac Fernández Blanco. Buenos Aires, Argentina.

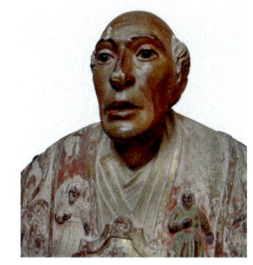

Fig. 8. Unknown artist, *Saint Gregory Magnus.* Jesuit Guaraní Mission of Trinidad, 1700s. Polychrome wood, 44⅛ × 27½ × 15 in. Museo de La Plata. Universidad Nacional de La Plata. Province of Buenos Aires, Argentina.

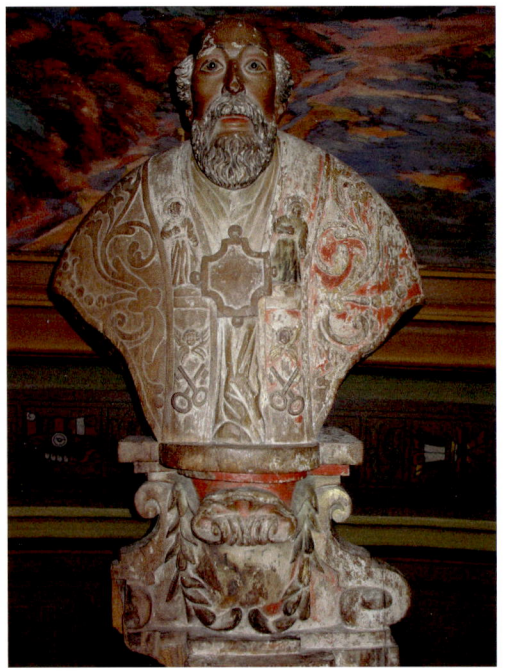

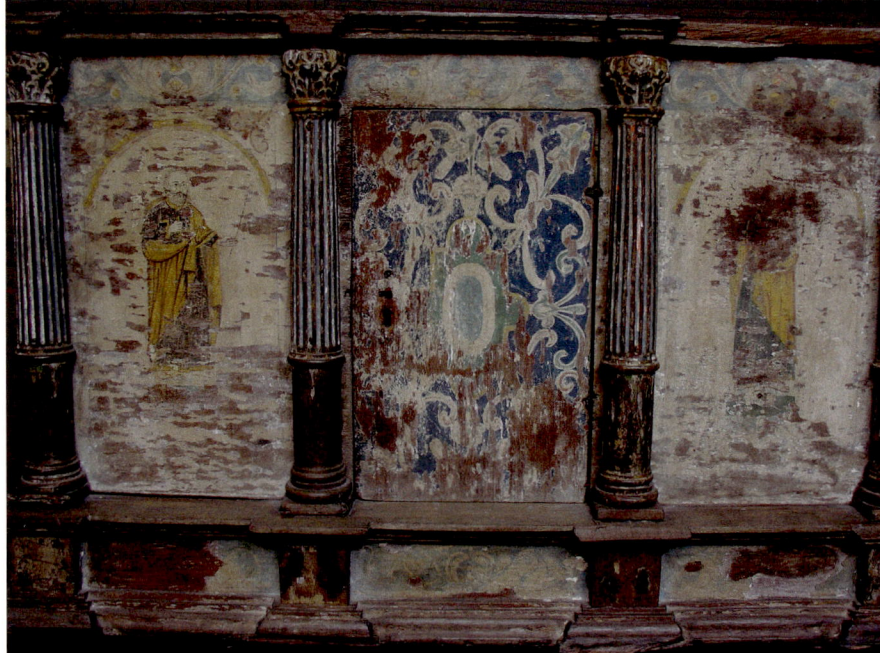

Left: Fig. 9. Unknown artist, *Saint Leon Pope.* Jesuit Guaraní Mission of Trinidad, 1700s. Polychrome wood, 44⅛ × 27½ × 11¾ in. Museo de La Plata. Universidad Nacional de La Plata. Province of Buenos Aires, Argentina.

Right: Fig. 10. Unknown artist, *Niche for a Tabernacle.* Jesuit Guaraní Mission of Trinidad, 1700s. Polychrome wood, 59 × 98⅜ × 27 in. Museo de La Plata. Universidad Nacional de La Plata. Province of Buenos Aires, Argentina.

become necessary for painting, as it replaces very well the ultramarine blue made of lapis lazuli," and also noted that the Indians from the missions could use it for their paintings.[27]

Within Guaraní cultural horizons, these materials would be appropriated by combining and matching them with their own. *Samu'ü,*[28] cedar, mud, shells, colorful parrot and other bird feathers, *urucú* (*Bixa Orellana,* or achiote), *kuudé* (hematite), and *ñandypá* (a blue substance from the *Harrisia bonplandii* species) were part of their aesthetic tradition and embodied their visual material epistemologies, which also implied festive, ritual, and healing connotations. To track these ancestral uses, we must look at some ethnographical records. Urucú (or *yruku* for the Chiripá and the Pai) is used for colorful face painting related to festive and feminine mythic meanings. As for the kuudé, or hematite, the Jesudi communities in Paraguay still use it for body painting on young single males during the Hobedei feast. Additionally, the ñandypá not only provided beautiful blue dyes but was also linked to heroes Avá-Nandí (a hunter for

the Chiripá culture) and Hy'apúguasuva and mythical figures with "glowing blue eyes," as Escobar notes.[29]

The healing and sacred quality that native Guaraní cultures granted to many of these materials ended up overflowing the limits of aesthetics, invading the very functions of the representations that held them. Balsams, resins, pigments, and dyes that were manipulated by different craftsmen in order to give brightness and color to these simulacra were also ground in mortars in the reduction's pharmacies. Resins, gums, and balsams like incense, sandaracca, mangays, turpentine, copal, balsam of Pará, Elemi gum, dragon's blood, or Aguaribay balm were the bases of varnishes, lacquers, and resinates applied for a matte or polished carnation, or to achieve a good estofado, but they also offered the power to heal the pains of the body. Félix de Azara said about Aguaribay:

In the missions of the Jesuits, . . . one finds in abundance the Aguaribay. . . . When [its branches] are rubbed comes a sticky liquid, whose smell resembles that of turpentine. . . . Fifty arrobas of leaves produce

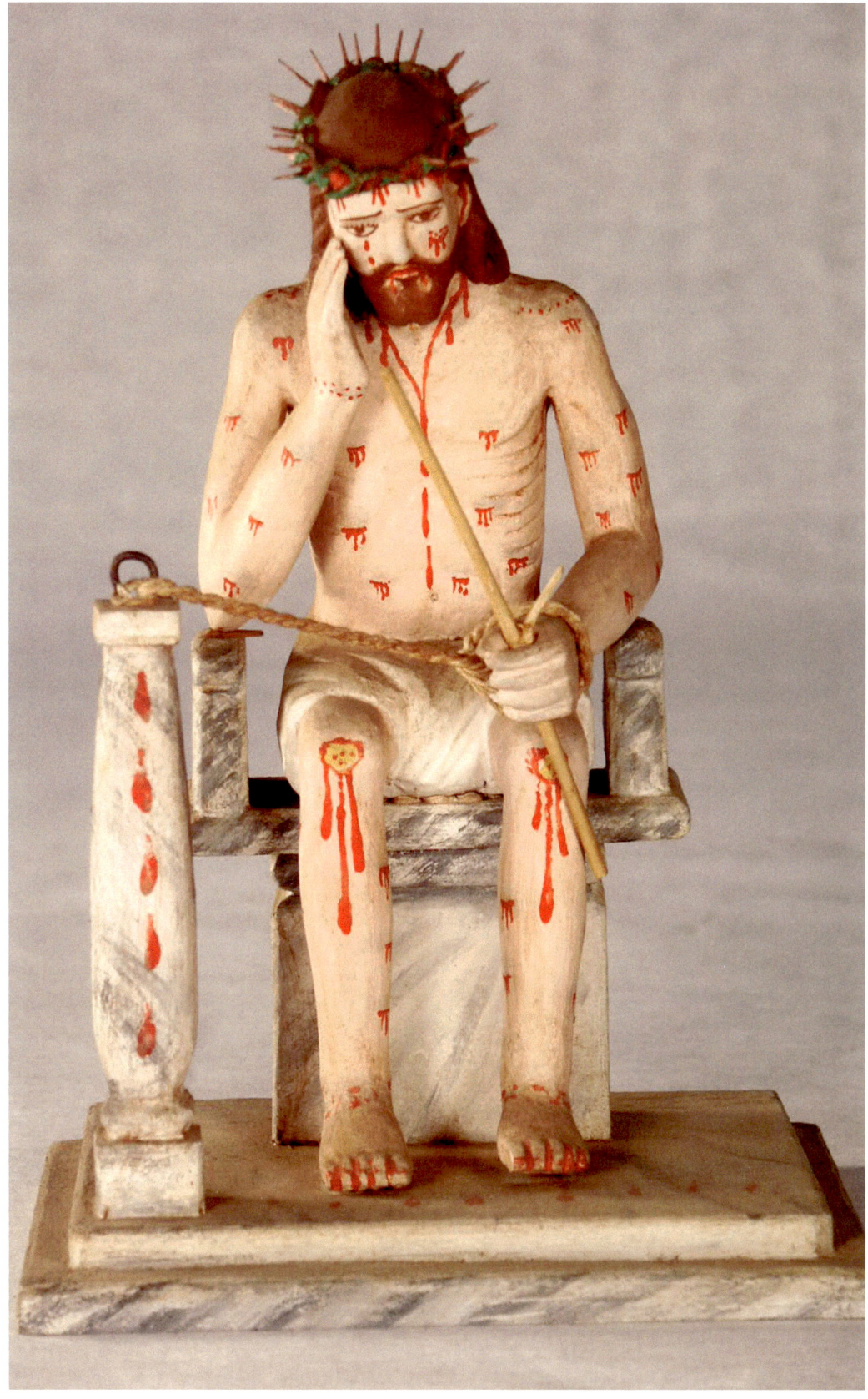

Fig. 11. Juan Bautista
Rojas, *Our Lord of Patience.*
Yaguarón (Paraguay), about
1985. Polychrome wood,
11 × 5½ × 7½ in. Centro de
Artes Visuales/Museo del
Barro. Asunción, Paraguay.

one of balm. Each of the Indian villages in which this tree is produced is obliged to provide at least two pounds every year, to be sent to the King's Pharmacy in Madrid. . . . It is ordinarily called cúralotodo, because it is a cure-all."[30]

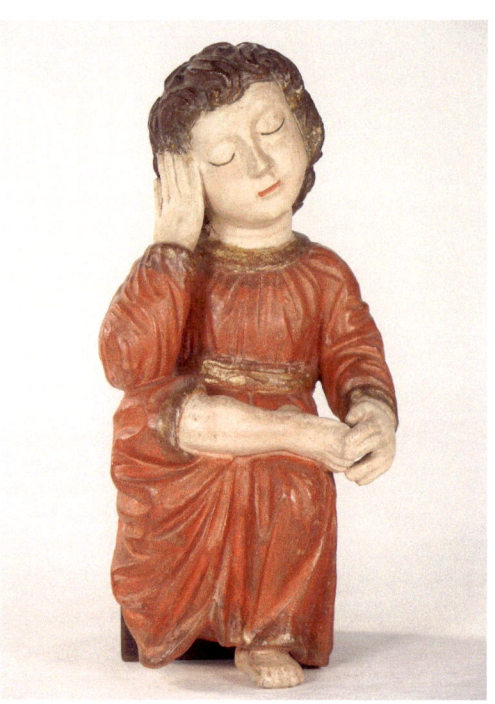

Fig. 12. Unknown artist, *The Child of the Spine.* Jesuit Guaraní Missions, 1700s. Polychrome wood, 11 × 5½ × 4¾ in. Centro de Artes Visuales/Museo del Barro, Asunción, Paraguay.

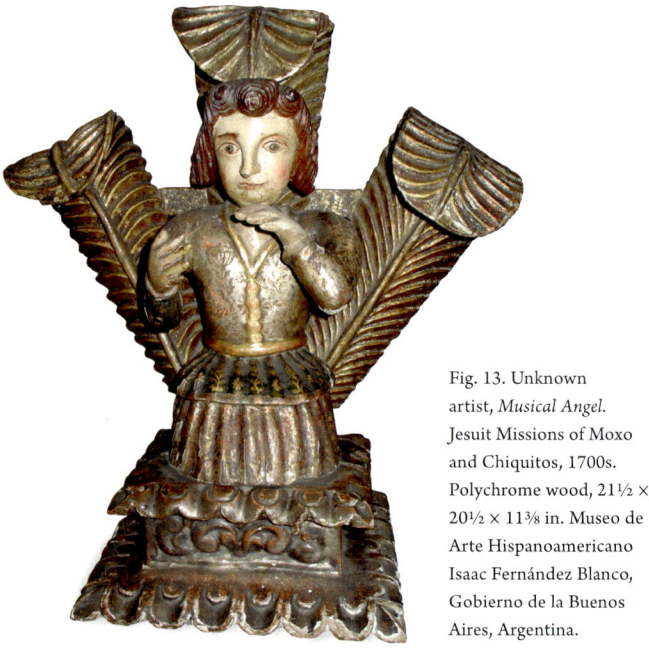

Fig. 13. Unknown artist, *Musical Angel.* Jesuit Missions of Moxo and Chiquitos, 1700s. Polychrome wood, 21½ × 20½ × 11⅜ in. Museo de Arte Hispanoamericano Isaac Fernández Blanco, Gobierno de la Buenos Aires, Argentina.

These and other materials would give "life" to sculptures (fig. 11) that, in many cases, offered a body and soul therapy. There are many testimonies talking about the faculty of crosses and images of saints healing ailments (usually associated with sinful practices), whether by touch, contemplation, or even ingestion of the powders from scratches.[31]

Regarding the woods used, cedar (*Cedrela fissilis*) was the most common. For the Guaraní it is the mythical ygary, which in Guaraní means "sacred tree from which the word flows." This wood, which is still used by Guaraní artisans to make zoomorphic carvings called *kagka* and *ta'anga,* served as support for the construction of most of the Jesuit and Franciscan images. Other species selected by the artisans were the Tembetary *guazú, anangapiry, arazay, querandy, yuatiy, ibiraucay* ("beautiful to make hands"), *guaribay, curiy,* and the Brazilian pine, or "tree of the missions." In the second half of the eighteenth century, Father José Guevara warned about the Brazilian pine's quality of sweating a natural purple varnish if a sculpture was exposed to heat. It is easy to imagine how this peculiarity was activated every time an image, while exposed to candles or the warm weather of the rainforest, seemed to be sweating blood, an interaction between materiality and ritual practices that contributed to their agency in religious and social terms.

Now, from a cognitive but also spiritual sense, the manipulation and domain of the Native people of this colorful and sensorial world of substances and matters go together with the way they managed to deal with a new representational system, so different from their Native cultural beliefs (or practices). Their chromatic universe (sometimes full of colors, like the Mbyá culture, and sometimes absent of them, like the Aché) was made up masks, body painting, basketry, pottery, flowers, and feathers (in diadems, plumes, chokers, and kilts), all forms that helped to establish social hierarchies among the community and to strengthen the social unit. As Escobar writes, "Like the myths (but also through them) those forms act as identity signifiers and guarantees of the social contract. . . . The beauty of the bodies garrisoned for the ritual and that of the exalted objects in their ornaments and their contours are not valid by themselves but as endorsements of the prosaic crafts and the serious certainties that the community needs to survive."[32] These features and qualities integrated an aesthetic based in a synthetic, frontal, and solid sense of forms, volumes, and bodies, a conceptual synthesis that also included stillness.

So, from the moment they became part of a new social and cultural order imposed by the Jesuits and even after their expulsion, at the time when some were relocated in the Franciscans' missions or just left the system to start new careers as *santo apoavá* (santo makers), a whole internal movement toward a creative process must have taken place in their impulse to copy or appropriate the new iconographies and their

ways of being part of a new numinous space but also to maintain and not betray their own, an impulse that still remains.

Many of the images held in the collections I have mentioned here have been attributed to the hands of Jesuits such as Louis Berger, Luis de la Croix, or José Brasanelli. Others have often been attributed to a nonskilled hand; therefore, to unknown Native artisans. Beauty, grace, fluency in the movement, proportion, rhythm, decency, expressiveness, and dramatism are the qualities mostly used to define the former; roughness, hardness, economy of lines, rigidness, volumetric, unexpressive, and schematic stand as marks of the latter.

In between, Jesuit and Native hands built this visual tale, surely negotiating traditions and expressive formulae. The Habiyú portrait is an example of this. The gaze and the solid bodies of many other Jesuit Guaraní images share with it that quiet expression that must have hidden their creators' internal feelings and ideas about divinity, or the sacred, and how to represent it (figs. 12, 13, 14, and 15). A whole inside movement differing

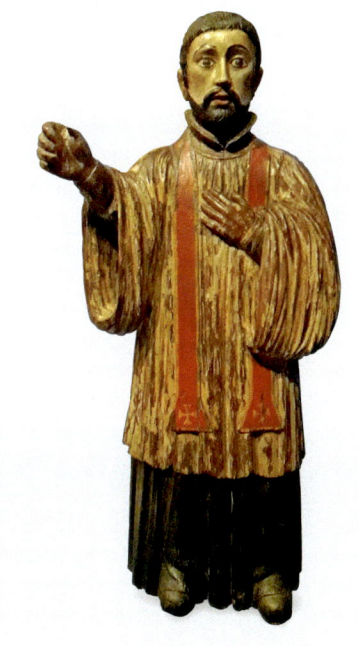

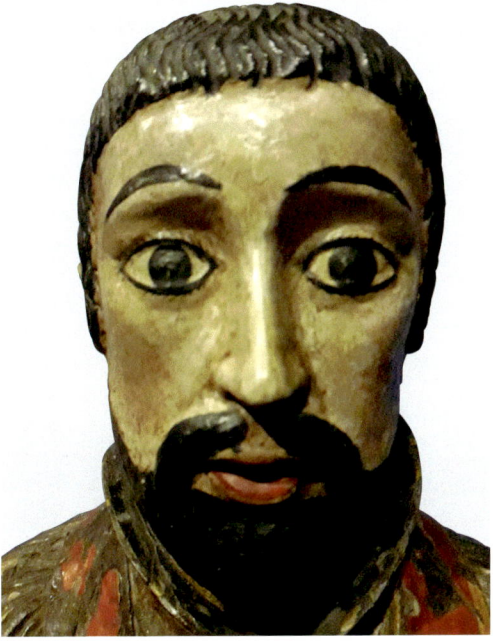

Far left: Fig. 14. Unknown artist, *Saint Francis Xavier.* Jesuit (Franciscan?) Guaraní Missions, 1700s. Polychrome wood , 33⅛ × 16½ × 10⅞ in. Museo de Arte Hispanoamericano Isaac Fernández Blanco, Gobierno de la Buenos Aires, Argentina.

Left: Fig. 15. Unknown artist, *Saint Francis Xavier* (detail). Jesuit or Franciscan Guaraní Missions, 1700s. Polychrome wood. Museo de Arte Hispanoamericano Isaac Fernández Blanco, Gobierno de la Buenos Aires, Argentina.

from what Cobo believed, that the artisans were thinking about nothing, as if no feelings or thoughts could emerge from those bodies.

The manual labor organization necessary for making the images (carvers; guilders; painters; eye, hands, feet, and face makers, etc.) must have found its correlate in the communitarian and cooperative form of work that Bartomeu Melià, one of the most important linguists and anthropologists in Paraguay, identified for the Guaraní with the word *potiró* (its translation is *manos a la obra*, which means "let's get to work").[33] This word, says Melià, derives, according to Antonio Ruiz de Montoya, from *po*, which means "all the hands," hands that, within a creative process very far from passivity and stillness, manipulated near and distant forms and materials in a way we still need to understand. The interdisciplinary study of materiality is a way to do this. In this sense, I wish that this idea of potiró would function as a trigger in our discussions, in order to help us rethink the intersections between art, science, and heritage as a key to taking into account all the hands and all the gazes.[34]

✝ ✝ ✝

Notes

1 Bernabé Cobo, *History of the Inca Empire: an account of the Indians' customs and their origin, together with a treatise on Inca legends, history, and social institutions,* trans. and ed. Roland Hamilton (Austin: University of Texas Press, 1979), book I, chapter 5, 22.

"*Muéstrense tan cortos de discurso e insensatos, que parece andan abobados sin pensar en cosa. No pocas veces, por hacer yo experiencia desto, les suelo preguntar en su lengua, cuando los veo parados o sentados, que es lo que están pensando. A lo cual responden ordinariamente que no piensan nada. Preguntando una vez un amigo mío a un indio ladino y de razón que yo conocía, estando trabajando en su oficio, que era sastre, en que pensaba mientras cosía, le respondió que como podía pensar en nada estando trabajando. A la verdad, esta, pienso, es la causa de salir estos indios tan bien con cualquiera oficio mecánico que se ponen a aprender: el no divertir y derramar la imaginación a otra cosa, sino que todos los sentidos y potencias ocupan y emplean en solo aquello que tienen entre manos.*"

Bernabé Cobo, *Historia del Nuevo Mundo,* vol. 3 (Seville: Sociedad de Bibliófilos Andaluces, [1653] 1892), book I, chapter 5, 29.

2 "Vulgarmente llamamos ingenio una fuerza natural de entendimiento investigadora de lo que por razón y discurso se puede alcanzar en todo género de ciencias, disciplinas, artes liberales, y mecánica, sutilezas, invenciones y engaños." Sebastián de Covarrubias, *Tesoro de la lengua castellana o española* (Madrid: Luis Sánchez, 1611), 504v.

3 José de Acosta, *Historia natural y moral de las Indias* (Seville: Juan de León, 1590), book 6, chapter 14, 419. Unless otherwise noted, all translations are my own.

4 "Verles otra suerte de quipos, que usan de granos de maíz es cosa que encanta. Porque una cuenta muy embarazosa, en que tendrá un muy buen contador que hacer por pluma y tinta, para ver a como les cabe entre tantos tanto de contribución, sacando tanto de acullá, y añadiendo tanto de acá, con cien retartalillas, tomarán estos Indios sus granos, y pondrán uno aquí, otro acullá, ocho no se donde: pasarán un grano de aquí, trocarán tres de acullá, y en efecto ellos salen con su cuenta hecha puntualísimamente sin errar un tilde, y mucho mejor se saben ellos poner en cuenta y razón, de lo que cabe a cada uno de pagar, o dar, que sabremos nosotros dárselo por pluma y tinta averiguado. Si esto no es ingenio, y si estos hombres son bestias, júzguelo quien quisiere, que lo que yo juzgo de cierto es, que en aquello a que se aplican, nos hacen grandes ventajas." Acosta, *Historia natural,* book 6, chapter 8, 411–12.

5 "Primer Nueva Corónica de las Indias del Peru y provechoso a los dichos fieles cristianos, escrito y dibujado de mi mano e ingenio, para que la variedad de ellas y de las pinturas y la invención y dibujo a que Vuestra Majestad es inclinada, haga fácil aquel peso y molestia de una lectura falta de invención y de aquel ornamento e pulido estilo que en los grandes ingenio se hallan." Felipe Guamán Poma de Ayala, *El primer nueva corónica y buen gobierno* (1615) (Copenhagen, Det Kongelige Bibliotek [Royal Library of Denmark], GKS 2232 4°, http://www5. kb.dk/permalink/2006/poma/info/en/frontpage. htm). See also Thomas B. F. Cummins, "*Dibujado de Mi Mano:* Martín de Murúa as Artista," in *Manuscript Cultures of Colonial Mexico and Peru: New Questions and Approaches,* ed. Thomas B. F. Cummins, Emily Engel, Barbara Anderson, and Juan M. Ossio A. (Los Angeles: Getty Research Institute, 2014), 35–64.

6 Ticio Escobar, *La belleza de los otros: Arte indígena del Paraguay* (Asunción, Paraguay: Centro de Documentación e Investigaciones de Arte Popular e Indígena del Centro de Artes Visuales, 1993), 28.

7 Eugenia P. Tomasini, Fernando Marte, Valeria P. Careaga, Carlos Rúa Landa, Gabriela Siracusano, and Marta S. Maier, "Virtuous Colours for Mary: Identification of Lapis Lazuli, Smalt and Cochineal in the Andean Colonial Image of Our Lady of

Copacabana (Bolivia)," *Philosophical Transactions of the Royal Society A: Mathematical, Physical and Engineering Sciences* 374 (2016), https://doi.org/10.1098/rsta.2016.0047.

8 Alonso Ramos Gavilán, *Historia del Santuario de Nuestra Señora de Copacabana* (Lima, Peru: Ignacio Prado, [1621] 1988), 219.

9 Eugenia P. Tomasini et al., "Virtuous Colours for Mary."

10 Gabriela Siracusano and Agustina Rodríguez Romero, eds., *Materia Americana: El cuerpo de las imágenes hispanoamericanas (siglos XVI a mediados del XIX)* (Buenos Aires: UNTREF, 2020), 259–69.

11 José Emilio Burucúa, Alejandro Bustillo, Mercedes de las Carreras, Victoria Filipelli, Andrea Jauregui, José X. Martini, Diego Ortiz, Héctor H. Schenone, Alicia Seldes, and Gabriela Siracusano, *Tarea de diez años* (Buenos Aires: Ediciones Fundación Antorchas, 2000).

12 Antonio Sepp, *Continuación de las labores Apostólicas: Edicion Crítica de la Obras del Padre Antonio Sepp S.J., Misionero en la Argentina desde 1691 hasta 1733 / a cargo de Werner Hoffman.* (Buenos Aires: Eudeba, 1973), 3:270.

13 Guillermo Furlong, *Historia social y cultural del Río de la Plata 1536–1810: El trasplante cultural: Arte* (Buenos Aires: Tipográfica Editora Argentina, 1969).

14 "El trazo seguro y fluido devela la mano de un artista con sólida formación y experiencia que no podía ser otro que Berger, pues no había por entonces pintores con calidad artística de esta naturaleza. También ha quedado registrado el nombre de otro discípulo del H. Berger llamado Esteban, como se escribe en la Carta Anua que brinda la noticia de su muerte, expresando hace tiempo instruido por nuestro hermano Luis Berger en el arte de pintar. Este indio inmortalizó por sus sagradas imágenes, con las que ha provisto a varias reducciones y diferentes colegios." Carlos Page, "El jesuita francés Luis Berger: Un artista del Paraguay en los albores del siglo XVII," *Temas Antropológicos* 38, no. 2 (April–September 2016): 73.

15 Josefina Plá, *El Barroco Hispano-Guaraní* (Asunción, Paraguay: Universidad Católica "Nuestra Señora de la Asunción"; Intercontinental Editora, 2006).

16 Bozidar Darko Sustersic, *Imágenes Guaraní-Jesuíticas* (Asunción, Paraguay: Centro de Artes Visuales/Museo del Barro, 2010), 71.

17 The Tarea Foundation is an enterprise established by Argentina's National Academy of Fine Arts and the Antorchas Foundation.

18 Burucúa et al., *Tarea de diez años,* 263.

19 Burucúa et al., *Tarea de diez años,* 263.

20 Bozidar Darko Sustersic, "Arte Jesuítico Guaraní y sus estilos: Argentina-Paraguay-Brasil" (PhD diss., Universidad de Buenos Aires, Buenos Aires, Argentina, 2010), 72–73.

21 Gabriela Siracusano, "El eterno destello," in *Catálogo de Imaginería religiosa* (Asunción, Paraguay: Centro de Artes Visuales/Museo del Barro, 2008), 1:63–79. See also A. T. Fazio, L. Papinutti, B. A. Gómez, S. D. Parera, A. Rodríguez Romero, G. Siracusano, and M. S. Maier, "Fungal Deterioration of a Jesuit South American Polychrome Wood Sculpture," *International Biodeterioration and Biodegradation* 64, no. 8 (December 2010): 694–701.

22 Archivo General de la Nación (AGN) Buenos Aires, Argentina, Colonia, Gobierno section, Temporalidades de Misiones, 1768–78.

23 See Gabriela Siracusano, *Pigments and Power in the Andes: From the Material to the Symbolic in Andean Cultural Practices 1500–1800* (London: Archetype, 2010), 10–22.

24 Siracusano, *Pigments and Power,* 10–22.

25 See Adolfo Ribera and Héctor Schenone, *El arte de la imaginería en el Río de La Plata* (Buenos Aires: Instituto de Arte Americano e Investigaciones Estéticas, 1948), 110.

26 Gabriela Siracusano, Marta Maier, Blanca Gomez, Eugenia Tomasini, and Leontina Etchelecu, "Entre todas las manos: La dimensión material de la imaginería jesuítica guaraní," in Siracusano and Romero, *Materia Americana,* 259–69.

27 The original handwritten version of this unpublished manuscript is held by the Archivum Romanum Societatis Iesu (ARSI), the Jesuit archives in Rome.

28 The *palo borracho de flor blanca* (white silk floss tree; *Ceiba chodatii*), also called *yuchán,* is a botanical species from a tree coming from the subfamily Bombacoideae, originally from the tropical and subtropical jungles of South America.

29 Escobar, *La belleza de los otros,* 28.

30 Félix de Azara, *Viajes por América Meridional,* vol. 1 (Buenos Aires: Elefante Blanco, 1998), 101–2.

31 See Gabriela Siracusano, *El poder de los colores* (Buenos Aires: FCE, 2005), chap. 4; and Elianne C. Deckmann Fleck, "Las reducciones jesuítico-guaraníes: Un espacio de creación y de resignificación (Provincia Jesuítica de Paraguay, siglo XVII)," *Cuadernos de Historia: Serie Economía y Sociedad* 7 (2005): 71–96.

32 Ticio Escobar, *El mito del arte y el mito del pueblo* (Santiago: Metales Pesados, 2008), 57.

33 Bartomeu Melià, "Potirõ: Las formas del trabajo entre los Guaraní antiguos 'reducidos' y modernos," *Revista Complutense de Historia de América* 22 (1996): 183–208, http://revistas.ucm.es/index.php/RCHA/article/view/RCHA9696110183A.

34 This research has been possible thanks to the Complejo Museográfico Enrique Udaondo of Luján, Museo de Arte Hispanoamericano Isaac Fernández Blanco, Museo de La Plata of Argentina, and the Museo del Barro of Paraguay.

EMMANUEL ORTEGA

Consuming the Host
The Materiality of Franciscan Anxiety in Eighteenth-Century New Spain

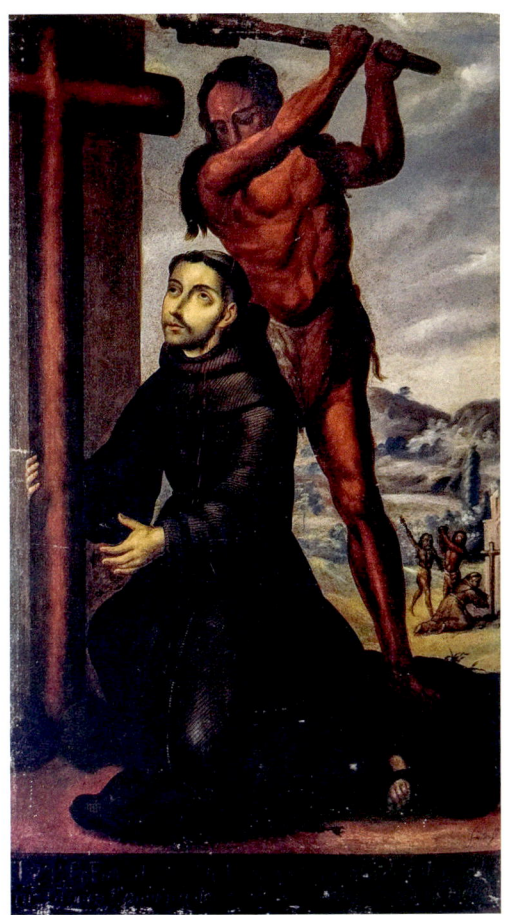

Fig. 1. Diego Sanabria, *Portrait of Fray Francisco Casañas de Jesús*. Mexico, mid-1700s. Oil paint on canvas. Museo de Guadalupe, Zacatecas, Mexico.

The *Chronica apostolica y seraphica de todos los colegios de Propaganda Fide,* written in 1746 by Isidro Félix de Espinosa, recounts the lives and deaths of several Novohispanic martyrs who died at the service of the order in the far lands of places like Sonora, Costa Rica, and New Mexico. According to these types of accounts, the zeal of these holy missionaries began early in their lives. Fray Francisco Casañas de Jesús (fig. 1), for instance, was infatuated with the cross as a kid, thus foreshadowing his future death as a missionary in New Mexico. As a child, Casañas de Jesús directed his attention to the cross:

He was always constructing small chapels, far away from his house, made out of sedge and other branches. On top of those chapels he would place a cross made out of wood and he would decorate it with flowers.[1] . . . [Years later,] the Apache Indians, who were rioting with the Pueblos and who represent the cruelest of people . . . saw him all alone at the cemetery. . . . When the time arrived, [Fray Francisco] quickened his step to hug the cross that he had placed in the cemetery, and after kneeling in front of the sacred wood, they discharged on his head a macana with such fury that they broke his skull, bathing his entire body with his own blood.[2]

To entice other novices to follow in the footsteps of Fray Casañas de Jesús and other martyrs, a genre of painting known as hagiographic martyr portraiture developed in New Spain. Diego Sanabria's portrait dates back to the mid-1700s when the production of hagiographic images intensified, partly as a consequence of the numerous battles of Native resistance in the provinces of the Spanish Empire in the Americas. The paintings were displayed in portrait galleries inside Franciscan colleges and monastic spaces to showcase the zeal and commitment the seraphic order practiced in defense and expansion of the colonies (fig. 2).

Daniel Miller defines material culture as a set of objects that exist "not through our consciousness or body, but as an exterior environment that habituates and prompts us" and argues that objects have the capacity "to implicitly condition human actors" and become "the primary means by which people are socialized as social beings."[3] As such, for the purpose of this chapter, I propose that the supremacy of Franciscan authority over their colonized subjects, the supposed divine call that allowed for many atrocities to take place during the campaigns of spiritual conquest, will be defined through the material culture represented in these images. More specifically, I will analyze the ideological juxtaposition between the instruments of conquest (e.g., the crucifixes present in almost every hagiographic portrait), Native weapons (e.g., bows, arrows, macanas, and axes), and the theological arguments used to define them. An analysis of these objects will permit us to better understand the modes in which the Franciscans sought to define their history in the Americas and their superiority over Natives.

The Paintings

No clear stylistic claim can be made in regard to these portraits; however, their instructional qualities are undeniable. All images exalt the precise moment when the flesh turned into spirit, and the earthly existence of the missionary is transformed into a holy martyr presence, a missionary goal highlighted in many hagiographies written in New Spain. The paintings, similar to the writings they were abstracted from, urged novices' scrutiny and affective response by placing the suffering of the martyr in the foreground of the composition. Natives' defiance against conversion is represented as aggression against the Franciscans and not as defensive actions of resistance. Thus, most portraits typically feature the first blow directed at the monk in the foreground of the compositions. In Casañas de Jesús's portrait, for instance, the barbarian towers over the kneeling friar, augmenting the threat of the action he is about to commit. As your eye moves toward the back of the images, the sequential narrative culminates in the middle ground. The barbarian, once again, appears in action, perpetrating visceral murders against seemingly helpless missionaries. This

Fig. 2. Ex Colegio Apostólico de Propaganda Fide de Nuestra Señora de Guadalupe (Old Apostolic School of the Propagation of Faith of Our Lady of Guadalupe), Guadalupe, Zacatecas, view of the present portrait gallery, 2018. Museo de Guadalupe, Zacatecas, Mexico.

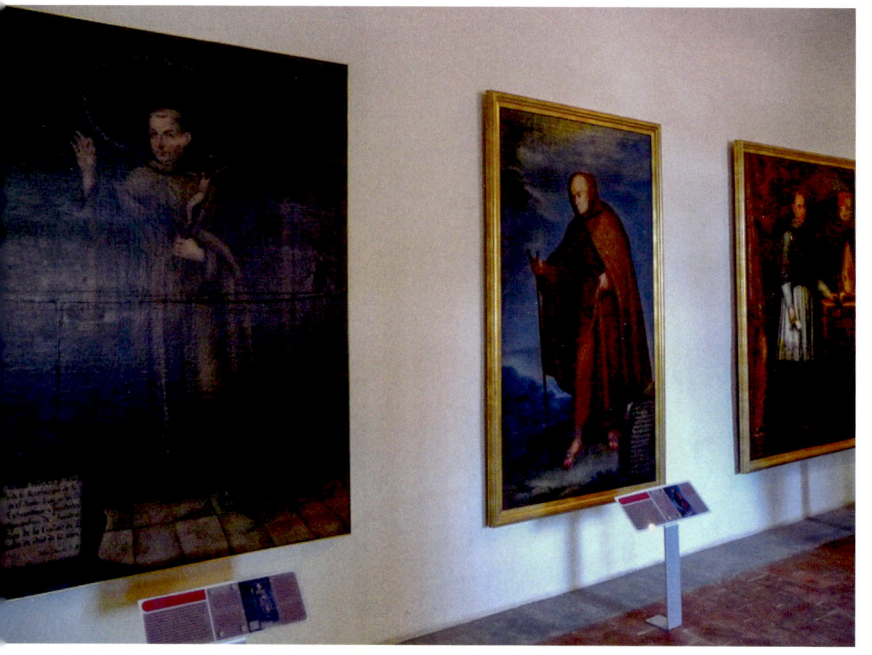

helped consolidate a narrative corresponding to hagiographic works that always rendered Native uprisings as savage aggressions.

The Revolt

The New Mexican Pueblo Revolt of 1680 (hereafter referred to as the "Pueblo Revolt") gave rise to a generalized anxiety about the internal provinces of New Spain. The insurrection was driven by a long period of administrative instability, missionary intolerance, excessive demands from the governors, abuses, and, overall, more than four decades of conflict. Generally speaking, Native resistance was a constant threat that fed the imaginations of Franciscans and viceregal authorities alike. The administration of the missions was also affected by the events of 1680. New tactics were developed to secure the safety of the territories. Luis Navarro García notes a correlation between the construction of the presidios (fortified base establishments that were under direct Spanish control) and the Pueblo Revolt, noting that "the catastrophe of Nuevo Mexico . . . had shaken the tranquility in which matters were conducted at the Council of Indies . . . , [and] that in repeated occasions the inaction of the viceroy was violently reprimanded, and the simultaneous construction of four different presidios was ordered."[4] Furthermore, fueled by the fear of viceregal authorities of being scolded directly by the Crown, the frequency and implementation of royal *visitas* (inspections of missions and presidios to the north) increased after 1685. Thus, the Pueblo Revolt created a collective administrative anxiety, which changed the empire. The rise of a new genre of images depicting the conflicts in the north was then necessary.

The College of Propaganda Fide, which housed most of the paintings analyzed here, appropriated this fear as a tool for recruiting novices to become missionaries. This monastic institution was established in New Spain in

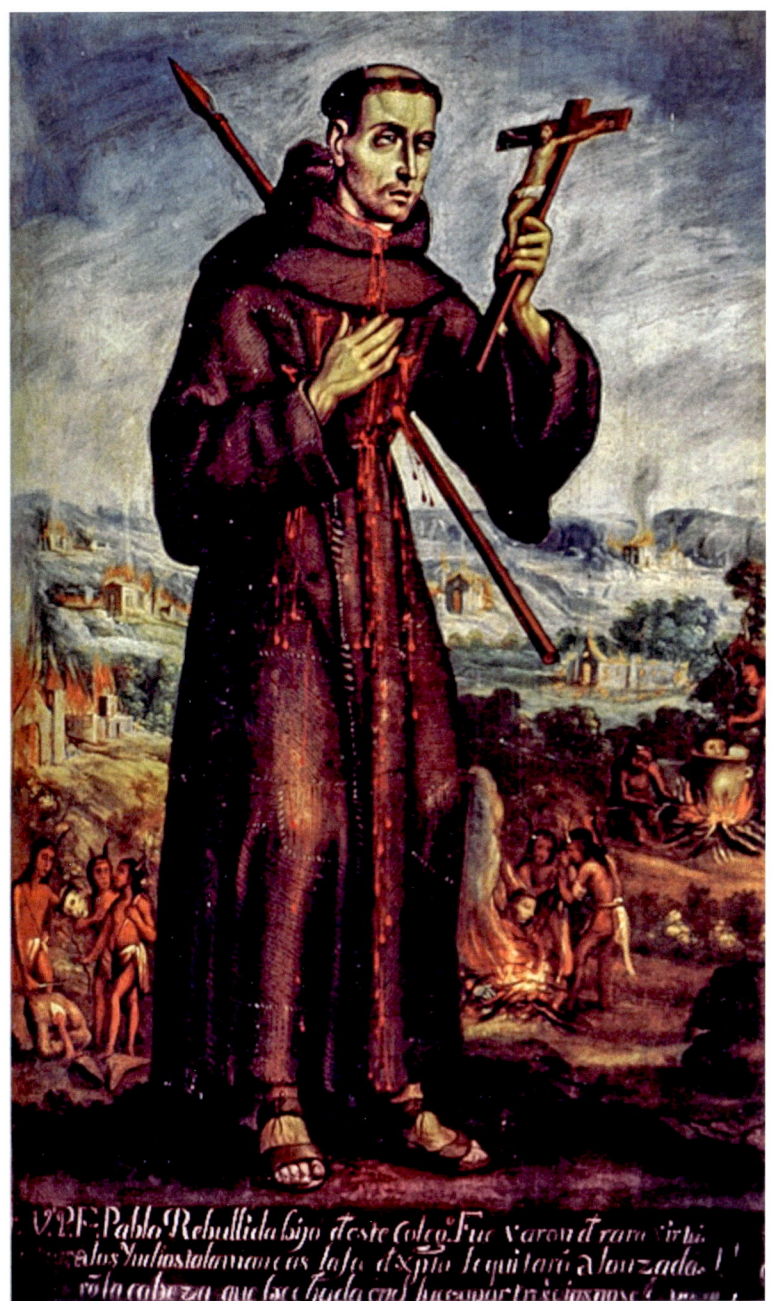

Fig. 3. Unknown artist, *Portrait of Pablo Rebullida*. Mexico, mid-1700s. Oil paint on canvas. Museo Regional de Querétaro, Querétaro, Mexico.

1683, only three years after the Pueblo Revolt, to promote missionary expansion into the northern and southern provinces of the viceroyalty where many of these martyrdoms occurred. In order to adapt to the necessities brought forth by the anxieties caused by the Pueblo Revolt, and the threat of losing the northern territories to the French, the visual culture of the "barbarian" had to be reinvented to fit new political needs. The figure of the "savage," which predominates in maps and chronicles of the sixteenth century, fed the European imaginary and distorted the representations of Native peoples of central Mexico. Two hundred years later, the Native peoples of the northern territories were transformed into *mecos* (short for Chichimecos, or Chichimecs) via a set of visual tools that rendered them violent and untamed. Antonio Rubial and María Teresa Suárez Molina note that hagiographic portraits' formulaic representations of New Mexico Pueblo peoples constitute "rhetoric and formal concepts of the Indigenous savage from the sixteenth century, created in Europe and replicated in the Americas."[5] Given this assessment, I find it necessary to contextualize the purpose of these recycled rhetorical devices to understand their place in the visual culture of the tumultuous eighteenth century. These include the contrast between the martyred figure and the sensualized naked body of the "savage" and the objects that emphasize their piety and pagan aggression, respectively.

In most of the images presented here, the protagonists firmly hold a crucifix as their only weapon of defense. Natives with weapons are contrasted with the unarmed friars, whose only tools of defense were ostensibly effigies of the Virgin Mary, bibles, crucifixes (as in the case of Pablo Rebullida who died in Talamanca, Costa Rica, in 1709 [fig. 3]; and Fray Francisco de Arvide de Jesús who was killed by the Zuni in 1632 [fig. 4]), or a wooden cross (as in the case

of Fray Casañas de Jesús who died in Jemez Pueblo, New Mexico, in 1691).[6] The instruments of theological defense aim to emphasize their narrative, which constantly reaffirmed their zeal toward the Franciscan enterprise and the Rule of Saint Francis. In fact, in rules of both 1221 and 1223, Saint Francis emphasized the poverty of his brothers by declaring they were forbidden from earthly possessions, like money and property. These rules also indicated the need to die following the example of Christ: naked on the cross, in pain, and divorced of any material concerns.[7]

Hagiographic portraits allow us to better understand how Novohispanic Franciscans partly defined their existence in relation to northern Natives. In order to reveal the Franciscan enterprise as an extension of the Crown—that is, the Franciscan Imperial Being—a revision of the materials that engendered Natives as savages in these portraits needs to be contextualized.

The Formation of the Franciscan Imperial Being

Ramón Grosfoguel, aided by Enrique Dussel's writings, helps explain the ideological contradictions that constituted the agency of the European conqueror at the turn of the fifteenth century, which is fitting in our discussion concerning Franciscans of the eighteenth century. He notes, "Descartes' 'I think, therefore I am' is preceded by 150 years of 'I conquer, therefore I am.' The *ego conquiro* is the condition of possibility of Descartes *ego cogito*. . . . The 'I conquer' that began with the European men colonial expansion in 1492, is the foundation and condition of possibility of the 'I think' that secularizes all the attributes of the Christian God and replaces God as the new foundation of knowledge."[8]

For the Franciscans, the contact with the Americas brought forth a new series of ethical confrontations that allowed Europeans to redefine what Enrique Dussel refers to as the "Imperial Being." Since 1492, European man's subjectivity has depended on the existence and the elimination of his colonized subjects.[9] I argue that in a similar fashion, Franciscans began to define their existence in the Americas based on this imperial alliance. From the time the Franciscans set foot in Veracruz with Hernán Cortés, the colonial enterprise was dependent on their spiritual guidance and missionary commitment. In fact, these hagiographic portraits aimed to erase the Franciscans' complicity with the Crown while heightening their credo.[10]

The Franciscans thrived in the medieval archetypal community that was to survive in the interstices of the world, divorced from all material and structural possessions. However, the eighteenth-century Franciscan missions, created among other reasons to defend the Bourbon territories of the northern provinces, betrayed this ideology and aligned their brotherhood with a colonial enterprise over two centuries old. When the instruments of evangelization presented in hagiographic portraits are discerned as products of a Franciscan imperial existence, we can thus make sense of this mendicant order as both a brotherhood engaged in the supposed salvation of the souls of "savages" and a royal institution at the service of the Crown. At the core of this ideological dichotomy and disparity lies the construction of the savage through their instruments of attack: bows, arrows, and macanas are always matched against the defenseless martyr's crucifixes, Marian statues, bibles, etc.

The Weapons of Resistance

In his 1681 sermon dedicated to the Pueblo Revolt's twenty-one martyrs, preached in the Cathedral of Mexico City, Dr. Isidro Sariñana y Cuenca connected Indigenous armament to Psalm 11 to explain the fury of the Pueblo Natives: "For look, the wicked bend the bow,

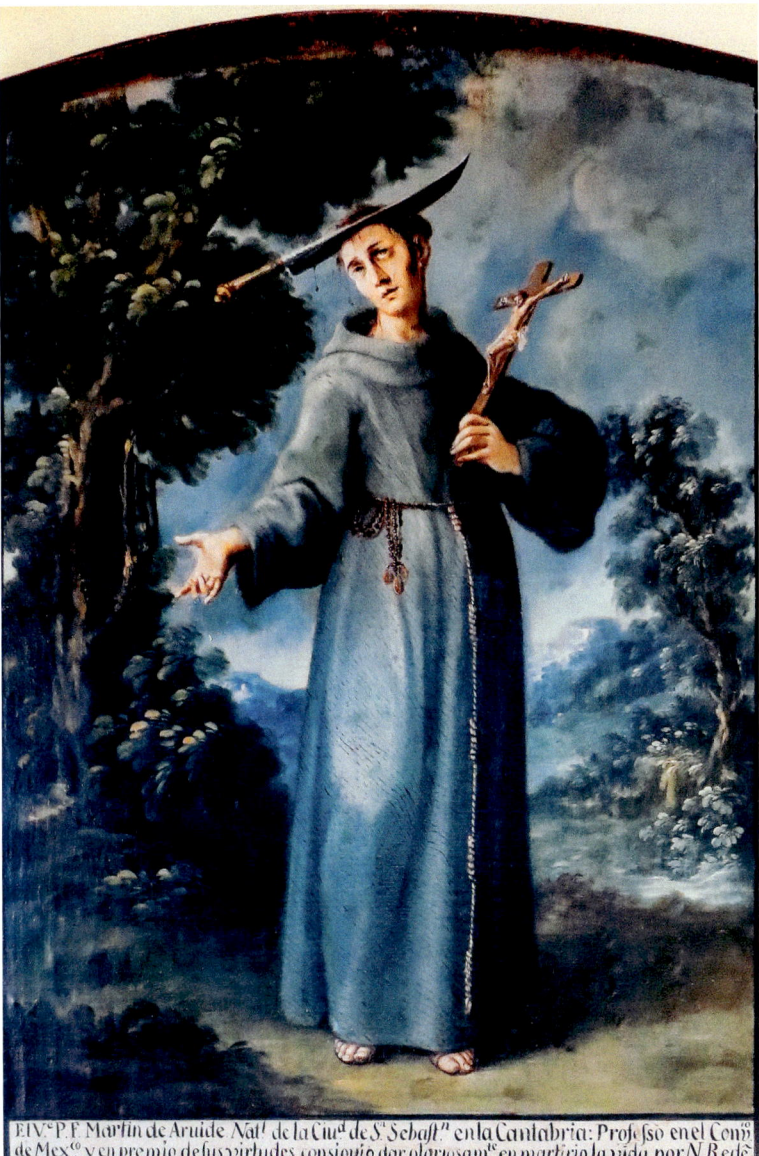

ElV.ᵉ P.F. Marfin de Aruide Natˡ de la Ciuᵈ de Sᵗ Sebaftⁿ en la Cantabria: Profeſſo en el Conᵛⁿ de Mexᶜᵒ y en premio de fus virtudes, consiguio dar gloriosamᵗᵉ en martirio la vida por N. Redē̄ ptor en el nuevo Mexᶜᵒ en 27 de febrero de 1632 aˢ

they have fitted their arrow to the string, to shoot in the dark at the upright in heart."[11] The arrows, which are prominent in many martyr images, symbolized for Sariñana y Cuenca the embodiment of treason. In general, Native weaponry represented, in Novohispanic martyr scenes, American manifestations of a new type of *arma christi*; that is, the instruments that penetrated Christ's body during his passion and death on the cross. Sariñana y Cuenca expresses the quiver to be a womb full of darts and a "symbol of

Fig. 4. Unknown artist, *Portrait of Francisco de Arvide.* Mexico, mid-1700s. Oil paint on canvas. Museo de Guadalupe, Zacatecas, Mexico.

dissimulation, in which treason is concealed."[12] Through a reference made by the prophet Jeremiah in the book of Lamentations, Sariñana y Cuenca attributed the agony these arrows provoked in the martyrs to the will of God: "I see that in this place Jeremiah uses the words 'Quiver of God,' *'pharetrae suae,'* for those most mysterious Divine judgments and secret designs from which God permitted that He should suffer, like arrows which pierced Him through, in all calamities, which in His persecution afflicted Him."[13]

Here, suffering gains a new layer of meaning. In this telling homily, the will of God and the grief of Jeremiah are directly linked to the pain inflicted by the arrows of Pueblo Natives. A pain that is twofold, the agent of their anguish is the product of treachery yet fulfills the will of God. This connection between the willful torment of the twenty-one martyrs of 1680 and God's plan made it a crucial element of the martyr-making process.[14] In other words, "savagery" becomes a theological agent by which the pain of martyrdom is achieved, and misery resides in the

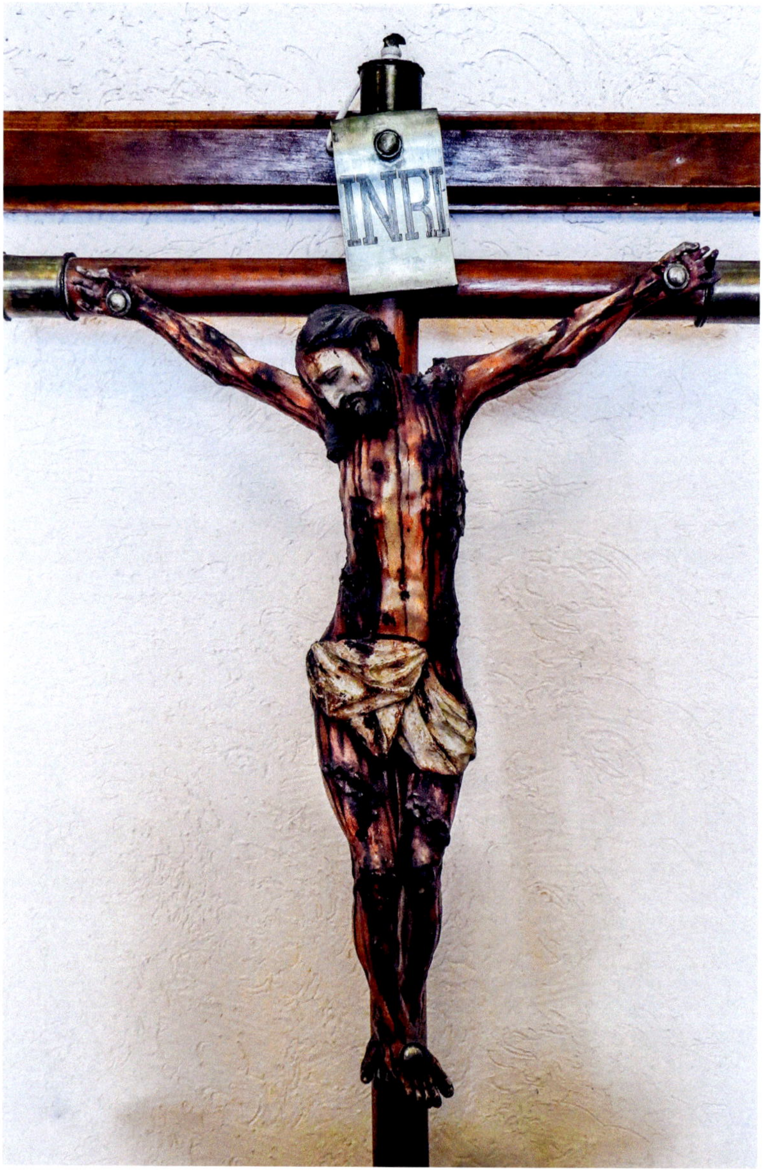

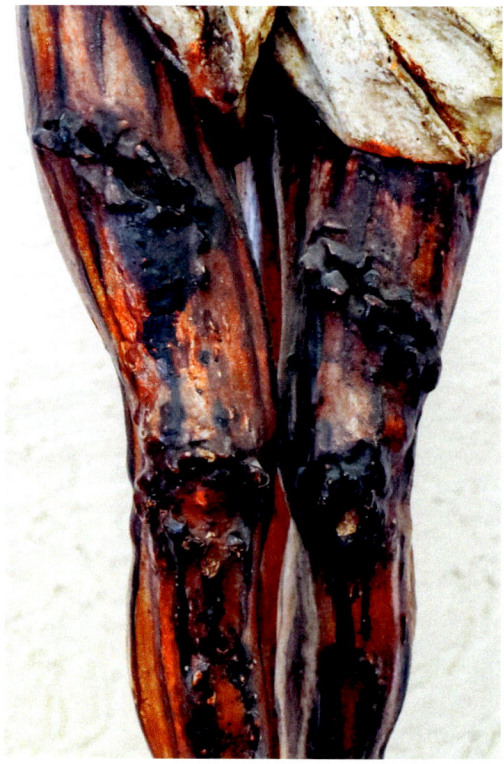

Fig. 5. Unknown artist, *Cristo de la Mordida*. Mexico, mid-1700s. Wood and pigment. Church of San Francisco, Puebla, Mexico.

Fig. 6. Unknown artist, detail of *Cristo de la Mordida*. Mexico, mid-1700s. Wood and pigment. Church of San Francisco, Puebla, Mexico.

excess of violence, which is produced by the constructed *"indio"* figure and his uncivilized actions upon friars' bodies. The inflicted agony operates as a required link to the suffering of Christ and as a tool that combined Pueblo Natives' barbarism, hatred, and God's will, all within a single act.

Cristo de la Mordida

Sometime during the eighteenth century, a convoy of Franciscans from Puebla was sent to New Mexico to evangelize the souls of Pueblo peoples. They carried with them a crucifix, in a similar fashion as in the portraits of Rebullida and Fray Arvide de Jesús. Allegedly, when the crucifix was presented as the host and naked body of Christ, a Pueblo person took a bite of the effigy (fig. 5). This action would have corroborated the Spanish presumptions of Natives' savagery, cannibalistic tendencies, and inability to understand the teachings of the Eucharist. The fictional cannibalism of New Mexico Pueblo peoples must have also validated the anxiety depicted in the portrait of Arvide de Jesús, which was located in the same church in San Francisco, Puebla. When the crucifix is analyzed, one can clearly discern the supposed site of the Native's teeth marks (fig. 6). They were sculpted on both legs, and the unnatural placement and exaggerated bite marks remind us of the monstrousness that Natives in the north represented to central Novohispanic audiences.

The host as the site of theological confusion among peoples of the Americas is a topic that has been explored by scholars of the sixteenth century.[15] However, *Cristo de la Mordida,* as it is popularly known in Puebla, demonstrates how the visual, recycled tropes of the savage performed similarly two hundred years after their introduction to the Americas. It is precisely the alleged inability of Pueblo peoples to understand the doctrines of transubstantiation that triggered

a change in the collective colonial imagination. As the edges of the empire expanded, so did the visual rhetoric of the barbarian. The location of the savage and the cannibal had been transplanted from central Mexico to the provinces of New Spain. To consume the host as flesh, instead of being spiritually transformed through the body of Christ, is to misinterpret the epistemologies of the colonizer. In other words, the capacity of Natives to understand the scriptures, or for that matter any spiritual or civilizing technology, was a determining factor for their subjectivity to be framed as either nuanced human beings or typecast as savages.

The New Savage

The portrayal of northern Natives as the new savage reaffirms and corresponds to sixteenth-century hagiographic descriptions of Chichimecs. According to historian Rubial García, this type of narrative that underplayed Native resistance became a literary formula after the first Novohispanic hagiography appeared in Jeronimo de Mendieta's *Historia eclesiástica indiana* (1595).[16]

Mendieta's tale of Fray Juan Calero, who met his martyrdom in 1541 in Tequila at the hands of the Caxcan peoples, corresponds to the narratives presented in eighteenth-century portraits and hagiographies. To persuade audiences that the possible failure of the mission in this region was a product of Native hostility, and not the friars' unfair procedures, Mendieta stressed the good work of Calero and described an arduous eighteen-month-long mission among the Caxcan peoples. Mendieta describes Calero's martyrdom in gruesome detail:

The barbarians shot arrows at him, and wounded he fell to the ground, confessing the Name of God among all those unbelievers. Not content with their doings, with macanas they broke his teeth . . . saying,

"You won't preach heaven and hell things no more, we neither need it, nor want your doctrine." They also struck his head with a *macana*, and even when blood ran from several body parts, seeing that he was not entirely dead, they finished killing him by stoning.[17]

Historia eclesiástica indiana gave visibility to a new cult of martyrs that was developing in Mexico at the end of the sixteenth century. It helped define the new relationship between Franciscan missionaries and Natives. It also outlined the parameters of later conceptions of the figure of the northern *chichimeco*. In his writing, Mendieta described Chichimecs as *nervosos* (nervous), *fornidos* (burly), *desbarbados* (beardless), and *brutos* (brutes). Mendieta's accounts are some of the first Franciscan portrayals of Native peoples outside of the Valley of Mexico. They are described and illustrated with images in book five titled "Franciscanos ilustres, fallecidos de muerte natural o por martirio" (Illustrious Franciscans, Killed by Natural Death and Martyrdom) under the visual rubric of the Chichimecs, as subjects of the Crown, and needing to acquire a spiritual education. Understanding the hagiographic historiography of the Franciscan mission enterprise allows us to reiterate how the anxiety against Chichimec resistance was transplanted in the 1700s to the northern provinces.[18]

The pictorial formula of the new savage was reinforced with the hagiographic portraits presented here, the production of maps of places like present-day Texas and New Mexico, and the development of *casta* paintings, which often included bands of Chichimecs as part of their vocabulary.[19] Beginning in the early 1700s, artists such as Diego Sanabria (see figs. 1–3) created images that must have ignited the imagination and anxieties of novices and *visitadores* (administrative visitors) and similar authorities.

Throughout the eighteenth century, the monstrosity of northern Natives was a reminder of the dangers that lurked throughout the then frontiers. Given the devastating result of the Seven Years' War, the fear of losing more territory (this time to the French Empire), and the increasing tensions with the Comanche, who by 1760 were trading guns and ammunition with the enemy, it is no surprise that the reintroduction of Natives as chichimecos was to center around the northern provinces. In 1726, Pedro Rivera Villalón, visitador of the presidios, described the Comanche as "very barbarian and bellicose. . . . Their origin is ignored given that they are always in pilgrimage, ready for battle, and always in war against all nations, they set up camp anywhere. . . . Men are not covered above the belly button, and women below their knees."[20]

Rivera's description of the Comanche as wandering, barbarian, bellicose, and half-naked is consistent with all visual representations of chichimecos in the images of the eighteenth century. In other words, the opposition against the Crown by Pueblo peoples, the Comanche, and the Apache, who for decades were seen as simply rebellious, must have been a principal source of anxiety for the Franciscans and hegemonic authorities alike. It also helps explain why the artists of hagiographic portraits continually chose northern Natives as central characters, especially considering the fact that there are many additional nations described by the chroniclers in their hagiographies.[21]

Conclusions

In summary, hagiographic martyr portraits functioned beyond their role of illustrating the history of the Franciscans in America first recorded in their literature. When the material culture represented in these images is analyzed beyond the perception of "recycled rhetorical devices," we begin to see how the iconography of the Chichimec in the eighteenth century, even when it appears similar to the ways it manifested in the sixteenth century, reveals new political tensions that need to be further studied. Hagiographic portraits aimed to veil the Franciscan complacency with a colonial enterprise, while simultaneously referencing their zeal and willingness to die for the expansion of the church. This dichotomy required the creation of a new genre of painting in which the objects illustrated represented more than traditional iconographies. The theological meaning of crucifixes is always juxtaposed with rudimentary weapons of attack that bear the task of creating new martyrs. However, their main role within these images was to reveal Natives' limitations and unwillingness to understand and accept their intended spiritual message. As the concept of the barbarian migrated to the northern and southern poles of the viceroyalty of New Spain, so did the anxieties for attack in those places. One of the most important consequences of the Pueblo Revolt of 1680, as noted by Navarro García, was the renewed urge to protect the neglected territories of the north, "but perhaps the most important consequence was the jolt it produced in the governors' consciousness."[22] These anxieties are represented in the visual and material culture of eighteenth-century spiritual conquest. Understanding these objects as products of such anxiety allows us to highlight the fact that Native peoples of the Americas never stopped resisting during the colonial period, and how their battles were, perhaps, not all in vain.

✜ ✜ ✜

Notes

1 "Magestad divina, de esta talla fueron las diversions de este joven virtuoso pues siempre andaba formando capillas de juncia, y otras ramas en lo más retirado de su casa, y en ellas colocaba una cruz de madera y la tenía muy adornada de flores." Isidro Félix de Espinosa (and Juan Domingo Arricivita), *Chronica apostolica y seraphica de todos los colegios de Propaganda Fide de esta Nueva-España, de missioneros franciscanos observantes: Erigidos con autoridad pontificia y regia para la reformacion de los fieles y conversion de los gentiles* (Mexico City: La Viuda de don J. B. de Hogal, 1746), 262–63. Unless otherwise stated, all translations are my own.

2 The original full quote reads as follows: "Estando allí ocultos los Indios Apaches, gente cruelísima, con quien se habían colgado los amotinados del Pueblo, y apenas lo vieron solo en le cementerio, lo entregaron a estos carniceros lobos, sedientos de sangre de Cristianos, y . . . ya llegada la hora, apresuró el paso para abrazarse con la cruz, que había puesto en el cementerio, y al hincarse delante aquel sagrado madero, le descargaron sobre la cabeza con una macana tan recio golpe, que le partieron el casco, y le bañaron todo el cuerpo con su misma sangre." Espinosa, *Chronica apostolica y seraphica,* 285. A macana was a wooden club with obsidian blades associated with the Nahua peoples of central Mexico.

3 Daniel Miller, "Materiality: An Introduction," in *Materiality,* ed. Daniel Miller (Durham, NC: Duke University Press, 2005), 6.

4 "La catástrofe de Nuevo Mexico . . . había sacudido el tranquilo despacho de los asuntos en el Consejo de Indias . . . y en repetidas ocasiones, se recriminase violentamente la inacción del virrey, se ordenase la erección simultanea de cuatro presidios." Luis Navarro García, *Don José de Gálvez y la Comandancia General de las Provincias Internas del norte de Nueva España* (Seville: Consejo Superior de Investigaciones Científicas, 1964), 32.

5 Antonio Rubial and María Teresa Suárez Molina, "Mártires y predicadores: La conquista de las fronteras y su representación plastica," in *Los pinceles de la nación: De la patria criolla a la nación mexicana, 1750–1860,* ed. Jaime Soler Frost (Mexico City: Banamex, 2000), 64.

6 Fray Francisco de Arvide de Jesús's life and death are documented by two chronicles. He sporadically appears in the *Memorial* of Fray Alonso de Benavides (1630) and in Agustín de Vetancurt's *Menologio Franciscano* (1697). See Alonso de Benavides, *Benavides' Memorial of 1630,* trans. Peter P. Forrestal (Washington, DC: Academy of American Franciscan History, 1954); and Agustín de Vetancurt, *Teatro mexicano: Descripción breve*

de los sucesos ejemplares, históricos y religiosos del Nuevo Mundo de las Indias (Mexico City: Editorial Porrúa, 1971). As noted in the text accompanying the painting, Arvide de Jesús was from the port of San Sebastián, Cantabria, in Spain, and took his vows in the convent of San Francisco in Mexico City circa 1612. He was appointed to "appease" the Jemez Pueblo peoples, who had begun to disperse throughout the surrounding mountains, and remained a leading figure there for several years. He was killed by the Zuni as he migrated to convert the Zipias of present-day eastern Arizona. According to the text accompanying the painting of Pablo Rebullida, he was a friar from Fraga, Aragon, joining the order in Tortosa in the late seventeenth century. He traveled to the Americas and attended the Colegio de Propaganda Fide de la Santa Cruz, Querétaro. There, he was commissioned to travel to Central America to evangelize the resistant tribes of the Talamanca region. From Guatemala, Rebullida was sent to Costa Rica in 1695. Felix de Espinosa in his hagiography expressed Rebullida's fervent zeal and desire for martyrdom. He frequently noted, "He de morir martyr: he de ser martyr" (I will die a martyr: I will be a martyr). These are the words he uttered as he sailed to the Americas."

7 Carl F. Starkloff, "Church as Structure and Communitas: Victor Turner and Ecclesiology," Theological Studies 58, no. 4 (1997): 643–68. Starkloff notes that Franciscans were to follow "the poor and naked Christ . . . [and] always be in a state of temporal passage until they entered the unchanging state of heaven. And this was the condition, quite literally, in which Francis died" (654).

8 Ramón Grosfoguel, "The Structure of Knowledge in Westernized Universities: Epistemic Racism/Sexism and the Four Genocides/Epistemicides of the Long 16th Century," Human Architecture: Journal of the Sociology of Self-Knowledge 11, no. 1, Article 8 (2013): 77.

9 Grosfoguel, "Structure of Knowledge," 77.

10 Emmanuel Ortega, "Hagiographical Misery and the Liminal Witness: Novohispanic Franciscan Martyr Portraits and the Politics of Imperial Expansion," in Visualizing Sensuous Suffering and Affective Pain in Early Modern Europe and the Spanish Americas, ed. Heather Graham and Lauren G. Kilroy-Ewbank (Leiden, Netherlands: Brill, 2018), 246.

11 Ps. 11:2 (New Revised Standard Version).

12 Isidro Sariñana y Cuenca, The Franciscan Martyrs of 1680: Funeral Oration Over the Twenty-one Franciscan Missionaries Killed by the Pueblo Indians, August 10, 1680 (Santa Fe: New Mexican Printing Company, 1906), 12–13.

13 Sariñana y Cuenca, Franciscan Martyrs of 1680, 12. The passage that Sariñana y Cuenca is referring to is Lam. 3:12–13 (New Revised Standard Version), which reads as follows: "He bent his bow and sent me as a mark for his arrow. He shot into my vitals the arrows of his quiver."

14 The meaning of the arrow as a symbol of barbarism in literature of chronicles of conquest was present throughout the Spanish colonial period. This is a topic that can be explored in the realms of literature, art history, anthropology, and other disciplines. Also, these disciplines trace the development of Native weaponry as a symbol with many layers of signification. A good example of arrow as a symbol of barbarism and civilization is observed in Álvar Núñez Cabeza de Vaca's Naufragios (1542). See Álvar Núñez Cabeza de Vaca, Naufragios, trans. Juan Francisco Maura (Madrid: Cátedra, 1989).

15 See Jaime Lara, Christian Texts for Aztecs: Art and Liturgy in Colonial Mexico (Notre Dame, IN: University of Notre Dame Press, 2008); Louise M. Burkhart, ed., Aztecs on Stage: Religious Theater in Colonial Mexico, trans. Louise M. Burkhart, Barry D. Sell, and Stafford Poole (Norman: University of Oklahoma Press, 2011); Carolyn Dean, Inka Bodies and the Body of Christ: Corpus Christi in Colonial Cuzco, Peru (Durham, NC: Duke University Press, 1999); and Christopher Elwood, The Body Broken: The Calvinist Doctrine of the Eucharist and the Symbolization of Power in Sixteenth-Century France (New York: Oxford University Press, 1999).

16 Antonio Rubial García, "El mártir colonial: Evolución de una figura heroica," in El héroe entre el mito y la historia, ed. Federico Navarrete Linares and Guilhem Olivier (Mexico City: Centro de Estudios Mexicanos y Centroamericanos, 2000), 75–87, accessed April 9, 2017, DOI: 10.4000/books.cemca.1302.

17 "Los bárbaros dispararon en el sus flechas, y asaetado cayó en tierra, confesando el Nombre de Dios entre aquellos descreídos. Los cuales no contentos con lo hecho, con las macanas le quebraron los dientes y muelas en la boca, diciendo: 'Ya no nos predicarás más cosas del cielo, ni del infierno, ni hemos menester ni queremos tu doctrina.' Dieronle también macanazos en la cabeza, y aunque de muchas partes le corría sangre, viendo que aún no estaba del todo muerto, le acabaron de matar a pedradas." Fray Gerónimo de Mendieta, Historia eclesiástica indiana, obra escrita a fines del siglo XVI por fray Gerónimo de Mendieta, de la Orden de San Francisco: La pública por primera vez Joaquín García Icazbalceta (Mexico City: Antigua Librería, 1870), 738, http://cdigital.dgb.uanl.mx/la/1080012505/1080012505_143.pdf.

18 See also Juan Focher, Itinerarium Catholicum proficiscentium ad infideles convertendos / Itinerario del misionero en América, ed. Antonio Eguiluz (Madrid: Victoriano Suárez, 1960). The original text was compiled by Diego de Valadez and published in 1574. Mendieta uses Itinerario as a basis for many of his ideas on missionizing and spiritual conversion. A

careful study on the ways *Itinerario* influenced our perspective on the Chichimecs is yet to be done.

19 *Casta* paintings were typically produced in the eighteenth century to illustrate different families that, as a product of racial mixing in the viceroyalties, generated mixed-blood children.

20 "Tan barbaros y belicosos . . . su origen se ignora, porque siempre andan peregrinando y en forma de batalla, por tener guerra con todas las naciones, y así se acampan en cualquier paraje. . . . Su vestuario de los hombres no pasa del ombligo, y el de las mujeres les pasa de la rodilla." Navarro García, *Don José de Gálvez,* 104.

21 The wars against the Apache and Comanche continued for decades. For example, one of the most important encounters between New Mexican Pueblos and the Comanche occurred in 1772 when five hundred men attacked Pecos, New Mexico. By 1770, José de Gálvez, Marquis of Sonora and *visitador* in New Spain, declared that the subjection of the barbarian tribes of the north was not as easy as he believed prior to leaving Mexico City for his *visitas* to the north a few years before. See Navarro García, *Don José de Gálvez,* 201.

22 "Pero quizá su más importante consecuencia fue la sacudida que produjo en la conciencia de los gobernantes." Navarro García, *Don José de Gálvez,* 26.

OLAYA SANFUENTES

Cognitive Ecologies and Cabinetization
The Bishop of Trujillo's Eighteenth-Century Index

An eighteenth-century English etching of Noah's Ark, a metaphor for history's first collection, visually relates that century's way of understanding the world around it and conceiving of historical and Biblical events. The artist, Edward Wells, illustrates a plan for housing the animals on the ark and saving them from the Great Flood.[1] The crates in which the animals were transported, as well as their classification and separation into enclosures based on their survival needs, share the concept of cabinetization discussed in this chapter. The etching represents the biblical ship with regard to floating crates (fig. 1).

In *Sorting Things Out: Classification and Its Consequences*, Geoffrey C. Bowker and Susan Leigh Star state that a classification system is one in which metaphorical or literal crates contain material for subsequent use.[2] This idea is at the heart of my chapter. I will attempt to outline a historic case of classification of objects and their packing in crates with the idea that behind these crates lie ways of thinking and organizing the world. "Cognitive ecologies," as some contemporary scholars call them, are the crates and object containers that reveal the dialectic relationship between ways people understand their surroundings and the practices associated with this cognitive exercise. Human attempts to understand reality and its associated products are evident throughout history; they relate to other phenomena such as governing visual regimes, forms of acquisition and documentation of information, and media representations and their subsequent circulation. Using the case of Bishop Baltasar Jaime Martínez Compañón's index, I aim to show, via diverse historical sources and conjecture based on these sources, the many dimensions involved in the creation of a collection.[3] Bishop Martínez Compañón's index, written in Trujillo, Peru, dates to December 26,

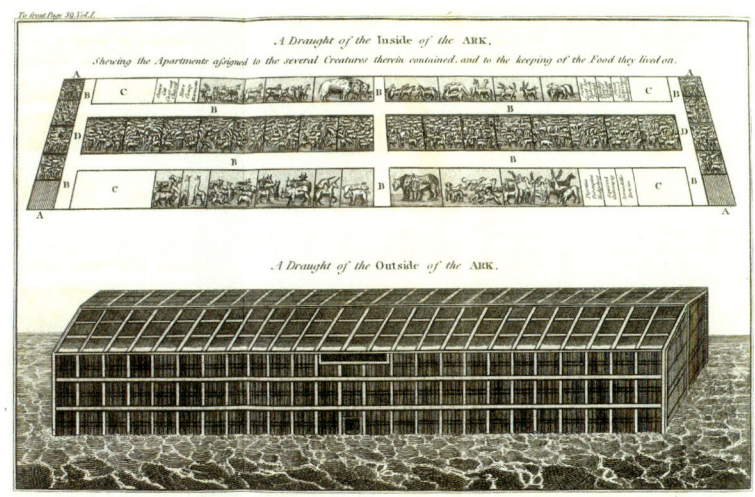

Fig. 1. "A Draught of the Inside of the Ark" and "A Draught of the Outside of the Ark." Oxford, 1809. Printed in Edward Wells, *An Historical Geography of the Old and New Testament,* vol. 1 (Oxford: Clarendon Press, 1809), opposite p. 39.

1788.[4] In it are listed the twenty-four crates, and their corresponding packed objects, sent to Spain in response to an order by King Carlos III.

The relationship between metaphorical and real crates is dialectic and dialogical. Mental collections, lists, and inventories manifest physically in the world; they are found in bookstores, museums, medal collections, cabinets, and image galleries, among other places. The mind needs the surrounding material world in order to incorporate new information in mnemonic compartments that accommodate this information and facilitate its learning and memorization. At the same time, interventions in the environment are mediated by our mental categories. Thus, this chapter is based on Lambros Malafouris's hypothesis that knowledge is acquired through articulations among the mind, body, and surroundings: "Contrary to what classical cognitive science believes and cognitive archaeology often implicitly reiterates, what is outside the head may not necessarily be outside the mind."[5] Furthermore, as Jonathan Spackman and Stephen C. Yanchar attest, "Central to this shift is the conviction that perception, thinking, use of metaphor, and related phenomena are inextricably connected with the physical-temporal position occupied by the body itself, including embodied perception, mobility, perspective taking, and skilled activity in a world of physical objects and events."[6]

The Manuscript

Bishop Martínez Compañón's manuscript is in keeping with eighteenth-century endeavors, habits, and practices for discovering and interpreting reality. These approaches were also marked by the Bourbon dynasty's philosophy of absolutism, which emphasized the use of knowledge to improve land administration and to optimize the use of resources. The Spanish Crown made visits to and sponsored many scientific expeditions to

its empire throughout the eighteenth century. Species were collected on these expeditions for the newly established Real Jardín Botánico (Royal Botanical Garden; founded 1755) and the Real Gabinete de Historia Natural (Royal Cabinet of Natural History; founded 1771). Meanwhile, within colonial Spain, functionaries of the royal court shared the illuminated spirit of the times. In the eighteenth century, planning for a natural history museum in Peru had begun, and it was to feature specimens from the territory and would prove that this type of institution was the incarnation of imperial forms of acquisition, documentation, and knowledge sharing. Martínez Compañón's entire work, when analyzed in conjunction with its visual encyclopedia and the objects sent to Spain, form part of a personal and individual effort to bring into existence a royal natural history museum.

Arbitrariness, as displayed by Martínez Compañón in choosing the species that formed his collection, is also present in this chapter, which has been structured in a way intuitive to me and makes clear a personal process for organizing information in an attempt to share and understand a phenomenon. Events are presented in tandem with physical evidence but are revealed in a subjective order. While here, in this instance, the actions are presented as separate occurrences, many of them must have happened simultaneously. Above all, arbitrariness is present in the handling of the aforementioned dialectical relationship between the acquisition of knowledge from the perceptible world and the practices associated with this process.

Collection of the Objects

Martínez Compañón's index is a catalogue of the objects collected, crated, and sent to Spain. As with any classification system, it is a cultural representation of a reality; it is arbitrary and artificial, but, as such, it provides information about its time. The result is the illusion of an organized reality or, as in this case, a portion of reality, via documentation of the animal, plant, and mineral world as well as the registration of many arts and antiques from a colonial territory. Subjectivity is present from the beginning: in the choice of objects collected, in the ways of grouping them, in the use of adjectives to describe them, and in the revelation of their main characteristics and uses.

The choices made and work done served to motivate a mandate to acquire objects for the king's collection. Each object numbered and described in the index passed through different valuations and experienced what Arjun Appadurai calls a "social life."[7] First, they were selected as representative of a specific context, and then they were collected and handled to become part of a royal collection. Although the objects were supposed to go to King Carlos III, their destiny was subject to the whims of history. The final resting place of most of the specimens is unknown, although we are certain about some and can draw conclusions about others. Some objects became part of Madrid's Royal Cabinet of Natural History, were later integrated into collections at Spain's Museo Arqueológico Nacional (National Archeological Museum; founded 1867), and found their final home at the Museo de América (Museum of the Americas; founded in 1941). These objects might have been moved in 1965, when the building that currently houses the museum was inaugurated. Furthermore, other species went to the Royal Botanical Garden, while several others went to Madrid's Buen Retiro Park. Some of the objects ended up in the Royal Aranjuez Palace.

The index's order allows some conclusions to be drawn about the period in which the process of collecting took place. The many objects collected, packed, and sent to Madrid—in the case of Martínez Compañón—are related to

variable mandates he received: the king's orders influenced by the illuminated ideals of the time, the viceroy's orders for the bishop of Trujillo, and the orders the bishop gave to the diocese priests through questionnaires sent out prior to his visit. However, no one knows how those involved carried out these orders or how the objects ended up in the crates presented by the index. Behind the image of a catalogued collection of Peruvian objects hides the specific accounts of how they were made and how they were obtained from their owners.[8]

In order to carry out this tremendous project, many actors and instruments were involved. Martínez Compañón chose a group to accompany him and make ecclesiastic visits to the territory, which included his secretary, Pedro de Echevarri; a missionary; a chaplain; a scribe; a Spaniard named Antonio de Narbona; his nephew, José Ignacio Lecuanda; and six slaves. After the bishop chose his companions, he wrote a pastoral letter to the priests so they might be received in an austere manner and respond to the two questionnaires they had received prior to the visit.[9] The first questionnaire referred to ecclesiastical issues and the second referred to worldly issues related to natural history and local resources.[10]

Emily Berquist Soule claims that without Indigenous knowledge and expertise this enormous task could not have been carried out. Already in place was a European tradition of using the services of locals to assist collectors, a system the bishop of Trujillo would surely have used. In a treaty from the sixteenth century, and still in force in the eighteenth, collectors, rich or not, were urged to send suitable, intelligent men to the regions in search of valuable objects.[11] Since there was no possibility of the bishop finishing a project of this magnitude himself, he invited a group of Native people to collaborate with him over a decade's time.[12]

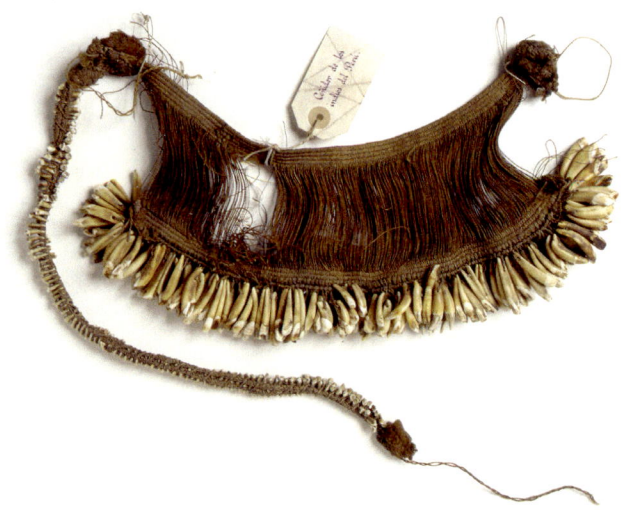

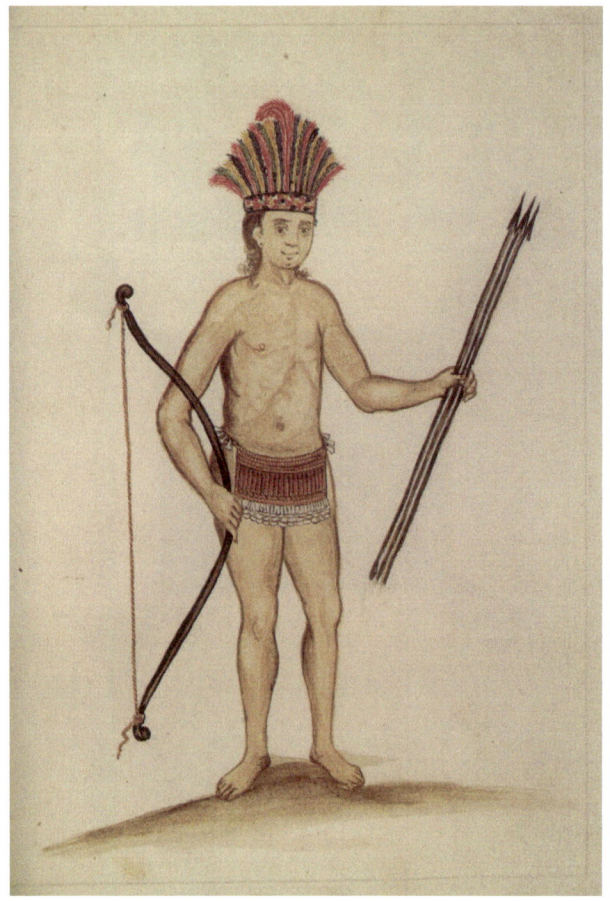

Top: Fig. 2. *Taparrabo* (loincloth). Peru, about 1788. Monkey teeth, and plant fiber on fabric, 30¾ in. Museo de América, Madrid.

Above: Fig. 3. Unknown artist, *Indio selvático, desnudo, con arco y tres flechas* (Naked Indian from the forest, with bow and three arrows). Peru, about 1782–90. Watercolor and pen on paper, 9⅜ × 6½ in. Real Biblioteca, Madrid.

Much of the information included about the indexed objects must have come from Native and mestizo popular knowledge, as is the case with the traditional medicine associated with many of the plant species.[13] This idea can be extrapolated to all instances of the acquisition of knowledge on American soil since the arrival of the first Europeans in the sixteenth century. From Christopher Columbus himself, who explored the Antilles guided by Natives, to Hernán Cortés, who used Aztec geographic representations to discover the territory and sent his findings to Carlos V along with a map of Mexico and Tenochtitlan, the Spanish made use of Native knowledge. European tradition was not the only explanation for the success of the collections. Regarding Andean territory, scholars Lisa Trever and Joanne Pillsbury claim that before the Europeans' arrival, Andean men were already familiar with the general terms of collection practices.[14] Over the course of three years, the bishop traveled the territory with a group of Natives who helped him collect specimens. They even took objects from Native tombs; the decision to do so was probably informed by the Christian belief that since the objects belonged to pagan Natives, they were therefore not respectable and fell outside of what was considered "truly religious."[15]

The heterogeneity contained within the territory of the Trujillo diocese is clear from the great number of objects collected and the categories created to ensure a meaningful sample. The objects are grouped and presented based on a subjective classification system. First, the definition of the term "object" for the purposes of the index is quite broad. Everything from within the diocese and anything that could be wrapped and transported was used. This definition included, therefore, species from throughout the natural world, as well as cultural and artisanal artifacts. In terms of the natural world, both plant and animal samples were sent. One way of understanding the incoherence of grouping man-made objects with natural ones has to do with the Christian idea that all of God's works are artistic creations.[16] This inclusive system was also influenced by George Louis Leclerc de Buffon's sociological relativism regarding nature: the idea that humans can only understand nature through their own social and cultural world.[17] For this reason, ethnographic objects make up part of the collection with 108 specimens illustrated.

Visual Documentation

Unless one reviews all of Bishop Martínez Compañón's projects of the time, it is impossible to understand the 1788 index in which he descriptively enumerates the objects catalogued and packed in crates to be sent to Spain. Along with specimens and their classification in the index, the bishop requested 1,400 illustrations of the natural and cultural world of his diocese. The complementary nature of the documents belongs to a long history of museum samples accompanied by illustrations and maps (figs. 2–5). It was of utmost importance to complete both the physical specimen collection and to obtain botanical illustrations (fig. 6) in order to satisfy the interest in thoroughness held by companies involved in scientific exploration and their associated cabinets,[18] the most prevalent manner of showing evidence of the acquisition and circulation of knowledge from the sixteenth through the eighteenth centuries.[19]

Berquist Soule claims that the bishop of Trujillo's organizational system and his approach to the commissioned botanical illustrations were rather unscientific. She argues that the images were more or less impressionistic and captured details that were not very useful to contemporary specialists, who were particularly interested in details such as plant reproductive organs.[20]

The illustrations of some species are similar to those collected. Such is the case, for example,

of the anteater that was brought to Spain both as a species and as an illustration. Other animals that were collected and illustrated were the woodpecker and many types of quail. The amount and the complexity of the mediums Martínez Compañón used to register his jurisdiction makes his work one of the most complete material and visual compendiums of the Peruvian colonial period.[21] They also reveal an encyclopedic interest and his more general and grandiose objective of making his own natural history collection, as so many scholarly travelers did toward the end of the eighteenth century. The organizational strategy behind these initiatives was that of the museum, a sort of miniature world.[22]

Packing

The objects were wrapped and packed in crates. It can be deduced that the crates were wooden, as it is known that contemporary scientific expeditions, such as those for which specimens were sent from the British colonies to England, employed wooden cases. The deposits at

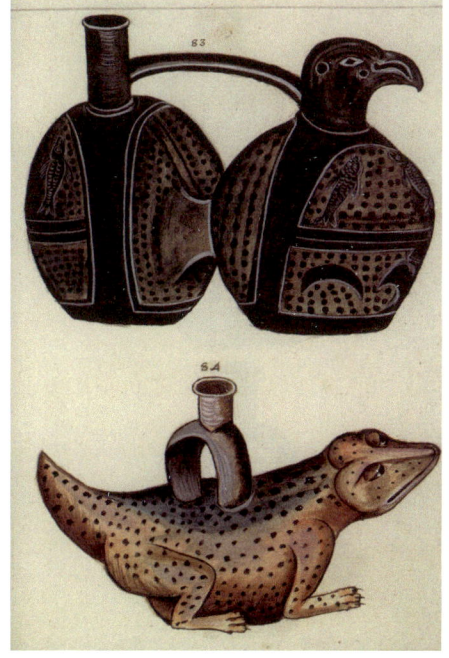

Fig. 5. Unknown artist, *Dos vasijas, no. 38* (two vessels). Peru, about 1782–90. Watercolor and pen on paper, 9¾ × 6½ in. Real Biblioteca, Madrid.

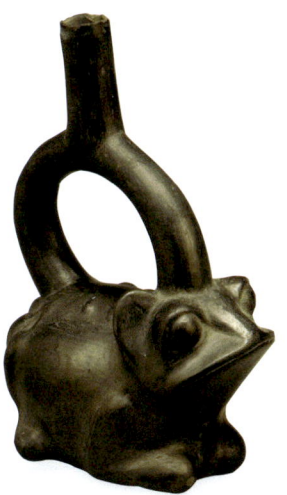

Fig. 4. *Vasija zoomorfa* (zoomorphic vessel). Peru, about 1000–1470. Black clay, 6⅝ × 8⅝ in. Museo de América, Madrid.

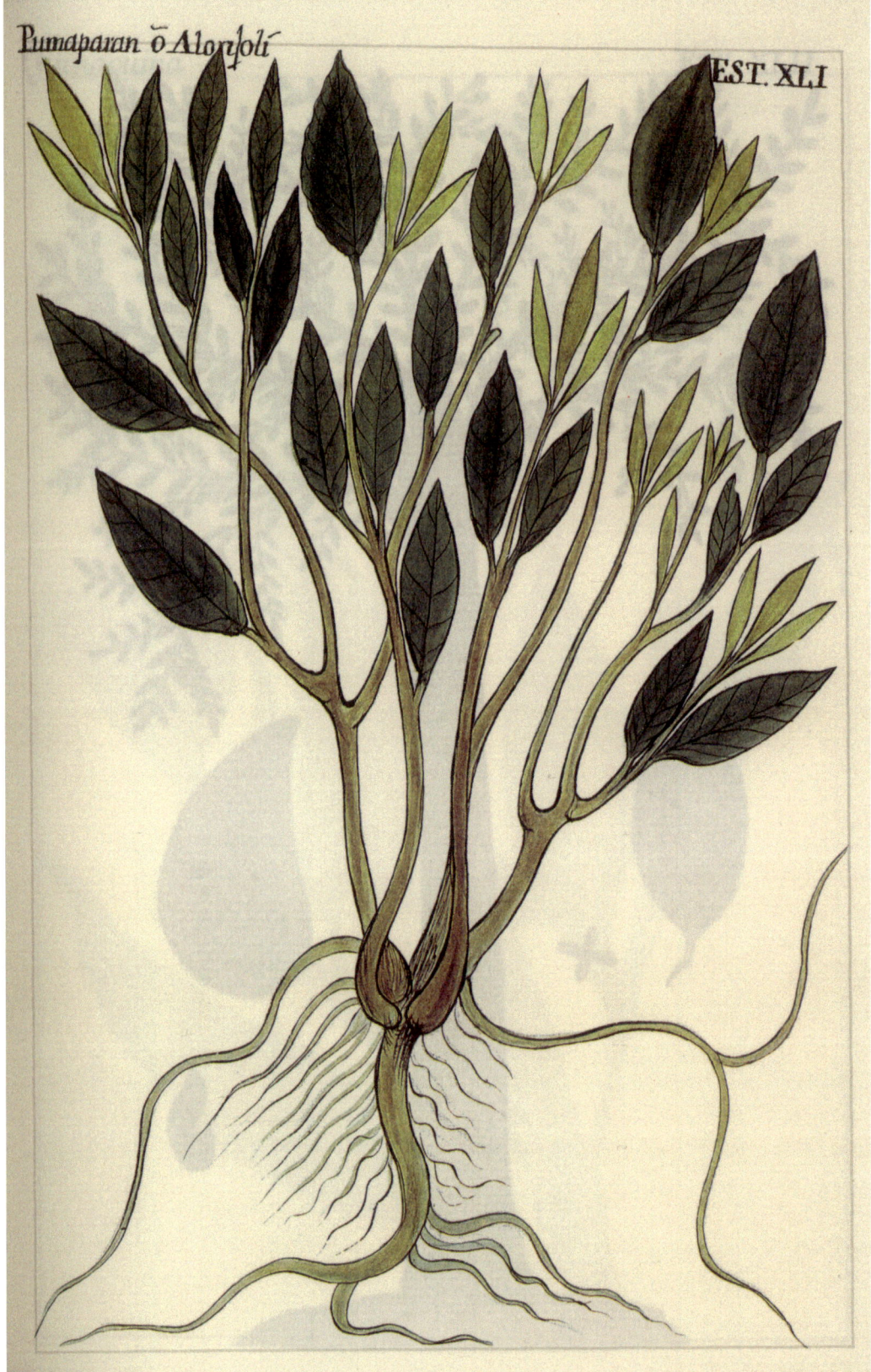

Fig. 6. Unknown artist, *Pumaparan, o Ajonjoli* (sesame). Peru, about 1782–90. Watercolor and pen on paper, 9½ × 6½ in. Real Biblioteca, Madrid.

Madrid's botanical garden contain wooden crates used for other contemporary expeditions, similar in nature to the one studied here.

The crates were divided into many compartments. In Crate 2, for example, clay objects representing Native women were separated from those representing Native men (figs. 7 and 8). Sometimes the crates were separated into levels. Crate 9 contained minerals and had two levels, each level with its own further divisions. On the bottom level there were ten divisions, and on the top there were five. The levels were separated by a wooden board, and if the crates were of the same size, it might be said that the mineral samples contained therein were small and representative, since each division contained several mineral samples. Ribbons in many colors were often used to identify and differentiate among the specimens. Today, we know of indigo-, red-, and mother-of-pearl–colored ribbons as well as blue and white ones.

Classification and the Term "Index"

The source under consideration is an index. While it is similar to lists and inventories, it has some particularities. It is not just any given list, because it functions as the index of a book and tries to create an order for the reader to go through the crates containing collected objects. It could be said, however, that it is a list with an established order, if what matters most is the integrated system it achieves. It is not quite an inventory, because studies of cultural material tend to use this term for documents that state "what is found here," referring to those objects in a house or factory that make up a closed system and are referred to in legal terms due to their uses or natures. The index here is rather a list of things that have been chosen to represent a universe. For this reason, it does not attempt to represent the entire universe either quantitatively or qualitatively. Perhaps we could use

the concept of inventory if we understand it as that which is collected and packed as a universe itself, offering information about the cultural products of a specific place, a diocese in this case, and its associated values. Along these lines, we might apply methodological approaches used for inventories, such as that of Giorgio Riello, who states that there is no such thing as a model inventory (or index, for the purposes of this chapter); inventories are subjective because they are conditioned by social values, assumptions, beliefs, and conventions.[23]

In order to describe the objects in a manner accessible to everyone (including intermediaries, scientists, and royalty), Martínez Compañón used colloquial language. This was a rather unscientific approach as science tended to use Latin names for specimens. Since 1752, Spanish nature expeditions to America had used Carl Linnaeus's classification system, but Martínez Compañón's work prioritized local dialects and Spanish.[24] Flora, fauna, and mineral specimens

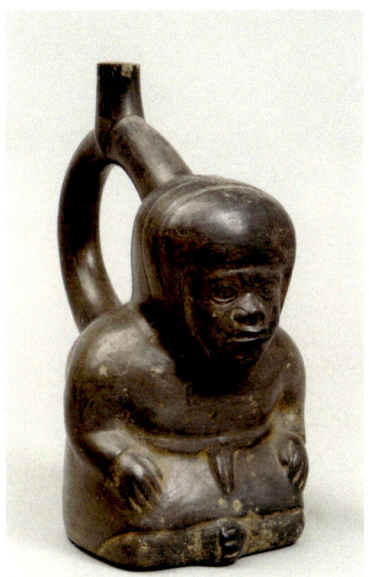 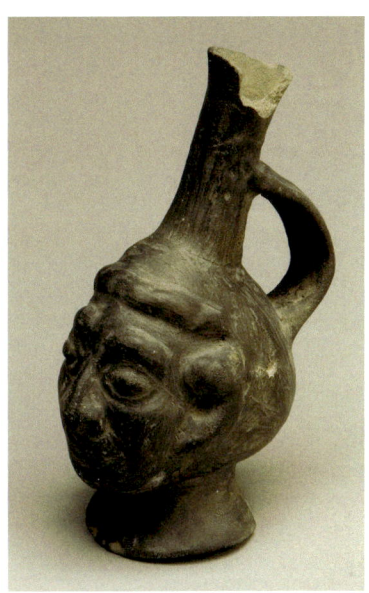

Fig. 7. *Vasija antropomorfa* (anthropomorphic vessel). Peru, about 100–750. Black clay, 8⅝ × 7¼ in. Museo de América, Madrid.

Fig. 8. *Vasija cefalomorfa* (cephalomorphic vessel). Peru, about 1000–1470. Black clay, 7⅛ × 3⅛ × 2 in. Museo de América, Madrid.

were described using methods applied since the time of Ulisse Aldrovandi, which favored the external, observable aspects of objects.[25]

Transport

The bishop's crates shipped aboard the commercial boat *La Rosa* sailed from the Port of Callao in February 1779. According to José Araneda's calculations regarding mail service between America and Spain, the boat probably took at least four months to arrive in Cadiz.[26] This long travel time was a direct assault on the physical integrity of some species, which were threatened by the humidity onboard, the salty ocean water, insects, and other such problems.[27]

For some of the crates, it is possible to infer the methods used to transport the species. Such is the case of Crate 11, which indicates that the leaves and flowers of plant species were pressed beforehand. Evidence of the storage practices used in North America around the same time in history is also of interest as it can be assumed that the bishop of Trujillo might have used similar practices. John Bartram, from Philadelphia, made a living collecting species to send to clients in London. Documents indicate that he sold one hundred species to a Peter Collinson for a hundred guineas, sending approximately twenty crates from North America between 1735 and 1760. Through Collinson, Bartram came to know Hans Sloane, whom he sent a box of insects in gratitude for having received a piece from Sloane from his natural history collection.[28] Years later, while searching for curiosities and novelties for Sloane, Bartram sent him Native American artifacts, the function of which even he was uncertain. John Bartram collected and packed them for shipping from Philadelphia.

From the letters narrating this process, it is clear that the same practice of sending flowers and plants, pressed and dried, was used in the northern hemisphere. Furthermore, the documents provide a wealth of information regarding how collection and shipping processes were intricately woven with the ways in which knowledge was acquired. Bartram had to send two samples of each of the dried, pressed plants and tag each one with a number. Another recommendation was to wrap seeds in paper, separating each one from the others, and then place them in leather bags, although there were those who preferred to put them in crates with sand in order to maintain the dry conditions they required. Linnaeus suggested these ways of transporting seeds to keep them dry, adding that salt helped with this process. Other plants were sent in glass jars filled with alcohol, and still others were sent planted in soil-filled crates.[29] The dehydration of animal specimens was recommended to kill the pests living inside some of them. The British colonies suggested packing specimens in cotton or chaff. Shells, minerals, and corals "ought to be rolled up carefully in a piece of paper . . . by themselves to prevent rubbing, fretting, or breaking in carriage: and then all put together into some box, trunk, or old barrel, placing the heaviest and hardest at the bottom".[30]

Exhibition

Eighteenth-century theoretical approaches to nature were linked to the ways in which objects were exhibited as a compartmentalized system with divisions governed by preestablished criteria, as well as material containers appropriate for these systems. These containers were a sort of embodiment of the governing mental and visual system, which allowed both those imparting and obtaining knowledge to visualize and manipulate the results.

At the same time, collections affected the way the surrounding reality was catalogued and inventoried. In some cases, such as the bishop of Trujillo's, for example, ways of approaching the world around him were motivated not only by scientific growth, which was the governing interest of the time, but also by how the observed object might prove practical and useful. This not only explains the stimuli that inspired knowledge of the land but also the categories, nomenclature, and descriptions used for the chosen specimens. These categories, created to group certain objects within the same class, were the result of rational thought. The categories were created to organize both the discourse and the action. Humans who invent complex organizing systems also organize their lives and explain their world.[31] In fact, Bishop Martínez Compañón, and many other scholars from his time, were imbued with the ideas of illumination and therefore created documents and completed tasks to serve a useful function or for the benefit of science. Practically speaking, thorough and organized knowledge of the territory and its specimens could only benefit industry.[32]

This proposal for ordering and representing reality also corresponded with other parallel, contemporary ways of approaching the world with other man-made classifying systems such as, for example, the first scientific cabinets, which were organized in compartments and shelves housing series and objects related to one another. Hence, ways of thinking had a relationship with ways of collecting: cultural material was organized to reveal these ways of thinking.

This way of approaching the environment and supporting the acquisition of knowledge was inserted into a tradition originating in the sixteenth century for which organization of the specimens was as important as the specimens themselves; the act of grouping, organizing, and systemizing was what produced knowledge. Classifications and collections shared the same spirit in their approaches to reality. As John Elsner and Roger Cardinal argue, "Collecting is classification lived, experienced in three dimensions."[33] The history of collecting is, therefore, the story of how humans have accommodated, taken ownership of, and extended the taxonomies and knowledge systems they have inherited.[34]

These ways of compartmentalizing the collections appear to be mirrored in the compartmentalized way they are stored in material containers. Imagining such cases full of divisions and subdivisions leads immediately to thoughts of the cabinets these objects were usually displayed in. Glenn Adamson calls this phenomenon the "cabinetization of knowledge," by which he means that ways of organizing the mind have their equivalencies in the way material containers are organized to exhibit specimens.[35] I would like to insert a stage between the two: the ways collections are packed for shipping.

Ways of cataloguing objects in an inventory, of packing crates, of storing them, and/or exhibiting them in a cabinet, reveal ways of thinking and functioning. Storage solutions gradually evolved over time, revealing a shift in the approach to nature from the object of human admiration to an unknown that ought to be discovered and scientifically analyzed. Furniture that was created to store these collections was, likewise, part of this

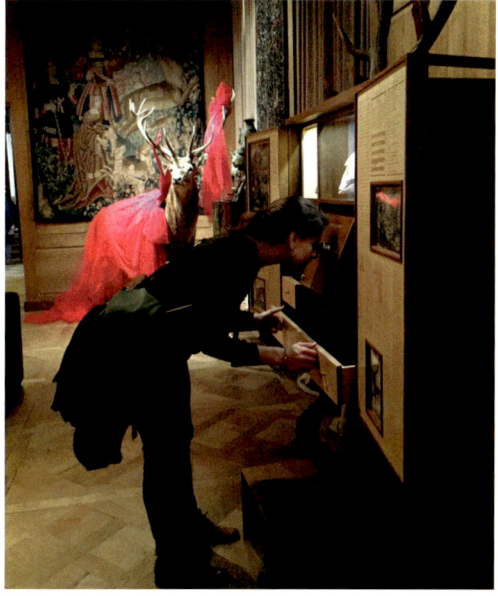

Fig. 9. Daniela Serra at the Musée de la Chasse et de la Nature, Paris, 2017.

process. It allowed for the movement of objects previously merely admired on the ceiling or wall to be lowered so an interested observer might analyze them in detail.[36] Cabinets of wonder (with birds of paradise, unicorns, salamanders, etc.) displayed at a distance were replaced by cabinets of curiosities (with magnifying glasses and lenses for personal inspection and accompanying information so the objects might be better understood). This, however, was a process, and it began in some parts of Europe as early as the end of the sixteenth century. This makes it possible

to say that there was no single way of collecting the world, and no two collections were exactly alike.[37] As early as the sixteenth century, Seville's collectors were stockpiling objects from America, not only to satisfy the needs of many for wonders and curiosities but also to meet with the scientific spirit growing among others. One example of the latter was Nicolás Monardes, who was in possession of a collection of diverse American specimens and a structure for his research and experiments aimed at creating new medicines.

Many of the species sent from different parts of the world hung in sixteenth-century collections, but they were more performative than scientific and were meant more to amaze than to explain. The seventeenth- and eighteenth-century cabinets, on the other hand, offered viewers and users up-close sensorial contact with the specimen, "a more analytical mode of presentation."[38] Previously, animals had been viewed in macro terms: their mere presence amazed their audience, which was stupefied by their sizes and shapes. With time, a micro approach became important, the opportunity to relate an object's details to its whole, for a viewer to learn by coming in close contact (fig. 9). Thus, these cabinets were important as observatories that presented a model of this world of objects in their classifications and relations.[39] To this end, material structures had to be designed in a way that allowed for careful scrutiny of the objects within. New scientific paradigms required a perspective that could focus in on the details without losing the big picture. Little by little, isolated fragments of the world would make way for the parts of a lineal and organized whole.[40] Kircher's baroque and esoteric puzzle would become an organized and rational whole.[41] Paraphrasing Stephen Greenblatt, a world of wonders became one of resonance in which displayed objects were capable of evoking systematic universes, mnemonic

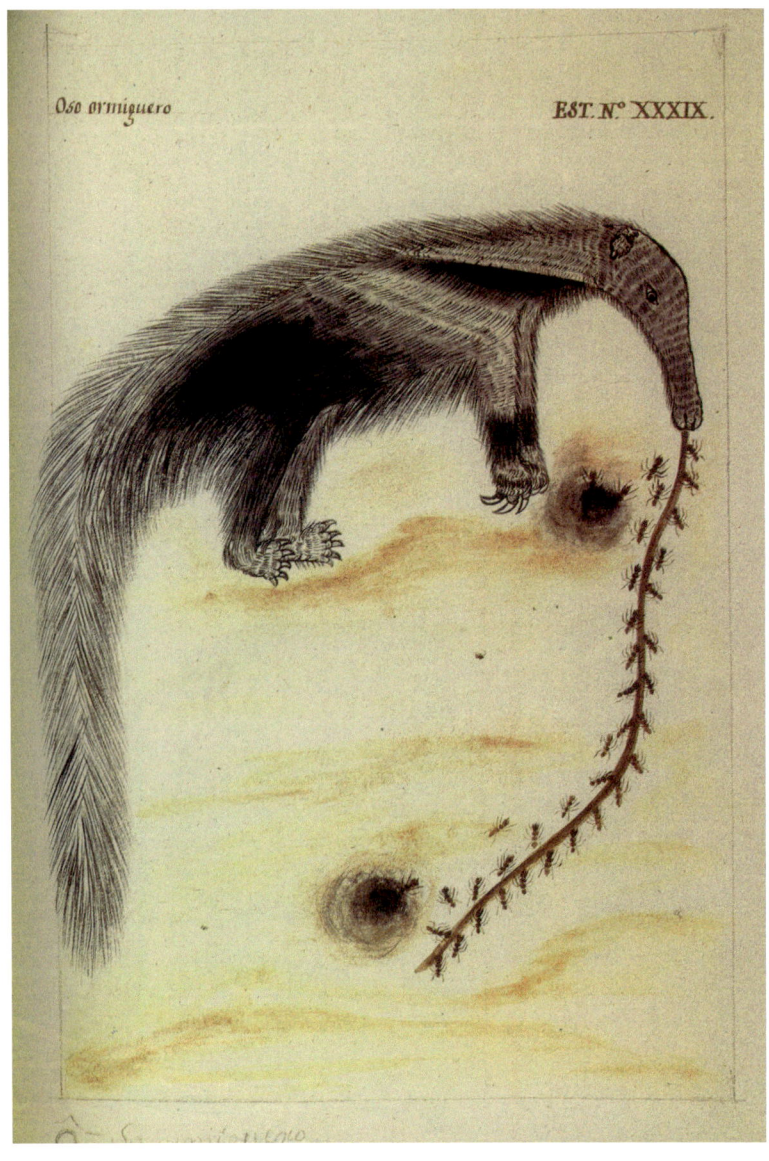

Fig. 10. Baltasar Jaime Martínez Compañón, *Oso hormiguero* (anteater). Peru, about 1782–90. Watercolor and pen on paper, 9½ × 6½ in. Real Biblioteca, Madrid.

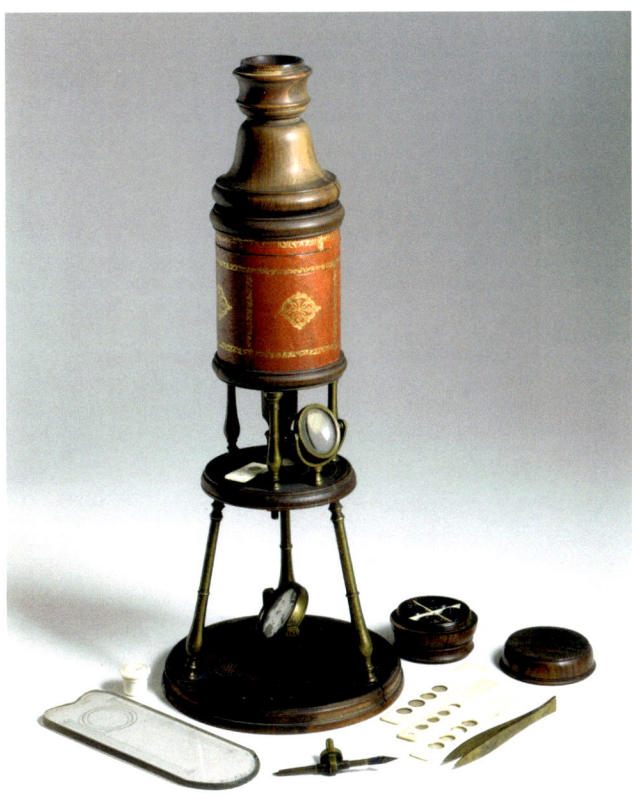

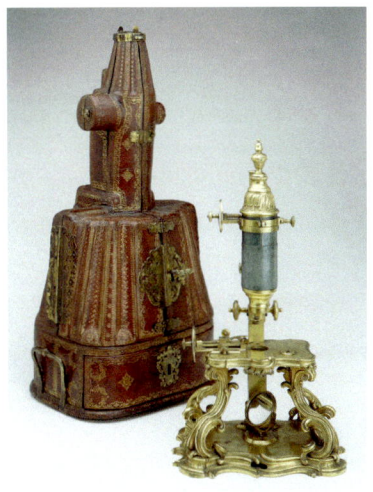

Fig. 12. Michel-Ferdinand d'Albert d'Ailly (inventor), compound microscope and case. Bronze mounts are attributed to Jacques Caffieri, France, about 1751. Gilt bronze, enamel, shagreen, and glass; wood, tooled leather, brass, velvet, silver galon, and various natural specimens. J. Paul Getty Museum, Los Angeles, California.

Fig. 11. Early Culpeper type microscope. England, about 1725. Brass, leather, pasteboard, and wood. Science Museum, London.

signs of a complex world being organized in the minds, the writings, and the facilities of the era.[42]

This would appear to explain the fact that many of the samples of animals included in Martínez Compañón's crates were sent in parts, thereby sacrificing perhaps the overall effect of the specimen but making a priority of maintaining intact those parts that could be damaged when crated. Such is the case of the anteater in Crate 18, whose tongue (probably this animal's most important and distinctive part) was packed separately from the rest of its body (fig. 10). To do so, the tongue was rolled up and wrapped in paper. Once it arrived in Spain, the tongue became one of the attractions at King Carlos III's Aranjuez Palace. Something similar happened with Crate 19, which included several birds. The bird called "majoma" was packed both as a whole specimen and in parts with the head, skin, and tail feathers separate from the bones and wings.

The case also contained the loose beaks of several (other?) birds.

Ways of cataloguing, packing, and exhibiting fragments of collections were also related to practices associated with the scientific method of the time, where the details of objects and specimens were the most important. The modern microscope was invented in 1830, but prior attempts to examine objects in detail, and a culture that was mostly visual and had epistemological preferences for detail, date back to the end of the seventeenth century and carry on through the eighteenth century (figs. 11 and 12). These instruments guaranteed the possibility of achieving the new type of visual knowledge required.

The index reveals another practice leading to a more scientific world: the direct relationship between things that were packed and the individual identity they assumed once registered in the index. Each object from the bishop of Trujillo's collection had its own identity. Cabinets of curiosities, on the other hand, subordinated the objects to rhetorical categories that prioritized wonders, causing the objects to lose their identity and become part of a category of things that embodied histories, fables, proverbs, and other maxims that were largely unscientific.[43] The objects collected from colonial Spain would no longer be considered mere curiosities and eccentricities from a person's private treasure, reserved so a few chosen people could see them in secrecy and with special permission; they were individual objects that could be seen and admired in a public space. The practice of utilitarian encyclopedism was still in use, in which folklore and oral history had a place in the description of objects and their exhibition.[44]

Final Thoughts

This chapter has revealed how eighteenth-century methods for acquiring knowledge, with features that can be traced back to the sixteenth century, were related to classification systems being developed and how, in turn, these were related to collection, packing, documentation, and information sharing practices. Traditional forms of acquiring knowledge and classifications based on classic texts and the Bible gave way to new cognitive ecologies that were more closely related to exploration of the physical world and experimentation.[45]

Notes

1 There is, however, a previous version by Atanasius Kircher; it inspired this print, and Noah's Ark appears in his work.

2 Geoffrey C. Bowker and Susan Leigh Star, *Sorting Things Out: Classification and Its Consequences* (Cambridge, MA: MIT Press, 1999).

3 Carlo Ginzburg, *Mitos, Emblemas e Indicios: Morfología e Historia* (Barcelona: Gedisa, 2008), 185–239.

4 Baltasar Jaime Martínez Compañón, *Razón de las especies de la naturaleza y del arte del obispado de Trujillo del Perú* (Seville: 1789).

5 Lambros Malafouris, *How Things Shape the Mind: A Theory of Material Engagement* (Cambridge, MA: MIT Press, 2013), 3. Malafouris's ideas are revealing. His contribution includes the "Material Engagement Theory": MET is the notion of the extended mind.

6 Jonathan Spackman and Stephen C. Yanchar, "Embodied Cognition, Representationalism, and Mechanism: A Review and Analysis," *Journal for the Theory of Social Behaviour* 44, no. 1 (2013): 47.

7 Arjun Appadurai, "Introduction: Commodities and the Politics of Value," in *The Social Life of Things: Commodities in Cultural Perspective,* ed. Arjun Appadurai (Cambridge: Cambridge University Press, 1986), 3–63.

8 James Clifford, *Dilemas de la cultura: Antropología, literatura y arte en la perspectiva posmoderna* (Barcelona: Gedisa, 1996), 262.

9 Emily Berquist Soule, *The Bishop's Utopia: Envisioning Improvement in Colonial Peru* (Philadelphia: University of Pennsylvania Press, 2014), 51.

10 Berquist Soule, *Bishop's Utopia,* 53.

11 Mark A. Meadow, "Introduction," in *The First Treatise on Museums: Samuel Quiccheberg's Inscriptions 1565,* trans. Mark A. Meadow and Bruce Robertson (Los Angeles, CA: Getty Publications, 2013), 30–31.

12 Berquist Soule, *Bishop's Utopia,* 2.

13 The assistance of locals in the recognition and collection of native species was likewise employed by the British colonies where slaves played an important role in the acquisition of species, according to accounts associated with the Hans Sloane collection. Sir Hans Sloane (1660–1753) was an Irish physician, naturalist, and collector. His collection provided the foundation of the British Museum, the British Library, and the Natural History Museum in London.

14 Lisa Trever and Joanne Pillsbury, "Martínez Compañón and His Illustrated 'Museum,'" in *Collecting across Cultures: Material Exchanges in the Early Modern Atlantic World,* ed. Daniela Bleichmar and Peter C. Mancall (Philadelphia: University of Pennsylvania Press, 2011), 240.

15 See Serge Gruzinski, *La guerra de las imágenes: De Cristóbal Colón, a "Blade Runner" (1492–2019)* (Mexico City: Fondo de Cultura Económica, 2013).

16 Christine Davenne, *Cabinets of Wonder* (New York: Abrams, 2012), 9.

17 George Louis Leclerc de Buffon, *Buffon's Natural History: Containing a Theory of the Earth, a General History of Man, of the Brute Creation, and of*

Vegetables, Minerals, &c. &c., 10 vols. (London: H. D. Symonds, 1797).

18 Davenne, *Cabinets of Wonder,* 85.

19 Daniela Bleichmar, "The Imperial Visual Archive: Images, Evidence, and Knowledge in the Early Modern Hispanic World," *Colonial Latin American Review* 24, no. 2 (2015): 236.

20 Berquist Soule, *Bishop's Utopia,* 4.

21 Berquist Soule, *Bishop's Utopia,* 10.

22 Berquist Soule, *Bishop's Utopia,* 3.

23 For an excellent essay about inventories in the modern world, see Giorgio Riello, "Things Seen and Unseen: The Material Culture of Early Modern Inventories and Their Representation of Domestic Interiors," in *Early Modern Things: Objects and their Histories, 1500–1800,* ed. Paula Findlen (New York: Routledge, 2013), 125–50.

24 Hans Sloane also described his species in English and not in Latin, the language used for natural history at that time.

25 Marco Beretta, "Collected, Analysed, Displayed: Lavoisier and Minerals," in *From Private to Public: Natural Collections and Museums,* ed. Marco Beretta (Sagamore Beach, MA: Science History Publications, 2005), 113.

26 José Joaquín Araneda Riquelme, "Un gobierno de papel: Los correos y las rutas de comunicación en tiempos de la reforma imperial en Chile (1764–1796)" (master's thesis, Pontificia Universidad Católica de Chile, 2017).

27 Bleichmar, "The Imperial Visual Archive," 239.

28 James Delbourgo, *Collecting the World: Hans Sloane and the Origins of the British Museum* (Cambridge, MA: Belknap Press of Harvard University Press, 2017), 243.

29 Delbourgo, *Collecting the World,* 174.

30 Delbourgo, *Collecting the World,* 121.

31 Mary Douglas, *Estilos de pensar: Ensayos críticos sobre el buen gusto* (Barcelona: Gedisa, 1998), 155.

32 The spirit behind eighteenth-century classification and collection of American objects was very different from that apparent in the sixteenth and seventeenth centuries, which generally demonstrated the divinity of creation, and specifically revealed medieval thought and tastes. In this sense, at first American objects showed the extent of paganism and later on showed the exoticism of faraway lands.

33 John Elsner and Roger Cardinal, "Introduction," in *The Cultures of Collecting,* ed. John Elsner and Roger Cardinal (London: Reaktion Books, 1994), 2.

34 Elsner and Cardinal, "Introduction," 2.

35 Glenn Adamson, "The Labor of Division: Cabinetmaking and the Production of Knowledge," in *Ways of Making and Knowing: The Material Culture of Empirical Knowledge,* ed. Pamela H. Smith, Amy R. W. Meyers, and Harold J. Cook (Ann Arbor: University of Michigan Press, 2014), 248.

36 Celeste Olalquiaga, "Object Lesson/Transitional Object: The Cabinet of Baron de la Mosson," *Cabinet Magazine* 20 (2005–6), http://www.cabinetmagazine.org/issues/20/olalquiaga.php.

37 Delbourgo, *Collecting the World,* 25.

38 Olalquiaga, "Object Lesson/Transitional Object."

39 Brent Nelson, "Investigate Tagging: Modelling the Early Modern Cabinet of Curiosities," *Digital Studies/ le Champ Numérique* 5, no. 1 (2014): https://www.digitalstudies.org/articles/10.16995/dscn.49.

40 Carla Yanni, *Nature's Museums: Victorian Science and the Architecture of Display* (New York: Princeton Architectural Press, 2005), 23.

41 Delbourgo, *Collecting the World,* 25.

42 Stephen Greenblatt, "Resonance and Wonder," *Bulletin of the American Academy of Arts and Sciences* 43, no. 4 (1990): 19.

43 Alessandro Tosi, "Wunderkammer vs. Museum? Natural History and Collecting during the Renaissance," in Beretta, *Private to Public,* 48.

44 This term is used to describe Hans Sloane's work, and I think it is applicable to this case presented here. Delbourgo, *Collecting the World,* 114.

45 See Anthony Grafton, *New Worlds, Ancient Texts: The Power of Tradition and the Shock of Discovery* (Cambridge, MA: Belknap Press of Harvard University Press, 1992).

MARÍA PAOLA RODRÍGUEZ PRADA

Ammonites, Gourds, Watercolors, and Lithograph Prints
Scientific Objects and Images for a Cultural History

This survey stresses the scientific character of material culture resulting from scientific practices carried out during the founding period of the Museo Nacional de Colombia (National Museum of Colombia). It emphasizes a cultural production circumscribed to a breakthrough political period between the Spanish colonial regime and the instauration of the republic by means of war. This cultural production, however, is embedded not only in a specific history of science but also in a history of mentalities forged in Europe and conveyed throughout Spanish America during the late Enlightenment period and the late eighteenth and early nineteenth centuries.

I follow James Secord's discussions about the history of science in terms of knowledge as a form of practice and, therefore, science as a practical activity. Science as a process includes experiment, fieldwork, and theory-making.[1] Evidence for these practices resides historically, as he puts it, in "experimental instruments, natural history specimens, and three-dimensional models. But it is equally true of pamphlets, drawings, journal articles, notebooks, diagrams, paintings, and engravings."[2] The material culture

or, better yet, this material scientific culture is what I will discuss here.

Colombia's museum was conceived, together with a school of mines, as a scientific and technical apparatus for the republic, and it was imbued with a sense of civilization and progress. The duration of the complex process in which they took shape, their concrete existence (with the technical expertise implied in such specific institutions), and the international diplomacy required (under which all recruitment of personnel was carried out) must not be separated from the broad social and cultural context in which they developed.[3] To promote public welfare and prosperity and to foster public instruction—purposes underlying the founding of this museum in Colombia—were significant values for humanity during the European Age of Enlightenment.[4] These values also shaped a generation of young people who were coming of age during the late viceroyalty period, and who then became the agents of renewal at the turning point in Colombia's independence.[5] Their behaviors, attitudes, and "mental equipment" were in keeping with local colonial Spanish mentalities.[6] Therefore, the material scientific culture I refer to is rooted not only in a matrix of public instruction and educational institutions but also in a long philosophical tradition in which reason was entitled to question nature, and science tended toward the intelligibility of natural problems and natural phenomena.[7]

This discussion on material culture will focus on three elements: the first, a newspaper article written in 1824 about the opening of the museum, which introduces the political context for the institution under which material scientific culture will be discussed. This press review supports the method adopted by this research in which printed material culture and manuscripts, as well as museum collections, are deemed legitimate sources for an exercise in microhistory. Secondly, with regard to the concept of material scientific culture, I engage in a case study of collections gathered at the national museum during its first decade of existence, particularly fossil specimens. In doing so, some problems in the discipline concerning ammonites will be discussed, bringing to light scientific practices of collection, description, and classification by means of scientific books and engravings. By this time, fossils were coveted specimens that would help unravel the age of Earth, and Madrid's Real Gabinete de Historia Natural (Royal Cabinet of Natural History, now Spain's National Museum of Natural Sciences) held a valuable keystone in solving this problem. Finally, I will discuss several watercolors and objects collected during the early 1820s and 1830s that provide an account of additional material culture that continued to be forged in other scientific practices during the museum's foundational period. These, however, were cultivated within an added private sphere in which agents linked to the museum facilitated the extensive circulation of objects among public and private academic circles while also furnishing public museum collections in France and Colombia.

Written Press: Traces of a New Country in a Newspaper Article about a Museum

On July 18, 1824, the *Gaceta de Colombia* (Gazette of Colombia; 1821–31), the government's weekly periodical, carried an account of the museum's official opening in Bogotá. It announced that the vice president of the republic, the secretary of the interior, and the secretary of war were in attendance, along with an "additional retinue." The *Gaceta* also briefly described a part of the collections exhibited, citing mineralogical samples, exogenous rocks (meteorites), and paleontological and zoological specimens, in addition to archaeological and ethnographical objects. Certain mineral samples were classified according to the methods of René-Just Haüy (1743–1822). It also noted the inclusion of a chemistry lab and a drawing room.[8] Earlier that year, the *Gaceta* reported that the museum had published a scientific memoir about a meteorite, which included a lithographic engraving of the rock (fig. 1).[9]

I would like to draw attention to two significant issues presented by this newspaper article: first, the official cortège in attendance at the opening, and, second, the scientific material culture regarding the collections on display; they reveal museological practices implied in the recognition of specialized labs and work spaces. My main interest, however, is in stressing the significance of the presence of government dignitaries at the inauguration, since it sheds light on the political context of the museum's founding.

In July 1823, Colombia's vice president and congress founded both a museum and a mining school. The political context at the time was unique given the fact that the museum was founded in the midst of the War of Independence from Spain. In July and August 1819, the battles of Pantano de Vargas (July 25) and Puente de Boyacá (August 7) secured the central territory

MUSEO COLOMBIANO

*Tenemos el placer de anunciar al públic
que el dia 4 del corriente se abrió el museo d
historia natural. S. E. el vicepresidente c
los secretaries del interior y de la guerra y
guna comitiva concurrieron á la apertura.*

*El museo en su infancia posé ya algun
cosas raras; las siguientes son las principa
les. Una coleccion de minerales arreglada se
gun el sistema del celebre Hüy, en la qu
se encuentran algunas muestras singular
por su cristalisacion y escasez. La mayor par
de estos minerales vienen de Europa y d
otras partes muy remotas. Tiene algun
pedazos de hierro meteorico encontrados e
diferentes partes de la República y analizado
por los señores Rivero y Boussengault.*

*Muchos huesos de animales desconocid
sacados en Suacha que son muy curiosos pe
su tamaño. Una momia encontrada cerca d
Tunja con su manta bien conservada, y se su
pone tener mas de 400 años. Algunos insec
tos de estraordinaria hermosura. Tambien pose
varios mamíferos, reptiles y peces y a
gunos instrumentos muy bien hechos; tiene
demas el establecimiento un laboratorio, y sal
de dibujo.*

*Deseoso el gobierno de fomentar un esta
blecimiento que es indispensable para prob*

Fig. 1. "Museo Colombiano," *Gaceta de Colombia* 144. Colombia, July 18, 1824. Letterpress printing on paper, full newspaper page 15.35 × 9.84 in. Biblioteca de la Presidencia de la República, Bogotá, Colombia.

of the viceroyalty of New Granada (est. 1717), by that time already christened Cundinamarca. In December of that same year, the transitional Congress of Angostura, recently installed in the city of Santo Tomás de Angostura (in present-day Venezuela), proclaimed the new Republic of Colombia, comprising the territories of Cundinamarca (now Colombia), which at the time included Panama and the former Captaincy General of Venezuela and the Real Audiencia of Quito. This congressional body, however, had been granted temporary status, valid only until 1821, when a more formal representative body would be instated in Bogotá. During the subsequent years, from 1821 to 1824, absolute

independence was gained: first in Venezuela with the Battle of Carabobo (June 24, 1821), and then in the Quito region in 1822 with the Battles of Bomboná (April 7) and Pichincha (May 24). Finally, in 1824, with the Battles of Junín (August 6) and Ayacucho (December 9), the Colombian army played a key role in securing Peru's independence.

In fact, in December 1819, the Congress of Angostura appointed a diplomatic corps to represent the new country before other states and European powers. Plenipotentiary delegate Francisco Antonio Zea (1766–1822) approached government circles in Spain, England, and France, seeking political recognition for Colombia, negotiating a loan to fund the war, and transacting all necessary means with which to promote development in Colombia. This included the recruitment in Paris and London, between 1821 and 1822, of a number of experts in the fields of geography, mechanics, mining engineering and exploitation, natural sciences, and lithographic printing techniques. The goal was to establish in Colombia a geographical engineering corps, a mining school and a corps of mining engineers, a museum, and a lithography workshop. This, as mentioned above, gave rise to the Museo de Colombia and the Escuela de Minas (School of Mines).

The *Gaceta* reported the museum's opening and emphasized the presence of the high-ranking officials, thus confirming the museum's place as part of the governmental apparatus. The presence of the vice president of the republic, Francisco de Paula Santander (1792–1840), implied representation from the highest level of the new executive government, for he was also acting president while President Simón Bolívar (1783–1830) was leading independence campaigns on the battlefield. In addition, Secretary of the Interior José Manuel Restrepo Vélez (1781–1863) attended not only in

Fig. 2. J. Delarue (lith.)—
Lemercier, Benard et
Cᵉ. (Imp.)—P. Bertrand
(Éditeur), Plate 1, Fossiles
de Colombie recueillis par
M. Boussingault (Fossils
from Colombia collected by
Mr. Boussingault). France,
1842. Lithography print
on paper, 12.59 × 9.84
in. Published in Alcide
d'Orbigny, *Coquilles et
échinodermes fossiles de
Colombie (Nouvelle-Grenade)*
(Paris: Bertrand Libraire-
Éditeur, 1842), [65].
Bibliothèque de l'École des
mines de Paris, MINES
ParisTech, Paris, France.

representation of the executive branch's main ministry but also as a member of the bureau to which public instruction, science, and fine arts organizations were ascribed. Finally, Secretary of War Pedro Briceño Méndez (1794–1836) was also present, presumably in keeping with his ministry's responsibilities with regard to engineering and engineering academies and schools.[10] A review of subsequent budgets signals that while national education expenses accounted for 1.15 percent of the secretary of the interior's total public expenditure in 1826, the museum's natural sciences chairs comprised 0.92 percent of that budget. Apparently, by the museum's third year,

the nation had invested in a single scientific institution more than 50 percent of the resources earmarked for all the educational institutions in the nation combined.[11]

A reading of the newspaper article in question suggests that natural resources, public instruction, and science appeared as one collective constituent feature of the process of forging the Republic of Colombia. Now I will discuss the scientific material culture in the museum's collections on display and some of the museological practices applied in its specialized workrooms.

Scientific Material Culture: The Search for Extinction in a Young Museum's Agenda

In 1842, French naturalist and traveler Alcide d'Orbigny (1802–1857) published in Paris a thorough description of a sampling of fossils titled *Coquilles et échinodermes fossiles de Colombie (Nouvelle-Grenade), recueillis de 1821 à 1833, par M. Boussingault, et décrits par Alcide D'Orbigny* (Fossil shells and echinoderms of Colombia [New Granada], collected from 1821 to 1833 by M. Boussingault and described by Alcide D'Orbigny).[12] The book included detailed lithographic engravings of the ammonite specimens mentioned in the title. These lithographs synthesize the processes of observation, collection, description, and classification of a scientific object, as well as the practices inherent in the legitimization of knowledge among a scientific community through publishing and circulation of print material culture. This mid-nineteenth-century publication presented specimens discovered during the founding period of Colombia's national museum and encompassed an even earlier period of scientific quest (fig. 2).

As the oeuvre's complete title suggests, the fossils described were collected by Jean-Baptiste Dieudonné Boussingault (1801–1887), one of

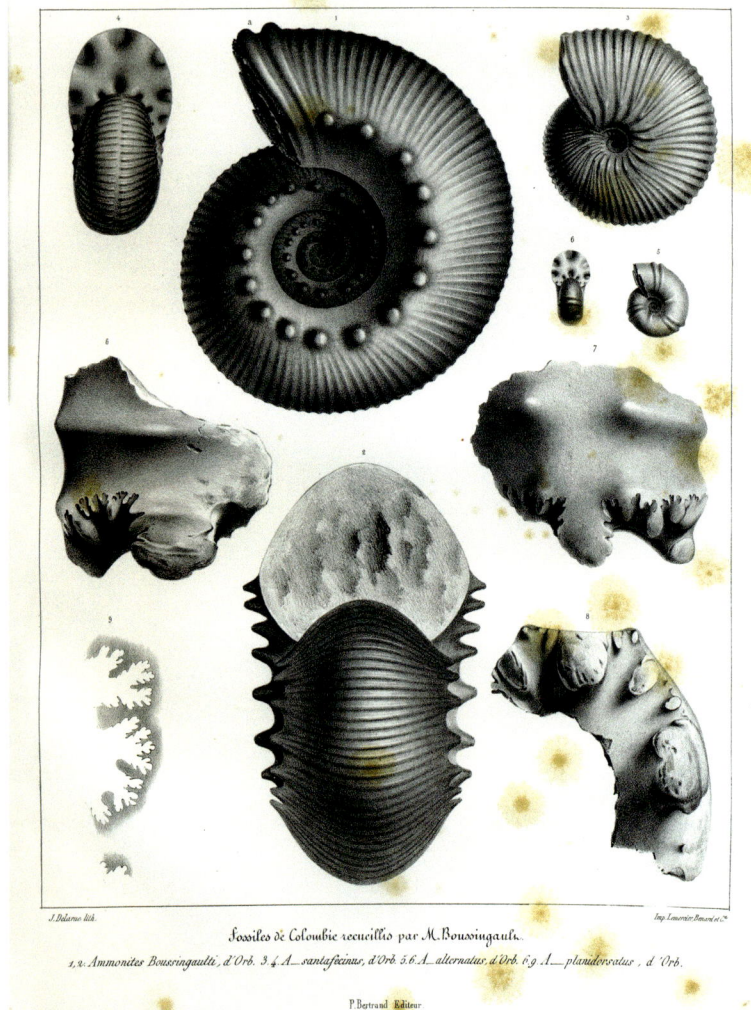

Fossiles de Colombie recueillis par M. Boussingault.

1, 2. Ammonites Boussingaulti, d'Orb. 3, 4. A. santafecinus, d'Orb. 5, 6. A. alternatus, d'Orb. 6, 9. A. planidorsatus, d'Orb.

P. Bertrand Éditeur.

the mining technicians appointed by Zea to serve in the mining corps in Colombia and to teach at the mining school, working under Mariano Eduardo de Rivero (1798–1857) to organize the school's mineralogical cabinet.[13] During Boussingault's stay in Colombia, working at the mining school and afterward with private British mining entrepreneurs, he gathered fossils and sent them to geologist and mining engineer Alexandre Brongniart (1770–1847), a teacher at the Muséum d'Histoire Naturelle in Paris since 1822 and a member of France's Académie des Sciences. Because Brongniart's other duties kept him busy, he delegated the study of these samples to d'Orbigny, who had recently arrived from his own expedition to meridional South America (1826–1833).[14]

These material traces of natural and geological specimens, and of the person who collected them, enable us to speculate about the types of collections present at the museum in Colombia while Boussingault worked for the mining school. The museum and the mining school shared premises and, therefore, study collections. Boussingault collected specimens mainly from three places: in the province of Carache in the southwestern part of the department of Venezuela, and later, in the provinces of Socorro and Bogotá in the northeastern part of the department of Cundinamarca.[15] The established route through these territories at the time suggests the course followed by Boussingault during his early expeditions in Colombia. The paucity of evidence regarding collections at the museum in Bogotá limits our knowledge of the extent of paleontological studies carried out there. Nevertheless, a cross-examination of other printed documents and manuscripts sheds light not only on these disciplinary practices at the museum but also on its participation in a larger quest to unravel the age of Earth and the changes in its fauna.

Indeed, Maria Margaret Lopes states that "letters, journals, scientific periodicals and literary and science publications" revealed the "diverse scientific cultural frameworks" under which "debates on the importance of fossils for explanations on the origin and transformation of life on Earth" took place.[16] These Colombian fossils exemplify the material scientific culture sustaining Lopes's alleged frameworks. The circuit for the specific geological knowledge-building in which these fossils were embedded can be observed by following Boussingault's collecting practice, their shipment to an Académie des Sciences member (Brongniart), their further submission for description and classification by another geologist whose travels to South America had gained him authority on the field (d'Orbigny), and, finally, the knowledge-building validation when classification results were corroborated by the Académie des Sciences, following submission of d'Orbigny's paper during academy sessions in September 1842 and January 1843. French intelligentsia was, therefore, well aware of these works.

At a meeting of the academy on January 23, 1843, a summary report on d'Orbigny's memoir was prepared and read by commissioners Élie de Beaumont (1798–1874), Armand Dufrénoy (1792–1857), Henri Milne-Edwards (1800–1885), and Alexandre Brongniart (as rapporteur).[17] The expertise of these members on crustacean or geological matters was well acknowledged; several of them belonged to France's Corps des Mines and had been or were currently teachers at the École des Mines in Paris and at the Muséum d'Histoire Naturelle, where they had shaped and augmented geological and mineralogical collections. De Beaumont had, in addition, participated in the making of France's geological maps.

D'Orbigny described the forty-three specimens sent by Boussingault and identified among them cephalopods (eight types of ammonites),

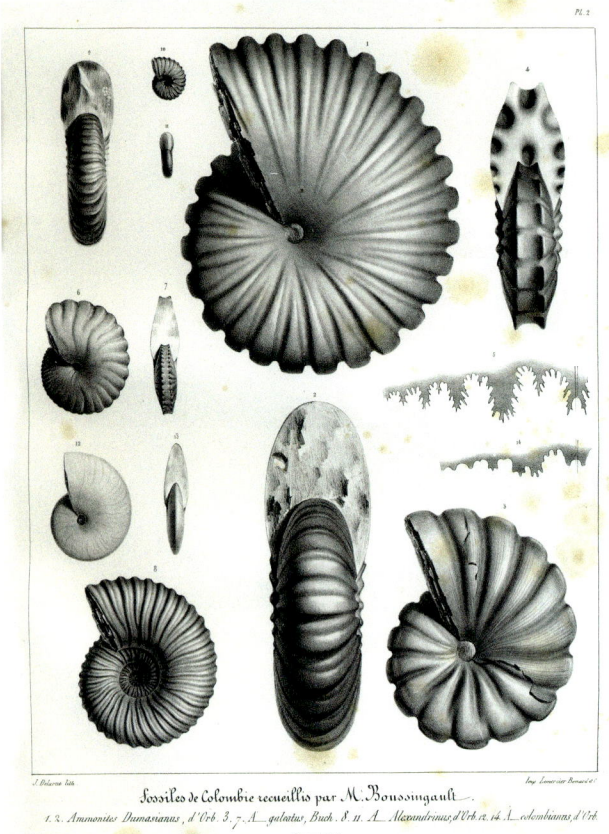

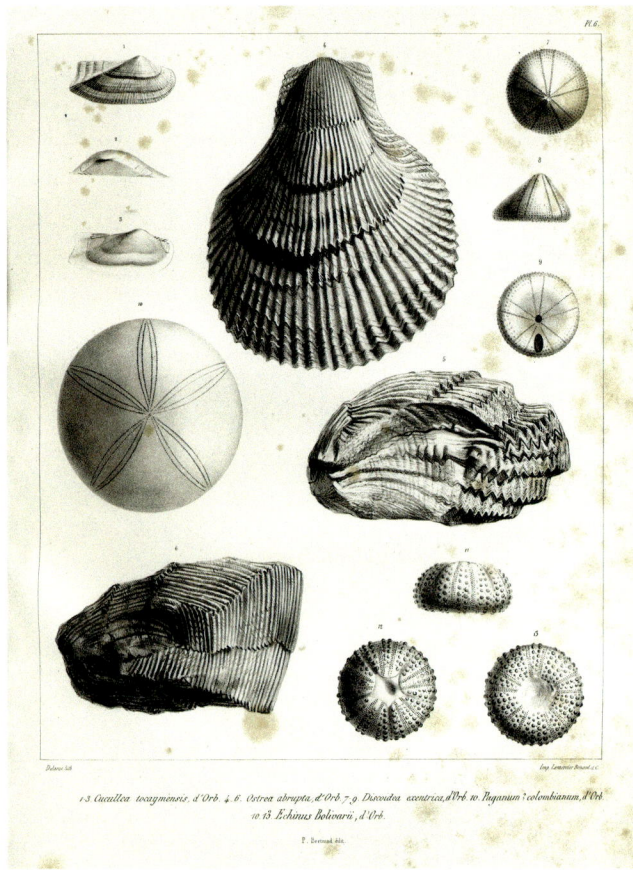

Fig. 3. J. Delarue (lith.)—Lemercier, Benard et Cᶜ. (Imp.)—
P. Bertrand (Éditeur), Plate 2, Fossiles de Colombie recueillis
par M. Boussingault (Fossils from Colombia collected by
Mr. Boussingault) France, 1842. Lithography print on paper,
12.59 × 9.84 in. Published in Alcide d'Orbigny, *Coquilles et
échinodermes fossiles de Colombie (Nouvelle-Grenade)* (Paris:
Bertrand Libraire-Éditeur, 1842), [67]. Bibliothèque de l'École
des mines de Paris, MINES ParisTech, Paris, France.

Fig. 4. J. Delarue (lith.)—Lemercier, Benard et Cᶜ. (Imp.)—
P. Bertrand (Éditeur), Plate 6, "1.3. Cucullea tocaymensis,
d'Orb. 4-6. Ostrea abrupta, d'Orb. 7-9. Discoidea exentrica,
d'Orb. 10. Paganum ? colombianum, d'Orb. 10.13. Echinus
Bolivarii, d'Orb. France, 1842. Lithography print on paper,
12.59 × 9.84 in. Published in Alcide d'Orbigny, *Coquilles et
échinodermes fossiles de Colombie (Nouvelle-Grenade)* (Paris:
Bertrand Libraire-Éditeur, 1842), [75]. Bibliothèque de l'École
des mines de Paris, MINES ParisTech, Paris, France.

gastropods (six total from genera *Natica, Acteon,*
and *Rostellaria*), lamellibranchs (twenty-six types
from genera *Cardium, Venus, Astarte, Lucina,
Tellina, Anatina, Nucula, Trigonia, Cuculloea,
Modiola, Lithodamus, Inoceramus, Ostrea,* and
Exogyra) and echinoderms (three genera:
Echinus, Discoidea, and *"Paganum [??]"*) (figs. 3
and 4).[18] After comparing these with European
specimens and other American samples, he con-
cluded that the Colombian fauna must have existed between the last strata of the Carboniferous
period and the first Tertiary deposits. He stated
that "this interval is composed in Europe by
Triassic terrains, Jurassic terrains and Cetacean
terrains."[19] Academy commissioners acknowledged this work by recognizing its "thorough
description" and "application to geological
matters": the precise identification of genera and
species as well as their comparison with those
similar to European specimens and the type of
terrains in which they were found as well as the
resulting geological period that they must have

been related to. Commissioners also praised the "critical considerations" that led d'Orbigny to establish new species until then unknown to science, as well as his application of a "comparison method" by which he contrasted the fossils with earlier classifications for marine fauna fossils collected in other South American countries in addition to Colombia.[20] This included, for instance, Léopold de Buch's (1774–1853) classifications in 1839 of Colombian fossils collected by Alexander von Humboldt (1769–1859) and Carl H. Degenhardt (1790–1848), and also Isaac Lea's (1792–1886) classifications in 1840 of samples gathered by J. H. Gibbon.[21] The marine fauna fossils collected by Boussingault, therefore, served this complex process of geological knowledge-building, which Lopes describes as "between fieldwork and laboratory science."[22]

The outcome of Boussingault's fieldwork would quite naturally have converged in the Colombian Escuela de Minas mineral and geological collections, thereby revealing a wider and collective scientific practice cultivated by personnel at the school and the museum. Recall the aforementioned newspaper article describing the opening of the Colombian museum and examine again its brief account of the collections exhibited there: mineral samples, meteorites, entomology and ichthyology specimens, reptiles and mammals, and, apparently, several paleontological, archaeological, and ethnographical objects. The reported paleontological specimens were bones from "unknown animals" excavated in a place called Sucha (now Soacha) and were "curious for their size."[23] Georges Cuvier (1769–1832) had specifically commissioned the bones to Rivero, himself appointed by Zea to establish and act as chief director of the museum and school of mines in Bogotá, and to set up the mining corps.[24] Cuvier was the perpetual secretary of the Académie des Sciences and director of the Muséum d'Histoire Naturelle. Zea consulted

with him, asking for the Parisian museum's graduate specialists who "could establish in Colombia the basis of science teaching."[25]

Since 1796, Cuvier had presented his studies of living and fossilized elephant species to the academy, thus introducing the notion of extinction. He was head of the animal anatomy department (1802), which he later reformulated as "compared anatomy." Martin Rudwick explains that by 1812, with his work *Recherches sur les ossemens fossiles de quadrupèdes, où l'on rétablit les caractères de plusieurs espèces d'animaux que les révolutions du globe paroissent avoir détruites* (Research on the fossilized bones of quadrupeds, where are restored the characters of various species of animals which the revolutions of the globe appear to have destroyed), Cuvier's theories had already coalesced. The nature of bones varied depending on the strata where they were found. Conclusions on stratigraphy were drawn by the shared works of Cuvier and geologist Alexandre Brongniart. Theories related to anatomy and their relationship to particular periods in Earth's evolution imbricated stratigraphic research performed at the time with the unification of geological terminology.[26] The circumstances surrounding Cuvier's paleontological work, and the official posts he held at the French scientific institutions contacted by Zea, therefore explain why the bones excavated in Soacha (and from the so-called Ground of Giants) among the collections at the museum in Bogotá were anything but random. They have direct links to scientific practices applied in Paris, especially at the Muséum d'Histoire Naturelle. Although Cuvier's knowledge of extinct fauna's archaeological sites in Colombia was undoubtedly based on Humboldt's earlier travels to New Granada and his specimen collections, not to mention Humboldt's scientific liaisons with local intelligentsia such as Francisco José de Caldas (1768–1816),[27] Cuvier explicitly charged Rivero

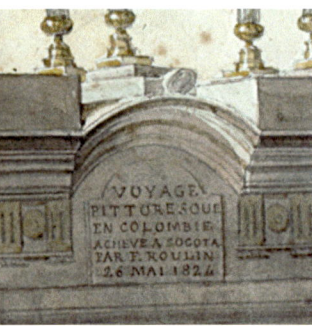

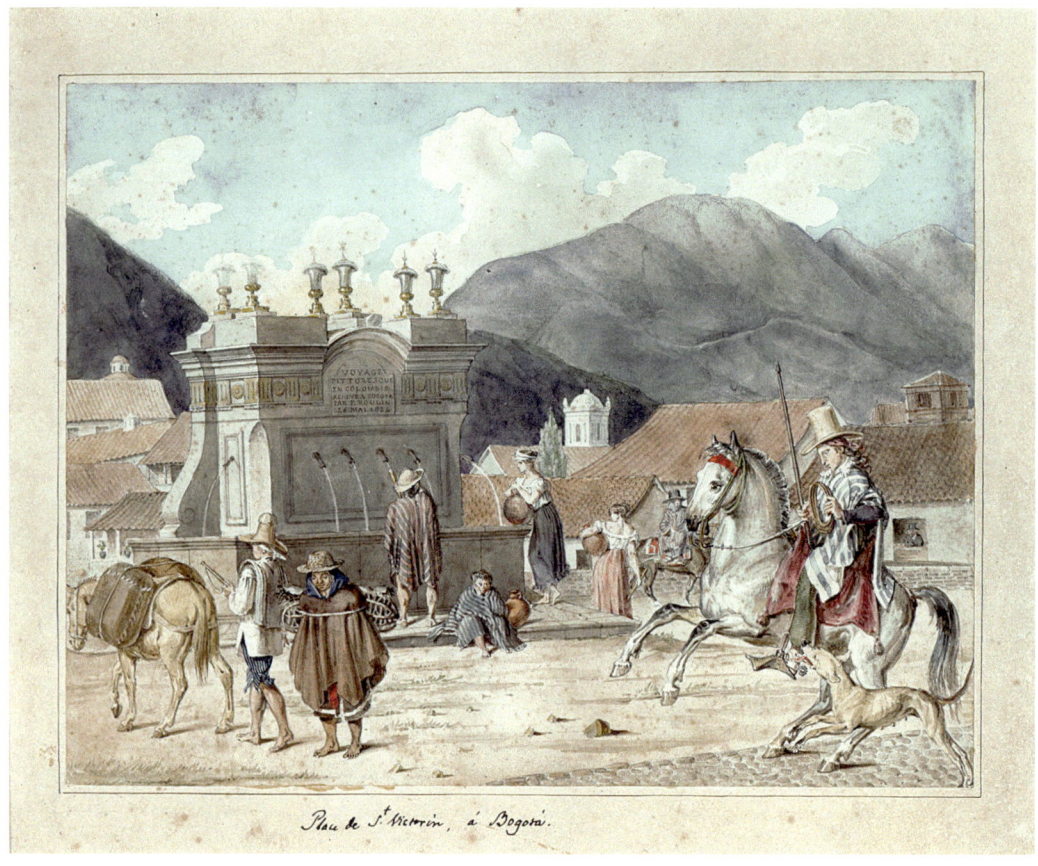

Fig. 5. François-Désiré Roulin, *Place de St. Victorin, à Bogotá (Plaza de San Victorino, en Bogotá)* [Plaza of San Victorino in Bogotá]. Colombia, May 26, 1824. Watercolor on paper, 7.87 × 10.23 in. AP4088, Colección de Arte del Banco de la República, Bogotá, Colombia.

Place de S.t Victorin, à Bogotá.

with the task of collecting these bones, and Rivero, in doing so, integrated the scientific apparatus of knowledge-building into the museum's collections and research in Colombia.[28]

Rivero's search for and excavation of the giant bones, as well as their shipment to Cuvier, were well accomplished.[29] The shipment's arrival in Paris is documented in writing, as is Cuvier's description of the shipment as "mastodon bones."[30] Scholars have closely studied Cuvier's paradigmatic search for extinct mammal fossils since 1796.[31] This included his eagerness to access the coveted *Megatherium* at Madrid's Real Gabinete de Historia Natural, reconstructed in 1793 by Juan Bautista Bru (1740–1799) following its discovery in 1787 by Dominican friar Manuel Torres in the Luján region near Buenos Aires,[32] as well as several enterprises to ship other dinosaur skeletons to Europe by means of keen

British, French, and German diplomatic agency and what Irina Podgorny calls the "recording practices of public servants and instructions of colonial administrators."[33] Cuvier's scientific practice was sustained not only by cabinet comparative work performed on natural specimens but also by wider analyses that included the study of "substitute specimen samples." The latter were based on drawings and molds exchanged among various correspondents throughout Europe and the Americas.[34]

Since the late 1780s, Spanish America under Bourbon rule had provided Madrid's Real Gabinete with a remarkable fossil specimen (the *Megatherium*), and European intelligentsia attempted to unravel its mysteries. Thus, physical bones, drawings, molds, engravings, and written descriptions constituted the material scientific culture that helped to forge the discipline of

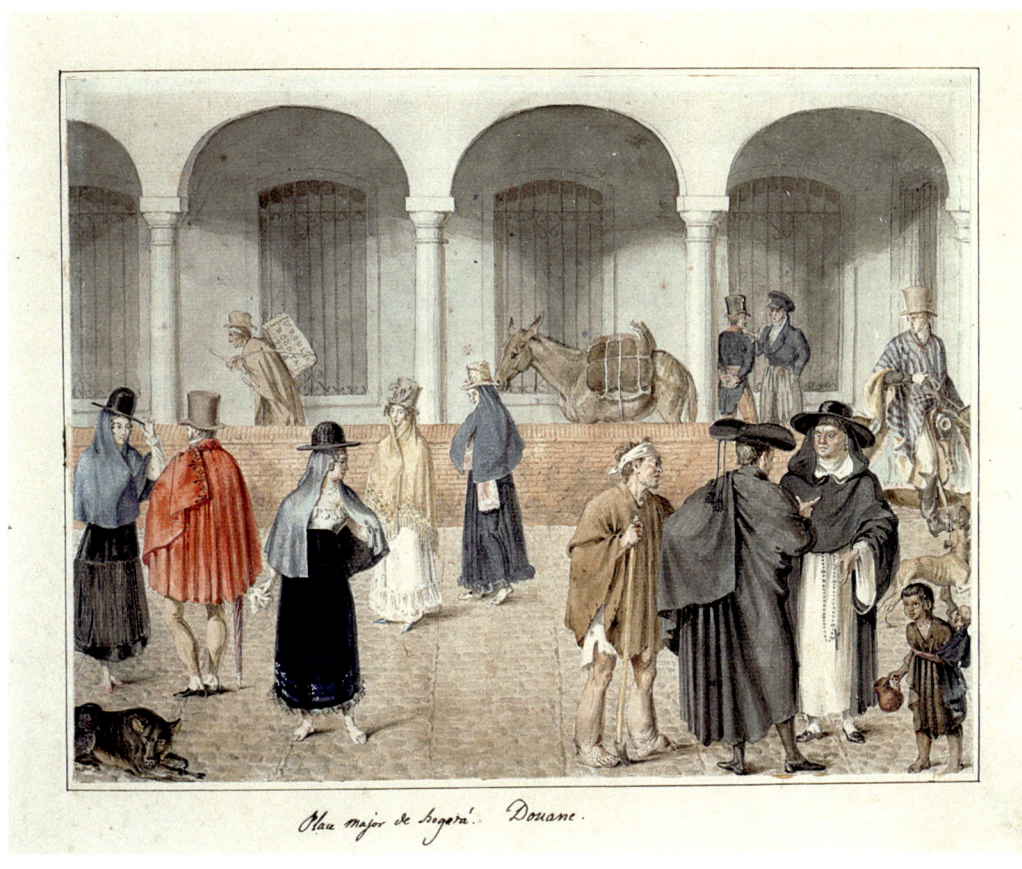

Plau major de bogotá. Douane.

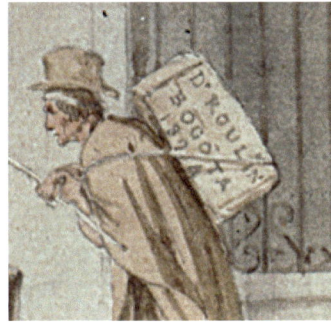

Fig. 6. François-Désiré Roulin, *Place major de Bogotá: Douane (Plaza mayor de Bogotá: Aduana)* [Main square in Bogotá: Customs building]. Colombia, 1824. Watercolor on paper, 7.87 × 10.23 in. AP4087, Colección de Arte del Banco de la República, Bogotá, Colombia.

paleontology, while geology continued to shape answers about the age of the planet throughout the nineteenth century. The lithographic engravings of the ammonites discussed here contributed to this long chain of material scientific culture.

Observing the Locals: The Picturesque as an Ethnographic Concern

On April 21, 1825, before returning home to Peru, Rivero wrote a letter to Humboldt from Bogotá. Among his accounts, Rivero spoke of the museum he founded and of its collections, of his latest travels to various mining sites, and a project he was working on with one of his museum colleagues, François-Désiré Roulin (1796–1874). He wrote, "In the company of Dr. Roulin, whom you know very well for his different talents, we have decided to publish a short work on the monuments of

the ancient Yndios of Cundinamarca. We have a nice collection of gold and copper *tunjos* [votive anthropomorphic figurines], several vases, and 18 drawings of the curious and colossal statues that are found in San Agustín, 3 days from Neyba."[35] Watercolors by Roulin and certain objects currently preserved in different French museums can therefore be traced to the official scientific framework of the national museum in Bogotá, regardless of their parallel development in the private sphere of these individuals' personal interests. As a physician who specialized in physiology, Roulin was also recruited by Zea in July 1822. Roulin requested that Zea allow him to engage in comparative human physiology, but because he had studied at the École Polytechnique in Paris, he ended up lecturing at the mining school in Bogotá on elemental mathematics, descriptive geometry, mechanics, and drawing.[36] While Roulin was at secondary school in Rennes, the French Comité d'Instruction Publique (Committee for Public Instruction) introduced drawing into the general studies curriculum, and Roulin was trained in linear drawing, landscape perspective, and human anatomy drawing. He went on to exploit these artistic skills during his subsequent physiology studies and, later on, as part of his natural science observations while in Colombia.

Roulin's artistic ability interests us not only with regard to the "short work on the monuments of the ancient Yndios of Cundinamarca" he was planning to publish with Rivero[37] but also because of a series of watercolors he painted (generally undated, except for two, inscribed with the following legends: "Picturesque Journey in Colombia / Finished in Bogota by F. Roulin May 26, 1824" and "Dr Roulin / Bogota / 1824") (figs. 5 and 6).[38] Although there are indications that he planned to publish a book, the compendium—like the one mentioned by Rivero—either never came to fruition or remains as yet unknown. However,

in his existing watercolors depicting part of his travels in Colombia, Roulin recorded scenarios, landscapes, local inhabitants, and daily activities under a particular ethnographic gaze. These images are among the few references for daily life and customs of the early nineteenth-century Colombian republic period. Although a complete "picturesque journey" was never published under Roulin's authorship, his images served as visual sources for later printed journals, books written by other travelers, and scientific texts.[39]

One of the most noteworthy examples of these books was printed in 1841. Under d'Orbigny's direction, the editors of *Voyage pittoresque autour du monde* published a well-known miscellany of travel accounts to the Americas since the seventeenth century titled *Voyage pittoresque dans les deux Amériques.*[40] It was profusely illustrated with maps and engravings (soft-ground etchings on steel plates) drawn by Louis-Auguste de Sainson (1801–1887). Among these illustrations

Fig. 7. François-Désiré Roulin, *Danse du pays (Baile típico)* [Country dance]. Colombia, ca. 1823. Watercolor on paper, 7.87 × 10.23 in. AP4090, Colección de Arte del Banco de la República, Bogotá, Colombia.

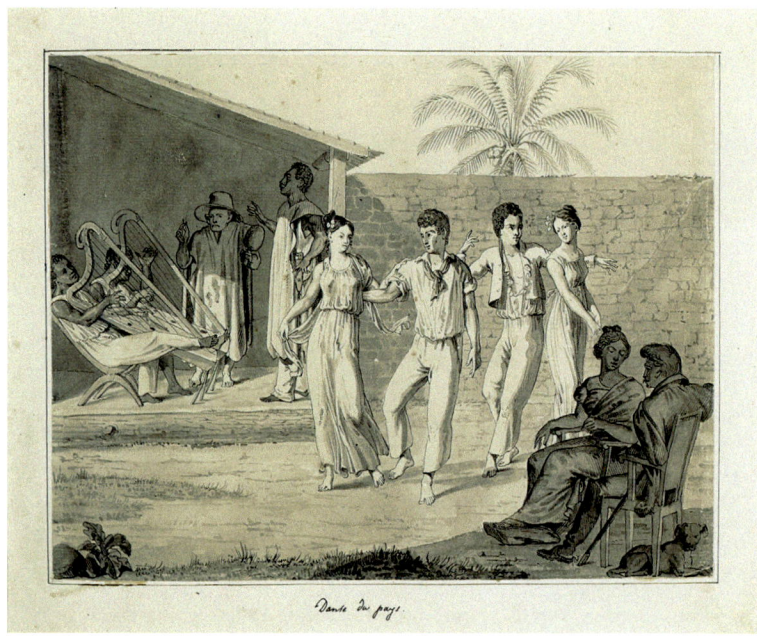

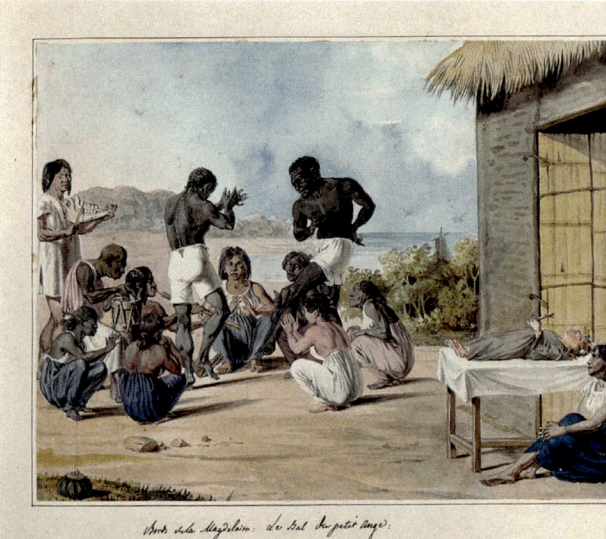

Fig. 8. François-Désiré Roulin, *Bords de la Magdelaine: Le bal du petit ange (Orillas del Magdalena: El baile del angelito)* [Edges of the Magdalena river: The little angel's ball]. Colombia, ca. 1823. Watercolor on paper, 7.87 × 10.23 in. AP4077, Colección de Arte del Banco de la República, Bogotá, Colombia.

were several Colombian scenes based on original sketches drawn from real life by Roulin. In addition to providing the customary genre scenes, their rich iconography has served material culture studies in terms of portraying lasting traditions dating from the late Spanish colonial period as well as cultural mixtures (figs. 7–10).[41]

In support of the argument about material scientific culture, I shall point out two of Roulin's watercolors, *Bords de la Magdelaine: Ménage d'une famille de pêcheur* (Banks of the Magdalena: Fisherman family's household; AP4080) and *Le Vagre, poisson de la Magdelaine: Selles, ustensiles* (The Catfish, fish of the Magdalena: Saddles, utensils; AP4085), both dated approximately 1823 (figs. 11 and 12). The overriding anthropological perspective of these images portrays, for example in the first watercolor, Native figures placed in front of detailed representations of natural specimens. On the painting's right side is a depiction of what looks like a *Crescentia cujete*,

commonly known as a calabash tree. The second watercolor adheres to a more descriptive and scientific composition style in which elements are represented naturalistically on a single plane, with no atmospheric background and no concern for comparative scale between depicted objects. In the lower right-hand corner of the watercolor are a number of traditional, locally made utensils manufactured from the fruit of the aforementioned calabash tree. And so, an example of the natural flora carefully observed and studied in the first watercolor under scientific practices carried out by museum personnel is further explored for its anthropological interest in the second watercolor, despite the fact that this field of study had not yet been epistemologically constituted at the time these paintings were created.

Known visual documentation of Native as well as local household paraphernalia in the early 1820s in Colombia is very rare, and these watercolors provide evidence of daily life at the

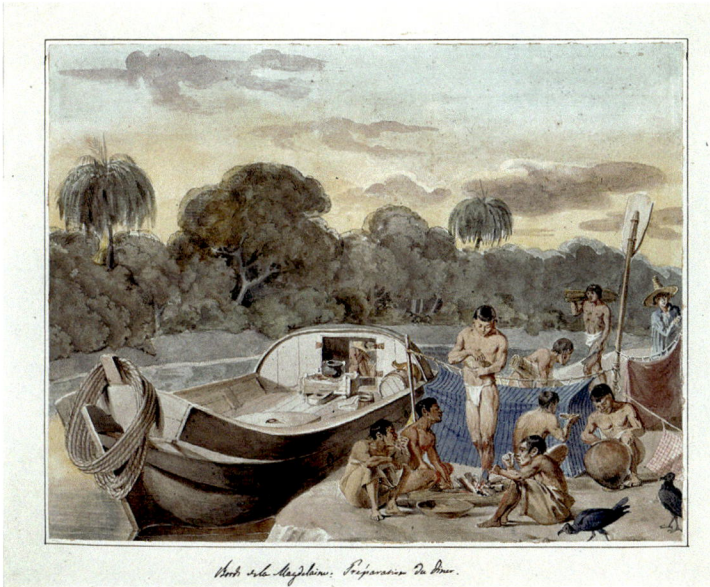

Fig. 9. François-Désiré Roulin, *Bords de la Magdelaine: Préparation du dîner (Orillas del Magdalena: Preparación de la cena)* [Edges of the Magdalena river: Preparing dinner]. Colombia, ca. 1823. Watercolor on paper, 7.87 × 10.23 in. AP4081, Colección de Arte del Banco de la República, Bogotá, Colombia.

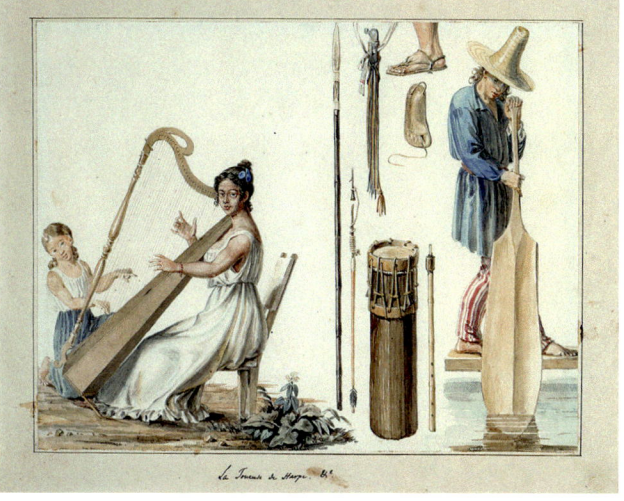

Fig. 10. François-Désiré Roulin, *La joueuse de harpe (La intérprete de arpa)* [The harp player]. Colombia, ca. 1823. Watercolor on paper, 7.87 × 10.23 in. AP4086, Colección de Arte del Banco de la República, Bogotá, Colombia.

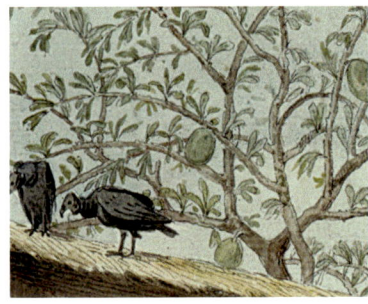

Fig. 11. François-Désiré Roulin, *Bords de la Magdelaine: Ménage d'une famille de pêcheur (Orillas del Magdalena: Hogar de una familia de Pescadores)* [Edges of the Magdalena river: Household of a fishing family]. Colombia, ca. 1823. Watercolor on paper, 7.87 × 10.23 in. AP4080, Colección de Arte del Banco de la República, Bogotá, Colombia.

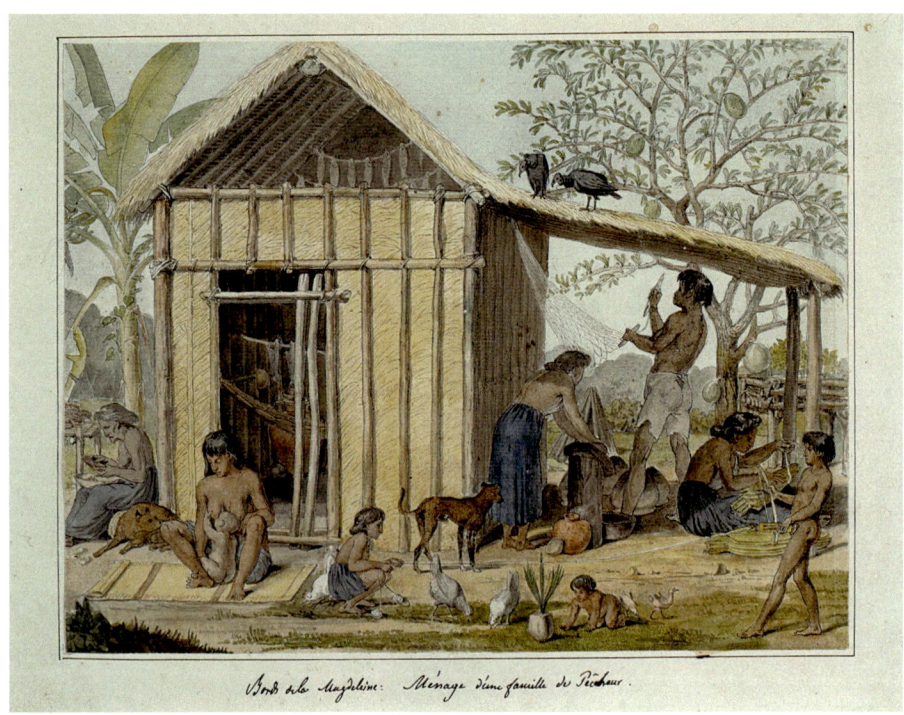

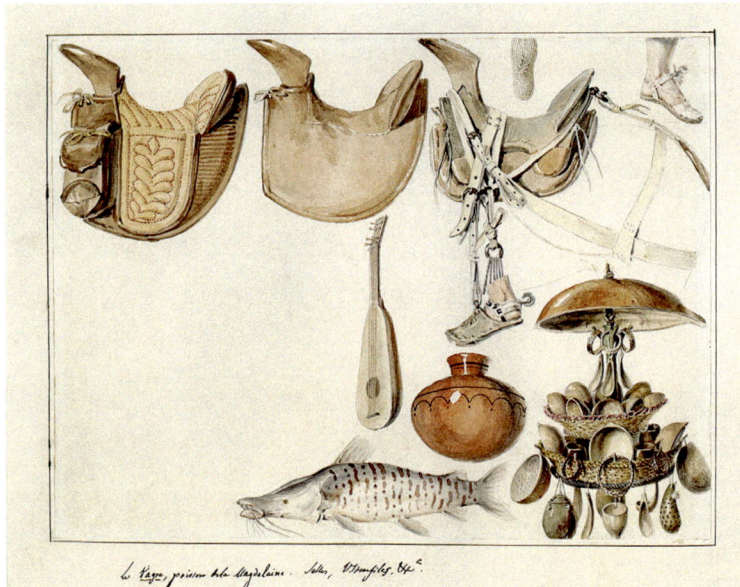

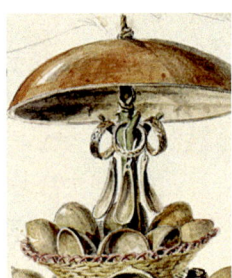

Fig. 12. François-Désiré Roulin, *Le Vagre, poisson de la Magdelaine: Selles, ustensiles (El bagre, pescado del Magdalena: Sillas, utensilios)* [The catfish of the Magdalena river: Saddles, utensils]. Colombia, ca. 1823. Watercolor on paper, 7.87 × 10.23 in. AP4085, Colección de Arte del Banco de la República, Bogotá, Colombia.

time, including the utilitarian appropriation of local flora. Although antiquities, curiosities, and *artificialia* were previously observed and collected by travelers during the early Spanish America colonial period, and have been well documented by scholars,[42] Roulin's visual descriptions seem to be part of a systematic exercise in observation and description that can only be fully comprehended by placing the fragmented objects into their wider general context.

Conclusion: When Images Become Museum Objects

The calabash utensils depicted in the watercolor were obviously re-signified by the observer's interest. Their significance as material culture or, better yet, as material scientific culture, would later be reinstated when they became collectible objects and were sent to various museums. The Musée des Beaux-Arts at Lons-le-Saunier in France lists among its collections object numbers 5061 and 5062, described as "Bowl" and "Bowl with a golden frieze decoration," respectively (figs. 13–15).[43] These bowls made from gourds were donated by a certain Mr. Goudot, apparently in 1843. Tracing the objects and the surname of their donor leads us back to the Museo Nacional de Colombia of 1823, and perhaps to the previously cited newspaper article stating that the museum possessed "several mammals, reptiles and fish and some very well made instruments."[44]

Francisco Antonio Zea recruited a certain Justin-Marie Goudot (1802–1847) for Colombia's museum as one of its natural history collectors.[45] Goudot's work was much appreciated by the museum's directors. Some records show that by 1826 he had increased the collection "twofold, with birds, amphibians, fish and insects" and "deposited 45 genera of plants," duly organized, in the museum's herbarium.[46] I have previously studied Goudot, citing his academic profile and the collections he carried back to France when he and his family returned in October 1842.[47] Goudot departed Colombia for France aboard the *Chaires* in company of his wife, Catalina Goudot, aged twenty-five, and their children Hipólito and Emilie, six and two years old, respectively. On their way home, the family stopped in New York on October 29,

1842.[48] Some of the specimens he imported to France were acquired by the Muséum d'Histoire Naturelle in Paris and by private collectors. While residing in Colombia, Justin-Marie Goudot also sent descriptions, drawings, and samples to his naturalist brother, Jules-Prosper (1803–ca. 1861) in Madagascar (April 23, 1828), who worked as a *voyageur-naturaliste* (naturalist-traveler) for the Muséum d'Histoire Naturelle in Paris.[49] Justin-Marie's Colombian sojourn apparently attracted a third Goudot brother as well, Etienne (1801–ca. 1863),[50] who arrived to Colombia in 1824, after embarking in Falmouth (England) on the schooner *George,* bound for Philadelphia (USA) where he landed on May 3.[51] Aside from the word "clerk" listed as Etienne Goudot's occupation on the ship's list of arrival, very little is known of his affairs in Colombia. He did, however, figure actively in Bogotá as a pharmacologist from 1825 until the early 1830s.[52] His pharmacy sold laboratory and medical equipment, as well as art supplies and other items imported from abroad.[53] On March 15, 1837, Etienne and his eighteen-year-old wife, Ignacia Goudot, sailed from the port of Cartagena in Colombia to New York aboard the *Marcelino,* and then

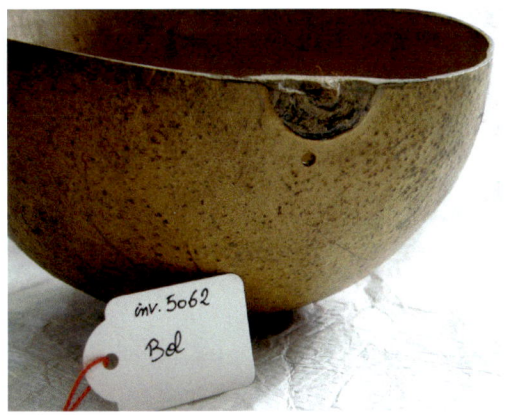

Fig. 13. Unknown artist, *Bol* (Bowl); detail. Colombia, n.d. [possibly collected 1830s]. Gourd pierced and cut, 3.14 × 6.29 × 5.51 in. Etienne Goudot (donor), 1843. Inv. 5062, Musée des Beaux-Arts, Lons-le-Saunier, France.

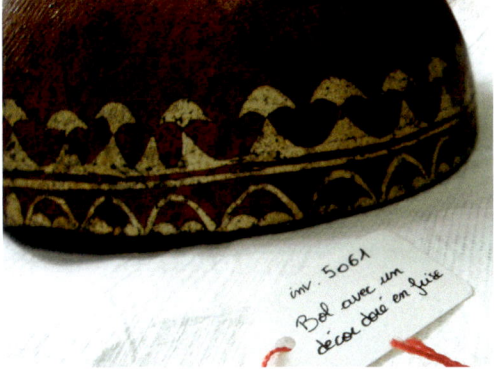

Fig. 14. Unknown artist, *Bol avec un décor doré en frise* (Bowl with a golden frieze ornament); detail. Colombia, n.d. [possibly collected 1830s]. Gourd pierced, cut, and painted, 3.54 × 7.08 × 6.29 in. Etienne Goudot (donor), 1843. Inv. 5061, Musée des Beaux-Arts, Lons-le-Saunier, France.

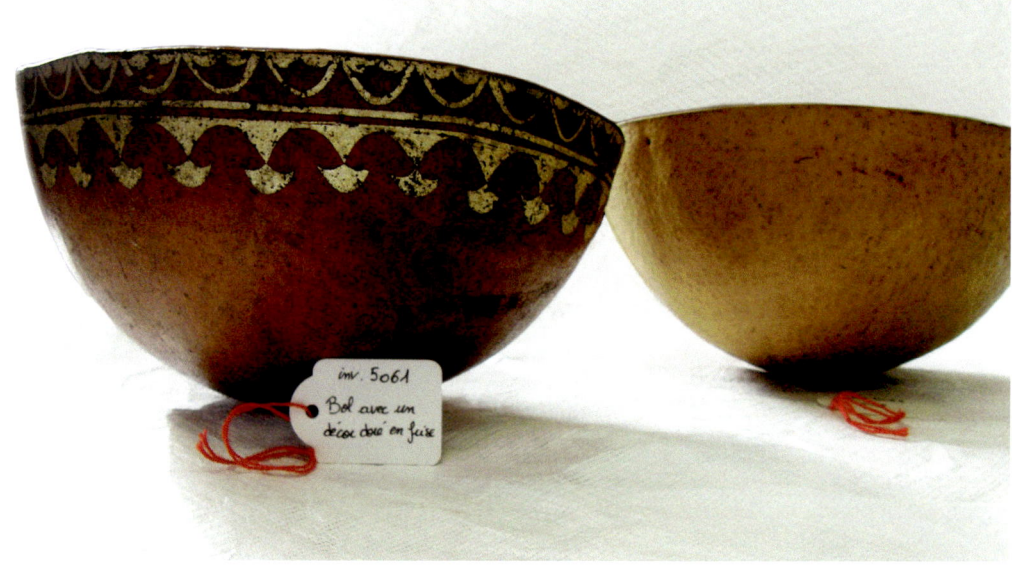

Fig. 15. Unknown artist, *Bol avec un décor doré en frise* (Bowl with a golden frieze ornament), and *Bol* (Bowl). Colombia, n.d. [possibly collected 1830s]. Gourds pierced, cut, and one of them painted. Etienne Goudot (donor), 1843. Inv. 5062 and 5061, Musée des Beaux-Arts, Lons-le-Saunier, France.

continued on to France.[54] He must have returned to Colombia, however, to carry on with his business since new manuscript evidence places him in Bogotá in 1838, supplying chemical equipment to the national museum.[55] Also, an infant Félix-Etienne Goudot was born in Bogotá on May 30, 1840, and was listed as accompanying a "merchant" E. Goudot traveling aboard the *Martin W Brett* to France via New York in May 1843.[56] Aside from transporting goods, Goudot's high mobility favored a widespread and frequent circulation of material scientific culture.

Between the 1830s and 1850s, all three Goudot brothers were registered members of the Société d'Émulation du Département du Jura in their hometown of Lons-le-Saunier. The society's annual reports listed the three Goudot brothers as society donors. In 1843, Justin-Marie donated sixty-two exotic birds, marine specimens, beetles, lobsters, and shells (fig. 16 is linked to J.-M. Goudot).[57] Prior to this, in May and September 1837, Étienne had donated "several natural history objects and others related to 'industry,' samples from gold, zinc and sulfide iron mines, along with Peruvian figurines made of gold, jasper, and terra-cotta" (fig. 17).[58] Other well-documented archaeological objects entered Lons-le-Saunier's collections in 1848,[59] some of which still remain in the Musée des Beaux-Arts (numbers 130 to 136) and the Musée d'Archéologie (numbers 137 to 139) (fig. 18).[60]

Among the Musée d'Archéologie's historical archives, a page from the "Catalog of the Museum of the City of Lons-Le-Saunier - dossier GOU / GOU-I [...]" provides the following description: "Two calabashes, one painted in red ocher, with gilded edges, and the second in natural ocher,"[61] and data regarding the donor is listed there as

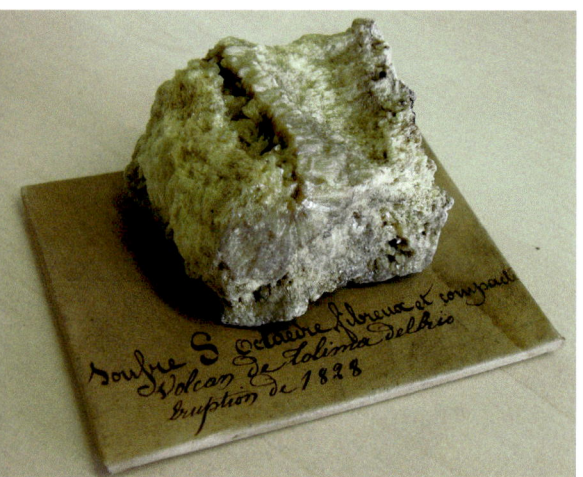

Fig. 16. "Soufre S octaèdre fibreux et compact, Volcan de Tolima del Rio [?], Eruption de 1828" (Sulfur S fibreux and compact octahedra, Tolima del Rio [?] Volcano, Eruption of 1828). Colombia, collected about 1828. [possibly collected by Justin-Marie Goudot] 1.18 [approx.] × 1.96 × 1.57 in., and cardboard 2.36 × 3.14 in. Etienne Goudot (donor), 1843 (?). Inv. 2017.00.12, Musée d'Archéologie, Lons-le-Saunier, France.

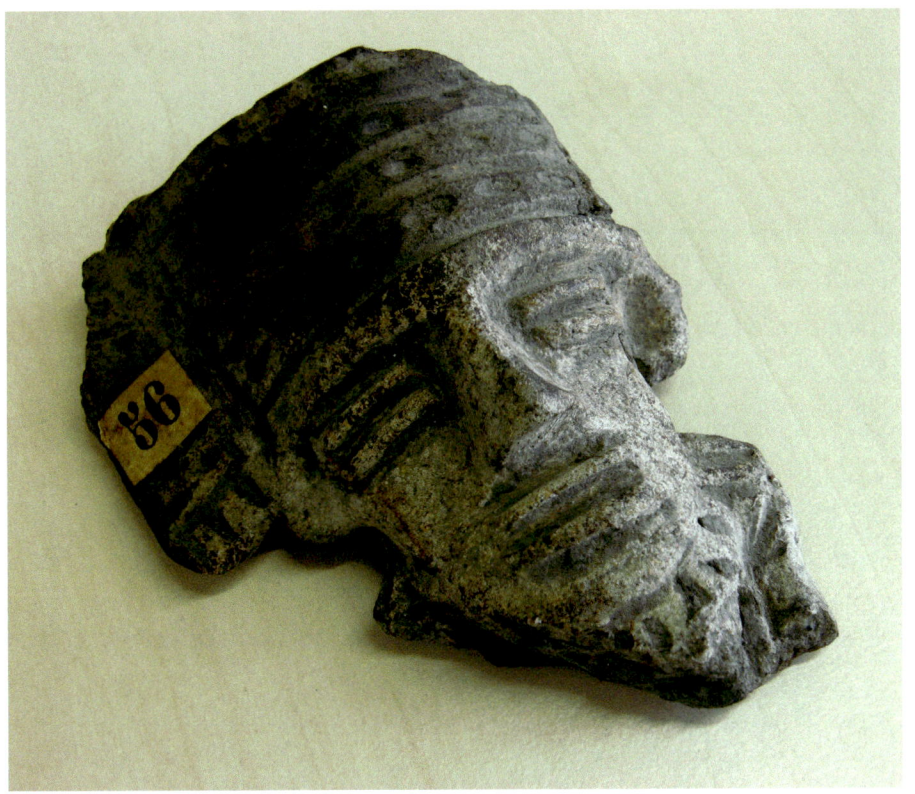

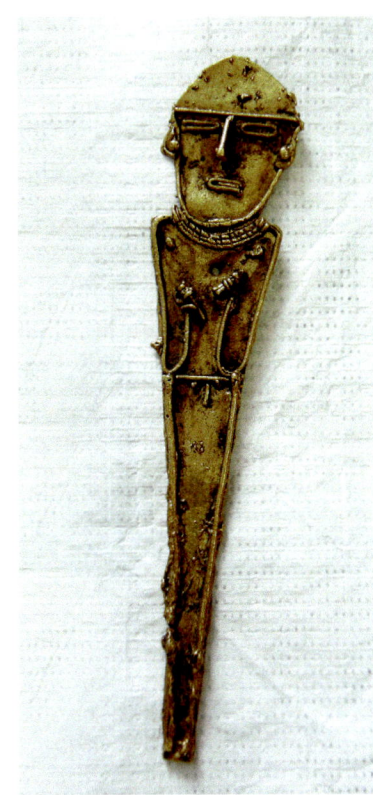

"Goudot, (Etienne) from Frébuans [Jura]. Living in Bogotá (Colombia)." These gourds are now associated with aforementioned objects 5061 and 5062. There is no information regarding their year of inclusion or collection; nevertheless, the Goudots' place of residence is specifically stated as "Colombia" and not "Nueva Granada" (the name adopted by Colombia after 1830 when the departments of Cundinamarca, Venezuela, and Quito separated), which seems to clearly establish the gourd's date of collection prior to 1830.

These gourds, as well as Roulin's ethnographic watercolors and d'Orbigny's ammonite engravings of Boussingault's fossil specimens, exemplify the material scientific culture of an emerging republic, a republic that was forged by agents formed under political, cultural, and intellectual frameworks conceived during the late Spanish American period. The concepts of civilization and progress justified the museum and mining school's specific scientific practices. While museum and mining school personnel such as Rivero, Justin-Marie Goudot, Boussingault, and Roulin assembled and studied both natural collections and archaeological and ethnographical objects under a certain scientific scrutiny, Etienne Goudot proceeded similarly, inspired nonetheless by other practical interests. The public and private spheres converged, as revealed by the outcome of the scientific practices in which these objects were embedded: newspaper articles; collections listed on display at the Museo Nacional de Colombia in Bogotá, as well as specimens conveyed to France, and their corresponding textual descriptions, classifications, drawings, and engravings; and painted representations that included natural surroundings and anthropological entourages. These objects were imbued with cultural significance and transformed into material scientific culture.

✛✛✛

Fig. 17. Muisca culture, "Tête de figurine anthropomorphe" (anthropomorphic figurine head). Colombia, 600–1600. Terra-cotta, 3.54 × 2.75 × 1.18 in. Etienne Goudot (donor ?), 1837. Inv. 4630, Musée d'Archéologie, Lons-le-Saunier, France.

Fig. 18. Muisca culture, *tunjo* (anthropomorphic figurine). Colombia, 600–1500. Hammered plate and filigree in tumbaga gold (gold-copper alloy), 3.14 × 0.39 in. Donation from Archbishop of Bogotá by means of Etienne Goudot (donor?), 1837. Inv. C 2, Musée des Beaux-Arts, Lons-le-Saunier, France.

Notes

1 James A. Secord, "Knowledge in Transit," *Isis* 95, no. 4 (2004): 654–72. About practices and material culture, see pp. 657–58.

2 Secord, "Knowledge in Transit," 665.

3 María Paola Rodríguez Prada, *Le Musée National de Colombie, 1823–1830: Histoire d'une création* (Paris: L'Harmattan, 2013).

4 Dominique Poulot, *Les Lumières* (Paris: Presses Universitaires de France, 2000), 246, 255, 262; and María Paola Rodríguez Prada, "'Promover la instrucción pública, especialmente en los ramos en que directamente se interesa la prosperidad de la Nación': El Museo Nacional de Colombia y la Escuela de Minas (1823–1830)," paper presented at the Congreso Internacional "Una mirada a las Independencias," Pontificia Universidad Católica del Perú, Lima, September 12–14, 2018.

5 See studies about intellectual and Enlightenment agency in the New Granada viceroyalty by Renán Silva, *Los ilustrados de Nueva Granada, 1760–1808: Genealogía de una comunidad de interpretación* (Medellín, Colombia: Banco de la República, 2002).

6 Robert Mandrou, *Introduction á la France Moderne (1500–1640): Essai de Psychologie historique* (Paris: Éditions Albin Michel, 1961), 347–48; Lucien Febvre, "Une vue d'ensemble: Histoire et psychologie," in *Combats pour l'histoire,* ed. Lucien Febvre (Paris: Librairie Armand Colin, 1953), 207–20; Jacques Le Goff, "Mentalities: A History of Ambiguities," in *Constructing the Past: Essays in Historical Methodology,* ed. Jacques Le Goff and Pierre Nora (Cambridge: Cambridge University Press; Paris: Éditions de la Maison des Sciences des l'Homme, [1974] 1985), 166–80; and Robert Darnton, *La gran matanza de gatos y otros episodios en la historia de la cultura francesa* (Mexico City: Fondo de Cultura Económica, [1984] 2015).

7 Poulot, *Les Lumières,* 25–27.

8 *Gaceta de Colombia* 144, July 18, 1824, n.p.

9 *Gaceta de Colombia* 111, February 30, 1823, n.p.

10 José María de Mier, La Gran Colombia, vol. 1, *Decretos de la Secretaría de Estado y del Interior 1821–1824* (Bogotá: Presidencia de la República, 1983), 3, 76–80.

11 Statistics are calculated after budget presented by José Manuel Restrepo Vélez, secretary of the interior, in "Esposición que el Secretario de Estado del Despacho del Interior del Gobierno de la Republica de Colombia hace al Congreso de 1827 sobre los negocios de su Departamento," Correspondance politique de l'origine à 1871, Colombie, t. 3, 1826–1828, fol. 48, Ministère des Affaires Étrangères, Archives, Paris, France. For a complete analysis of this public expenditure, see Rodríguez Prada, *Le Musée National de Colombie,* 394.

12 Alcide Dessalines d'Orbigny and J. B. (Jean Baptiste) Boussingault, *Coquilles et échinodermes fossiles de Colombie (Nouvelle-Grenade), recueillis de 1821 à 1833* (Paris: P. Bertrand, 1842).

13 Contract signed between Francisco Antonio Zea and Jean-Baptiste Boussingault, Generales y Civiles 1819–1825, box 98, folder 86, fol. 40, Enrique Ortega Ricaurte (EOR), Section Colecciones (hereafter, SC), Archivo General de la Nación (hereafter, AGN), Bogotá, Colombia.

14 D'Orbigny, *Coquilles et échinodermes fossiles,* 1–2.

15 According to d'Orbigny's descriptions, fossils from Cundinamarca were collected in the Magdalena River valley between the mountainous chain of Sumapaz on the east and the mountain chain of Quindío on the west, while bordered by the territories of Vélez on the north and those of Ibagué and Tocaima on the south, estimating a long 75-league strip. Socorro Province's sites where the specimens were collected are Villa de Capitanejo, La Roca de Cal (?), Cacota de Matanza, Sube (?), Vélez, San Gil, Oyba, and Las Palmas. In regard to what d'Orbigny designates as the Province of Santa-Fe de Bogotá, precise sites were Tocaima, Ibagué, Anapoima, Chipaqui (*sic;* Chipaque), Zapatore (?), and Pitaquiro (?) between the river port Honda and the capital city of Bogotá. Regarding specimens collected in Venezuela, Boussingault must have gathered them in Carache during his first journey toward Bogotá, after arrival from France and debarking at the port of La Guaira, in the Colombian state of Venezuela. D'Orbigny, *Coquilles et échinodermes fossiles,* 21.

16 Maria Margaret Lopes, "'Scenes from deep times': Bones, Travels, and Memories in the Cultures of Nature in Brazil," *História, Ciências, Saúde—Manguinhos* 15, no. 3 (2008): 615–34; quotes on p. 616.

17 Élie de Beaumont, Armand Dufrénoy, Henri Milne-Edwards (commissaires), and Alexandre Brongniart (rapporteur), "Paléontologie—Rapport sur un Mémoire de M. Alcide d'Orbigny intitulé: Coquilles fossiles de Colombie recueillies par M. Boussingault," in *Comptes rendus hebdomadaires des séances de l'Académie des sciences publiés conformément à une décision de l'Académie, En date du 13 Juillet 1835 par MM. les secrétaires perpétuels,* ed. Académie des Sciences, vol. 16, no. 1 (Paris: Bachelier, imprimeur-Libraire, 1843), 178–82.

18 D'Orbigny, *Coquilles et échinodermes fossiles,* 22–23.

19 D'Orbigny, *Coquilles et échinodermes fossiles,* 23–24.

20 Beaumont et al., "Paléontologie—Rapport sur un Mémoire," 181.

21 D'Orbigny, *Coquilles et échinodermes fossiles,* 13, 17, 19–20. A survey on Humboldt's extinct fauna

specimens collection in the New Granada viceroyalty and their delivery to the Muséum d'Histoire Naturelle in Paris has been thoroughly assembled by Alberto Gómez Gutiérrez, *Humboldtiana neogranadina,* vol. 3, *Scientia. Escritos científicos y disciplinares* (Bogotá: CESA, Pontificia Universidad Javeriana, Universidad de los Andes, Universidad del Rosario, Universidad EAFIT, and Universidad Externado de Colombia, 2018), 391–415.

22 Lopes, "'Scenes from deep times,'" 621.

23 *Gaceta de Colombia* 144, July 18, 1824, n.p.

24 Contract signed between Francisco Antonio Zea and Mariano de Rivero, Generales y Civiles 1819–1825, 98, 86, fol. 25, EOR, SC, AGN, Bogotá.

25 Fonds Papiers et correspondance du baron Georges Cuvier, mss. 3244, pièce 74, Manuscrits et papiers savants, Bibliothèque, Académie des Sciences, Institut de France.

26 Martin Rudwick, *El significado de los fósiles: Episodios de la historia de la paleontología* (Madrid: Hermann Blume, [1972] 1987).

27 Francisco José de Caldas, "Del influjo del Clima sobre los Seres Organizados, Por D. Francisco José de Caldas, individuo meritorio de la Expedición Botánica de Santa Fé de Bogotá, y encargado del Observatorio astronómico de esta capital," in *Seminario de la Nueva Granada: Miscelánea de ciencias, literatura, artes é industria,* ed. A. Lasserre (Paris: Librería Castellana, 1849), 110–55; excerpt pp. 119–20. Transcription and translation to Spanish of Humboldt's diaries and correspondence mentioning archaeological sites for fossil excavations during his travels in New Granada in Alberto Gómez Gutiérrez, *Humboldtiana neogranadina,* vol. 1, *Relatio: Apuntes y encuentros (vol. 1 1800–1801),* 362, 389–91.

28 Desiderata transcribed by Mariano Eduardo de Rivero to Francisco Antonio Zea, in a letter dated at Portsmouth, on board the *New York,* October 11, 1822, Generales y Civiles, 98, 85, fol. 19, EOR, SC, AGN, Bogotá.

29 On October 8, 1823, Rivero writes to Humboldt announcing delivery of "fossils bones" excavated from Pescadera near Soacha and from "caño del Fiscal," half an hour away from Bogotá. See letter from Rivero to Humboldt, transcribed by Monique Alaperrine-Bouyer, *Mariano Eduardo de Rivero en algunas de sus cartas al Barón Alexander von Humboldt* (Arequipa, Peru: Centro de Estudios Arequipeños-UNSA, 1999), 55–56.

30 Cuvier acknowledged receipt of these specimens, which he identified as "mastodon," and also registered other shipments received from Rivero and Boussingault: "Les mêmes naturalistes ont adressée au Muséum d'Histoire Naturelle, des ossements de Mastodonte à dents étroites, trouvés près de Bogota, et qui ajoutent à nos connaissances sur cet animal perdu." Excerpt from Académie des Sciences, "Histoire de l'Académie Royale des Sciences de l'Institut de France: Analyse des Travaux de l'Académie royale des Sciences, pendant l'année 1823: Partie Physique par M. le Baron Cuvier, Secrétaire perpétuel," in *Mémoires de l'Académie Royale des Sciences de l'Institut de France, Années 1823,* vol. 6 (Paris: Académie des Sciences, 1827), xc, xcj.

31 Martin Rudwick, "Recherches sur les ossements fossiles: Georges Cuvier et la collecte d'alliés internationaux," in *Le Muséum au premier siècle de son histoire,* ed. Claude Blanckaert, Claudine Cohen, Pietro Corsi, and Jean-Louis Fischer (Paris: Muséum National d'Histoire Naturelle, 1997), 591–606; and Irina Podgorny, "El camino de los fósiles: Las colecciones de Mamíferos pampeanos en los museos franceses e ingleses del siglo XIX," *Asclepio* 53, no. 2 (2001): 97–115, https://doi.org/10.3989/asclepio.2001.v53.i2.161.

32 Irina Podgorny, "Fossil Dealers, the Practices of Comparative Anatomy and British Diplomacy in Latin America, 1820–1840," *BJHS—The British Society for the History of Sciences* 46, no. 4 (2013): 647–74; specifically p. 648, https://doi.org/10.1017/S0007087412000702; and Irina Podgorny and Maria Margaret Lopes, *El desierto en una vitrina: Museos e historia natural en la Argentina, 1810–1890* (Rosario, Argentina: Prohistoria Ediciones, 2014), 34.

33 Podgorny, "Fossil dealers," 655; and Irina Podgorny, "Mercaderes del pasado: Teodoro Vilardebó, Pedro de Angelis y el comercio de huesos y documentos en el Río de la Plata, 1830–1850," *Circumscribere* 9 (2011): 29–77. For Brazilian case studies of dinosaur bones' circulation around Europe in the early nineteenth century, see also Lopes, "'Scenes from deep times,'" 619–23.

34 For Cuvier's scientific practices, see not only Rudwick, "Recherches sur les ossements fossiles," but also Claudine Cohen, "Stratégie et rhétorique de la preuve dans les *Recherches sur les ossements fossiles de quadrupèdes* de Cuvier," in *Le Muséum au premier siècle de son histoire,* ed. Claude Blanckaert, Claudine Cohen, Pietro Corsi, and Jean-Louis Fischer (Paris: Muséum National d'Histoire Naturelle, 1997), 523–39.

35 Following is the complete excerpt with precise citation of archaeological sites: "En compañía del Dr. Roulin a quien conoce Vd. muy bien por sus distinguidos talentos, pensamos publicar una obrita sobre los monumentos de los Yndios antiguos de Cundinamarca. Tenemos una bonita colección de tunjos de oro y de cobre, algunos vasos y 18 dibuxos de las estatuas curiosas y colosales que se encuentran en San Agustín a 3 días de Neyba. El año pasado mandé a Matis quien se acuerda de Vd. mucho, para que las dibuxase, y me ha traído una colección de ellos, una mesa sobre la cual hacían sus sacrificios, es digno de virse [sic], las figuras que la sostienen son muy grande[s] y se asemejan mucho a las que se ven en los Museos, traídas de Egypto."

Alaperrine-Bouyer, *Mariano Eduardo de Rivero,*
61–63; quote from p. 62.

36 Letter from François-Désiré Roulin to Francisco
Antonio Zea, dated in Paris, July 10, 1822. Generales
y Civiles 1819–1825, 98, 86, fol. 50, EOR, SC, AGN,
Bogotá. The original contract signed between
Roulin and Zea has not been discovered, but certain
correspondence between Rivero and Zea, as well as
the previously cited, suggests Roulin's recruitment
process. See details in Rodríguez Prada, *Le Musée
National de Colombie,* 284–89.

37 Other than Rivero's reference to this shared work
about Indian antiquities in his letter to Humboldt
(1825), it is also mentioned in a manuscript by
Boussingault, who acknowledges existence of this
project, apparently still unaccomplished by 1830.
"Boussingault au Dr F. Roulin, 4 avril 1830, X5(B9),
4 avril," fol. 2r: Correspondance classée par ordre
alphabétique, Manuscrits conservés à la Bibliothèque
de l'Observatoire de Paris: manuscrits cotés des
dix-huitième et dix-neuvième siècles, Bureau des
longitudes, Archives, Manuscrits et fonds d'archives,
Bibliothèque, Observatoire de Paris, France.

38 Original inscription "VOYAGE PITTORESQUE EN
COLOMBIE / ACHEVE A BOGOTA PAR F. ROULIN 26
MAI 1824" written on *Place de St. Victorin, à Bogotá
[Plaza de San Victorino, en Bogotá]* by François-
Désiré Roulin, watercolor on paper, 20.36 × 26.7 cm,
AP4088, Colección de Arte, Banco de la República
de Colombia. Original inscription for this second
image, "Dr ROULIN / BOGOTA / 1824," written in
*Place major de Bogotá: Douane [Plaza mayor de
Bogotá: Aduana]* by F.-D. Roulin, watercolor on
paper, 20.36 × 26.7 cm, AP4087, Colección de Arte,
Banco de la República de Colombia.

39 Such as *Le Globe,* the *Revue des Deux Mondes,*
Le Magasin Pittoresque, the travel accounts by
Gaspard Théodore Mollien (1796–1872), and some
scientific works by George Cuvier, Baronet William
Jardine (1784–1843), Mariano Eduardo de Rivero,
and Joaquín Acosta (1800–1852).

40 Alcide d'Orbigny, *Voyage pittoresque dans les
deux Amériques, Résumé général de tous les voyages
de Colomb, Las-Casas, Oviedo, Gomara, Garcilazo
de la Vega, Acosta, Dutertre, Labat, Stedman, La
Condamine, Ulloa, Humboldt, Hamilton, Cochrane,
Mawe, Auguste de Saint-Hilaire, Max. de Newied,
Spix et Martius, Rengger et Longchamp, Azara,
Fresier, Molina, Miers, Poeppig, Antonio del Rio,
Beltrami, Pike, Long, Adair, Chastellux, Bartram,
Collot, Lewis et Clarke, Bradbury, Ellis, Mackenzie,
Franklin, Parry, Back, Phipps, etc., etc. Par les
rédacteurs du Voyage Pittoresque autour du Monde*
(Paris: Furne et Cie., Libraires - Éditeurs, 1841).

41 Such is the case of the *butaca* chair presented
in Jorge F. Rivas Pérez, "Transforming Status: The
Genesis of the New World Butaca," in *Festivals and
Daily Life in the Arts of Colonial Latin America,
1492–1850: Papers from the 2012 Mayer Center
Symposium at the Denver Art Museum,* ed. Donna

Pierce (Denver: Denver Art Museum, 2014), 111–28.
See also general studies for South American
nineteenth-century travelers and genre scenes, such
as Beatriz Álvarez Rincón, *François-Désiré Roulin:
De la Guaira a Bogotá* (Bogotá: Colección Banco
de la República, 2003); and Patricia Londoño Vega,
*América Exótica: Panorámicas, tipos y costumbres
del siglo XIX: Obras sobre papel, colecciones de La
Banca Central, Colombia, Ecuador, México, Perú y
Venezuela* (Bogotá: Banco de la República, 2004). An
iconographic analysis approach from gender studies
can be seen in Mónica Merchán Sierra, "Nymphes
exotiques, indigènes victimes ou créatures vulgaires:
Images des femmes grande-colombiennes d'après
les voyageurs du XIXe siècle" (PhD diss., L'École
Normale Supérieure de Lyon, 2013), available at
http://www.theses.fr/2013ENSL0752.pdf, accessed
March 19, 2017.

42 Isabel Yaya, "Wonders of America: The Curiosity
Cabinet as a Site of Representation and Knowledge,"
Journal of the History of Collections 20, no. 2 (2008):
172–88, https://doi.org/10.1093/jhc/fhm038.

43 Inventory number 5061: *bol* and inventory
number 5062: *Bol avec un décor doré en frise,*
Collections Beaux-Arts, Musée des Beaux-Arts of
Lons-le-Saunier, France. I wish to thank Dorothée
Gillmann, Attachée de conservation du patrimoine,
Responsable des collections Beaux-Arts Musées
de Lons-le-Saunier at the Musée des Beaux-Arts,
who kindly hosted my visit to Lons-le-Saunier and
granted me full access to ethnographical collections
donated by Justin-Marie and Etienne Goudot.

44 The original excerpt is "varios mammíferos *[sic]*,
reptiles y peces y algunos *instrumentos muy bien
hechos.*" *Gaceta de Colombia* 144, July 18, 1824, n.p.
(emphasis mine).

45 Contract signed between Francisco Antonio
Zea and Justin-Marie Goudot, folder D 2, fol. 37,
Peticiones y Solicitudes Boyacá, Istmo, Zulia,
Orinoco Maturín, Cauca, Venezuela y Cundinamarca
10, Peticiones y Solicitudes 75, Section República
(hereafter, SR), AGN, Bogotá. Regarding Justin-Marie
Goudot's death, official archives list it on June 6,
1847, at the river port of Honda in Colombia, country
named by then Nueva Granada. Archives Portal
Europe, France, Archives nationales, Minutier central
des notaires de Paris, MC/RE/LVI/26, Minutes et
répertoires du notaire Benjamin Labarbe (étude
LVI), Répertoire numérique détaillé, 11 juin 1842–5
décembre 1850, "Inventaire après décès de Justin
Goudot, arrivé à Honda, province de Mariquita, le
6 juin 1847, à la requête de Catherine Velossa, sa
veuve à Belleville, rue de Paris, n° 95. 1er octobre
1850," http://www.archivesportaleurope.net/
ead-display/-/ead/pl/aicode/FR-FRAN/type/fa/
id/FRAN_IR_042325/dbid/C349000435/search/0/
goudot, accessed November 12, 2017.

46 Jerónimo Torres, "Museo Nacional," *Gaceta de
Colombia* 223, January 22, 1826, n.p.

47 María Paola Rodríguez Prada, "The Creation of the National Museum of Colombia (1823–1830): A History of Collections, Collectors, and Museums," *Museum History Journal* 9, no. 1 (2016): 29–44, https://doi.org/10.1080/19369816.2015.1118261.

48 This and the following information clarifying certain travel itineraries concerning Justin-Marie Goudot was possible thanks to Dominique Malécot from the Conservatoire d'espaces naturels de Franche-Comté in France, to whom I am grateful for his enthusiastic help. Dominique Malécot, email message to author, August 17, 2017. He drew my attention to passenger arrivals lists microfilmed by National Archives and Records Administration in Washington, DC. Immigration index card for "Gustino Goudat" can be viewed at "New York, New York, Index to Passenger Lists, 1820–1846," database with images, *FamilySearch* (https://familysearch.org/ark:/61903/3:1:33S7-9GXC-FSK?cc=1919703&wc=M6YK-568%3A212776301 : 21 May 2014), Gon - Grau > image 2499 of 5182; citing NARA microfilm publication M261 (Washington, DC: National Archives and Records Administration, n.d.). Immigration index card for "Catalina Goudat" can be viewed at "New York, New York, Index to Passenger Lists, 1820–1846," (https://familysearch.org/ark:/61903/3:1:33SQ-GGXC-F13?cc=1919703&wc=M6YK-568%3A212776301 : 21 May 2014), Gon - Grau > image 2497 of 5182; citing NARA microfilm publication M261 (Washington, DC: National Archives and Records Administration, n.d.). Immigration index card for "Hepolito Goudat" can be viewed at "New York, New York, Index to Passenger Lists, 1820–1846," (https://familysearch.org/ark:/61903/3:1:33S7-9GXC-FVD?cc=1919703&wc=M6YK-568%3A212776301 : 21 May 2014), Gon - Grau > image 2500 of 5182; citing NARA microfilm publication M261 (Washington, DC: National Archives and Records Administration, n.d.). Finally, immigration index card for "Emilie Goudat" can be viewed at "New York, New York, Index to Passenger Lists, 1820–1846," (https://familysearch.org/ark:/61903/3:1:33SQ-GGXC-FPJ?cc=1919703&wc=M6YK-568%3A212776301 : 21 May 2014), Gon - Grau > image 2498 of 5182; citing NARA microfilm publication M261 (Washington, DC: National Archives and Records Administration, n.d.). The above documents were accessed November 12, 2017.

49 "Goudot (Afrique, 1823–1830)," 1, 2, pièce 2 'Voyage à Madagascar 1828 1829', 575 Voyages et Missions, AJ15 MNHN, Archives nationales, Paris, France.

50 Again, I express gratitude to Dominique Malécot, who confirmed and provided me with birth dates for Goudot siblings, after consulting the Archives départementales du Jura (hereafter, ADJ). Rose Etienne Simon Goudot was born January 5, 1801, in Lons-le-Saunier (ADJ 3E 4667), Justin-Marie Goudot was born April 13, 1802, in the same town (ADJ 3E 4668), and Jules-Prosper Goudot was born December 12, 1803. Besides them, another four siblings can be accounted for: Ame Philippe Goudot (b. August 11, 1796), Joseph Amédé Goudot (b. July 26, 1799), Aimé Emmanuel Frédéric Goudot (b. January 21, 1805), and Elizé Joseph Goudot (b. June 4, 1809). Dominique Malécot, email message to author, April 27, 2017.

51 Travel itineraries concerning Etienne Goudot were possible thanks to Dominique Malécot. "Pennsylvania, Philadelphia Passenger Lists, 1880–1882," database with images, *FamilySearch* (https://familysearch.org/ark:/61903/1:1:K8C9-CKD : 29 December 2014), M Goudot, 1824; citing NARA microfilm publication M425 (Washington, DC: National Archives and Records Administration, n.d.); FHL microfilm. Manifest of Passengers document can be viewed at "Pennsylvania, Philadelphia Passenger Lists, 1800–1882," (https://familysearch.org/ark:/61903/3:1:9392-629Q-7B?cc=1908535&wc=M61G-VWP%3A179559401 : 21 May 2014), 034 - 3 Jan to 31 July 1824 > image 183 of 426; citing NARA microfilm publication M425 (Washington, DC: National Archives and Records Administration, n.d.). Verso of the manifest of Passengers document with date of arrival can be viewed at "Pennsylvania, Philadelphia Passenger Lists, 1800–1882," (https://familysearch.org/ark:/61903/3:1:9392-629Q-ZB?cc=1908535&wc=M61G-VWP%3A179559401 : 21 May 2014), 034 - 3 Jan to 31 July 1824 > image 182 of 426; citing NARA microfilm publication M425 (Washington, DC: National Archives and Records Administration, n.d.). The above documents were accessed November 12, 2017.

52 Several newspaper articles and ads as well as published leaflets left traces of Etienne Goudot's activities. Wan-Swietten, "Artículo Comunicado," *Gaceta de Colombia* 194, July 3, 1825, n.p.; Estevan Goudot, *Honorables señores de la Cámara de Representantes* (Bogotá: Imprenta de Nicomedes Lora, 1834), Fondo Anselmo Pineda (hereafter, F. Pineda) 466, pza. 26, Biblioteca Nacional de Colombia (hereafter, BNC); *Almanque Curioso para el año de 1861: Contiene datos estadísticos, recetas, anécdotas i avisos importantes calculado para la confederación granadina* (Bogotá: Imprenta de "El Mosaico," 1860), 23, F. Pineda 50, pza. 7, BNC; *Opiata Anti-Venerea curativa del Coto* (N.p.: n.d., ca. 1860?), F. Pineda 803, fol. 489, BNC.

53 "Aviso no Oficial," *Gaceta de la Nueva Granada* 355, July 1, 1838, n.p.

54 Immigration list document at "New York Passenger Lists, 1820–1891," *FamilySearch* (https://familysearch.org/ark:/61903/1:1:QVPX-BWR5 : 15 April 2015), Estevan Goudot, 1837; citing NARA microfilm publication M234 (Washington, DC: National Archives and Records Administration, n.d.); FHL microfilm. See also complete document at: "New York Passenger Lists, 1820–1891," *FamilySearch* (https://

familysearch.org/ark:/61903/3:1:939V-5T98-P6?cc=1849782&wc=MX62-229%3A165726601 November 2014), 033 - 16 Mar 1837–11 Jun 1837 > image 25 of 898; citing NARA microfilm publication M237 (Washington, DC: National Archives and Records Administration, n.d.). The above documents were accessed November 12, 2017.

55 Museum documents by Joaquín Acosta, Instrucción Pública, t. 126, año 1837–1840, fol. 9, SR, AGN, Bogotá. I am indebted to Libardo Sánchez Paredes, researcher in the history department of the Museo Nacional de Colombia, for drawing my attention to this source.

56 "New York Passenger Lists, 1820–1891," *FamilySearch* (https://familysearch.org/ark:/61903/3:1:939V-5FQX-J?cc=1849782&wc=MX&62-VZ9%3A165729201 : 7 January 2015), 051 - 26 Oct 1842–15 Jun 1843 > image 839 of 1206; citing NARA microfilm publication M237 (Washington, DC: National Archives and Records Administration, n.d.). The above documents were accessed November 12, 2017.

57 *Travaux de la Société d'émulation du département du Jura, pendant l'année 1843* (Lons-le-Saunier: Frédéric Gauthier, 1844), 101.

58 *Travaux de la Société d'émulation du département du Jura, pendant l'année 1837* (Lons-le-Saunier: Frédéric Gauthier, 1838), 176. See also Désiré Monnier, *Annuaire du département du Jura pour l'année 1842* (Lons-Le-Saunier: Imprimerie et Lithographie de Fréd Gauthier, 1842), 172, 181–82, who registers under the "Deuxième section. Annales Contemporaines, Simple Notes sur ce qui s'est passé de plus remarquable dans le Département du Jura, de 1830 à 1841," for the "Annales 1837," month of "Mai," the following excerpt from p. 182: "26. Arrivé de Santa-Fé de Bogotá (Nouvelle-Grenade) M. Goudot, de Lons-le-Saunier, dépose au musée départemental, entr'autres [*sic*] curiosités étrangères et précieuses, deux figures de divinités indiennes

en or, un petit sceptre de même métal, surmonté de deux oiseaux, et qui parait avoir été à la main de l'une des idoles; une petite statuette en pierre rouge; cinq têtes de dieux en terre cuite; une petite tête de Tunjo, en cuivre; autant d'objets d'une époque antérieure à la conquête des Espagnols, et dont la rareté augmente de beaucoup l'intérêt." For Goudot siblings' donations, see also Rodríguez Prada, "Creation of the National Museum," 37–38.

59 Donations to the Musée Départemental in 1847 are described under the *Annuaire*'s section "Antiquités": "M. Goudot, de Lons-le-Saunier, habitant St.-Yago, de l'Ile de Cuba, a fait parvenir, de la part de Mgr. l'archevêque de Bogotá, cinq figurines en or qui représentent des anciennes divinités du culte péruvien. Ces symboles ont beaucoup de rapport avec celles que l'on a trouvées en Egypte, et qui remontent à une autre antiquité." Désiré Monnier, *Annuaire du département du Jura, Pour l'année 1848, IX Année* (Lons-le-Saunier: Imprimerie et Lithographie de Frédéric Gauthier, 1848), 573–74.

60 I would like to express my gratitude to Sylvie Lourdaux-Jurietti, head of archaeological collections at the Musée Lons-le-Saunier, for generously hosting my visit and granting full access to archaeological and geological collections donated by the Goudot siblings. For further catalogue descriptions of the latter, see Musée des Beaux-arts et d'Archéologie de Besançon, *Nos petites amériques: Collections amerindiennes, archéologiques et ethnographiques des musées de Franche-Comté* (Besançon, France: Musée des Beaux-arts et d'Archéologie, 1993), 66–68.

61 "Deux callebasses [*sic*], une peînte en ocre rouge, à bords dorés, et la deuxième en ocre naturelle." *Catalogue du Musée de la Ville de Lons-Le-Saunier—Dossier GOU / GOU-I // Don de MM. Goudot,* document consulted at the Centre de Conservation et d'Etude René-Rémond in Lons-le Saunier based on Sylvie Lourdaux-Jurietti's advice.

Acknowledgments

I am very grateful for the generosity and contributions of colleagues from all over the Americas and Europe for this volume: Thomas B. F. Cummins, Emmanuel Ortega, Donna Pierce, Rafael Ramos Sosa, María Paola Rodríguez Prada, Olaya Sanfuentes, Gabriela Siracusano, Jonathan Tavares, and Antonio Urquízar-Herrera.

I would like to extend my sincerest gratitude to the staff of the Mayer Center for Ancient and Latin American Art for their efforts in organizing the Mayer Center Symposium XVIII: Julie Wilson Frick, our former Mayer Center program coordinator; Jesse Laird Ortega, senior curatorial assistant; Maria Luisa Minjares, curatorial assistant; Jared Katz, Mayer Fellow for Art of the Ancient Americas; and Sarah Krantz, former department intern.

The Denver Art Museum events and audiovisual staff, particularly Travis Moore and Ron Wilcox, as well as the security staff led by Tony Fortunato and Terri Cross, also provided significant support. In addition, I would also like to thank my colleague, Victoria Lyall, Frederick and Jan Mayer Curator of Art of the Ancient Americas, for her unconditional support. I am also grateful to the museum director, Christoph Heinrich, for his continued enthusiastic support of the Mayer Center Symposium series and subsequent publications.

In preparing this publication, I am grateful to Nancy D. Bratton for her extraordinary design skills, and the invaluable proofreading and editing provided by Maya Allen-Gallegos. Special thanks are due to Laura Caruso and Kati Woock, who are in charge of publications at the Denver Art Museum, for their expert advice, editing, and project management. An extensive thank you also goes out to Jeff Wells and Christina Jackson, who provided their expert assistance with the images.

I am grateful to Cassochrome, in Waregem, Belgium, for producing the volume and to the University of Oklahoma Press for its distribution. My deepest thanks go to Maria Luisa Minjares for communicating with the authors, editing, image gathering, compilation research, proofreading, gathering image permits, and translating in this publication.

On the behalf of the Denver Art Museum and the Mayer Center of Ancient and Latin American Art, I want to express my most sincere gratitude to the late Frederick Mayer and his wife, Jan, for providing the opportunity to gather in Denver such a distinguished group of scholars from across the Americas. The symposium and its accompanying publication would not have been possible without the Mayers' commitment to the fields of Latin and Ancient American art, and their generosity and enlightened vision to bring them to the world.

Jorge F. Rivas Perez
Frederick and Jan Mayer Curator
of Latin American Art
Denver Art Museum

✦ ✦ ✦

Image Credits

Published by the Mayer Center for
Ancient and Latin American Art at
the Denver Art Museum
100 W. 14th Ave. Pkwy
Denver, CO 80204

mayercenter.denverartmuseum.org

denverartmuseum.org

ISBN 978-1-945483-04-2

Library of Congress Cataloging-in-Publication Data

Names: Mayer Center Symposium (18th : 2018 : Denver Art Museum), author. | Rivas, Jorge, editor.

Title: Materiality : making Spanish America / Mayer Center Symposium XVIII; edited by Jorge F. Rivas Pérez.

Description: Denver, CO : Denver Art Museum, [2020] | Series: Readings in Latin American studies | Includes bibliographical references. | Summary: "This volume collects the work of nine scholars who shared their research at the 2018 symposium presented by the Frederick and Jan Mayer Center for Ancient and Latin American Art at the Denver Art Museum. This international group of scholars assembled to explore the theme of materiality in the Americas. The chapters consider materiality from a wide variety of angles, including hagiographic martyr portraiture, arms and armor in Spanish America, religious sculpture, the interpretation of the tocapu in post conquest Peru, and collections assembled both in the Americas and of goods sent back to Europe"-- Provided by publisher.

Identifiers: LCCN 2020040900 | ISBN 9781945483042 (paperback)

Subjects: LCSH: Art and society--Latin America--Congresses. | Material culture--Latin America--Congresses. | Latin America--Civilization--Congresses.

Classification: LCC N72.S6 M39 2018 | DDC 700.1/03--dc23

LC record available at https://lccn.loc.gov/2020040900

Copyeditor: Maya Allen-Gallegos

Design: Nancy Bratton Design

Project management: Kati Woock and Maria Luisa Minjares

Proofreaders: Laura Caruso and Kati Woock

Printed by Cassochrome, Waregem, Belgium

Distributed by University of Oklahoma Press, Norman, OK

Front cover (detail): Unknown artist, *Virgin Embroidering with Saints Anne and Joaquim*. Bolivia, late 1600s–1700s. Oil paint on canvas, 36½ × 40 in. Denver Art Museum: Gift of Dr. Belinda Straight, 1983.598.